God's Capitalist:
Asa Candler of Coca-Cola

Asa Candler
(1851–1929)

God's Capitalist

Asa Candler of Coca-Cola

by Kathryn W. Kemp

MERCER UNIVERSITY PRESS
MACON, GEORGIA
2002

For Jim and our family

ISBN 0-86554-782-3

© 2002 Mercer University Press
6316 Peake Road
Macon, Georgia 31210-3960
All rights reserved

First Edition.

Book design by Mary-Frances Burt
Burt & Burt Studio

The paper used in this publication meets the minimum requirements
of American National Standard for Information Sciences—Permanence
of Paper for Printed Library Materials, ANSI Z39.48-1984.

Library of Congress Cataloging-in-Publication Data

Kemp, Kathryn W.

God's Capitalist: Asa Candler of Coca-Cola / Kathryn W. Kemp.
p. cm. Includes bibliographical references and index.

ISBN 0-86554-782-3

1. Candler, Asa Griggs, 1851-1929. 2. Capitalists and financiers—Georgia—
Atlanta—Biography. 3. Capitalism—Religious aspects. I. Title

HC102.5.C34 K456 2002
338.7'66362'092—dc21

2002001096

TABLE OF CONTENTS

Who Was Asa Candler?

In the spring of 1917 a special train rolled northward, carrying a delegation of Atlanta's most prominent men to attend the inauguration of President Woodrow Wilson. Perhaps the most well-known of these passengers was Atlanta's mayor, Asa Griggs Candler. The newspapers reported that at every stop along the way, "the people swarm forward asking for Mayor Candler, anxious to shake the hand of the south's foremost capitalist and the mayor of the south's foremost city."[1] Now, at the turn of a new century, the name Asa Candler no longer triggers such instant recognition, although when Coca-Cola is mentioned, a belated connection sometimes takes place.

Asa Candler, the man who founded the Coca-Cola Company, died in 1929 but this is the first attempt to present a disinterested, systematic treatment of his life.[2] His son Charles Howard Candler at one time privately published an extensive and affectionate memoir of his father. However, those who are able to locate a copy of this book will conclude that it lacks the rigor of a work of serious scholarship. The son completely disregards the facts of a liaison that ended in a scandalous breech of promise suit and also ignores the fact of his father's turbulent second marriage. Perhaps this was unavoidable.

Few loving sons could engage in a dispassionate evaluation of a father's life and work—even though there is a ready market for nasty exposes by hurt or angry children. Howard Candler's *Asa Griggs Candler* is the recollection of an affectionate son rather than a critical study and, as such, it needs no apology.

Other Candler family memoirs show similar weaknesses, and studies of the Coca-Cola Company, by their very nature, treat only limited aspects of its founder's diverse activities. As a prominent figure in the gilded-age and progressive eras of Southern history, Asa Candler deserves a place in the record.

When I began to research his life, I encountered a few persistent ideas about Asa Candler that have survived the years.

A common reaction to Candler's name blends his *persona* with that of Robert Woodruff, the most widely recognized, more recent head of the Coca-Cola Company, well known for his large philanthropy. People often do not know where one left off and the other began, and some actually blend events of their two careers into one.

Asa Candler, the capitalist, evokes in some persons a kind of free-wheeling enthusiasm for negative innuendo.[3] For example, a group of young Methodist reformers, in a pamphlet attacking the "racist" and "imperialist" aspects of Coca-Cola, Emory University, and Methodist missionary exertions in Cuba, claimed that Asa Candler thought the Spanish-American War was "just what he needed" to open foreign markets for Coca-Cola.[4] These writers evidently did not know (or did not care) that Candler's younger brother John had suffered severe wounds while serving in that war.

On the other hand, some native Atlantans preserve the positive public image of Candler that seems to have predominated during his lifetime. A few of these, persons of four score years, actually saw him, or knew others who did. They remember "a good Christian man," who gave generously of his fabulous wealth and slipped pennies into the hands of children that they might drop them into the church collection plate.

None of these superficial judgments will satisfy serious readers of biography, who would desire a more thoughtful exploration of a life.

As is true of all persons, Asa Candler had both negative and positive qualities—and some observers will disagree on which is which. His aggressive business habits might seem wholly admirable to some, while others might find them distasteful. In like manner, his religious faith may be seen as either deep or merely narrow. Whatever individual responses his life inspires, he deserves to be remembered for the powerful influence he had, not only on his own time and place, but on the present as well. Atlanta without the Coca-Cola Company and Emory University would hardly be the same place.

To follow Candler's activities on the larger stage of Atlanta life is to illuminate some areas of the history of his beloved city. Aspects of the lives of his immediate family also require some attention. However, these secondary topics do not receive exhaustive treatment here. I have constantly reminded myself that this is the story of Asa Candler and have attempted to keep most of the focus on the man himself while including sufficient background information to provide context. My emphasis is on the public man, although some evidence of Candler's inner life has been inferred from his various writings, and some quite personal matters are treated in the last chapter. However, I make no attempt to develop a deep psychological analysis.

The principal sources of primary material relating to Asa Candler, his family, and associates are the various Candler family papers in several collections at Emory University's Woodruff Library Special Collections department and a small but extremely rich collection of Candler papers in the archives of the Coca-Cola Company. Unfortunately, these contain little direct documentation of Asa Candler's relationships with his three younger sons and his daughter in their adult years. A number of letters to the eldest son Howard and a few to his daughter have survived to stand witness to the mind of a stern and loving father.

Both primary and secondary sources thoroughly document his relationships with Atlanta's business and political elite; more problematical are the sentiments of the non-elite segment of the community with regard to Candler. As usual, the "voice of the people" in the documentary record remains muted. I have used two newspapers, the *Journal of Labor* and the African-American *Atlanta Independent* to speak for Atlanta's general public, but these sources should be read with caution. The labor paper served the skilled craftsman and not the common laborer; the *Independent* concerned itself largely with the somewhat narrow views and interests of its editor, who could not, of course, speak for a whole race of people.

Asa Candler did too many things at once to have his biography arranged in simple chronological order. I began with a chapter on his childhood, but his career in the prime of his life was so complex that an additional, topical scheme became necessary. Chapter titles such as "Prescriptionist," "Entrepreneur," "Philanthropist," and "Mayor," which are based on various social roles he occupied, arise from this organizational scheme. Chapters titled "Steward," "Elitist," and "Moralist," although they also deal with events in Candler's life, focus on his ideas, motivations, and beliefs. Additional roles, such as father, husband, or churchman, are treated wherever convenient or appropriate. The difficult events of his last decade, many of which Howard Candler omitted when he wrote his father's life story, comprise the chapter called "First Citizen."

As I pursued this subject, many research facilities and staffs gave generously of their help and I thank them all: Emory University's Woodruff Library Special Collections Department, the Coca-Cola Company's archives, the Atlanta History Center Library/Archives, the Georgia Department of Archives and History, the Atlanta Federal Records Center branch of the National Archives, Georgia State's Pullen Library and Southern Labor Archives, the special collections and microfilm sections of the Decatur Branch of the DeKalb County Public Library, the Special Collections Department of the Atlanta Public Library, the Atlanta Chamber of Commerce Research Department, the office of the Clerk of the Superior Court of Fulton County, the DeKalb County Historical Society, Atlanta University's Woodruff Library Special Collections Department, the medical library at Crawford Long Hospital, the special collections department of the Baker Library of the Harvard Business School, and the

Special Collections Department of the Perkins Library at Duke University all contributed in some significant way. Professors Stuart Galishoff and Tim Crimmins of Georgia State University read an earlier version of this manuscript and offered invaluable criticisms. Finally, Professor John Matthews also of GSU, who also read the manuscript, and was the person who originally suggested that a full biography of Asa Candler might be useful. He has my deepest gratitude.

[1] "Leading Citizens of Atlanta to March in Inaugural Parade," *Atlanta Journal* 4 (March 1917): 3.

[2] Charles Howard Candler, *Asa Griggs Candler* (Georgia: Emory University, 1950) is the only published, full-length biography of Asa Candler; see also, Mark K. Bauman, "Candler, Asa Griggs," in *Dictionary of Georgia Biography* vol. 1, Kenneth Coleman and Charles Stephen Gurr, eds. (Athens: University of Georgia Press, 1983) 183. Unpublished materials include Asa Candler's papers and those of his brother Warren, both in the Special Collections department of the Robert W. Woodruff Library at Emory University, Atlanta, which will be identified below as "AGC Papers" and "WAC Papers" respectively. Also in Woodruff Library's Special Collections are the papers of Candler's son, Charles Howard Candler, cited below as "CHC Papers"; these include the research materials used by Candler to write his account of his father's life; one such source is an untitled, brief biographical sketch of Asa Candler, with addenda and corrections, written by his brother John S. Candler, ca. 1929, cited below as "John Candler manuscript." The Archives, The Coca-Cola Company holds a small collection of Candler family papers and reminiscences of early associates of Asa Candler in the Coca-Cola Company.

[3] See the discussion of AGC's speech on child labor in the "Elitist" chapter.

[4] Institute for Southern Studies, "Georgia Methodism and Coca-Cola," circulated by the Youth/Young Adult Caucus of the United Methodist General Conference in Atlanta, n.d.; a copy is in the AGC papers, Emory. "Case Study: Coca-Cola and Methodism," a 1977 article by Bob Hall in *Southern Exposure* magazine (issue No. 3) rehashes the same material.

CHAPTER ONE

Country Boy

In the later 1830s, Samuel Candler and his fourteen-year-old bride, Martha, came to the rolling hills of Carroll County, Georgia, bringing with them two wedding gifts from her father: an Indian pony named Picayune and a slave girl named Mary. Several streams watered the 300 acres of land where they began to farm. There, Samuel and Martha built their home on the crest of a ridge surrounded by oak and hickory trees. Facing south, it began as a "dog trot" house—two small structures with doors that opened on a covered hall or breezeway between them. Large porches sheltered the front and rear of the building. Following the custom of the time, one large room, warmed by a fireplace in winter, doubled as a dining room and sitting room. The kitchen was a separate building. Over the years, Samuel and Martha had eight sons and three daughters and as the family expanded, so did the house. Eventually, their "comfortable but not ostentatious" home contained many books and a piano, enough evidence for their grandson's opinion that "both were unusually cultured for their period and place."[1]

The farm was, of course, a commercial enterprise, but Samuel's business interests extended far beyond its boundaries. He also occasionally held public office. Early in Samuel Candler's childhood his father had died, so he grew up partly in the care of a kinsman, Dr. Ignatius W. Few, who became the founder and first president of Emory College in Oxford, Georgia. Candler's large extended family was moderately comfortable, but as an orphan, he had to make his own way in the world.[2]

As Samuel Candler entered adulthood, a new opportunity for wealth appeared. In the spring of 1830, tales of gold nuggets snagged in the roots of fallen trees and gold dust in the gravel of mountain streams brought thousands of prospectors into the lands of the Cherokees in the northwest quarter of the present state of Georgia. No one knows the exact place or time of the original discovery, but by the end of the year it was clear that the prospectors had come to stay. The Cherokees resisted for nearly a decade before they were forced to march west on the Trail of Tears to the Oklahoma Indian Territory. The state of Georgia divided the former Cherokee lands to form all or parts of twenty-four new counties.[3]

The history of northwest Georgia now became a story of miners and farmers and men who built new cities. The miners came first, probing to discover the diagonal band of gold deposits that ran from Carroll County, west of Atlanta, to Rabun County in the state's extreme northeast corner. The most intense activity clustered in the Dahlonega area and in the area between Acworth and Canton; about thirty miles west of Atlanta, another cluster of activity developed in Carroll County. All sorts of people tried their luck in the hunt for gold. After bringing in their harvests, small farmers left their fields to prospect; prosperous planters leased gold lots, sending their slaves to work at panning or placer mining. Some full-time miners prospected the countryside on their own; others sought employment with mining companies.[4]

As a young man during the Georgia gold rush of the early 1830s, Samuel Candler pursued various mining activities, first in Carroll County and then in Cherokee County. It was in 1833, during this stay in Cherokee County, that he married Martha Bernetta Beall. Samuel made a good impression on his neighbors who elected him sheriff in

1834 and then sent him as a representative to the legislature in 1835. However, the newlyweds soon moved to the farm in Carroll County.[5]

Acting as the agent for a group of Macon investors who leased out gold prospecting rights on land they owned in the area, Candler received ten percent of the rents he collected for them.[6] He also began to diversify his business interests. With several partners, he developed the site that became the present town of Villa Rica. Candler then borrowed $1500 to open a store in the town and was successful enough to repay the sum promptly.[7] This general store—Villa Rica's first—usually contained $2,000 in stock. Miners came to the store with gold dust that they packed in goose quills for safe-keeping; thus the storekeeper became a small dealer in gold. Through these and other investments, Samuel Candler became one of the most prosperous men of his region.[8]

As Carroll County matured, although its gold deposits dwindled, the area retained its simple, frontier qualities. The inhabitants continued some mining, and they also raised stock or engaged in subsistence farming. Only those like Candler, who could afford the best acreage, undertook commercial agriculture and speculated in land: in 1847 Samuel Candler owned 7,800 acres in Carroll and Paulding counties.[9]

In the nineteenth century, the R. G. Dun Company—predecessor to today's Dun and Bradstreet—collected credit information on American firms from respected local businessmen. In their confidential reports on Samuel Candler, his fellow merchants consistently rate him as a safe, reliable man with good business capacity. In 1848 the entry calls him "a careful money saving money loving man," worth between $5,000 and $10,000. According to this report, he invested equally in real estate, stock in trade (for his store), and Negroes.[10]

When the market value of slaves rose more rapidly than the value of land, slave ownership indicated the location of the true wealth of Carroll County. In 1850 this was the case, when 3.5 percent of the county's ten thousand free inhabitants owned the county's 1500 slaves. The largest Carroll County owner was Elijah Dobbs, who owned forty-five slaves in 1860. Candler—with just under twenty slaves—ranked among the county's larger slave holders, in terms of the number of individuals owned. Some of the area's more prosperous men may have bought slaves for speculative purposes. Many of Candler's slaves must have been engaged in working on his farm, but whether all were doing so is unknown. In June 1860 Candler owned four "slave houses" occupied by seventeen persons of various ages and both sexes. At the same time, acting as an agent for S. B. Chapman (possibly as executor of an estate), Candler reported an additional nineteen persons and three houses.[11]

By the time of the birth in 1851 of his eighth child, Asa, the elder Candler had retired from the store, leaving it in the charge of William, one of his older sons. However, he continued his involvement in public affairs and Democratic party politics. During his long residence in Carroll county he served a term in each house of the legislature and was elected judge of the Inferior Court (justice of the peace). Other members of the Candler family served in similar ways; at one point Samuel sat in the legislature at the same time as his brother Ezekiel and Ezekiel's son Milton.[12]

While Samuel secured the family's fortunes, Martha took a strong role in their home. She led her eleven children in daily family worship, aided by the "English book of prayer." For many years she took the children to the Primitive Baptist Church, although the Candler family later became Methodist. Samuel himself did not join a church until later in life, but strong habits of hard work and sober living certainly contributed to the family's growing prosperity. In keeping with such principles, the Candlers, although comfortable, did not indulge themselves.

Following the practice of most rural families of their day, Samuel and Martha required the children to help with the work of the farm. A friend of the family later claimed that the Candler boys "found play in work" under their father's firm discipline: "Even on Saturdays, when other boys would be idle, the Candler boys were busy doing something." A small, wiry child, Asa lost the hearing in one ear when he fell from a loaded wagon while helping to harvest a field of corn. One of the wheels struck his head. However, if the discipline was firm, it was not so rigid as to stifle the children's sense of fun. One night, Asa hid under the bed of his youngest brother Charlie, a boy who suffered from a great fear of cats. Asa let out a life-like feline yowl and his terrified brother ran to their mother. Samuel was forced to rise from his bed to restore order to the agitated household.[13]

In a photographic portrait from this time the boy Asa looks at the camera with the same direct, skeptical gaze that was to be seen on the front pages of Atlanta's newspapers more than half a century later. Perhaps he remembered his own youth years later, when Asa Candler described a typical boy: "A boy…loves to do things that he imagines makes him appear to be a man. See him raking his upper lip vainly endeavoring to coax to the surface a mustache before its time, nauseating his stomach trying to chew tobacco and spit amber,…all to make himself believe that he is a man."[14]

Samuel and Martha gave particular, tender care to their third child, Noble Daniel Candler, who was mentally impaired. According to one family history, Noble had been a normal child until he suffered "a disease of the brain" when he was four years old. His brother John described Noble as "a man in stature, but less than a child in mind." He lived all his life with his mother, who cared for him until his death in 1887.[15] Asa Candler's heartfelt expressions of love and concern for his own children and the life-long bonds that connected him with his brothers and sisters bear silent witness to the fundamentally sound character of Martha and Samuel's child-rearing methods, stern though they might have been.

Even in his youth, Asa demonstrated an acute business sense. One enterprise began when a marauding mink disturbed the peace of the hens that lived under his mother's kitchen. Asa went to the rescue, diving under the house to rout the predator. He scrambled after the mink, out of the yard, through the woods and into a creek, where he caught up with it. The mink bit him, leaving a permanent scar on his arm, but young Candler triumphed, forever ending the mink's menace to the family chickens. He decided to send the pelt to Atlanta by wagon, hoping to sell it for twenty-five cents. To his delighted surprise, it brought a dollar. Young Candler's entrepreneurial character immediately asserted itself. "The man who bought it wanted more. I started people in the neighborhood to catching minks, and the skins we sold brought quite a sum." Alert to the interests of his neighbors, he diversified, investing some of his profit in "plain, every-day pins" to sell to rural housewives. He must have spent a good bit of time visiting prospective buyers around the countryside. He told a writer, "Seems you couldn't make anything off pins doesn't it? But when I went away to school, I had more than $100 saved up through the sale of mink skins and speculation in pins."[16]

Asa Candler approached his teens as the promising son of a prosperous and respected father and a pious and affectionate mother. In the midst of his large family he lived a busy and satisfying life, but the Civil War brought an abrupt end to this boyhood idyll.

Along with many of his Carroll County neighbors, Samuel Candler at first opposed secession. They sent him to the fateful 1860 Charleston convention that saw the Democratic Party split over the issue, but, when war came he and his neighbors supported the Confederacy. Candler's two older sons, Milton and Ezekiel, fought for the South.[17]

In common with many other southerners, the Candler family suffered as a result of the conflict. The Candler home near Villa Rica, more than thirty miles west of Atlanta, was on the fringes of the Federal campaign that demolished the city. Although no set battles took place in Carroll County, the area experienced some action. Stoneman's Raiders visited the county, and about ten days before Lee's surrender a large force under General Croxton looted and attempted to burn the county seat, Carrollton. In addition to the natural concerns of a mother whose sons were at war, Martha had special fear for the mentally disabled Noble, because he appeared to be an able-bodied man. If discovered, either army might take him away. However, the Candlers faced the hardships of the war with typical energy and resourcefulness. They boiled dirt from the smokehouse floor to recover valuable salt, for example. They probably lost crops and goods, but Mrs. Candler hid grain and meat for the family's sustenance and kept their small store of "hard" money concealed on her person. The family also managed to save some cotton from destruction.[18]

On the first post-war Christmas, the children received only gingerbread cakes but the sale of the cotton provided a bit of capital to begin the family's economic recovery. As a first step, Samuel began to build up his farming operations.[19] In 1865, his neighbors again elected him to the Georgia legislature. The general store reopened; R. G. Dun's credit reports on Candler & Son resumed with the March 1868 information that he was "Doing well selling for cash & making money[;] is an old Merchant & well qualified for bus[iness]."[20] By 1870, Samuel Candler owned $3,500 worth of real property and $3,750 in personal property. Compared to his prewar assets of $5,700 real and $13,280 personal property, this represents a considerable setback. Nonetheless, he continued to be numbered among the more prosperous residents of the area.[21]

In 1866, a one-armed former Confederate chaplain, William C. Dunlap, came to Villa Rica to lead a Methodist revival meeting. Like many southern men, Samuel Candler had taken little interest in formal religion before the war, but Dunlap's passionate preaching finally persuaded him to join the Methodist church. In addition to the influence of the Reverend Dunlap, the elder Candler's preferences on the sacrament of baptism affected his choice of denomination. As a new convert, he would be baptized, but his son John remembered that Samuel "would not consent...to be immersed" even though Mrs. Candler had been a life-long Baptist. This reluctance is understandable, since rural congregations commonly adjourned to any convenient stock pond or stream to carry out the sacrament. Methodists, by contrast, could be baptized with a dignified sprinkling. In any case, Martha's Baptist opinions were not without influence in the family; on the same day that Samuel Candler joined the body of believers by a Methodist rite, their daughter Jessie insisted on a total immersion, Baptist-fashion. In support of Samuel's conversion, Mrs. Candler left the Old Pleasant Grove Missionary Baptist Church and followed her husband to the Methodist congregation in Villa Rica, where she became the Assistant Superintendent of the Sunday school. Samuel also taught Sunday school; the four younger boys, Asa, Warren, John, and Charles, shared a pew in their father's class for young boys.[22]

Asa Candler, speaking in 1898, provided a glimpse into the church services his family once attended, when he recalled the religious music of his boyhood with a mixture of rue and affection. In his opinion, the "classics" such as the hymns of Watts, Wesley, and Newton, failed "to touch the young." He added, "the improvisations of the old preachers which they called solos…were sung when they got happy and were not fit for any other state, the fervent shout of the singer covered like charity…many of the blemishes of his music…."[23]

Whatever his opinion of the music of the old-time church, Methodist doctrines remained with Asa Candler and his three younger brothers. Methodists sought to conduct their lives along the lines of a Christ-inspired method that combined faith with upright living and with good works for the benefit of others.[24] Family prayers and church services planted these principles in the minds of the Candler children so firmly that Asa's beloved younger brother Warren became a Methodist clergyman and eventually rose to the rank of bishop in the Methodist Episcopal Church, South. Young Asa became a full member of the Methodist church at Villa Rica in 1869.[25] The Southern Methodist Church shaped him and he devoted a great part of his energies and wealth to its service. His faith was the pole star of his life.

The war and its aftermath had undermined the family's economic condition, and it also interfered with the younger Candlers' schooling. Asa had entered a local primary school shortly after his fifth birthday and continued there until it closed, when Georgia joined the Confederacy, a few days after Asa's ninth birthday. During the critical years of his early teens, no formal schooling was available in the area. Of course, education in rural antebellum Georgia had often been haphazard. Before the war, the Candlers had found it necessary to hire a young man to prepare their two oldest boys for college. Asa Griggs Candler was the namesake of this tutor, Asa W. Griggs, a distant relative and a medical student who later became a prominent physician. According to his brother John, Asa "was expected by his father to be a physician" as well.[26]

The young Candler children finally attended a school that citizens of Villa Rica organized in 1869, but the following year Asa went to Huntsville, Alabama, to live with his eldest sister Florence and her husband James W. Harris, while attending a high school "of fine reputation" taught by a Professor Slaymaker. Asa then moved with the Harrises to Cartersville, Georgia, where his education continued under the tutelage of Rev. S. G. Hillyer. Had he continued on this course he would have entered Emory College and pursued his—or his father's—plan that he study medicine. Meanwhile, to help meet expenses, he served as an apprentice in an apothecary shop operated by two family doctors, Best and Kirkpatrick. He learned the "prescriptionist" trade rapidly and soon the two doctors left their drug business entirely in his hands.[27]

This apprenticeship began on 1 July 1870. Within two years, young Candler abandoned his plans for a future in medicine. In a letter, written in 1872 to his namesake, Dr. Asa Griggs, he set down an early example of his pragmatic business sense, comparing the prospects of a career in medicine with the possibilities open to a pharmacist. In this cool analysis of the relative economic advantages of the two careers, he tartly observed that there was no shortage of doctors in the area, but that their considerable number compensated for their limited abilities. "Besides I think there is more money to be made as a druggist than as a physician & I know it can be done with a great deal less trouble of soul and body.... I want next year to go to a larger establishment in a larger place, where I can get sufficient compensation for my services."[28]

Later in life, Candler alluded to a youthful ambition to be a physician, which, as he remembered, poverty had thwarted. In fact, at the time he wrote his letter to Dr. Griggs explaining his new career choice, he was in a position to gain access to a medical education if he wanted one. Just one year later, the Candler family was able to send his younger brother Warren to Emory College in respectable style, and to keep him there in spite of the death of their father.[29] Asa made his career decision when he was twenty years old, mature enough to assert his independence of his elderly father's plans for his professional future and to follow his own inclination to enter a profitable profession. Candler's recollection of a medical career frustrated by reconstruction-era poverty has the aura of middle-aged nostalgia for roads not taken, rather than an air of deep personal disappointment. As the letter to Dr. Griggs makes clear, Asa Candler's warm appreciation of the dollar strongly influenced his decision at the time. Armed with a profession, he set out in the fashion of millions of young men of his day, to seek "sufficient compensation" for his services. He moved to Atlanta in the summer of 1873.

As Asa Candler became prominent, a whimsical version of his arrival in the city gained currency and persisted through his obituaries and into Atlanta legend. The tale echoes Benjamin Franklin's autobiographical account of a wide eyed, penniless youth wandering the streets of a great city in search of a means of livelihood. In his lifetime, Candler himself encouraged the impression of the friendless poor boy who made good: "I came to Atlanta, where after days of fruitless search, I secured a position with George J. Howard, a wholesale and retail druggist."[30] When Candler's son Howard retold the family legend in his memoir of his father's life, he added that the young Asa had arrived in Atlanta with $1.75 in the pockets of his homemade clothes. In this variation, the job search lasted until 9:00 P.M. on the first day. Furthermore, "No salary was offered until he could prove himself worthy of compensation... [H]e stayed that night until midnight."[31]

Some thirty years after his arrival in the city, Candler—conveniently within earshot of a newspaper reporter—entertained some associates in a committee meeting with the story of his first residence in Atlanta. The writer for the *Atlanta Constitution* included the anecdote in a florid account of Candler's "early struggles": on that first day, the young prescriptionist had sought inexpensive lodging in a boarding house, where he paid in advance for space in a bed—to be shared with two other lodgers—and a hook to hang his coat. The two bedfellows returned home late and objected to finding a stranger in their space. They suggested with "pugilistic playfulness" that he sleep hanging from the coat hook. The young man appealed to his employer, and "with his bundle for a pillow, gladly...sought out the softest side of the tenderest plank of the counter in the drug store where he worked." Candler, whom his son tactfully described as "a man of less than medium height," later joked that his room in the back of Howard's store was so cramped that even he couldn't stand up straight in it.[32]

Candler's brother John has also left a biographical sketch of Asa, which is less Franklinesque, but may be more accurate. In spite of a one-year discrepancy in the date, it is convincing in its detail: "Mr. George W. Howard [a druggist in Atlanta].... while on a visit to his farm in Cartersville was attracted by the young prescriptionist at the drug store of Best & Kirkpatrick and offered him a position as prescriptionist in his drug store at 47 Peachtree Street and thus it was that in 1872 [SIC] Asa Griggs Candler became a resident of Atlanta."[33]

The young man with calculating eyes, who wore his cap at a jaunty angle, attacked his responsibilities at Howard's drug store with typical energy. He wrote personal notes to potential customers to assure them that he would give them the best service because "my success depends on the amount of good I can do my proprietor in the way of trade." Such enterprise impressed Howard, who soon made him chief clerk.[34]

Meanwhile, in Villa Rica, Candler's aged father fell ill. In mid-September Dr. J. L. Slaughter began regular visits to the Candler home, bringing medicines that included an occasional half-pint of brandy. Death claimed Samuel Candler on 17 November and Asa left Atlanta to return to the farm to help his mother and young brothers cope with the new situation.[35] One of the older brothers, William Beall Candler, previously had been taken into business with his father to operate the store. Samuel Charles, who was between Asa and Warren in age, left school to assist in this part of the family business, but Warren remained at Emory College in Oxford, in accordance with his father's intentions for him. Asa helped his mother operate the farm and care for both his youngest brother John and the mentally deficient Noble.[36]

More troubles came the next fall when William and Samuel contracted typhoid in an epidemic that swept the state. Asa took over management of the store while the youngest boy, thirteen-year-old John, supervised the harvesting and ginning of the family's cotton. At this point the Candlers determined to reorganize their affairs. They sold the farm, and Mrs. Candler took young John to Cartersville in February 1875. Her daughter Florence enrolled John and two of his cousins into her high school for girls, where they prepared for college. The brothers Samuel and William became partners in the Villa Rica store, which continued the success begun by its founder. Meanwhile, Warren completed his studies in theology at Emory and graduated in July 1875.[37]

Asa, having discharged his responsibilities in Villa Rica, returned to Atlanta where he resumed his employment at George Howard's 47 Peachtree Street pharmacy. He also renewed his association with Trinity Methodist Church, where the young prescriptionist served as a steward of the church and assistant superintendent of the Sunday School. In his later years he recalled his Villa Rica childhood tenderly: "When I think of those golden days amid these parched years of care and distractions, I sometimes feel that once I lived in Heaven, and wandering, lost my way."[38] But he also told an audience, "I love Atlanta." The city had become his home and remained so for the rest of his life.

---

[1]Charles Howard Candler, *Asa Griggs Candler* (Atlanta: Emory University, 1950) 28, 31, 39-40.

[2]Candler, *Asa Griggs Candler*, 18-19. According to Dr. Charles C. Jarrell, *Oxford Echoes* (Historical Society of the North Georgia Conference and the Wesleyan Christian Advocate, 1967) 11-12, Ignatius Alfonso Few, DD, LLD, was a Princeton graduate who also had read law with his uncle, Col. William Few. He experienced a religious conversion after surviving a nearly fatal hemorrhage of the lungs. Although his health limited his ability to travel, he became a noted Methodist preacher and promoter of Christian education.

[3]"Big Ten's Map of Georgia Gold," (Cocoa Beach, FL: Big Ten, Inc., n.d.); W. Larry Otwell, *Panning Georgia's Gold: The Gold Panner's Guidebook* (Cleveland GA: Rainbow Sequoia, Pub., 1985) 2 ; Ray C. Rensi and H. David Williams, *Gold Fever: America's First Gold Rush* Georgia History and Culture Series (Atlanta: Georgia Humanities Council, 1988) 1-15; Rev. Lloyd G. Marlin, *The History of Cherokee County* (Atlanta: Walter W. Brown Publishing Co., 1932) 35, 144-49.

[4]"Big Ten's Map of Georgia Gold"; Rensi, 19-23.

[5]Candler, *Asa Griggs Candler*, 22-24, 43-44; transcription of obituary notice for Hon. Samuel C. Candler, identified "*Southern Christian Advocate* 10 December 1873" in box 7, CHC papers, Emory; Mark K. Bauman, *Warren Akin Candler: The Conservative as Idealist* (Metuchen, NJ: The Scarecrow Press, Inc., 1981) 6; John Candler manuscript, CHC papers, Emory; Rev. Lloyd G. Marlin, *The History of Cherokee County* (Atlanta: Walter W. Brown Publishing Company, 1932) 184, 191. On page 12 of *Cherokee County* Marlin reproduces the 1833 Cherokee County juror's list, which includes Ignatius W. Few, a prominent lawyer and Methodist layman who sheltered young Samuel after the early loss of his parents.

[6]Ibid.

[7]Veterans of McDaniel (Curtis Camp) and the Annie Wheeler Chapter, United Daughters of the Confederacy, sponsors, *Carroll County, Georgia: Souvenir—Historical Edition* (Carrollton GA: R. Lee Sharpe-Modern Printing Company, 1908; repr. Carroll County Genealogical Society, 1988) 31; R. G. Dun & Co. credit reports, Georgia vol. 5, section 101, R. G. Dun & Co. Collection, Baker Library, Harvard University Graduate School of Business Administration [Cited below as Dun, vol. 5]. R. G. Dun & Co., a predecessor of Dun & Bradstreet, collected credit reports throughout the United States and entered them in volumes organized by state; the citation above refers to the third volume of reports from the state of Georgia. Each volume consists of numbered sections representing an individual businessman or a firm; over a span of several years, one or more reports per year might be entered in each section.

[8]Candler, *Asa Griggs Candler*, 28; Bauman, 7; Ray C. Rensi and H. David Williams, *Gold Fever: America's First Gold Rush* (Georgia History and Culture Series, Atlanta: Georgia Humanities Council, 1988) 21; *Carroll County Souvenir*, 31; R. G. Dun & Co. credit reports, Georgia vol. 3:101; Candler, *Asa Griggs Candler*, 28. See Rensi on gold dust as a medium of exchange.

[9]James C. Bonner, *Georgia's Last Frontier: The Development of Carroll County* (Athens: University of Georgia Press, 1971) 51, 72-74.

[10]Dun, vol. 5.

[11]Bonner, *Georgia's Last Frontier*, 74-75; "Carroll County Slave Owners of 1860 as taken by George W. Awtry beginning th June 1860, Second District: Post Office—Villa Rica" reproduced in *Carroll County Genealogical Quarterly* (Spring 1981): 12-13. Ten persons held more than 20 slaves; 45 (including Candler) owned between 10 and 19, 87 owned between 5 and 10 slaves, and 212 owned fewer than 5.

[12]Candler, *Asa Griggs Candler*, 27. Another kinsman, Allen D. Candler, was governor of the state at the end of the century.

[13]Candler, *Asa Griggs Candler*, 42-43, 46-47. The source of the "play in work" quotation is identified only as "a friend of the family" who made this comment "while Father was still a relatively young man."

[14]Candler, *Asa Griggs Candler*, 41 [photograph]; AGC, untitled fragment, manuscript of speech, fol. 37, box 2, AGC papers, Emory.

[15]Allen D. Candler, *Colonel William Candler: His Ancestry and Progeny* (Atlanta: Foote and Davies, 1896) 114.

[16]"How I Made My First Dollar, Confessions By Atlanta Business Men," *Atlanta Journal* (15 February 1914).

[17]Bonner, *Georgia's Last Frontier*, 76-77; Lucian Lamar Knight, *Reminiscences of Famous Georgians*, 2 vols. (Atlanta: Franklin-Turner Co., 1908) 2: 358-59. Knight claims that Candler was burned in effigy for his views, although the unionist sentiments of his neighbors cast some doubt on the idea; Knight certainly erred in his statement that Samuel Candler "grew to manhood under the paternal roof-tree," when, in fact, he had lived with Augustus W. Few.

[18]Candler, *Asa Griggs Candler*, 49; Bauman, *Warren Akin Candler*, 27.

[19]Bauman, *Warren Akin Candler*, 27; John Candler manuscript, CHC papers, Emory.

[20]Dun, vol. 5.

[21]Candler, *Asa Griggs Candler*, 49; Bauman, 8-9; Dun , vol. 5. The 1870 manuscript census report confirms the Dun & Co. estimate of Candler's estimated worth in 1871 at $2,000 or $3,000. After Samuel's death, when William Candler took over the firm, his entry in Dun's Georgia vol. 51, section 116K estimated his worth at $8,000, information that provides further evidence of the mending of the Candler fortunes after the war. As Mark Bauman asserts, the wartime sufferings of Candler's family should not be exaggerated: "the financial hardship of the Candlers may have been severe only in relation to their prior circumstances."

[22]John Candler manuscript, CHC papers, Emory.

[23]AGC, manuscript of speech [1894], fol. 37, box 2, AGC papers, Emory.

[24]Robert E. Cushman, "The Wesleyan Tradition" in *Encyclopedia of Religion in the South*, Samuel S. Hill, ed. (Macon GA: Mercer University Press, 1984) 825-27.

[25]John Candler manuscript, CHC papers, Emory.

[26]Candler, *Asa Griggs Candler*, 48; John Candler manuscript, CHC papers, Emory. Candler was born on 30 December 1851; Georgia seceded on 19 January 1861.

[27]"What December Sixth Means to the Candler Family," *Atlanta Journal* (19 December 1920): 5; John Candler manuscript, CHC papers, Emory. Charles Howard Candler's version of his father's postbellum schooling and apprenticeship differs in some details from this account. I have chosen to rely on John Candler's chronology of events because it was written more than twenty years before Charles Howard Candler's book, and because the author was personally present during the time described. In any case both agree that Asa went away to stay with his married sister and go to school.

[28]Asa G. Candler to Dr. A. W. Griggs, quoted in Candler, *Asa Griggs Candler*, 55.

[29]John Candler manuscript, CHC papers, Emory; Microfilm copy, records of the administration of Samuel Candler's estate, Court of Ordinary, Book G, Appraisements and Vouchers, 1874-1876, Carroll County, Georgia Department of Archives and History. The records of the administration of Samuel Candler's estate show that Warren received $352.60 "to pay for clothing, colledge [SIC] tuition and current expenses for the year 1875."

[30]"What December Sixth Means to the Candler Family," *Atlanta Journal*, 19 December 1920, 5.

[31]Candler, *Asa Griggs Candler*, 63-64.

[32]Alan Rogers, "Rise of Asa G. Candler from Poverty to Wealth," *Atlanta Constitution*, 17 June 1907, 6; John Candler manuscript, CHC papers, Emory. The 1874 Atlanta *City Directory* confirms Candler's residence at 47 Peachtree Street.

[33]John Candler manuscript, CHC papers, Emory. The sources disagree on the year of Candler's move to Atlanta. John Candler uses only the year 1872. The letter to Asa Griggs, written in Cartersville, is dated 11 September 1872. Charles Howard Candler reports that his father left Cartersville on Monday, 7 July 1873.

[34]Candler, *Asa Griggs Candler*, 62 [photograph], 65. Quotation from: AGC to Leak & Williams, 10 January 1873, The Archives, The Coca-Cola Company.

[35]Microfilm copy, records of the administration of Samuel Candler's estate, Court of Ordinary, Book G, Appraisements and Vouchers, 1874-1876, Carroll County, Georgia Department of Archives and History. These include a transcription of the statement of charges for the services of Dr. Slaughter. These records also reveal the existence of yet another Candler enterprise, a tannery.

[36]John Candler manuscript, CHC papers, Emory; Allen D. Candler, *Colonel William Candler*, 114.

[37]John Candler manuscript, CHC papers, Emory.

[38]AGC, "Rural Sunday School Celebration," manuscript of speech, fol. 28, box 2, AGC papers, Emory.

CHAPTER TWO

Prescriptionist

When Asa Candler returned in 1876, Atlanta was earning its "Resurgens" motto, rapidly rebuilding after the almost total destruction that General Sherman had visited on the city. Visitors at the time thought that the city resembled a boomtown of the western frontier more than the traditional, "sleepy" cities of the old South. Youthful, energetic, and absorbed in commercial life, Atlanta's go-getter atmosphere matched Asa Candler's character to perfection. In this year, Martha Candler, still seeking a suitable education for her youngest son John, brought him to Atlanta to enroll in Boys' High School. They rented a place three blocks from Howard's store. Asa joined them; the city directory described Asa as a boarder in his mother's home. The three Candlers attended Trinity Church briefly, but transferred their membership to First Methodist to accommodate Mrs. Candler. The walk was shorter, and her son John remembered "she was never strong." As usual, both Asa and his mother took an active part in the Sunday school, where both taught classes.[1]

Perhaps Mrs. Candler "was never strong" in the physical sense, but she seems to have had a character of steel. A few photographs record her deep-set eyes and down-turned mouth as she gazes levelly at the camera. The resemblance to later photos of Asa is striking. In one 1895 image, the tiny woman sits out of doors in a straight chair, surrounded by seven imposing adult sons, the perfect image of the indomitable pioneer mother. One could easily imagine that this tiny woman—she weighed less than a hundred pounds—could face down marauding Yankee foragers, as the family legend claims. Now that her Villa Rica home had been sold and her youngest children settled, she lived close to Asa for the rest of her years. She also helped him launch his extraordinary business career, which began in a business partnership in the wholesale and retail drug business.[2]

In the fall of 1876 Candler's employer, George Howard, decided to relocate his drug business to Marietta Street, but Candler did not go with him. Instead, early in 1877, he and a co-worker, Marcellus Hallman, took over Howard's old 47 Peachtree Street location where they also began to sell drugs at wholesale and retail. Asa's brother John wrote that Hallman and Candler financed their partnership with their personal savings, a loan from Mrs. Candler and possibly a loan from Hallman's brother. The young partners promptly captured some of Howard's customary patronage.[3]

Their former employer fought back with a large notice in the *Constitution*, beginning on 22 April. It trumpeted his "REMOVAL!" to the new location. He wished to "respectfully call the attention of my friends and the public" to his new location and reassured them that he had hired two new prescriptionists, Charles H. Greene and Dr. J. S. Pemberton, "whose skill and experience in the drug business requires no comment." He extended to his former patrons "a hearty invitation to call on me in my new quarters."[4]

On 29 April, a few days after Howard's removal notice began its series of appearances, Candler and Hallman purchased a "card" or notice in the advertising section of the daily paper to counter their former employer's bid to keep his established customers, they insinuated that someone dealt in shoddy goods:

> Having for a number of years met and welcomed our friends at No. 47 Peachtree street and believing that a change

of base is not always best, we have decided to remain at THE OLD STAND, where we will continue the Drug Business in all its Details. Our entire stock and fixtures are FRESH AND NEW and have been BOUGHT WITH THE CASH, Hence we are enabled to furnish fresh and PURE MEDICINES as low as is asked for OLD AND INERT ONES. Our Prescription Desk will be in charge of Asa Candler, known in Atlanta as THE prescription clerk with Mr. Howard and has been supplied with medicines selected especially for prescription purposes.

The medical profession and public generally are respectfully informed that all prescriptions sent to us will be sent out CORRECT.

With sincere and grateful acknowledgements to our friends for past attentions and soliciting encouragement from them in our new role, we make our bow under the firm name of HALLMAN & CANDLER, formerly with Geo. J. Howard.[5]

Hallman & Candler's "card" ran only once, in the Sunday paper, but Howard must have felt considerable pressure. He had not advertised in the paper for several months before, but now found it advisable to run the removal notice for about two weeks and to follow it with another, listing seventy-five items available at his establishment in the Norcross building. He kept this announcement in the daily paper into the summer months. Meanwhile, Hallman & Candler shamelessly traded on the reputation of Howard's old location and used the phrase "Howard's Old Stand" on their letterhead. Perhaps the fight was too much for Howard; the following year he went into an entirely new line of work as a commission merchant with offices at 29 Alabama Street. Pemberton and two partners operated the drug business at No. 2 Marietta Street.[6]

The firm of Hallman & Candler seems to have prospered from the beginning. In 1877, Atlanta sources reported positively to R. G. Dun on the new partnership. Evidently the informants were unaware of any family loans involved in its founding. The report stated that the two young clerks had jointly saved about three thousand dollars from their salaries to invest in the business. The salary Howard paid his prescriptionists and clerks is unknown, but if the informants believed that the young men had saved their startup costs in about two years of employment, they must have thought them to be very thrifty fellows. Additional entries in Dun's "Georgia" volume over the ensuing three years trace the firm's continuing reputation for reliability. They estimate that its capital stock increased in value to five thousand dollars. Informants characterized Hallman and Candler as "shrewd active stirring young men" who "Stand well as to char[acter,] prudent & temp[erate] & consid[ered] safe."[7]

George Howard's troubles at the hands of the aggressive young prescriptionist were not limited to the world of commerce. While Candler still worked for Howard, Howard's daughter Lucy Elizabeth—called Lizzie by her family—had often found reasons to visit her father's place of business. Her photograph shows a sweet-faced young woman with a soft smile and dark eyes. When she met Candler, she was enrolled at La Grange College, in La Grange, Georgia. Her studies centered on music and art; her crayon drawing of an angel adorned the Candler home for many years. According to her son, Lizzie found pretexts to visit her father's store in order to watch Candler mix medicines and family lore reports that the young prescriptionist fell in love at first sight. Evidently, the relationship had become quite serious before Candler left Howard's employ, because when Lizzie came home for her Christmas holiday in 1877, she and Candler decided to marry. Whatever stormy scenes this decision may have engendered have remained private, but the young woman refused to return to La Grange after Christmas. George Howard opposed the match and denied his consent, but the couple proceeded with their plan and made their marriage vows in the First Baptist Church on the following 15 January. The father of the bride refused to attend.[8]

In his memoir of his father's life, Howard Candler speculates that George Howard objected to the wedding because of the bride's age or because she "had been reared in a social atmosphere which he considered would be strange to her husband." Neither reason seems convincing. Eighteen is not an unusual age to marry, and Asa Candler, although from a rural family, was no yokel. He was a church-going youth from a "good" family. If he was not wealthy, he was in business for himself and doing well, as Howard certainly knew. The latter fact provides a more plausible source of Howard's hostility. Very likely, he had not forgiven the events of the previous spring, when the prospective groom had made a raid on the clientele of "Howard's Old Stand." Adding his daughter to the list of Candler conquests must have rankled considerably. Howard continued his open hostility for some months.[9]

Asa, who preferred to call his bride Lucy rather than Lizzie, brought her to his home on Pryor Street where he and his mother had lived since the fall of 1877. Even before the addition of Lucy Howard, the composition of the Candler household had changed. Asa's brother John had finally completed his high school education and, in the fall of 1876, followed his brother Warren's path to Emory College at Oxford. Meanwhile, Warren, who had discovered his vocation for preaching, studied to become a Methodist pastor. He also married in November 1877, shortly before his brother Asa. The church now sent him to his first post at Sixth Methodist in Atlanta, where he received a very small salary. This necessitated careful economies, so Warren and his wife joined Asa and Lucy, the elder Mrs. Candler, and her son Noble in the cottage on Pryor Street.[10]

The two young couples evidently lived together amicably, probably because of the deep affection that bonded the brothers for all of their lives. Although he was older than Warren, Asa turned regularly to his brother for moral and spiritual advice. John, who pursued a career in law, also became a business associate of Asa. His law firm represented various large Candler enterprises in later years. Candler also kept close ties with his other brothers, particularly the two who had remained in Villa Rica: William Beall Candler, a merchant and banker and Samuel Charles Candler, Jr., a planter. Asa also became the protector of his sisters when they were widowed and involved several of their sons in his business enterprises. Warmly demonstrative, the brothers embraced whenever they met one another in public or in private.[11] In January of 1878, Asa and Warren took their wives in a two-horse carriage to visit the scenes of their country childhood. In later years, they regaled the family with their adventures in the muddy back roads and swollen streams of Carroll County.

The ever-expanding household rented larger quarters on Ivy Street and soon the two young couples produced their first children, Asa's son Charles Howard and Warren's daughter Florence.[12] A few days before Lucy went into labor, her father extended a slender olive branch, writing a terse note to his son-in-law: "Sir—I am disposed to 'bury the hatchet' and to be friendly in the future—if this should meet your approval you can let me know."

Asa accepted the gesture. He and Lucy named their first-born Charles Howard, reserving the name of Asa, Jr. for their second son. Thus, the family mended its fabric.[13]

Asa Candler, writing to his son on his twenty-first birthday, described the event of his birth 2 December 1878: "Twenty one years ago, in the early bleak cold December morning after a night of anxious expectancy you were placed in my arms, a wee wrinkled baby boy. They said 'He is without a blemish.' Your mama said "Oh how good that he is not deformed." Your grandmother my sainted mother kissed you & thank[ed] God for you."[14]

The crowded situation at Ivy Street sent Asa Candler into the real estate market for the first time. He purchased a residence at 66 Walton Street, paying $2,975. John, fresh from Emory, rejoined the household in the summer of 1880 and Asa Candler, Junior, first saw the light of day there in August. Warren's family left later the same year, when he received the appointment as presiding elder of the Dahlonega District.

The constant change in the composition of this household as it crammed into crowded quarters testifies to the adaptable temperament of its members. However, although Lucy had the aid of a servant, Fannie Walker, and Walker's twelve-year-old daughter, the situation began to wear on her. Her son described her as "superintendent and well-nigh slave" of a crowded establishment that included small children, her elderly mother-in-law, the mentally feeble Noble Daniel, and the various other kin who came and went. In 1882, the Candler family was again on the move, this time to the eastern suburbs of the city.[15]

Early Atlanta sat in a constellation of small settled areas, barely urban enough to have acquired names. Today, traces of these places remain on the map of the metropolitan area, preserved in the names of neighborhoods, shopping strips, or schools. The distinct identities of Cross Keys, West End, Buckhead, Oak Grove and a multitude of other small settlements have been subsumed into that of greater Atlanta. One such neighborhood (its name now usually recognized as a rapid transit train stop) was Edgewood. Near the western margin of Edgewood, Candler purchased Mrs. Mary E. Jones's "place"—ten acres and a cottage planted all about in field peas—for $3,250.

The rustic character of the area Candler chose may be seen in the records of the town council of Edgewood, a village near the family's new home. In addition to running two small schools (white and "colored"), the council concerned itself with matters such as "livestock running at large in the town" and the need to keep privies "clean and well limed." One marshal provided all the law enforcement needed to round up and fine the occasional drunk and disorderly citizen who disrupted the peace of the town.[16]

While building a new house, the family lived in the Jones cottage, which was close to the Georgia railroad as well as the road connecting Atlanta with the town of Decatur. (The Jones site is in the area of present Elizabeth, Hurt, and Edgewood streets in the Inman Park neighborhood.) They located the new home, which eventually expanded to contain fourteen rooms, on the opposite side of the railroad. Before it could be completed, Candler's only daughter, Lucy Beall Candler, was born. The two younger Candler boys were born in the new house: Walter, in 1885 and William, in 1890.[17] Candler provided his mother, Martha, with a house of her own, just two doors down the street, where she continued to care for Noble, until he died in 1887.[18] John also lived in this house with his mother until his marriage. A succession of her grandsons (Asa's nephews) stayed with her until her death in 1897. In 1914, her son Asa remembered his mother in a letter of condolence to a friend whose own mother had recently died: "This is…your greatest loss in life. I cannot, however, think that the loss is entire. Her influence over you will remain. When you would go wrong, her face will deter you. I do not believe a good Mother can ever die. Mine has not, though absent from the flesh since 1897."[19]

Candler left the center of the city of Atlanta at a time when many of the city's most affluent citizens were also on the move. In the immediate post-war period, members of Atlanta's budding elite had lived near to one another in simple houses or apartments close to the junction of the railroad lines that had created the commercial center of Atlanta. With increasing affluence, these people began to construct more opulent homes that clustered along Peachtree Street—a series of "castles" that "represented the fortunes built before 1890."[20] However, Asa Candler's choice of residence had little to do with this migration of Atlanta's wealthiest citizens. In fact, although he operated a prospering small business in 1882, he had not yet ascended to the company of those who could claim to hold a fortune. While others sought residences located on prestigious avenues, Asa Candler's move beyond the outskirts of the city reflected his conscious decision to avoid the urban environment.

The kind of life Asa Candler devised in his new home recalled the atmosphere of his own Carroll County childhood. His house and barn sat in the midst of a vegetable garden, orchard, grape arbor, and pasture. Howard Candler recalled, "On this acreage, Father provided every feature of a miniature farm." Miniature, it may have been, but it was a real farm. There, Candler supervised an early winter ritual that is familiar to the rural south. The hogs he raised in the previous year were slaughtered and the meat preserved in a smokehouse for the winter's sustenance, to be consumed along with produce from the garden, "put up" by Lucy. With this meal, they drank home-made cider, "sweet, never hard," according to Howard. Mules and a pure-bred bull lived in the barn. The children played with and cared for chickens, pigeons, and pet dogs. A billy goat, fitted out with a harness, pulled Howard and his brother Buddie (Asa, Junior) in a wagon. Mrs. Candler had a horse and buggy and the two younger boys, Walter and Willie, drove a pony and cart to school in good weather.[21]

They also kept saddle horses. The little boys sometimes rode "Sorrel" to school, and Howard remembers that his father rode "a splendid, spirited stallion named Stonewall." Candler himself wrote, in a letter to his daughter, a tender description of a mare that died in October 1897: "I did hate to give up [Fannie?]...she never failed me in her life. Worked anywhere. You all loved her. She went fast, but would not run away—stayed where I put her. She was so docile— took any medicine or any treatment that I had to give her without resistance. She died standing up. Never layed down."[22]

The career of Candler the capitalist obscures the image of Candler as a horseman, but as a rural youth in the nineteenth century, he learned his equestrian skills quite naturally. It follows that he would join the Governor's Horse Guard, a largely ceremonial cavalry unit organized in 1883. According to the *Atlanta Constitution*, some fifty "quiet, unostentatious gentlemen, for the most part well known and substantial business and professional men" formed the troop. The Guard's founder, Captain John A. Miller, and many of its senior members were Confederate veterans. Guardsmen paid a small fee to join (five dollars in 1886) and provided their own mounts. Officially a cavalry unit of the state militia, the Horse Guard participated in parades and other ceremonial occasions and held an annual encampment. They organized a team to engage in "tilting" contests. Occasionally the duties of the Horse Guard took them to other cities, for example accompanying the governor to the International Cotton Exposition in New Orleans. They formed an honor guard for the visit of President Cleveland to Atlanta's Piedmont Exposition in 1887.[23]

By 1890, Candler held the rank of second sergeant and in January 1898 he rose to first sergeant. In a letter to her daughter, Mrs. Candler wrote, "Today being memorial day papa and Walter turned out." Presumably, they took their places in the day's ceremonies and parades, while Mrs. Candler and Willie, her youngest child, joined some other family members to watch the procession. Candler retired from active participation in the Guard in 1903 with the rank of first lieutenant, but he continued to support the organization. "Lieut. Col. Asa G. Candler, Sr." appears in a list of "staff officers" who made donations for a gift to the governor in 1913. In 1916, when regular units of the Georgia National Guard went to the Mexican border to resist the revolutionary bandit Pancho Villa, Candler spoke on behalf of the Governor's Horse Guard Association, volunteering their services as a military guard for the city: "Mr. Candler, a well known millionaire and capitalist, told the Governor that he and his associates were ready to shoulder guns and get busy if it should become necessary."[24]

Candler brought another aspect of his Carroll County childhood into the life of his own young family. In 1882, when the family came to Edgewood, Candler moved his church membership to the Edgewood Methodist Episcopal Church. Religious faith and observance already occupied the center of family attention. Each morning the Candlers gathered before breakfast to worship. Led by their father, they knelt together to pray. Brief and in an unostentatious style, this prayer usually expressed gratitude for God's blessings and asked for guidance and protection for the family. Candler would then read a short scripture. Each meal began with a blessing. When a respected guest was present—a visiting clergyman or one of the children's several uncles—he would be invited to ask this blessing or to lead the family worship. Howard Candler remembered that the children preferred their father's crisp style to that of the sort of visitor who was "a long-winded egotist" who exhausted them with his ostentatious piety.[25]

The family kept the Sabbath scrupulously. When Christmas fell on a Sunday, the children had to wait until the next day to receive their gifts. Although domestic responsibilities occasionally kept their mother at home, the rest of the Candlers unfailingly attended Sunday school, where Asa usually taught a class, and then went to morning and evening services. In the middle of the week a prayer meeting reinforced their faith. In addition to these regularly scheduled events, there were special "protracted meetings" of an inspirational nature. Candler gave money and services, attending to small concerns as well as large. For example, when his church changed pastors (a regular practice for Methodists) Candler arranged for the moving of their household goods and saw to it that the new minister found his pantry fully stocked with food.[26]

This was not a life of grim piety, however; deep pleasures came with strong belief. Candler took satisfaction when his teachings moved one of his Sunday school pupils to conversion. He loved to conduct congregational singing, although his tenor voice sometimes led him to begin in a key too high for ordinary singers. On such occasions, he often ended up singing solo for a giggling audience, a situation that his son said "bothered him not a whit."[27]

Family letters written to Candler's daughter Lucy when she went away to school in the late 1890s convey something of the more homely side of Asa Candler's life. He signed himself, "Your old possum-headed Daddy."[28] Domestic and motherly (although not much of a speller), Mrs. Candler wrote newsy and affectionate letters describing her daily life. She usually had some sort of household help, but she also cooked for her family in the classic southern tradition, meals of baked pork, turnips, cornbread, and buttermilk. She baked tea cakes and soft gingerbread cake and "the best wafers you ever ate." She sewed: a waist to wear with her "pretty suit" and, with help from an unnamed "lady," winter clothes for the two younger boys. Howard wrote that she constantly mended his pockets, worn through by "such junk as is usually hoarded by small boys."[29] She grew flowers in her front yard. Tuberoses were favorites, and she also planted "nashturtians" with the help of young Willie.

She signed her long letters to Lucy "Your devoted mother," a true depiction of her character. In the late 1890s, when her two older boys were also away at Emory, she missed her only daughter a great deal. At times she picked flowers from her garden for Lucy, sending them by the train to Macon. She wrote, "I went to give Aunt Julia dinner yesterday morning she said something about you and I began to cry, she said hush Miss Lucy it is hard to give our girl up, but it is for her good."[30]

Mrs. Candler's tender feelings extended beyond her family. When she attended the Memorial Day parade with Willie and his aunt, the sight of the old Confederate veterans "made me cry, as it always does." One warm Tuesday night, while "papa has gone to a meeting of some kind and hasn't got back yet," she sat down to write to Lucy. An ink mark slashes a line across a portion of the letter: "The scratch you see above was mad[e] by me trying to keep the musquitoes off. I tell you they are simpley terible here we can hardly read or write at all. I have off my shoes and I cant keep them off my feet no way I fix them…your pap named our place musquitoesville that is a very appropriate name dont you think."[31]

In the same letter, Mrs. Candler told her daughter of a wedding soon to take place in Atlanta: "[T]hey are to be married with two rings. I never heard of that before I would like to see it."[32]

The press of business often meant that Candler missed the family's evening meal. At times Lucy would pack a dinner and send young Howard on the one-mile walk to catch the Edgewood Avenue streetcar, to carry the meal to his father. On other occasions she kept a late supper warm on a rack in front of the fire in their bedroom, waiting for her husband's late return. These irregular eating habits, coupled with the fact that he usually skipped lunch, may have contributed to his complaints of chronic dyspepsia. The tensions associated with his business concerns may also have been a factor. Business worries—possibly combined with poor eyesight—may also have been the cause of his frequent and severe headaches. Howard remembered his mother pouring pitchers of cool water over the back of his father's head and neck in an attempt to ease his pain.[33]

In spite of these occasional difficulties, the Candlers' family life on the "miniature farm" was warm, simple, and satisfying. Church activities provided the central focus for their life, but they enjoyed other entertainments. They sang together while Mrs. Candler played the piano and they listened to their father read humorous short stories that gave him the chance to demonstrate his skill in imitating rural dialects. The children attended the circus on several occasions. Writing to his daughter Lucy, Candler described a recital attended by the family: "[It] was splendid, Louisa played a solo. Asa Warren [John's son] made a speech and William [Asa's youngest son] recited 3 times. Miss Hufficar sang 'Comin' through the Rye' & other pieces. Miss Baldwin played & Walter & William ate ice cream & we all had a big time."[34]

As his children grew and thrived, so did Candler's business interests. After three years of partnership in Hallman & Candler's Peachtree Street store, Candler in 1881 bought out his partner Hallman and organized Asa G. Candler & Company. This development in Candler's affairs reflects his strong desire for complete personal control of his investments. His son commented, "The '& Company' was a euphemism, since Asa G. Candler owned it all personally." However, according to John Candler, family members assisted this transaction. His mother, his brother Samuel, who was a lawyer in Alabama, and his brother William, still keeping the store in Villa Rica, put funds at his disposal. Two other investors were Major Campbell Wallace, president of Merchant's Bank, and J. H. Porter, cashier of the Lowry Bank. John Candler does not comment on the source of Mrs. Candler's funds or on any settlement of the estate of Samuel Candler, but it is logical to assume that the elder Candler's assets and the sale of the family farm probably provided some of these monies. John Candler says that as a result of hard work, Asa soon repaid the obligations he originally incurred in founding his company. However, complete autonomy escaped Candler for a time. In the year that followed the creation of Asa G. Candler & Company, he sold his father-in-law a half interest in the firm, which became known as Howard & Candler.

Other difficulties ensued. A fire on 13 October 1883, wiped out most of the stock of this company. Fortunately, an insurance settlement enabled the purchase of the goods of another drug firm, Pemberton, Iverson & Denison. Finally, in 1886, Candler bought Howard's share of their firm and restored the name Asa G. Candler & Company to the enterprise. Whenever possible in his future business arrangements, Candler would retain control, allowing only a few minority share holdings to family or close friends.[35]

Asa G. Candler & Company, like Hallman & Candler before, manufactured and sold patent medicines and cosmetic products. In the basement laboratory in his thirty by one-hundred twenty foot building, Candler produced a number of the products sold by Candler & Company, which included not only patent medicines but also basic drugstore items such as paregoric, camphor and ammonia. A retail store and offices occupied the street level of the Peachtree Street location, while packaging and shipping activities occupied the second and third floors. From this center several agents traveled through south Georgia and east Alabama by horse and buggy, drumming Candler products to rural druggists.[36]

Among Candler's successful products were Everlasting Cologne, a dentifrice labeled Delectalave, and a "blood purifier" called B.B.B (Botanic Blood Balm). B.B.B., in addition to purifying the blood, cured skin diseases, rheumatism, catarrh, and kidney troubles. According to Howard Candler, it had a strong taste, which his father considered an essential quality for patent medicines. Although he manufactured them, Candler did not necessarily invent these products. For example, the formula for Everlasting Cologne passed from its original developer to a New York manufacturer and thence to Hallman & Candler and its successor firms. In another instance, Candler purchased and later sold the company that owned B.B.B.[37]

A calendar and an almanac preserved in the Emory archives show Candler's energetic use of advertising from this earliest period of his business career. They also identify more items, produced by other manufacturers and handled by his company. Candler's men offered Georgia merchants a group of products under the brand name of "Streetman's" that included their Champion of Pain, Nerve and Bone Liniment, Plasters, and Dyspepsia and Liver Cure. Other products were Hallman's Vermifuge, Howard's Hair Dye ("25 cts. a box"), Rock Candy Cough Syrup and the preparations of Parke, Davis & Company. Eagle Brand Baking Powder was proclaimed: "Pure and Powerful. Will make more from a given amount of flour than any other." Candler also sold two brands of house paints. The advertising matter in the almanac included "A Bit of History" about Asa G. Candler & Company: "Our stock is complete, our Store as commodious and well adapted for the transaction of the business as can be found...TRY US."[38] The *Atlanta Journal* and the *Constitution* of the late eighties regularly carried toothy ads touting Delectalave dentifrice.

A decade of enterprising activity established Asa Candler's position as a small manufacturer. Candler & Company enjoyed a gross annual volume of over $100,000 a year by the end of the eighties. Asa Candler husbanded his gains with care, reinvesting most of the profits back into the business. He made additional investments, some more profitable than others. His son reported that his father purchased stocks in a railroad and in a glass company that he held for the rest of his life, although they were essentially worthless. During this period Candler also invested in one project that was to leave its mark on the map of Atlanta. He was among the eleven incorporators of the Atlanta and Edgewood Street Railway Company, created on 24 December 1886.[39]

Joel Hurt, a visionary Atlanta businessman, had conceived a plan to create Inman Park, an elegant real estate development east of Atlanta. Part of the "Jones place" property Candler had purchased in 1882 had been, after he sold it, included in the new project. The plan included a street railway to carry commuters in a straight line from the city business district to the proposed residential development. In August 1889, with Hurt at the controls, the electrically powered yellow, gold, and orange car made the first trip to Inman Park. The ride was swift, quiet and smooth; passengers enjoyed the brass-fitted car's oak interior, illuminated by eight incandescent lights.[40] Although Inman Park failed to live up to its founder's grandiose expectations, it remained a highly desirable neighborhood. Eventually Candler built a mansion there, but even before, the family made regular use of the street railway, which was close to their "miniature farm."

As the nineteenth century entered its final decade, Asa Candler approached middle age as a moderately successful man, but was by no means to be ranked among the rich. In 1889 the *Atlanta Journal* profiled several city businessmen, including Candler. This set of articles has the air of the "business office must" in which the editorial department of a newspaper turns its skills to puff up the reputation of an advertising client. In any case, it offers an early glimpse of the up-and-coming entrepreneur. It characterized Candler as "the owner of possibly the largest drug business in the city of Atlanta" and included an engraving of Candler and an extensive description of the facilities at 47 Peachtree where the owner kept "a constant eye to every minute detail of the magnificent establishment…working diligently and faithfully and with that business tact that assures success in any undertaking." Appended to the profile of Candler and his firm were a number of testimonial letters for his products.[41]

The following year, an *Atlanta Constitution* article identified thirty-five of the city's great men, including five millionaires. Candler was not yet numbered among them, but if, at this juncture, he did not rank among the most important Atlanta men of business, his participation in the street railway enterprise demonstrates a respectable standing in the city's economy.[42]

Candler left a scrap of evidence about his financial status on January 1890, on a balance sheet written in his own hand on the stationery of Asa G. Candler & Co. His son says that this document, headed "We stood Jan 1st 1890," contained information to be submitted to Merchants' Bank, where he hoped to acquire a line of credit. His largest assets were his $6,000 home, which was mortgaged for half of its value, and the merchandise in his store, which was worth a bit over $30,000. Combining these with his interests in some patent medicine products with a few other assets, he claimed a net worth of about $50,000.[43]

Notably absent from this list is any mention of shares in the Atlanta and Edgewood Street Railroad. A great contest to control Atlanta's street railroad and electric power franchises had already begun. One step in this process was a reorganization of the Atlanta and Edgewood. Although he had earlier invested in the street railway, Candler was not among these new incorporators, who, the

Constitution estimated, shared close to a million dollars when a consolidation of Atlanta's several street railways absorbed their holdings.[44]

Perhaps Candler was not yet a big enough fish to swim in those rough waters, or perhaps he had simply determined to concentrate on the business he knew. This would have been a sensible plan for a man about to enter his forties, with a large family to support. He had recently acquired rights to a pain remedy after using it successfully to treat one of his own severe headaches. The new product promised to be at least as profitable as Delectalave or B.B.B. Its owner may not have suspected that it would soon make him a rich and influential man, but in any case, he was well prepared to make the most of any opportunity that "Coca-Cola" might provide.

---

[1]Sholes' Directory of the City of Atlanta for 1877; John Candler manuscript, CHC papers, Emory. [Hereafter all editions will be cited as "Atlanta City Directory" with the appropriate year added.] They lived at 31 Fairlie, at the corner of Griggs (now Poplar) St. See also, Truman Hartshorn and others, *Metropolis in Georgia: Atlanta's Rise as a Major Transaction Center* (Cambridge MA: Ballinger Publishing Company, A Subsidiary of J. B. Lippincott Company, 1976) 7-9. Hartshorn quotes an 1879 *Harper's Magazine* article on Atlanta as a western-style town.

[2]Charles Howard Candler, *Asa Griggs Candler* (Atlanta: Emory University, 1950) 32 [physical description], 33, 50 [photographs].

[3] *Atlanta Constitution*, 22 April 1877, 2. Dr. Pemberton later devised the original formula for Coca-Cola.

[4]Candler, *Asa Griggs Candler*, 69; John Candler manuscript, CHC papers, Emory;

[5]*Atlanta Constitution*, 29 April 1877, 4.

[6]Atlanta city directory (1878); Candler, *Asa Griggs Candler*, 70. According to the city directory, Candler's partner Marcellus Hallman resided in their store at 47 Peachtree. A photograph in the AHC collections shows a window painted "Hallman & Candler" at 49 Peachtree, but the end of a large sign on the 47 Peachtree location including a portion of a letter "H" that probably was part of Hallman's name can be seen at the edge of the picture. This photograph has led to some confusion about the location of the business, but it is likely that the Hallman & Candler enterprise occupied both the 47 and 49 storefronts, and used 47 as its official address.

[7]R. G. Dun & Co. credit reports, Georgia vol. 14, section 160. Quotations are from April 1879 report.

[8]Candler, *Asa Griggs Candler*, 71-74, 491; John Candler manuscript, CHC papers, Emory.

[9]Ibid., 74. Photographs of Candler (1873 and 1877) are on pages 62 and 73; Lizzie's 1877 image is also on page 73.

[10]John Candler manuscript, CHC papers, Emory; Atlanta city directory, 1878. The latter also

lists Warren Candler as a boarder at the N. Pryor Street location.

[11]In a letter of 11 May 1906, Asa called Warren his "pillar of strength." Such expressions are found throughout their correspondence; see box 1, AGC papers, Emory, for many examples. Candler, *Asa Griggs Candler*, 34-36, summarizes the lives of the siblings of Asa Candler; 242ff recount the deaths of brothers Milton and Samuel Charles (Charlie) who each received special care from Asa in their last months of life. The sons of Sarah Justina Candler Willard and Elizabeth Francis Candler Dobbs are prominent in the Coca-Cola Company of the Candler era. Florence Julia Candler Harris lived close to Asa's family after the loss of her husband.

[12]John Candler manuscript, CHC papers, Emory; Candler, *Asa Candler*, 76-78, 187.

[13]Candler, *Asa Griggs Candler*, 76. The original of this letter is preserved in the Asa Candler papers in the Woodruff Library Special Collections at Emory.

[14]AGC to Charles Howard Candler, 2 December 1899, box 1, AGC papers, Emory. Although he used his entire name as the author of the book on his father's life, Asa Candler's first son usually was known as Howard.

[15]Candler, *Asa Griggs Candler*, 77-78; John Candler manuscript, CHC papers, Emory; US Census Bureau, microfilm of manuscript census returns and indexes (1880) Federal Records Center, National Archives and Records Service, Atlanta.

[16]"Minutes of the Town of Edgewood from 2 February 1890 to 13 August 1906," in the records of the City of Atlanta, Atlanta History Center Library/Archives. The city of Atlanta annexed Edgewood in 1909.

[17]Candler, *Asa Griggs Candler*, 78-79, 188-90, 491.

[18]Atlanta city directories for the 1890s only identify Candler as a resident of Edgewood, but the 1901 and 1902 volumes identify the address as 893 Seaboard Avenue. A map prepared by H. B. Baylor and E. B. Latham, copyright 1894, but labeled "Baylor Atlas, 1893" can be found in both a bound volume and in the folder labeled "Plat Maps, 14th District, LL1-LL14" in the Atlanta History Center Library/Archives which shows the location of both Candler's and his mother's property. Another map in this folder, untitled but copyrighted by the city of Atlanta shows the "footprint" of the houses in this area as surveyed in 1928. An undated newspaper clipping in the DeKalb County Historical Society files identifies a photograph of a house at 1069 Seaboard Avenue, which had become an abandoned ruin slated for destruction, as Candler's 14-room house. A parking lot of the Inman Park/Reynoldstown MARTA rapid transit station now occupies a good part of this site. See also Candler, *Asa Griggs Candler*, 78-79

[19]AGC to Dr. W. H. Gallaway, 30 September 1914, AGC Papers and Biography, The Archives, The Coca-Cola Company. In the family burial plot at Villa Rica, Noble Daniel rests between Martha and Samuel Candler, sheltered by a tall magnolia tree. Noble's gravestone reflects the family's tenderness toward their weakest member: "God saw fit to cloud his brilliant intellect but cast no shadows on his noble heart causing his life to be a joy to all who knew him."

[20]Doyle, 191, 196.

[21]Candler, *Asa Griggs Candler*, 195-97; Mrs. Candler to Lucy, 3 September 1897, The Archives, The Coca-Cola Company.

[22]AGC to Lucy Candler, 19 October 1897, The Archives, The Coca-Cola Company. Candler's handwriting, often difficult to decipher, consigns the precise identity of this excellent animal to the realms of mystery.

[23]"Cavalry to the Front," *Atlanta Constitution*, 30 March 1890, 14; Governors' Horse Guard Membership Certificate with $5 membership fee noted (1886) Wright (Ralph) Memorabilia, Archives, Atlanta Historical Society; miscellaneous Governor's Horse Guard memorabilia, fol. 7, box 3, AGC papers, Emory.

[24]Mrs. Candler to Lucy, (1900) The Archives, The Coca-Cola Company; "Candler Proposes to Form Home Guard," *Coca-Cola Bottler*, September 1916, 16; Miscellaneous Correspondence (Box 1) Rolls and Registers (Box 2) Office of the Adjutant General, Georgia Department of Defense, Georgia Department of Archives and History, Atlanta.

[25]Candler, *Asa Griggs Candler*, 213. Throughout the records of Candler's life are recorded examples of the now less prevalent custom of beginning all sorts of meetings, public and private, with an invocation.

[26]Ibid., 338, 197, 209, 212-13. Candler served in dozens of church offices over his lifetime; for a complete list, see Candler, *Asa Griggs Candler*, 338-39.

[27]Ibid., 206, 215.

[28]The Archives, The Coca-Cola Company, has a file of these letters to Lucy; the following account of Candler family life at the end of the nineteenth century was largely gleaned from this source.

[29]Candler, *Asa Griggs Candler*, 202; see pages 202-209 for the full text of his affectionate recollection of his mother.

[30]Mrs. Candler to Lucy, 3 September 1897, The Archives, The Coca-Cola Company. Asa Candler's elder sister, Florence Julia Candler Harris, lived close to his family after the death of her husband; however, Charles Howard Candler consistently calls her "Aunt Florence" in *Asa Candler*. The exact identity of "Aunt Julia" remains uncertain,.

[31]Mrs. Candler to Lucy, The Archives, The Coca-Cola Company, Atlanta.

[32]Ibid.

[33]Candler, *Asa Griggs Candler*, 210-211.

[34]Ibid., 215; AGC to Lucy, 2 September 1897, The Archives, The Coca-Cola Company.

[35]John Candler manuscript, CHC papers, Emory; Candler, *Asa Griggs Candler*, 80-81. This account of Candler, Howard, and Hallman's various partnerships is largely corroborated by a "Registry of Merchants, 1873-1882," [actually a record of business licenses] in the City of Atlanta records, Atlanta History Center; however, it contains no record of Asa G. Candler & Company. The 1881 license fee was recorded as paid in July by Hallman and Candler at 47 Peachtree; in the following July Howard & Candler paid at the same address. Charles Howard Candler states that Howard & Candler "sustained a crippling loss" because they had no insurance; John Candler says that the insurance firm of W. P and W. F. Patillo "secured a very prompt adjustment" of the insurance claim connected with this fire, and that business resumed quickly at the same location. According to E. Y. Clarke, *Illustrated History of Atlanta*, (1877; reprint, Atlanta: Cherokee Publishing Company, 1971) 128-30, the Patillo firm dominated the fire insurance business in the city. Charles Howard Candler identifies the source of the replacement stock, but does not explain how it was purchased. Evidently each source has a piece of the story.

[36]Candler, *Asa Griggs Candler*, 84-88.

[37]Candler, *Asa Griggs Candler*, 81-83.

[38]Almanac, box 7, AGC papers, Emory.

[39]Candler, *Asa Griggs Candler*, 89; Sarah Simms Edge, *Joel Hurt and the Development of Atlanta* (Atlanta: Atlanta Historical Society, 1955) 189.

[40]This discussion of the Atlanta and Edgewood Street Railroad draws on the following: Jean Martin, "Mule to MARTA, Volume I" in *Atlanta Historical Bulletin* 19/2 (1975): 22-29; Franklin M. Garrett, *Atlanta and Environs: A Chronicle of Its People and Events*, 2 vols. (Athens: University of Georgia Press, 1954) 2: 188-90; Don Lloyd Klima, "Land Barons Ride

the Rails: Real Estate Speculators and Street Railways in Late Nineteenth Century Atlanta" (MA thesis, Georgia State University, 1977) 66-78; David L. Williams, "The Development and Consolidation of Atlanta's Street Railways, 1866-1891" (MA thesis, Georgia State University, 1975) 52-55; Edge, *Joel Hurt*, 193-94.

[41] "Asa G. Candler & Co." *Atlanta Journal* 1 May 1889, 22.

[42] *Atlanta Constitution*, 7 April 1899, quoted in Garrett, *Atlanta and Environs*, 2 vols. 2: 179-80.

[43] AGC memorandum, "We Stood Jan 1st 1890" AGC Papers, box 1; Candler, *Asa Griggs Candler*, 89-90.

[44] Edge, 189; Williams, "Development of Atlanta's Street Railways," 63-139, passim; Klima, "Land Barons," 75-76.

CHAPTER THREE

Entrepreneur

"You know how I suffer with headaches..." Asa Candler wrote to his brother, Warren, in the spring of 1888. On this occasion, however, he had found relief, when "...a friend suggested that I try Coco-Cola." The headache went away and commercial curiosity took its place. After a brief investigation of the product, Candler found "...that it was owned by parties unable to put it fairly before the people. I determined to put money into it & a little influence." He didn't have the spelling quite right, but he had decided to invest $500 in Coca-Cola.[1]

Asa's letter to Warren is the earliest surviving evidence of his interest in this now legendary product. As befits a legend, the beginnings of the Coca-Cola Company are not perfectly clear, but combining information from a number of sources can develop a reasonably complete story.[2] Asa Candler's critical contribution to the product—like that of Henry Ford to the automobile—consisted mainly of popularizing it through effective production and merchandising methods. Its actual inventor, John Styth Pemberton, a Confederate veteran and long-time Atlanta druggist, was the same Dr. Pemberton who had joined George Howard's firm on Marietta

Street after Candler left his future father-in-law to strike out on his own. Pemberton had moved to Atlanta in 1869, where he involved himself in various business relationships for the next eighteen years. He made and sold Globe of Flower Cough syrup, Triplex Liver Pills, Indian Queen Hair Dye, Gingerine, Extract of Styllinger and French Wine of Coca—Ideal Tonic. The Pemberton Chemical Company, incorporated in 1885, manufactured patent medicines at 107 Marietta Street. At some point he began to develop a headache remedy that included fluid extracts of coca and of the kola nut in a simple-syrup base. It somewhat resembled "French Wine of Coca," an earlier product of Pemberton's. Frank Robinson, his partner, devised a distinctive cursive label with a revised spelling of "kola," thus establishing one of America's most recognizable trademarks: Coca-Cola.

The syrup went on sale in several local pharmacies. According to a traditional story, an unidentified headache sufferer allegedly purchased a bottle of the remedy at Jacobs' Drug Store, located in the downtown business district at Five Points. He asked Willis E. Venable, the soda fountain operator, to prepare a dose for him by mixing it with water. Venable suggested soda water, because the dispenser was more convenient. The customer pronounced the resulting drink to be both tasty and effective.[3] Other establishments soon adopted this method of preparation. By June, 1887, "Coca-Cola The Brain Tonic and Intellectual Soda Fountain Beverage" was advertised as "acclaimed by all who have used it." Its reputation as a beverage began to eclipse its original purpose of headache relief.

The elder Pemberton became seriously ill and could not promote his product effectively. On 8 July 1887, he sold two-thirds of his interest in the Coca-Cola formula, and the exclusive right to manufacture it, to two persons, the fountain operator Willis E. Venable and another individual, George S. Lowndes. At about this time, Candler had his historic headache. Many years after these events, in testimony offered in a patent office hearing in July 1914, Candler offered some explanation of what happened next, describing, in somewhat vague terms, his earliest involvement with the product. Before he became Coca-Cola's exclusive owner, "I was directing its policy in 1887, in 1888 more so…I don't know whether I bought it or not, I don't know what I had done; these gentlemen got to owing me a good deal of money in 1887 and the whole product had to be manufactured and sold through my business, that's my impression now.…I didn't own it, but I controlled it, because they owed me enough money for me to control it."[4]

In "directing its policy" he pressed to improve the product from the outset. In June of 1888 he grumbled in a letter to his brother Warren: "We are doing moderately well with Coco-Cola [SIC]. Its only obstacle is that Pemberton is continually offering a very poor article at a less price & the public who pay for Coco-Cola and are not benefited, erroneously decide that it is a fraud."[5]

The failure of his partners to meet his expectations probably moved him to want direct control of the product. In any case, a complex sequence of transactions did take place in which Asa Candler acquired Coca-Cola, a piece at a time. The production equipment, which had moved from place to place with a half dozen changes of ownership, finally went to Candler's facility at 47 Peachtree Street. Candler continued to increase his ownership of the product, and by April 1891 he owned it all.[6] A few months later Pemberton, the inventor of the original syrup formulation, died. Atlanta's druggists convened under Candler's chairmanship, meeting in his store to plan a demonstration of respect. They all closed their places of business for the hour of the funeral.

Candler later said that he "quit buying and selling" in 1890, although the drug company continued to exist: "people owed me, you know."[7] However, he did continue to distribute and advertise "DE-LEC-TA-LAVE" in the early 1890s. In the fall of 1891 he closed the Peachtree Street store and relocated his manufacturing activities to 42 -1/2 Decatur Street.[8] There he poured much of his energy into the development of his new product.

On 29 January 1892, the state of Georgia chartered the Coca-Cola Company as a corporation with capital stock of $100,000. Candler retained most of the shares, which were valued at $100, and thus was the president of the company. He was forty-one years old.

His brother John, with a single share, became vice president. Ten shares went to a former Pemberton associate, Frank M. Robinson, the man who designed the Coca-Cola trademark. He had become a close friend of Candler's and was made Secretary-Treasurer of the new firm. A short, stocky native of the state of Maine who always wore a coat even when he was without a tie, Robinson was Candler's right-hand man in the daily operations of the company. Candler and Robinson, for example, relied on their senses of taste and smell for quality control; Robinson could detect any imitation and Candler's "perception of flavor and savor could always be relied upon," according to Howard Candler. Even after Candler passed management of the company to Howard, the elder Candler still taste-tested Coca-Cola samples.[9]

Ten shares in the original corporation went to Candler's nephew, Samuel Candler Dobbs, who worked for Coca-Cola as early as 1891. The company also distributed a few shares to retailers to induce them to market the product enthusiastically. One share went to Asa's clergyman brother Warren, who seems to have taken no part in the operation of the business. Two early Candler associates who wrote histories of the company's earliest years, S. L. Willard and D. S. Candler, later said that an effort to sell some of the stock through the office of Phil Haralson of Atlanta did not succeed.[10]

After he acquired control of Coca-Cola, Candler consulted outside experts and used his own skills as a chemist to revise the Pemberton formula, which Pemberton or his son Charlie cooked up in the back yard in a three-legged, fifteen-gallon pot that stood over a fire.[11] According to Howard Candler, his father "worked it over" to eliminate some ingredients and change the proportions of others, thus making the mixture more stable and better tasting. The drink contained a flavoring agent that was derived from the coca plant but was free of narcotic effects. If Coca-Cola actually contained any cocaine, the tee-totaling Candler certainly would have eliminated it from the beverage at this point. He also switched storage of the syrup from tin cans to refurbished whiskey barrels. The inclusion of a "very desirable constituent" (possibly phosphoric acid) had made storage in metal containers undesirable.[12]

The laboratory on Decatur Street occupied the second floor of a building that also housed a saloon and a clothing store with a Negro clientele. Although he altered the formula, Candler's early methods of production were little better than the original boiling pot in Pemberton's back yard. At a 1913 sales meeting, a Candler associate described the early days of Coca-Cola, while obliviously demonstrating the racial attitudes of the time. "We had a large copper kettle for boiling the syrup and one big-footed Negro to handle the paddles. Boys, it was some equipment." At first, Candler and his assistants spent the greater part of the week brewing up batches of B.B.B. and Delectalave, but during the last day or two they made Coca-Cola syrup. Candler, his clothing protected by a tightly belted long blue gown, personally mixed the elements of the syrup. They cooked three ingredients in the forty-gallon copper kettle, and then used a dipper or a hand pump to move this base into clean whiskey barrels. Then they added five more components and vigorously agitated the mixture to complete the process. Unfortunately, during the transfer, they occasionally spilled the sticky syrup, which leaked through the floor to soil the clothing on sale below.[13]

Coca-Cola sold well in spite of the national financial crisis of 1893. The company declared its first dividend of $20 a share in that year. Beginning with the shipment of a barrel of syrup to Rome, Georgia, the company soon developed dispensers throughout the South and as far away as New England, Pennsylvania, and Ohio. In 1894, Coca-Cola's first branch manufacturing plant opened in Dallas, Texas. As business increased, Candler moved the Atlanta factory from the Decatur street location to an old house at the corner of Wheat and Ivy streets. By 1898 thirsty Hawaiians and Canadians could join the residents of every US state in enjoying the delicious, refreshing beverage; negotiations with Mexico were under way. Success was such that Candler felt ready to build a new, four-story Atlanta plant. He bought a triangular lot on Edgewood Avenue; the side street became Coca-Cola Place. He fitted it out with new production equipment, and said that it would be "sufficient for all our needs for all time to come."[14]

Candler made and shipped Coca-Cola syrup on the street and basement levels of his building. The upper two floors contained company offices and the office of Candler's brother John, a lawyer and judge, who was also vice-president of the company, its legal counsel, and its second largest stockholder. The "point" of the triangular building at the intersection of Edgewood Avenue and Coca-Cola Place contained a laboratory where Candler (or his associate Robinson) secluded himself to mix the secret flavoring components of the beverage. A vault-like iron door with a combination lock controlled access to the laboratory. Shipments of the essential ingredients were immediately stored in this room and the labels removed or defaced. Candler closely guarded his formula, which included powdered caffeine, a fluid extract of coca leaves and kola nuts that he called "C and C tincture," and a secret proprietary ingredient that later came to be known only as "Ingredient 7x." Asa Candler opened all the mail personally and did not permit any of the office staff to handle transactions regarding the critical ingredients. Eventually Candler initiated his son Howard into the mysteries of the process. Howard called the occasion "one of the proudest days of my long experience with The Coca-Cola Company."[15] During all of Candler's years, he trusted only a handful of close associates, many of them family members, with the full formula. The exact recipe for Coca-Cola and the identity of "Ingredient 7x" remain among the world's most closely guarded trade secrets after more than a century.

The early Coca-Cola Company personnel, in addition to Candler, consisted of Frank Robinson (the former Pemberton associate who devised the Coca-Cola trademark), Candler's nephew, S. J. Willard and one full-time salesman named Mr. Little. Candler also arranged for commercial travelers who sold other products, such as B.B.B. or the products of the Atlanta Perfumery Company, to take orders for Coca-Cola as well. In fact, Coca-Cola's Mr. Little also wrote orders for B.B.B.; it was, after all, another Candler product.

Coca-Cola was the first soft drink to enter the national market, where it vigorously defended its position with aggressive marketing. Ambition moved Asa Candler to imbue his enterprise with a kind of missionary fervor. Modeling his speech after the Great Commission of Christianity, Candler reported to his board of directors in 1897 that "we have not lagged in our efforts to go into all the world, teaching that Coca-Cola is the article, par excellence, for the health and good feeling of all the people."[16]

This was a new kind of business, made possible by the rise of mass manufacturing and transportation technology in the late nineteenth century. Products such as chewing gum and cigarettes—and Coca-Cola—pioneered the manufacturing of low-cost, prepackaged items for retail sale. They kept up a steady, high-volume flow of products to markets with large numbers of consumers. Competition among such producers emphasized advertising and service, rather than price.[17]

One key opportunity to tap the national market came to Candler by chance, when two Chattanooga attorneys, Benjamin Franklin Thomas and Joseph Brown Whitehead, approached him in the summer of 1899 with a scheme to bottle Coca-Cola, which was available only at soda fountains. Candler had originally rejected the idea of going into bottling himself, because of bad experiences with early bottled drinks. Although skeptical of the possibility of success, he agreed that Coca-Cola would franchise "parent bottlers" who could themselves franchise other bottlers. Candler's firm provided the syrup and promotion of the brand name. Bottlers made no other cola drinks—though they could bottle other flavors. Bottlers held their franchises for life and could pass them on to their heirs. Creation of this network of franchised bottlers helped shape the final structure of the Coca-Cola Company.

The first bottling operation opened in December 1899. After including another partner, John T. Lupton, these "parent bottlers" then extended bottling rights to local franchises over most of the country, thus establishing a distribution system that remains in effect to the present. At times the bottlers found themselves in competition with fountain dispensers for the trade of the same thirsty customers, but the company usually managed to keep both groups happy. Candler's Coca-Cola had developed into a type of organization that could control retail outlets through advertising and promotion, without the headaches of outright ownership. Growth continued steadily. The first decade of success could be measured in gallons: Coca-Cola sold 9,000 gallons of syrup in 1890; in 1900 the company made 370,877 gallons. At the end of Candler's administrative tenure, in 1916, Coca-Cola boasted assets of $27 million, and ranked 212 on a list of 500 of the largest US industrial enterprises.[18]

At first, Candler clearly considered this new product to be another patent medicine. He solicited sales for his "tonic stimulant" with a form letter extolling the "Ideal Brain Tonic, Coca-Cola ... a medical preparation of great value, which the best physicians unhesitatingly endorse and recommend for mental and physical exhaustion, headache, tired feeling, mental depression, etc."[19]

However, it was the "delicious, refreshing" soft drink rather than the "tonic stimulant" that Candler finally chose to promote. In fact, the use of Coca-Cola as a beverage seems to go back to the beginning. In his original 1888 letter to Warren he set out an aggressive promotional program to distribute tickets for free sample drinks at soda fountains. Coca-Cola would supply the syrup *gratis* to fountain operators who were willing to participate. He wrote to his clergyman brother, first reassuring him, " Now I dont want to make a merchant or peddler out of you," but asked if he might know of a Nashville fountain operator who would be interested in the promotion.[20] (This plan may have been Frank Robinson's idea, since he had given out tickets for free Coca-Cola in the Pemberton days.) In addition, Candler used advertising extensively, continuing the "Delicious— Refreshing" slogan, that Robinson had coined.[21]

The development of mass circulation national magazines and newspapers in the late nineteenth century opened new possibilities for "salesmanship in print" in the form of advertising. Even as he exerted every care in the manufacturing and merchandising of his product, Candler also took advantage of every opportunity to put the

Coca-Cola brand name before the consuming public. At first Frank Robinson managed both advertising and sales, but in 1906 Candler set up a separate sales department under Dobbs, leaving Robinson solely in charge of advertising. Robinson was more willing to allocate funds for advertising than Dobbs, and both would air their views at the annual stockholders' meetings. Candler, as the only major stockholder, made the final decision, and he accepted Robinson's view, spending freely to promote Coca-Cola. At a time when other manufacturers usually thought advertising represented money wasted, he understood that brand recognition, although intangible, constituted a valuable asset, even when promoting it did not pay an obvious return within the immediate fiscal year. As early as 1892, he put $11,401 into his advertising budget; by 1901 this sum had increased to $100,000. Coca-Cola spent a million dollars to advertise in 1911.[22]

The Massengale Advertising Agency of Atlanta handled the Coca-Cola account through most of the 1890s to 1904. Although the "Delicious! Refreshing!" approach predominated, the old patent medicine theme persisted in some 1890s ads, claiming that it "Relieves Headache Immediately." This approach ended at the turn of the century, when the company began to market Coca-Cola exclusively as a beverage.[23] Massengale's agency favored elaborate lithographs of elegantly clothed consumers enjoying Coca-Cola.

Some time prior to 1904, W. C. D'Arcy, a man who had sold advertising space on streetcars, somehow came to the attention of both Candler and Dobbs. They encouraged him to establish his own agency in 1904. By 1906 D'Arcy's firm had acquired almost all of the Coca-Cola account, while Massengale was left with the task of promoting the product only in religious publications. D'Arcy began to place Coca-Cola ads in national magazines. He took a more informal approach, using illustrations of pretty girls (including modestly clad bathing beauties) and "modern businessmen" engaged in leisure activities. Since these images met with Candler's full approval, D'Arcy's vision of a world of wholesome middle-class prosperity may well be seen as representative of Candler's own view of the ideal society in its moments of diversion. The utterly respectable inhabitants of D'Arcy's Coca-Cola displays could have put on their Sunday best and seemed quite at home in any Methodist Church in Atlanta.[24]

In addition to ads in publications, Coca-Cola found other ways to put its name before the public. Bill-boards and signs on the sides of buildings covered 2.5 million square feet by 1908. Massengale's gorgeous lithographs embellished ten-cent sheet music of sentimental songs and hymns. Over the years, Coca-Cola's trade mark decorated eight-day clocks, matches, pocket knives, blotters, watch fobs, and wagon umbrellas. The familiar red-and-white round metal sign began to appear everywhere. When Americans sat at the drugstore soda fountain, they could look up and see a cardboard festoon of handsome, wholesome and cheerful Coca-Cola drinkers, keyed to the season. Eventually, even Santa had a Coke at Christmas. In 1909 a dirigible "plastered with Coca-Cola advertising" floated over Washington, DC.[25]

Beyond seeing the value of brand-name recognition Candler also wanted to assure Coca-Cola's respectable reputation. Perhaps because of its name, many Americans believed that the drink contained the drug cocaine, an opinion that vexed the tee-totaling Candler. Although a flavor extract used in Coca-Cola and the narcotic cocaine both derive from the coca leaf, the soft drink had no narcotic properties. Candler always insisted that the product be called by its full, four syllable name. People who asked for "coke" or "dope," popular slang names for his product, outraged him. To squelch such notions, the company arranged to test Coca-Cola. Extensive advertising proclaimed testimonials from the state chemist of Alabama, the Medicine Department of Tulane University, and the Chemical Department of South Carolina College, all declaring Coca-Cola free of harmful drugs. For those with a less scientific turn of mind, men like "the great Cleveland batsman-manager" Napoleon Lajoie and Umpire Frank "Silk" O'Loughlin endorsed the drink as suitable for athletes in training.[26]

Candler also had to fend off imitators who sought to ride on the wake of Coca-Cola's success. In 1896, Candler began a campaign of legal action against "unscrupulous pirates" who peddled counterfeit

Coca-Cola. The firm began a permanent policy, using detectives to expose the imitators and law suits to drive them out of business. John Candler's law firm did battle with the makers of Koke, Taka-Kola, Caro-Kola, El-Cola, Takola, Toca-Coca, Caro-Cola, Ko-Cola, Coke-Ola, Cold-Cola—and more.[27] Until the turn of the twentieth century, the earning power or physical assets of a firm established its value; however, relentless litigation against imitators put Candler and Coca-Cola among the pioneers of the idea that a trademark had value in itself. In 1900, when Henry Havemeyer of the American Sugar Refining Company of New Orleans "claimed that a trademark (brand name) could be just as valuable as (or more so than) a physical asset." Perhaps he learned the value of a trademark from one of his important customers—Asa Candler's Coca-Cola Company.[28]

In this defense of the trademark, as in his use of advertising, and his development of an innovative system of distribution, Asa Candler was on the leading edge of American business practice. On the other hand, he continued some old-fashioned management methods as well. In the early twentieth century, professional managers began to replace owners of large enterprises in directing the day-to-day operation of their businesses. Stockholders, who demanded maximum efficiency energized this trend. However, high volume firms did not experience such stockholder pressure. They always had plenty of cash and never needed to issue large amounts of stock to raise capital funds. Therefore, the founders of these companies remained in direct control, feeling no need for the new management professionals.[29] A typical founder-manager, Candler kept his hand firmly on the reins of Coca-Cola and sought his subordinates among close family members. And in any case, Asa Candler always owned most of the stock of his various enterprises.

At Hallman & Candler he had come to work early, stayed late, and kept a close eye on the inventory. As head of a multi-million dollar international firm, he did much the same. Examples of Candler's obsession with detail abound. The famous Coca-Cola fountain glass had a dual purpose, carefully thought out by the head of the firm. "Our main object is to advertise Coca-Cola and the use of the glasses will enable them to dispense in proper proportions." He also insisted that the glass be "of first quality." Candler rigorously enforced quality control, at times relying on his acute sense of taste. Indignantly, he instructed a representative to inquire into a particular bottling plant that had put out a bottle of "something purporting to be Coca-Cola" that was not up to his standards. In letters written to his son in 1899 he fretted: "It takes every moment of our time looking after traveling men. We now have 12 working from this office;" and "We are 5000 gals. behind with orders not with standing we are turning out above 3000 gals. daily." Candler's immediate subordinates followed his example in dealing with individual dispensers in patient detail. Eighteen years later—theoretically retired from active management of Coca-Cola—he would urge his youngest son William to "go occasionally to see what was going on down at the factory," adding with underlining for emphasis, "I always found that watching by owners was good policy."[30]

Given the attitude that the company was his personal property and its management his personal concern, his business relationships sometimes took on a personal coloring as well. He took great pains to cultivate the bottling franchise holders. Arthur W. Pratt, an early Coca-Cola bottler, remembered Candler's fatherly encouragement during the difficulties he experienced when starting in the business: "I came to regard him as a member of my family and called him 'Uncle Asa.' He used to visit me at the bottling plant in New York, and we would sit on a syrup barrel and talk about the future of Coca-Cola. When he left, I would be full of enthusiasm and eager to work for that future."[31]

The relative scarcity of documentary evidence of Candler's business activities is a mute example of Candler's old-fashioned managerial style. When men like Candler began to develop their enterprises, record-keeping standards and methods of modern business practice had not yet evolved. The nineteenth-century businessman valued secrecy. He handled his own correspondence personally and did not rely on secretaries. He kept few files, disposing of the letters he received, and expected his correspondents to do likewise. Even investors could not expect detailed or accurate financial reports. Asa Candler, who was nearly fifty at the turn of the century, most certainly formed his ideas of appropriate business behavior on this older model of privacy and secrecy.[32] In many ways, Asa Candler's approach to his affairs remained that of the small-town business man, rather than that of the gilded-age capitalist.

Nor was he a great optimist. In August 1899, he wrote to his son Howard, who was traveling for the company during his summer vacation, "If I felt sure that this business would hold out perpetually, I believe I would resign & give you the place. But my boy I cant take such risk on your future...."[33] However, if Asa Candler once believed that his son's future would be more secure if the young man continued to study medicine, he soon altered his opinion. The process of this alteration reflected the tendency of pioneer entrepreneurs such as Candler to involve family members in the management of their firms. For Howard, the change of plans accompanied the coming of the new century.

At the end of his medical school term in March 1900, Howard again went on the road for Coke, first joining his brother Buddie who had been sent (fresh from Emory College) to work in Coca-Cola's Los Angeles plant. Howard traveled up the coast to Seattle, where he vied for hotel space with adventurers on the way to the Klondike gold fields. On a brief visit into Canada, he discovered that a few merchants already had made Coca-Cola an "international" product by purchasing it in Seattle for resale in Vancouver and Victoria, British Columbia. In early summer he returned to the east coast to join a party of eleven recent Emory graduates on a European tour, under the guidance of Reverend Julius Magath, a professor of modern languages. Howard's father instructed him to scout the possibilities for selling Coca-Cola while he visited Europe. In London, he took a break from his grand tour to call on John T. Ralphs, an American expatriate who operated a soda fountain in the basement of Spence's Department Store. Howard had brought along a sample of syrup, so Ralphs was able to taste the drink. Impressed, he immediately placed the first transatlantic order for Coca-Cola.[34]

While Howard was still in Europe, his father wrote to him about problems in his New York office. In his opinion, some of his New York personnel were "good, honest fellows, but not strong in the matter of directing subordinates." Candler asked Howard to transfer his medical studies to a New York City college, so that he might, "go there and look after our interests… If it will be to your professional interest to take your next course there, I doubt not that it will be a wise policy for the company to station you there."[35]

Other letters followed, discussing the plan "to boom Coca-Cola" in New York and worrying that the current manager did not "appear to be able to make it go." When Howard returned to the US, he first went to Atlantic City to circulate advertising matter and then proceeded to New York where he was to assist in merchandising Coca-Cola and incidentally to find a place in a medical college. Although he was accepted at Bellevue medical school, he decided to put it off "because my physical condition was below par" and to do "some outdoor work" instead. He became a salesman for Coca-Cola, both because it kept him outdoors a good deal and, as he later wrote, it was "helpful to my father."[36]

As his father had done before him, Howard abandoned his brief flirtation with medicine to undertake a life in business. The father's increasing reliance on his eldest son's services probably contributed to the change, but Howard has left no evidence that he ever regretted making it. Over time, all four of Candler's sons took roles in Coca-Cola or in other Candler business enterprises, which grew to include significant real estate and banking activity.

A true patriarch, Asa Candler mixed love and power. He gave generous demonstrations of affection to his children while he sought to inculcate in them his own serious attitude toward money and business. Candler never gave his sons an allowance or spending money, although when Howard was a boy he had the job of chopping vanilla beans for his father's preparation of vanilla extract. Candler "adhered strictly to a policy of putting back into his business everything that could be spared from the actual living expenses of his family."[37] He involved his sons in his business and treated their financial relationships with him in a business-like manner, demanding careful accounts of their expenses while at college. Candler agreed to advance the costs of Howard's medical education and his transportation to and from New York City, a total of $1500, but expected to be repaid, with interest. The fact that Howard became his agent in the city did not cancel the debt; Howard was married for several years before he was able to repay his obligation to his father. His starting salary as a Coca-Cola salesman had been $12.50 a week.[38]

If Asa Candler kept control of the company by keeping its management in family hands; perhaps he also kept a measure of control over his family by the same means. None of the brothers, nephews, sons or life-long friends who ran Coca-Cola had more than 25 shares—while Candler's ownership hovered around 400—until Candler became mayor of Atlanta in 1917 and passed most of his stock in Coca-Cola to his children. Even then, as holder of only seven shares, he seemed to dominate the company. He continued to hold office as a director, attended all board meetings, and nominated slates of officers. In January 1919 the board of directors, as usual, elected him chairman.[39]

Candler wanted absolute control of his enterprises in an age when progressive reformers sought to impose all sorts of government regulations on commercial activities. A new idea had developed that businesses should compete on what today is sometimes called a "level playing field." A few businesses accepted the new standard of behavior voluntarily, but more commonly, competitive concerns used less "sporting" policies. New standards of business behavior could only be enforced by regulatory laws.[40]

One practical result of this ethical evolution came when Congress passed "excess profits" tax legislation that forced corporate managers to respond to the wishes of small shareholders and distribute a portion of profits in dividends. As his son said, managers like Candler preferred to plow most of profits back into the business, in a surplus account. As early as 1898 the Coca-Cola president's annual report showed $59,466 in a surplus account; a decade later this line on the balance sheet approached $1 million. Candler invested these funds in real estate, stocks, and bonds, to be held by the Coca-Cola Company. Another item found in the annual balance sheet, "Bills Receivable" stood for "time loans secured by Atlanta Real Estate and bond of manufacturing concerns, with personal endorsements" that yielded 6 percent. The statement does not show any relation of these loans to the production or sale of Coca-Cola, and it lists ordinary accounts receivable as a separate item. Clearly Candler used the Coca-Cola company for business activity not directly related to the manufacture and sale of a soft drink.[41] Excess profits regulations had the effect of forcing Coca-Cola to stop such accumulation of assets and to distribute $5 million of capital funds plus a $3,000 per share dividend to stockholders. To Candler, who owned the overwhelming majority of the shares in Coca-Cola, such regulation seemed to be an unwarranted intrusion in his personal affairs. He had no desire to pay himself a dividend and saw no need to provide one for stockholders who were almost all his close family. Of course, he also responded to the imposition of the new income tax with similar outrage. First he was forced to pay himself a dividend and then he was taxed for it. These laws had acted in tandem to pluck a portion of his hard-won fortune from his hands and deliver it to the national treasury. In his annual report to stockholders presented in December 1914; he decried the tendency of taxation to "grow as Hagar's gourd vine" and said that he regarded such interference "as offensive as gourd vines in wheat fields."[42]

Not only did he resent taxation and excess profits legislation, but Candler's preferences also clashed with the progressive trend toward government-imposed standards for the manufacture of his product. Perhaps the greatest struggle between Candler and the government was Coca-Cola's marathon battle with the enforcers of the Pure Food and Drug Act of 1906. According to Dr. Harvey W. Wylie, head of the Bureau of Chemistry of the Department of Agriculture and a fanatical prohibitionist, caffeine-containing beverages were poisonous. To him, people like Asa Candler, who sold such drinks, were "dope-peddlers." In 1909, under the authority of the pure food act, the government moved against Coca-Cola, seizing a shipment of syrup sent from Atlanta to Chattanooga. In the case styled *United States of America v. Forty Barrels and Twenty Kegs of Coca-Cola* the government charged that Coca-Cola syrup was adulterated by the addition of caffeine. Furthermore, in an odd twist of the intent of the legislation, Coca-Cola was accused of misleading labeling because it contained no coca and only a little cola. The trial in the federal court at Chattanooga resulted in more than three thousand pages of transcript, mostly devoted to a duel of experts. Rabbits, frogs and guinea pigs gave their lives in experiments that showed some experts that Coca-Cola was a menace to health and convinced others that it was totally harmless. The government produced witnesses who claimed that the drink had addicted them and made them into nervous wrecks. Coca-Cola countered with testimony from nearly a hundred healthy and satisfied consumers.

Government witnesses also testified to conditions at the Edgewood Avenue plant in 1908, claiming that it was filthy and manned by ill-clad, sweating, tobacco-chewing Negroes. They said that they saw a toilet opening off of the manufacturing area and described a basement sewer drain as a "cess pool." Coca-Cola countered that its workers dressed in clean overalls and sturdy shoes and that the work place was clean. They said that the offending water closet did not exist. The disputed facts of this case are now beyond clarification. In like fashion, two conflicting pictures of the head of the Coca-Cola Company emerged from the testimony.[43]

Government inspectors had visited the Edgewood Avenue plant three times before bringing the charges. On the first two visits, the inspectors toured the facility, guided by Howard Candler, who had become its manager. Then, in October 1909, Dr. L. F. Kebler, chief of the Drug Division of the Department of Agriculture's Bureau of Chemistry, accompanied by inspector J. L. Lynch, arrived at the Atlanta factory without announcing themselves. They began to examine the street-level manufacturing area where a workman made sugar syrup and then moved to the basement area where this syrup, in large containers, was cooled and mixed with flavorings. Howard Candler arrived at the plant, learned of the inspection and, without pausing to remove his hat, rushed to the basement to find Kebler and Lynch. The government men asked to purchase samples of Coca-Cola syrup and some of its ingredients for analysis. Howard, claiming to be uncertain of how to carry out this transaction, went to consult his father. The two Candlers returned to the basement. They found Dr. Kebler climbing upon the framework that held the cooling tanks, peering into the tanks and up into the rafters close above him. According to Lynch, Candler responded to the situation with rage: "He was very angry and very excited and in the conversation referred to Dr. Kebler as 'A God-damned carpenter,' if I remember the conversation. He was very excited and very much worked up and very nervous."[44] At the time no one asked why Candler would have used "carpenter" as a term of abuse. Possibly Lynch misunderstood another, uniquely southern insult, "carpetbagger," which might have been, for Candler, an apt description of a federal inspector. In any case it remains doubtful that the church-going Candler used a sacrilegious oath; no other instance of his cursing has been preserved.

Later in the proceedings, Howard Candler denied that his father had ever used profane language and called Lynch's testimony far-fetched. In any case, the inspectors received a quantity of Coca-Cola syrup, although Candler refused to provide samples of any of the separate ingredients. Analysis of the syrup sample provided the basis of the government's case.[45]

Litigation and appeals of *The United States v. Forty Barrels and Twenty Kegs of Coca-Cola* ran for over nine years. The case reached the Supreme Court, which remanded it back to the federal district court in Chattanooga. There, in November, 1918, the Coca-Cola Company and the United States of America settled their differences when Coca-Cola agreed to make some minor modifications in its manufacturing processes. The fact that Dr. Wylie, the implacable foe of caffeine, was no longer with the government probably eased the way to the conclusion of the case. The contest cost Coca-Cola over $85,000.[46]

On a lesser scale the state of Georgia at times added to Candler's distress. He wrote to Howard in 1902, "Never in all my life have I

---

been so harassed." After the legislature had subjected his product to "abuse," it had imposed "a special tax of $400." However, in spite of such occasional outbursts of frustration, his years of struggle with the government over the quality of his product and the right to manage its profits as he saw fit did not occupy all of Asa Candler's time and energy. While he built Coca-Cola in the 1890s, he continued to give attention to his growing children and to participate actively and generously in church activities. As the new century began Coca-Cola had become well-established and profitable and Asa Candler began to broaden the horizons of his business interests. The early minutes of The Coca-Cola Company confirm Howard Candler's report that from the beginning his father had invested the company's surplus funds in real estate. Numerous and scattered, these small parcels of land represented Candler's first ventures outside of the manufacturing activities that had provided his original financial successes. Larger projects were to follow. By the turn of the century, the Atlanta business elite had acquired a new and increasingly preeminent member who was soon to surpass all of his earlier accomplishments.

[1] AGC to "Dear Warren" 10 April 1888, box 1, AGC papers, Emory.

[2] The following account of the founding of the Coca-Cola Company draws on: Candler, *Asa Griggs Candler*, 106-13; Charles Howard Candler, "The True Origin of Coca-Cola: Additional Facts Relating to Its Early History," [typed manuscript, 1952], Charles Howard Candler Papers and Biography, The Archives, The Coca-Cola Company [cited below as "True Origin"]; Charles Howard Candler, "Thirty-three Years with Coca-Cola" [typed manuscript], The Archives, The Coca-Cola Company [cited below as "Thirty-three Years], 1-30; Garrett, *Atlanta and Environs*, 2 vols. 2:120-26; Walter G. Cooper, *Official History of Fulton County* (Atlanta: Walter Brown Publishing Co., 1934) 798-801; E. J. Kahn, Jr., *The Big Drink* (New York: Random House, 1950) passim; and Pat Watters, *Coca-Cola, An Illustrated History* (Garden City NJ: Doubleday, Inc, 1978) *passim.* See also: Frederick Allen, *Secret Formula: How Brilliant Marketing and Relentless Salesmanship Made Coca-Cola the Best-known Product in the World* (New York: Harper Business, 1994).

[3] According to Howard Candler's "True Origins," Dr. Jacobs "disclaimed any knowledge" of this legendary transaction, although Venable did keep a bottle of Coca-Cola on the back bar of his fountain.

[4] Testimony of Asa G. Candler, The Coca-Cola Company, *Opposer vs. The Koke Company Company of America*, Appellant, Before the Examiner of Interferences, printed transcript, vol. 1, The Archives, The Coca-Cola Company, Atlanta.

[5] AGC to WAC, 2 June 1888, quoted in Candler, "True Origin." Pemberton had sold his interest the previous April.

[6]The following "chain of title" for Coca-Cola draws on several sources: Charles Howard Candler's *Asa Candler*, The Coca-Cola Company, *Coca-Cola: Opinions, Orders, Injunctions, and Decrees relating to Unfair Competition and Infringement of Trade Mark* (1923) 636 *et passim*; and the transcript of *The United Sates v. Forty Barrels and Twenty Kegs of Coca Cola*, a case discussed later in this chapter, which included certified copies of the pertinent documents. Because the Forty Barrels case eventually reached the Supreme Court, the *Opinions, Orders, Injunctions, and Decrees* volume cites this case as 241 US 995 (22 May 1916) but the original transcripts of testimony, were recorded in the US District Court for the Eastern District of Tennessee, Southern Division, Chattanooga, (1911) and are available at the Federal Archives and Records Center, Atlanta.

The sequence of sales is as follows: after Venable's purchase, the equipment for manufacture (which probably included the three-legged kettle) was moved to the basement of Jacob's Drug Store, where Venable was to produce the syrup. When he failed to work at the project, his partner Lowndes bought out his share; on 14 December 1887, Lowndes then sold his entire two-thirds interest to Woolfolk Walker, formerly a salesmen for Pemberton Chemical, and to Walker's sister, Mrs. M. C. Dozier. Pemberton still retained his original third of the company and the equipment went back to Pemberton Chemical's Marietta Street location. Walker and his sister still owned two-thirds of Coca-Cola when they bought out Pemberton's original third in 1888 for the sum of $550. At this juncture Woolfolk Walker apparently needed money: in April 1888 Asa Candler entered the picture and Walker, Candler & Company came into being. This company shared the ownership in Coca-Cola with Walker and his sister. A few days after Pemberton's sale to Walker and his sister, Candler, acting as an individual investor, bought half of their shares. He now owned one-third of the company in his own right and also was a partner in Walker, Candler & Company, which owned another portion of the company. On 30 August 1891, Candler bought out the remaining shares owned by Walker and Mrs. Dozier; all Coca-Cola shares now belonged to either Walker, Candler & Company or to Asa G. Candler as an individual. Finally, on 22 April 1891, he personally acquired the shares that had belonged to the company of Walker, Candler, & Co. That firm became defunct and Coca-Cola now became entirely Asa Candler's personal property.

[7]Testimony of Asa G. Candler, The Coca-Cola Company, *Opposer vs. The Koke Company Company of America*, Appellant, Before the Examiner of Interferences, printed transcript, vol. 1, The Archives, The Coca-Cola Company, Atlanta.

[8]1891 calendar, fol. 7, box 7, AGC papers, Emory. As will be seen in the following pages, some descriptions of early Coca-Cola manufacturing activities also include mention of other Candler products, such as B.B.B.

[9]"Minutes of the Coca Cola Company, vol. I, 1892-1910" typed transcript, bound, The Archives, The Coca-Cola Company, Atlanta; Kahn, *The Big Drink*, 6-7; Watters *Coca-Cola*, 14, 23-24; Candler, "True Origin."

[10]"Minutes of the Coca-Cola Company, vol. I"; Candler, *Asa Griggs Candler*, 93, 106; Candler, "Thirty-three Years," 6-7; D. B. Candler, "Brief History" and Samuel Willard, untitled history. The directors were Seth W. Fowle, E. A. Prescott, and John S. Candler.

[11]Kahn, *The Big Drink*, 18. Kahn found this item in an "archives document" that he does not identify further.

[12]D[aniel] B. Candler, "A Brief History of Coca-Cola," manuscript in Daniel B. Candler file [cited below as "Brief History"]; Samuel Willard, untitled history of Coca-Cola, 1891-1903, in Samuel Willard file, [cited below as "untitled history"]; electrostatic copies of two letters, Samuel Willard to Charles Howard Candler, 2 October 1929 and 10 October 1929, in Samuel Willard file; all in The Archives, The Coca-Cola Company. S.J. Willard, "The Early History of Coca-Cola as I Know It," part 5, The Coca-Cola Bottler, 33ff., clipping in Asa Griggs Candler,

Papers and Biography, The Archives, The Coca-Cola Company; Candler, "True Origin." Samuel Willard, Asa Candler's nephew, began working for his uncle in 1891. See also: "Coca Cola Recipe Given By Visitor" *Portland Oregon Journal* (16 July 1935), clipping in Walter Turner Candler file, The Archives, The Coca-Cola Company.
In revising the formula, he consulted Dr. W. H. Ingram, professor of pharmacy at Atlanta Medical College, Dr. H. S. Wright, a graduate chemist who ran his manufacturing department, and Mr. P. M. Christian, a Candler and Company prescriptionist. Howard Candler says nothing else about tin cans, but phosphoric acid, a common flavoring agent, might have reacted chemically with the metal containers. He told the *Portland Oregonian*, that the Pemberton mixture "would not hold together" until his father "worked it over."

[13]Watters, *Coca-Cola*, 35; Candler, "True Origin."

[14]Ibid.; Candler, *Asa Griggs Candler*, 129; D. B. Candler, "Brief History"; Willard, untitled history.

[15]Candler, "Thirty-three Years," 12.

[16]Richard S. Tedlow, *New and Improved: The Story of Mass Marketing in America*, (New York: Basic Books, Inc., 1990) 348-49; quotation from the Fifth Annual Report of the President, "Minutes of the Coca-Cola Company," vol. 1, The Archives, The Coca-Cola Company.

[17]Tedlow, *New and Improved*, 348-49.

[18]Ibid., 355-56, 366; *Asa G. Candler*, 179-84; Kahn, *Big Drink*, 69-78; Watters, *Coca-Cola*, 33; Alfred D.Chandler, *The Visible Hand: The Managerial Revolution in American Business* (Cambridge MA: the Belknap Press of Harvard University Press, 1977) Appendix A.

[19]AGC [form letter], 2 April 1890, in Asa Griggs Candler Papers and Biography box, The Archives, The Coca-Cola Company.

[20]AGC to "Dear Warren" 20 April 1888, box 1, AGC Papers, Emory.

[21]Robinson's tickets were passed out on the streets and mailed to lists of persons compiled from the city directory. Contrary to the myth that Candler invented the "Delicious—Refreshing" slogan, a form of it was used before he became involved with the product.

[22]Watters, *Coca-Cola*, 44, 88-89, 91; Tedlow, *New and Improved*, 364.

[23]Typical advertisements of this type are found in: Travelers' Protective Association of America, Georgia Division, *A Commercial History of the State of Georgia*, Edgar Harvey, ed. (1897) 79; Watters, *Coca-Cola*, 95; "History of the Atlanta Police Department," (1898) Published by the Policemen's Relief Association, Atlanta, Georgia, repr. with introduction by Herbert T. Jenkins, 1976. French Wine of Coca, Pemberton's old nostrum, still was available; see page 99 of *A Commercial History*....

[24]I am indebted to Professor Timothy J. Crimmins for the suggestion that Coca-Cola advertising might reflect Asa Candler's world-view.

[25]Watters, *Coca-Cola*, 96; Tedlow, *New and Improved*, 32; "Minutes of the Coca-Cola Company," vols. 1 and 2, *passim*, The Archives, The Coca-Cola Company.

[26]Watters, *Coca-Cola*, 95-97; "Great Success Coca Cola Won" and "A Cold Bottle on a Hot Day" [advertisement], *Atlanta Constitution*, 23 June 1907, 11; "Athletes Praise Coca-Cola" [advertisement], *Atlanta Constitution*, 9 June 1907, 7. Two letters, fol. 7, box 12, WAC papers, Emory, include reports from the Chemical Department of South Carolina College, ("the alkaloid is absent") and the Medicine Department of Tulane University in New Orleans ("fails to show the presence of Cocaine") attesting to Coca-Cola's purity.

[27]Watters, *Coca-Cola*, 33; Kahn, *The Big Drink*, 94-95. For many examples of the work of the sleuths who protected Coca-Cola's good name, see transcript of testimony, Coca-Cola Company, Opposer v. The Koke Company of America, The Archives, The Coca-Cola

Company. In thirty cases before 1929, various products were held to infringe on Coca-Cola's trademark. See The Coca-Cola Company, *Coca-Cola: Opinions, Orders, Injunctions, and Decrees, passim.*

[28]Saul Engelbourg, *Power and Morality: American Business Ethics, 1840-1914*, Contributions in Economics and Economic History, Number 28, Robert Sobel, ed. (Westport CN: Greenwood Press, 1980) 84; CHC, "Thirty-three Years," 45. Engelbourg quotes Havemeyer's testimony before the United States Industrial Commission whose report was published in 1900; Candler's manuscript identifies Coca-Cola's source of sugar.

[29]Chandler, *The Visible Hand*, 381.

[30]AGC to CHC, 21 July 1899, box 1, AGC Papers, Emory; AGC to CHC, 3 April 1889 and 6 August 1889, box 1, AGC papers, Emory; AGC to B. F. Thomas, "Correspondence" folder, Asa Griggs Candler Papers and Biography box, The Archives, The Coca-Cola Company; S. C. Dobbs to W. N. Broderick, 7 May 1900, "Business Announcements" subject file, Atlanta History Center Archives; AGC to "My dear Man" [CHC], 22 September 1917, box 1, AGC papers, Emory.

[31]Watters, *Coca-Cola*, 68.

[32]Engelbourg, *Power and Morality*, 87. Coca-Cola was in the "unregulated sector" until passage of Pure Food and Drug laws of the early twentieth century.

[33]AGC to CHC, 10 August 1899, box 1, AGC papers, Emory.

[34]Candler, "Thirty-three Years," 25-31.

[35]Ibid., 31.

[36]Candler, "Thirty-three Years," 32-33.

[37]Candler, "Thirty-three Years," 3. Chopping 30 pounds of vanilla beans is described on p. 49.

[38]Candler, "Thirty-three Years," 33-34.

[39]Minutes of The Coca-Cola Company, vol. 2, bound typescript, *passim*, The Archives, The Coca-Cola Company.

[40]Engelbourg, *Power and Morality*, 59, 129-140. Englebourg calls the newer, twentieth century ethic "universalistic" and characterizes the older, insider system of behavior as "particularistic."

[41]"Minutes of The Coca-Cola Company," vols. 1 and 2. As early as December 1893, in his second annual report Candler reported a "Stock & Bond" account holding $53,400.

[42]Quoted in Watters, *Coca-Cola*, 88-89. A survey of reference works has produced one entry on "Jonah's gourd vine" but no one—including the Georgia Agricultural Extension Service— seems to have any information on Hagar's vine.

[43]*United States of America v. Forty Barrels and Twenty Kegs of Coca-Cola*, US District Court for the Eastern District of Tennessee, Southern Division at Chattanooga, March 1911 [cited below as *US v. Forty Barrels*]; *Big Drink*, 106-08.

[44]Transcript of testimony, *US v. Forty Barrels*, 125.

[45]Testimony of L. F. Kebler, J. L. Lynch, Howard Candler, *US v. Forty Barrels.*

[46]Kahn, *Big Drink*, 106-108; Candler, *Asa G. Candler*, 147-52.

CHAPTER FOUR

Capitalist

A gentleman of eighty years, who once heard Asa Candler make a speech at his elementary school, remembered his high, reedy voice. He also remembered that when one of his schoolmates asked another to borrow a nickel, he got the reply, "Who do you think I am? Asa Candler?"[1] In early twentieth-century Atlanta, Asa Candler's name had become a by-word for wealth.

Coca-Cola remained his most significant (if sometimes troublesome) interest, but Candler used the profits it brought to launch into real estate and banking.[2] Although the newspapers followed his business interests closely, the public seldom bothered to distinguish between his activities in the soft-drink company and his growing investments in real estate and banking. The distinction, like that between the Coca-Cola bottling companies and the parent company, seemed to vanish in the minds of observers. They simply saw a rich man.

In spite of the increasing scope of Asa Candler's enterprises, they remained essentially a family business. At the turn of the century, he had already begun to involve his oldest son Howard in the operations of Coca-Cola. Now his second son and namesake, Asa, Junior, came of age and his father thought to follow a similar course with the young man everyone called "Buddie." Howard had fit into the Coca-Cola operation quite easily. Even as a college boy he had been an effective salesman in the mid-West and on the West Coast. After Buddie finished college at the turn of the century, Candler sent him to work briefly in the Los Angeles branch of Coca-Cola, but soon brought him back to Georgia where he planned to put the young man in charge of the newly acquired Witham Cotton Mills, in Hartwell, Georgia.

Candler bought this textile mill from W. S. Witham, a banker and a fellow Methodist Sunday school teacher in Atlanta. "Billy" Witham, although a native of Troup County, had spent twenty years in business in New York before he returned to Georgia to run a group of some thirty small banks. He resided in an elaborate Peachtree Road home christened Bide-a-Wee. He encouraged the officers of the member institutions of the "Witham Banking System" to develop their business skills and organized elaborate meetings to build morale. In the early summer of 1900 Candler, Witham, and their wives joined such a group of Witham executives on a two-week junket to Asbury, New York.[3]

Witham also was financial agent for eight textile mills, and in the course of the trip to New York, Candler and Witham arranged the sale of the textile mill at Hartwell. Shortly thereafter Coca-Cola (that is to say Asa Candler) purchased $65,000 of Witham Mill bonds. The value of these bonds covered the combined approximate worth of the mill, which Hart County assessed at $39,500 in 1900, plus the value of extensive improvements made at the time.[4] Although Candler was beginning to diversify his business interests, his concern for Buddie's future played an important part in his involvement in Witham Mills. Candler wrote to his elder son Howard, "I want to see my boys settled in honorable, useful callings while I am here if possible."[5] Buddie was to manage the mill, at least for a time. As Asa wrote in his letter to Howard, "If he takes hold well and is pleased with the business he will be made president in my place (I now hold that office) and will eventually own the stock."[6]

Buddie began his new occupation in September 1900, possibly traveling on the narrow gauge short line railroad that once a day made its way through the wooded mountains of northeast Georgia to Hartwell. For a few years, he made his home in the rural community a hundred miles from Atlanta. He found a wife there as well—Helen Magill, daughter of the editor of the local newspaper. They bought a house and furnished it in a style suited to his position as manager of an important local enterprise. Unfortunately, no record of Buddie's personal experience there can be found in the various archives that preserve parts of the Candler papers. Although property records show that he bought and sold various other parcels of real estate during his residence in Hartwell, his brother Howard later wrote that Buddie had been unfamiliar with his new vocation as a textile mill manager and proved unsuited to its demands.[7] By 1905, Buddie evidently was spending a great amount of time in Atlanta. He was an early and avid automobile driver, and the records of a garage he patronized in that year show that he made regular charges for services and purchases, although in one instance there was an express shipment of "oiler and fan belts" to Hartwell.[8] (Perhaps the inconvenience of travel to Hartwell on a once-a-day short-line railroad stimulated young Candler to try the new method of transportation.)

W. S. Witham continued to act as the mill's agent at the New York Cotton Exchange, but his performance did not always satisfy Buddie. His father reported to Howard: "Buddie is in a big huffy. Says he won't stay up there and work day and night for Mr. Witham to waste." As time wore on, Candler came to share Buddie's doubts about Witham's abilities. Of the mill, he complained, "that enterprise is a load" and complained of "the worry I am having at Hartwell."[9]

As his brother hinted, Asa, Jr. may have lacked the managerial talent to run the enterprise, but it is more likely that he lacked enthusiasm for a career thrust upon him by his father, which tied him to a place remote from Atlanta. The death of his young son (also named Asa) while a record snowstorm isolated Hartwell from outside contacts may also have undermined the charms of life in the small town. Buddie returned to Atlanta permanently in 1906, and spent the rest of his life in the city, successfully running various family real-estate enterprises.

Unlike most Candler undertakings, Witham Mills failed. Hart County tax records show a steady decline in the value of the mills to a low of just over $70,000 in 1907. The mill shut down in July 1909. In November, Candler moved Witham Mills from one pocket to another: the Coca-Cola Company (Asa G. Candler, president) purchased Witham Mills (Asa G. Candler, president) for $100,000. A few weeks later, in January 1910, Coca-Cola sold the entire property to J. M. Geer of South Carolina for $50,000.[10]

Candler used Coca-Cola to handle the various Witham Mills transactions, a strategy characteristic of his financial activity in the early years of the century. The Coca-Cola Company was a sort of holding company for Candler's real estate purchases until increasing government regulation of trade during the Progressive era made this arrangement impossible. Up to that time, acquisitions of the Coca-Cola Company often are indistinguishable from those of Asa Candler, the individual.

As Coca-Cola brought an increasing amount of money into his hands, Candler invested surplus funds in real estate, beginning with relatively small purchases. Howard Candler wrote that eventually the maintenance requirements of these scattered properties kept a full-time contractor and a small crew of mechanics busy. Coca-Cola's need for more office space led Candler to undertake his first major real estate enterprise. He built a modern seventeen-story "skyscraper" on a triangular lot at 127 Peachtree, just a short distance away from the old Hallman and Candler location.[11]

In the 1890s, few comparatively tall buildings arose on Atlanta's skyline. The ten-story Prudential Building and the eleven-story English-American Building were among the more dramatic city structures (in terms of height) at the turn of the century. In the next two decades, however, Atlanta began to take its place as one of the most urbanized of the southern cities.

Skyscrapers began to appear in American cities as the result of a number of closely related developments. Some factors were technological. Among these were the use of a skeleton of steel I-beams to support the great weight of the tall, slender buildings. Crucial was the development of reliable elevators that made the upper stories accessible to ordinary people who lacked the endurance to climb dozens of flights of steps. In Atlanta, because several railroad lines connected the city's central location to the rest of the South, many firms placed regional headquarters in the growing downtown. Local business and professional persons also preferred the convenience of modern, well-equipped locations where a tired businessman could visit a barber or dine in a pleasant restaurant. Increasing demand for office space, which stimulated this revolution in building design and construction, made the new structures themselves into profitable business ventures. These grand office buildings thus contributed to the city's success. In the years between the beginning of the century and the outbreak of the World War, one skyscraper after another rose above the low profile of the nineteenth-century city. Contemporary Atlantans judged Candler's building to be the finest of them all.[12]

The development of the Candler Building project demonstrates Candler's habit of using several of his enterprises interactively. As a first step, in December 1903 he organized the Candler Investment Company, a corporation that, according to his son, "owned the bulk of his personal real estate holdings." Then, acting through the Coca-Cola Company, Candler acquired the site for his building. After the fact, the board of directors of Coca-Cola ratified the already completed purchase of "Old First Methodist Church lot." In due course, the board not only voted to erect a building on that location but also approved negotiations to borrow $400,000 in construction funds from North Western Mutual Life Insurance Company. Such actions by the board of directors were formalities, since Candler controlled more than four hundred of its five hundred shares.

In January 1904 George E. Murphy, superintendent of the building department of the Coca-Cola Company, applied for construction permits and hired the architect George S. Stewart. The Candler Investment Company undertook the construction contracting, expecting the building to be completed by the spring of the following year. Coca-Cola's Murphy supervised most of the work on the seventeen-story steel and concrete skyscraper and Howard Candler, in the capacity of secretary-treasurer of Candler Investment, analyzed the bids of various sub-contractors and also conducted a good deal of on-site supervision.[13]

Sensitive to the needs of his future tenants, Candler himself made many of the design decisions that determined the layout and ornamentation of his building. As was true of all of his undertakings, he tolerated no shoddiness; the most skillful artisans—some brought from Europe—worked with the best materials. The offices received generous amounts of light from large windows. The latest mechanical equipment, including electric elevators and sophisticated steam heating, added to the building's comfort and convenience. Steam also powered an independent electrical system with generators situated deep in a second basement. The building possessed the best fireproofing precautions. (This was true of every Candler construction endeavor. Evidently the fire that wiped out Howard and Candler in the 'eighties made a lasting impression.) Three floors of the building were fitted out for the special needs of physicians and dentists. At the end of the day, a tenant of the Candler Building could leave his office and ride the electric elevator to the basement where a barber shop, baths, and a swimming pool awaited him.[14]

Some difficulties, which Howard Candler believed were the result of inexperience, hampered the project, but some of their problems belong in the "act of God" category. In one case, a construction worker fell from the fifteenth floor to his death. Delays came during a period of unusually bad winter weather in February 1905, when freezing rain coated the east side of the building with as much as three inches of ice. When the weather began to warm, large chunks of ice crashed down on Pryor Street, which had to be closed until the accumulation of ice melted away.

The storm also broke Atlanta's lines of communication with the outside world, and for almost three days the city had no news. Meanwhile, across the state in Hartwell, Asa Junior's small son became ill and died. As the bad weather abated, Asa Candler received a message to come to the railroad car shed. He arrived to discover that a coffin bearing the remains of his young grandson and namesake had arrived on the train from Hartwell. Because of storm damage to telephone lines, the child's father had been unable to contact Atlanta to inform his family of the child's sudden death.[15]

Work progressed on the building, but slowly. On 4 January 1906, still not quite complete in all details, the Candler Building opened to the public. Howard Candler candidly admitted, "[W]hile the building as finished was an exceptionally fine and substantial structure, its arrangement was not ideal and its cost was excessive."[16] Although the architect and contractor had dealt with the technical problems of construction, the building's style of construction and its embellishments came from Candler himself. It does not fit precisely into a stylistic category. Candler's European artisans had carved panels "illustrating the liberal arts and sciences" along with busts of great artists, inventors, and military heroes for his building's exterior. Massive twenty-six foot classic columns, each carved from a single block of marble, frame the Houston street entrance. Pairs of gigantic figures guard the Peachtree and Pryor Street doors. Inside, images of other distinguished persons, including heroes of the Confederacy and Candler family members, look down from "suitable niches" lining the grand stairway from the lobby; bronze birds support this stairway and a carved dolphin adorns the end of the marble handrail. Marble alligators guard the drinking fountains. It probably was no coincidence that Candler's seventeen-story skyscraper surpassed the height of the sixteen-story Fourth National Bank, which, since its opening the previous year, claimed the honor of being the tallest building in the South. The entire effect was—and still is—sumptuous, and the public found it pleasing. The editors of the *Journal of Labor* devoted a front page story to a description of the building and took the opportunity to note that its beauty was "a credit to the union men who built it."[17]

The Candler Building's elaborate appointments celebrated Candler's family, class, city, and region and signaled Asa Candler's presence in the front ranks of the Atlanta economy; it was a kind of trumpet fanfare in steel and concrete. It housed the headquarters of the Coca-Cola Company as well as another demonstration of his increasing stature, the Central Bank and Trust Corporation, which he organized while his building was under construction.

Candler Investment continued to manage the building until 1910, when Coca-Cola purchased its assets (that is, the building, well supplied with paying tenants) for $117,810. The investment company then liquidated, paying off its stock holders: Asa Candler, a few family members and close friends. Acting as an individual, he also undertook many real estate transactions on behalf of Coca-Cola for as long as he controlled the company, deals that usually involved less imposing structures in cities where the company had regional offices. These serviceable commercial properties included rental properties as well as facilities for making Coca-Cola syrup.[18]

The difficulties encountered in his first large-scale construction project did not discourage Candler from creating major buildings that bore his name in several American cities. In 1912, the Coca-Cola board once again voted to borrow funds, this time from the National Bank of Commerce in New York. In that city, Candler purchased a piece of property at 220-224 West Forty-first Street, a site formerly occupied by Central Baptist Church, which extended through the block to Forty-second Street. There he erected a twenty-five story sister to the structure already standing in Atlanta, also decorated in marble and terra cotta, and named the Candler Building. To "preserve the light and air" of this building from encroachment by future construction in the area, he purchased a neighboring property, the Bruce Library, "one of the famous old landmarks of New York and a relic of other days," where he built a five-story structure in architectural conformity to its larger neighbor.[19]

In its twenty-first annual meeting (January 1913) the Coca-Cola board voted a blanket authorization for the buying and selling of real estate at any time or place by the officers of the corporation. Candler then paid somewhat more than $100,000 for a lot in Washington, DC where, according to press reports, he planned to erect "a skyscraper." The *Atlanta Journal* knowingly announced, "It is Mr. Candler's ambition to put up large office buildings bearing his name in all prominent cities in the east." Candler confirmed the fact of the purchase but declined further comment.[20] Some fragments of correspondence relating to this property survive, but whatever Candler may have contemplated doing on this parcel of land remains unclear and nothing suggests that he undertook any major construction activity in the capital city.[21]

At this same time, Coca-Cola acquired a parcel of real estate in Baltimore, mortgaging it for a quarter-million dollars. In that city, yet another marble and terra cotta building, resembling those in Atlanta and New York, pierced the sky. In another echo of Candler's Atlanta enterprise, the Baltimore Commercial Bank (Asa Griggs Candler, president) occupied its main floor. By 1915, in addition to the trio of elegant skyscrapers in Atlanta, New York, and Baltimore, Candler or Coca-Cola also owned more modest office buildings in Winnipeg, Chicago, and Kansas City.[22]

Asa Candler's habit of buying and selling downtown Atlanta property stimulated periodic rumor-mongering in the daily press. In 1908, for example, when he purchased the Moore-Marsh building at the corner of Edgewood and Pryor, the *Journal* declared that it would be made into a vaudeville theater; four days later it announced that this plan had been abandoned and now there was to be a hotel. In the story, Candler denied having decided to make it a hotel "or anything else" but the writer disregarded his statement and went on to describe the fancied hotel anyway. In fact, it became a commercial loft building, rechristened "Commerce Hall."[23]

Of course, Candler generated real news as well, and his sons, as they reached maturity, also gained recognition in Atlanta's business community and in the press. For example, in 1909 Candler paid $125,000 to acquire the Lowndes building, a structure adjacent to the Candler building. Asa, Jr., identified as "active head" of Candler Investment Company, informed the *Atlanta Journal* that the structure would receive $25,000 in improvements, including an underground connection to the Candler building.[24] Howard would continue to serve his father in the Coca-Cola company, while Buddie became his right hand in his real estate concerns. As they came to maturity, the younger boys also joined in these interests and in banking, as well.

At the same time that he launched his career as a major developer of office buildings, Candler also built a new home for himself, another investment more suited to his status as a successful entrepreneur. The "miniature farm" had seen the older children through childhood and now they had married or were away at school. In 1903, the Candler household consisted only of Asa, his wife, and their youngest child Willie. Physically, they moved a short distance from the large, rambling frame house that faced the Southern Railroad line, but their sumptuous new home in Inman Park clearly bespoke their upward social movement. On the other hand, although it remained a desirable neighborhood, Inman Park no longer had the cachet of exclusivity its original residents had hoped for; as usual, Candler had balanced his desires for both quality and thrift. The red brick and granite house, designed for both beauty and comfort, boasted a large piazza and Doric columns; its owner named it "Callan Castle" to commemorate an ancestral residence in Kilkenney, Ireland.[25] The new house faced the intersection of Elizabeth and Euclid streets. Just across Euclid, on the other corner, lived Joel Hurt, the founder of Inman Park and of the Atlanta and Edgewood Street Railway in which Candler had invested in the late eighties.[26]

Hurt, although brilliant, energetic, and innovative, suffered bad luck in business. Financial setbacks in the early nineties had stunted the development of Inman Park, and Hurt had not fared well in the struggles over Atlanta's street railway and electric franchises. Ever optimistic, he also worked on the development of another suburb, a short distance to the northwest of Inman Park, which was to be called Druid Hills. The Olmsted Brothers, a famed firm of landscape designers based in Brookline, Massachusetts, laid out an ambitious plan for the project, but the inability to complete the necessary financing arrangements forced Hurt to abandon his intentions to develop the area. In the largest real estate transaction the city had seen, Hurt sold the land in June 1908, to the Druid Hills Corporation, which was entirely controlled by Asa Candler. He owned 2,250 of its 2,500 shares. Other stockholders of record included Preston W. Arkwright of the Georgia Railway and Power Company, the realtors Forrest and George Adair, William D. Thomson, Harold Hirsch, and John S. Candler and according to Howard Candler, the Coca-Cola Company provided the money that financed the Druid Hills operation. The Adair brothers became exclusive sales agents for the subdivision and continued to have close business relations with Candler for the rest of his active business life.[27]

The Olmsted firm, which also had designed Atlanta's Piedmont Park, followed the park-like style then in vogue for affluent suburbs. They sought to create a woodsy environment in which town and country were "married." Candler followed the general outlines of the Olmsted plan but eliminated its more extravagant features. A relic of this is Lakeside Drive, which now borders a sunken park rather than the artificial Lake Claire that the original plan proposed. Candler provided acreage for the establishment of the Druid Hills Golf Club, on the principle that it made his property more attractive to affluent buyers.

Deed covenants guaranteed the spacious, sylvan character of the subdivision. However, the Druid Hills board of directors specifically rejected the anti-Semitic restrictions that were commonplace at the time. W. D. Thomson, one of John Candler's law partners, made a motion that offers to purchase land in Druid Hills should not be refused "solely on the ground that the prospective purchaser is a Jew." The Adair brothers, who jointly owned only 25 shares, voted against the resolution, but the others present, including Candler with his controlling 2,250 shares, adopted it. One board member did not attend this meeting: Harold Hirsch, who was John Candler's other law partner and a Jew.[28]

Although Candler watched costs carefully, he did expend considerable sums of money on the creation of Druid Hills. Howard Candler believed that his father made little profit from the project, but that he enjoyed the development process itself. Candler and his grandson frequently rode in a buggy through the site, watching as workers built roads and installed utilities. In his account of his father's life, Howard Candler commented with some bitterness that the brothers Forrest and George Adair, exclusive sales agents for Druid Hills, had taken a "free ride" at his father's expense. Forming a company to sell the property, they made an agreement with Candler to cover their expenses: "In effect, Father granted Forrest and George Adair the privilege of speculating in real estate with his money. If they made a profit, he got half of it. If they lost money, he took the entire loss." However, the growth of Druid Hills indicates that Candler probably had few losses to absorb. In December 1909 the *Atlanta Journal* reported that $86,000 worth of lots had been sold and over $750,000 had been committed by various individuals who planned to construct new homes for themselves: Asa Candler, Jr. planned to erect a "palace" worth $100,000, and Forrest Adair intended to spend $30,000 on a new house. Eventually Candler himself, as well as his brother Warren, his long-time Coca-Cola associate Frank Robinson, and a number of other family members and friends built homes in Druid Hills. Nearly a century later, it remains a beautiful and desirable residential location, although the expiration of the original deed covenants has unfortunately allowed some new construction to be wedged between some of the original houses.[29]

Candler's expansion of his interests from the manufacture of Coca-Cola into real estate development and banking continued a life-long pattern of success built on careful management. More than a half-century after his death no comprehensive list of his interests exists. Obituary and *Who's Who* entries include only the most familiar firms, such as Coca-Cola or Central Bank and Trust, but his name appears in connection with many other enterprises and as president of several. Occasionally he faltered; some projects did better than others but overall the trend was upward. His career attracted considerable public attention, which led Asa Candler to translate his instinctive gift for advertising into a self-conscious management of his public image. He had a natural dignity and dressed impeccably. Many of his photographs show him in wing collar and morning coat, but he represented himself as an uncomplicated, democratic, countrified fellow.[30]

One example of Candler's image-molding survives from the winter of 1909, when Julian Harris, a local writer, approached Asa Candler for an interview. Harris wanted to prepare a biographical sketch for *Uncle Remus's Home Magazine*, a publication founded by his father, the famed writer Joel Chandler Harris. Candler demurred, claiming he was not a worthy subject, that he even lacked a college education. Harris seized on this as a possible theme for his story: Candler would be an inspiration to other young men who had no opportunity to obtain higher education. Candler, who was a trustee of Emory College, agreed but extracted from Harris a promise to point out that he might have done even better with an advanced education. From this interview, Harris created a personality sketch by arranging a bouquet of favorable anecdotes. The article said nothing important about Candler's lack of college training but it did constitute a demonstration of his masterful management of his public image. In fact, Julian Harris's interview tells less about the business capabilities of Asa Candler than it does about his personality.[31]

Early in the article, Harris admitted that Candler did have critics who accused him of being merely lucky or of being a schemer or who called him tight-fisted or arrogant, but Harris clearly shared the alternate view of Candler as "Atlanta's most important asset." During a long November evening in the library of Callan Castle, Candler clearly charmed the younger man. Harris found him to be "gentle, yet determined," with an undramatic manner of speech that Harris described as "cold and calm." Candler expressed himself in "plain, keen epigrammatic sentences."

Harris's sketch retold the traditional version of Candler's rural youth, the supposedly dire effects of war and poverty, and his arrival in Atlanta with only two dollars in the pocket of his home made clothes. Harris recorded Candler's dutiful return to Villa Rica to "assist his brothers to straighten out the farm and get it ready to sell" after their father's death. Candler gave no hint to Harris (or any other interviewer) that in addition to operating a farm his father had been a prosperous merchant and occasional dealer in gold dust who had left a legacy of real estate and small business investments.

The article moved quickly over the entry of its subject into business and his establishment of the Coca-Cola Company and focused on Candler's more recent activities in banking and real estate. At the time, the Candler Building was one of the city's most imposing new structures, and Candler gave Harris an account of how he had come to build it. He said that the plan of a syndicate to erect a number of small structures on the original site of the First Methodist Church moved him to intervene: "[S]ince the lot was to be used for commercial purposes,...[I]t seemed a shame not to put up a building that would be an honor to the old church site—a beautiful building."[32]

No dreary details of interest rates or mortgages or investment companies cluttered his story. According to Harris, Candler laid out $165,000 for the lot, money he raised by selling some unspecified real estate that he had picked up during the previous ten years. Harris accepted without question Candler's claim that he had no idea and was surprised to learn that his assorted real estate was worth $300,000. Candler was undaunted by his "new-found" wealth, according to Harris: "'Sell it,' Candler said; and the money from these sales was the starter for the $750,000 and more that must have gone into the Candler building."[33]

Although he pretended to be innocent of the value of land in Atlanta, later in the same interview Candler showed that he had a clear understanding of the local real estate market. "As a matter of fact, I bought property to help keep the price of real estate up, and where a number [of persons] wanted to buy property and hesitated, I guaranteed that they wouldn't lose. It didn't cost me a cent, but I stood ready to back up my belief in Atlanta to the limit. That's the main reason I bought Druid Hills. I paid $500,000 for it. It is a beautiful tract of land. I have faith in it as an investment."[34]

Candler also said that the abandonment of the elaborate landscaping begun by the previous owners of Druid Hills saddened him. Julian Harris praised the millionaire for salvaging the "water-gashed roads" of Druid Hills but seems hardly to have noticed that an investment opportunity probably constituted the principal charm of Druid Hills for Asa Candler.

For the young journalist sitting at the fireside of the aging millionaire, Candler's innocence seemingly knew no bounds. Recounting the story of the Candler Building, Harris depicted a naïve entrepreneur who impulsively erected his "remarkable and perfect office structure" with a "magnificent arrangement for a banking house" on its ground floor, although he lacked any prospective tenant to occupy it.[35] The unnamed president of one of Atlanta's better known banks supposedly refused the opportunity to rent the space: "The next day Asa Candler called a few friends together and to their complete astonishment announced: "I can't get a bank to move up here, so I'm going to start one myself. Any of you want to come in?" When they recovered, they guessed they'd come in."[36]

Could a bank ever have begun on such a combination of impulse and lack of foresight? Would such a feckless businessman have been chosen, as Asa Candler had been during this time, to manage the receivership of another failed bank, to guide the finances of a college or to lead a major fund-raising campaign for the Methodist Church?[37] Such questions went unasked; Julian Harris was no muckraker and *Uncle Remus's Home Magazine* hardly could be called a yellow sheet.

Candler actually organized the Central Bank and Trust Company in 1905 while the Candler Building was still under construction. In January of that year a reporter from the *Atlanta Journal* asked Candler if he would confirm a current rumor that he planned to put a bank in his new facility. Candler did so but insisted that the arrangements were not complete. He also took pains to insist, "Such an institution can in no way harm the other banking institutions of the city….Atlanta can stand another big bank and can make it profitable to the stockholders." He disingenuously denied that he would seek to control the bank: "I should prefer that outside citizens, on the merits of the growth of the city and the admirable location will take entire charge of the institution. You may say however, that a big bank will be in the new Candler building on Peachtree."[38]

In October, Candler revealed the details of the bank's organization. It would open for business on 1 January 1906, with a capital stock of $500,000. William S. Thomson, identified as "one of the promoters of the institution," told the *Journal* that even though Candler modestly urged that he not be considered for its presidency, "the other gentlemen are enthusiastically in favor of electing him to head the company."[39] In fact, Asa Candler dominated the Central Bank and Trust as he did any other enterprise in which he became involved. He held the office of president for as long as the bank continued to do business.[40]

Undoubtedly Asa Candler was pleased to see himself characterized as a poor boy that made good, and he also took care that he not be seen as calculating or ruthless. In this, as with all of his public revelations, he did not seriously misrepresent himself, but Candler practiced a calculated modesty. The man who used the most sophisticated advertising methods of the time to move Coca-Cola to the forefront of its market also tended his personal public image with care, a well-advised strategy in the era of muckraking journalism and a growing public demand for social responsibility on the part of business and businessmen.

---

[1]Franklin Garrett, personal communication, 1991.

[2]The relative importance of Candler's various holdings seems impossible to discover with certainty, since he kept his financial affairs private. Perhaps some inference may be drawn from the fact that although he divested himself of control of Coca-Cola (giving his shares to his wife and children) late in 1916, he kept his active interest in Central Bank and Trust—but inference is one thing and fact is another.

[3]*Dividend No. 3*, Grover Megahee, compiler, (1911) in the Atlanta Historical Society's library, contains the proceedings of one such convention of Witham bankers. It includes a photograph of "Bide-A-Wee," Witham's "country home" on Peachtree Road.

[4]Candler, *Asa Griggs Candler*, 299; Hart County tax digests; Minutes of the Coca-Cola Company, vols. 1 and 2, The Archives, The Coca-Cola Company. The exact nature of Candler's deal with Witham remains unclear. Howard Candler states only that his father bought "a considerable interest" in Witham Mills. The minutes of the Coca-Cola Company first identify the Witham bonds specifically in January 1904, but Howard Candler says that they were included in the unnamed stocks and bonds in the records of the preceding years. In any case, Witham issued $35,000 in bonds in 1899 and $30,000 in 1900; Candler seems to have bought them all.

[5]Ibid.

[6] AGC to Charles Howard Candler in Candler, *Asa Griggs Candler*, 299-300; the full discussion of Witham Mills covers pp. 298-302 of *Asa Griggs Candler*.

[7] Microfilm copies of Hart County Tax Digests, 1900, 1901, Georgia Department of Archives and History, Atlanta; [Asa G. Candler, Jr. obituary], *Atlanta Constitution* 12 January 1958, clipping in The Archives, The Coca-Cola Company; Candler, *Asa Griggs Candler*, 300-302. The obituary erroneously states that "his father sent him to Hartwell to supervise construction of the 30,000 spindle Hartwell Cotton Mill...." Asa, Junior, has apparently left no reply to his brother Howard's evaluation of his capabilities.

[8] Ledger [re-used as a scrapbook], Joseph Brown Connally Scrapbook, MSS 45, Atlanta History Center Library-Archives, Atlanta. Someone glued a collection of 8x10 photographs of Atlanta social events to the pages of this ledger book, obscuring the entries for the early months of 1905. From July to December, charges on Asa G. Candler, Jr.'s account averaged a bit over $70 per month.

[9] AGC to Charles Howard Candler, 10 May 1902, 13 December 1902, 21 February 1903, excerpts quoted in Candler, *Asa Griggs Candler*, 301.

[10] "Arrival of Remains Was First News of Death," and "For First Time in 60 Hours News From Outside World is Received by Journal," both in *Atlanta Journal*, 10 February 1905, 1; microfilm copies of Hart County Tax Digests, 1900-1910; Minutes of The Coca-Cola Company, vol. 2; microfilm copy of Hart County Deed Book "R", Georgia Department of Archives and History, Atlanta; Ralph Smith, "Candlers to Build a Big Cotton Mill in DeKalb County," *Atlanta Journal* 6 December 1909, 1, provides the date of the closing of Witham Mills, but the story's speculation about a future Candler investment seems to have been unsubstantiated gossip.

[11] Candler, "Thirty-three Years," 41; "Sky Scraper on Church Site," *Atlanta Journal*, 21 January 1904, 1.

[12] Elizabeth Anne Mack Lyon, "Business Buildings in Atlanta: A Study In Urban Growth and Form," (Ph.D. diss., Emory University, 1971) 224-27, 245; "Atlanta Architecture: A survey of the architecture of Atlanta for the last hundred years prepared by students of the School of Architecture, Georgia Institute of Technology, Winter Quarter, School Year 1948-49," (bound typescript cataloged in book collection) Atlanta History Center Library Archives, 33; Thomas Mashburn Deaton, "Atlanta During the Progressive Era," (Ph.D. diss., University of Chicago, 1969) 93-94.

[13] Minutes of the Coca-Cola Company; 8 April 1905, The Archives, The Coca-Cola Company; Candler Investment Company Minute Book, box 18, AGC Papers; Candler, "Thirty-three Years," 33-34, 42.

[14] "Atlanta Architecture" survey, 33-34; Lyon, "Business Buildings," 245, 247. The barber shop acquired an "electric light plunge" five feet square and ten feet high where sufferers of "lumbago, rheumatism and other uric acid troubles" sought relief in the dry heat of this electric light-lined cabinet; see "Town Talk: The Palace Lives and Other Stories," *Atlanta Magazine* (February 1970): 18.

[15] Candler, "Thirty-three Years;" "The Candler Building," pamphlet (1906) box 7, AGC Papers; "Arrival of Remains Was First News of Death," "For First Time in 60 Hours News From Outside World is Received by Journal," and "Tons of Ice Fall From Building," *Atlanta Journal*, 10 February 1905, 1.

[16] Candler, "Thirty-three Years," 43.

[17] Lyon, "Business Buildings," 239, 346-47; "Atlanta Architecture" survey, 34; Candler, "Thirty-three Years," 43; "The Candler Building," *Journal of Labor*, 2 March 1906, 1. "The Candler Building" pamphlet, AGC Papers. Fate still had a last blow to deal the project, how-

ever; a month after it opened, a wind storm smashed one of its large plate glass windows facing Peachtree Street.

[18]Minute Book, Candler Investment Company, AGC Papers, Emory; Minutes of the Coca-Cola Company, vols. 1 and 2, *passim*, The Archives, The Coca-Cola Company.

[19]Miscellaneous property documents, folders 2-5, box 20, AGC papers, Emory, Atlanta; Minutes of the Coca-Cola Company, vol. 2; Candler, "Thirty-three Years," 44; [untitled short notes on AGC activities], *Coca Cola Bottler*, February 1912, 13; March 1912, 10; August 1912, 14; September 1912, 18; November 1912, 16. The New York City building eventually became the property of Emory University. In 1948 the university had become the sole owner of the stock in Asa G. Candler, Inc., which had been Candler's real estate holding company. At this point the firm's only asset was the New York City Candler Building. By conveying ownership of the building to the university on 14 December 1949, Candler's old firm ceased to exist. The National Register of Historic Places lists the New York Candler Building.

[20]*Atlanta Journal* quoted in *Coca Cola Bottler*, March 1913, 15.

[21]Miscellaneous items, folders 7-9, box 19, AGC papers, Emory. This fragmentary evidence includes a chatty letter written in October 1911, by a business acquaintance named M. H. B. Hoffman; the letter does not show any close knowledge of Candler's plans, although it mentions the possibilities of a hotel or a bank. See folder 8. In folder 7 is a map with the lot in question labeled "Your Lot" and a neighboring square marked "New Hotel"; the location is close to the Union Station and about four blocks from the Capitol building.

[22]Minutes of the Coca-Cola Company, vol. 2; *Atlanta Journal* quoted in *Coca-Cola Bottler*, March 1913, 15; [various reports of AGC's activities], *Coca-Cola Bottler*, August 1915, 19; November 1915, 19; Charles F. Wilkinson, "Asa G. Candler, Pioneer-Capitalist," *Buildings and Management*, (September 1915) 56-57. AGC papers at Emory and at the Coca Cola Archives document several construction projects, large and small. No other archival evidence remains to clarify his plans for the property in Washington, DC During this era he also acquired the Forsyth Building in downtown Atlanta.

[23]"Moore-Marsh Building Is Sold," *Atlanta Journal*, 2 march 1908, 1; "Moore-Marsh Building To Be Theater," *Atlanta Journal*, 10 March 1908, 1; "Asa G. Candler To Make Hotel of Building," *Atlanta Journal*, 14 March 1908, 1.

[24]"Candler Buys Lowndes Building," *Atlanta Journal*, 4 December 1909, 6; "Lowndes Building To Be Made Annex for the Candler," *Atlanta Journal*, 6 December 1909, 1; microfilm of Sanborn Insurance Maps (1911) illustrates the physical relationship of the two structures.

[25]Candler, *Asa Griggs Candler*, 191-94.

[26]Klima, "Land Barons," 73-75, 78 describes the founding of Inman Park and discusses its failure to meet expectations after the financial crisis of 1893; Rick Beard, "Hurt's Deserted Village: Atlanta's Inman park, 1885-1911" in *Olmsted South: Old South Critic, New South Planner*, Dana F. White and Victor A. Kramer, eds., Contributions in American Studies, Number 43 (Westport CN: Greenwood Press, 1979) 204-209, also treats the shortcomings of the Inman Park project. On p. 208, Beard writes, "[B]y 1896 Inman Park was just a nice place to live; it was not Atlanta's ideal suburban community." The Candler and Hurt houses still stand.

[27]Elizabeth A. Lyon, "Frederick Law Olmsted and Joel Hurt: Planning for Atlanta," in *Olmsted South: Old south Critic, New South Planner*, Dana F. White and Victor A. Kramer, eds., Contributions in American Studies, Number 43 (Westport CN: Greenwood Press, 1979) 180-81; Candler, *Asa Griggs Candler*, 191, 270-74; Dana F. White, "Landscaped Atlanta: The Romantic Tradition in Cemetery, Park, and Suburban Development" *The Atlanta Historical Journal*, (Summer-Fall, 1982) 99-107; Sarah Simms Edge, *Joel Hurt and the Development of*

Atlanta, passim. According to Doyle, *New Men*, 99-101.

Forrest and George Adair, fixtures in the Atlanta real estate world throughout Candler's lifetime, inherited their business from their father George, a former aide-de-camp to the Confederate General Nathan Bedford Forrest. The elder Adair, formerly a partner in a firm of "Negro brokers," speculated in real estate after the Civil War.

[28]Druid Hills Minute Book, stockholders' meeting, 6 July 1910, box 9 , AGC Papers.

[29]Lyon, "Olmsted South," 181-82; Candler, *Asa Griggs Candler*, 272-74; "Over $750,000 Will Be Spent for Homes in Druid Hills Park," *Atlanta Journal*, 12 December 1909, 1.

[30]Examples may be seen in *Coca-Cola Bottler*, July 1916, 15; October 1918, 17; "Mayor Asa Candler Proves His Ability in Spelling Match," *Atlanta Constitution*, 27 January 1917, 8.

[31]Julian Harris, "Asa G. Candler: Georgia Cracker," *Uncle Remus's Home Magazine Emory University Quarterly* 7/4 (November 1909; reprint, December 1951): 196-207.

[32]Ibid., 201.

[33]Ibid., 201-202.

[34]Ibid., 207.

[35]The building opened with forty percent occupancy, according to the report of the secretary-treasurer on 6 January 1906; see Candler Investment Company minute book, box 18, AGC papers, Emory. The tenants, in addition to the bank, included: the US War Department's Department of the Gulf Headquarters, a florist, the American Bridge Company, Carnegie Steel, Atlantic [cotton] Compress Co., Otis Elevator, Atlanta Title Guarantee, Massengale Advertising, Lowman Advertising, Columbian Life Insurance, Northwestern Life, J. B. Whitehead, Lithia Springs Water Co., Ponce de Leon Amusement Co., Atlanta Skating Rink Co., Underwood Typewriters, the law firm of Candler, Thompson, and Hirsch, and the Coca-Cola Company.

[36]Ibid., 203.

[37]The major responsibilities that Candler assumed at various points in his career will be discussed below.

[38]"New Bank To Be Located in Candler Building," *Atlanta Journal*, 27 January 1905, 1. This establishment of an important commercial endeavor several blocks up Peachtree Street from the traditional economic center of the city was an early manifestation of the twentieth century trend of Atlanta's business district to move northward.

[39]"New Bank For Atlanta Is Organized," *Atlanta Journal*, 4 October 1905, 1. William S. Thomson should not be confused with John Candler's law partner, William D. Thomson.

[40]"Ask For Charter For Central Bank and Trust Co.," *Atlanta Journal*, 28 November 1905, 2; "Asa G. Candler Is President of New Bank," *Atlanta Journal* 8 December 1905, 5. Incorporators were Candler, John S. Owens, William H. Patterson, Samuel D. Jones, John C. Hallman, George E. King, James H. Nunnally, Isaac H. Hirsch, and William S. Thomson. Citizens' and Southern Bank purchased his shares and absorbed the bank in 1922; the circumstances of this sale are discussed in a later chapter of this work.

CHAPTER FIVE

Steward

In the spring of 1907 Asa Candler and his wife Lucy, took their youngest son William on an extensive tour of the West. As their railroad car rolled on, Candler wrote to his grown son Howard to describe the famous burro ride down a narrow trail cut in the side of the Grand Canyon: "I simply sat paralyzed as we slowly crept down on the backs of those little mules shod with shoes on which are sharp spikes—turning around sharp curves making SSSSS's—down and down we went…"[1]

When Asa and Willie and the others in the party reached the bottom, they rode a short distance across the level ground to a resting place where they shared a picnic lunch before returning up the cliff-side trail:

> I looked up…& realized that the only way I & William could ever get back to Mama was up a narrow steep crooked trail on a little mule's back & that I could not ever be allowed to guide him, just patiently sit on his back, not whip him, not scold him, not coax him, not try to talk…just hold my hands on the horn of the big saddle & trust him implicitly. I

thought oh why can't I thus tread life's hills—Trust God—go on be patient & after a while reach the high heights & see Him for my self who is "altogether lovely." Oh what a splendid illustration of real life....[2]

Such a sudden turn from a chatty account of a vacation adventure to an outflowing of religious feelings appear throughout Asa Candler's correspondence. In the space of a paragraph he could switch from a cool discussion of a business matter to expand on the glories of God's grace. A routine family letter could divert into a declaration of spiritual devotion and finish off with some other mundane matter. Candler's faith, ever foremost in his thoughts, set the course of his life. He lived by it.

Christian stewardship was a central aspect of his belief. Several of the great capitalists of the gilded age shared this principle, which holds that God gives wealth to individuals not for their personal enjoyment, but rather to be used for the advancement and improvement of His kingdom on earth.[3] Candler believed that although a duty of stewardship applies to both rich and poor, the rich Christian faces a special challenge: "The great principle underlying the teaching of Jesus concerning the dangers connected with wealth is that the increase of power of any sort increases responsibility and thereby multiplies the perils of the soul."[4] He deplored the fact that many fail this test, and "with unconscious atheism they begin to claim absolute ownership of properties and resources of which they are only trustees ... without reference to either the needs of their fellowman or the call of their Master."[5]

Candler's brother Warren held similar ideas. Bishop Candler called the new rich "all asses" and flatly stated, "Wealth makes a man rebellious and proud."[6] When Asa turned to Warren for advice on how to use the wealth that God had given him, the bishop replied in writing: "I pray God that you may be as great a christian as you are a business man...using money in a grand and statesmanlike way." Attached to this letter was a long memorandum that began, "The ability to make money is a gift of God (Deuteronomy viii: 10) just as any other sort of talent; and it must be consecrated to the service of God. It may no more be used selfishly than may a call to preach."[7] To this plain statement of the principle of stewardship, the bishop added a set of priorities to guide the rich Christian. Wealth should be applied to the needs of one's family first; then "to the maintenance of the business which God has given one to the end that he may serve Him by making money"; and finally "to the promotion of benevolent causes for the up-building of the kingdom of God." The wealthy man should be wary lest fascination with the kingdom of God lead him to forget his duties to family and business.[8]

As Warren Candler pointed out in his "Memoranda," the successful steward does make a profit; virtue is not his only reward. Thus, a cynical observer might see stewardship as a crude rationalization for greed. However, the weight of the evidence is on the side of Asa Candler's sincerity on this point. Stewardship provided the capitalist with a moral foundation for his energetic pursuit of profit, but it also channeled this pursuit in certain directions. Many of Candler's business undertakings reflect the spirit of capitalism as guided by stewardship, producing both a benefit to the public and a profit for his own interests. One of the first of these occasions came when his carefully managed Central Bank and Trust Company provided him with the means to ease the effects of the Panic of 1907 on the economy of Atlanta.

Most of the customers of a local bank do not pay much attention to their particular bank's place in the national network of financial institutions. Unfortunately, such minor participants in the American economy sometimes discover that they are vulnerable to economic forces originating far from home. The depositors in Atlanta's Neal Bank, which was actually a small family-owned business, received a rough lesson in economics in the winter of 1907. The crisis began in the banks of New York City, which formed the apex of a pyramid of American financial institutions. Small local banks deposited their reserve funds in various larger banks, and these major urban institutions, in their turn, placed reserves in the great banking houses of New York. These monies provided a reservoir of quick capital for investment at the discretion of the managers of the eastern banks. In August 1907, their reserves had become dangerously low, in part because of investments in over-valued securities, such as copper stocks. In October a drop in the price of some of these copper stocks triggered a panic among the depositors in New York's Mercantile National Bank. The panic spread to trust companies and other banks, all of which struggled desperately for survival. Some individuals who became aware of the situation hoarded cash, slowing economic activity so seriously that some businesses issued scrip when they could not find cash to meet payrolls. Although the situation frightened the nation's economic leadership, the faltering money market soon corrected itself. The scarcity of cash had created attractive conditions for those with the courage to risk putting money back in circulation. In addition, the Treasury Department deposited generous infusions of cash in troubled banks. These measures, along with an improved balance of trade, tended to ease the situation. Nonetheless, toward the end of the year, regions of the nation's economy remote from the center of the storm still felt its effects.[9]

At the height of the banking crisis, Atlanta's newspapers found the state fair at Piedmont Park more beguiling than financial news, which got short shrift. They reported on the resignation of F. Augustus Heinz, president of the troubled Mercantile National Bank, and the *Atlanta Journal* did follow the story of the panic. However, the paper seemed largely unconcerned by the connection between the banks of New York and those of Georgia.[10] At the end of the month Darwin G. Jones, manager of the Atlanta Clearing House, stated confidently "the New York disturbance has had not the slightest effect [on Atlanta]. Our local banks are going along in a normal way, caring for their customers...."[11] In fact, Atlanta's economy was in some trouble.

By December, the *Journal* had recognized the hard facts. However, the newspaper blamed the crisis on pessimism rather than large economic forces. To combat the problem, the newspaper offered the "Smile Club." Photographs of prominent citizens grinned from the front page while fatuous stories proclaimed their faith in Atlanta's economy. On December 11, the *Journal* highlighted eight bankers, including William F. Manry, cashier of the Neal Loan and Banking Company, whom the paper described as "another financial light and a member of the 'Smile' club." A majority of the Neal Bank's nine thousand depositors kept small savings accounts totaling about $723,000; the State of Georgia accounted for an additional amount, about $200,000. According to the Journal, "Mr. Manry is at once a prudent and conservative business man as well as an optimist, hence the illuminating smile on his face." [12]

As Christmas approached, Mr. Manry's smile must have faded. Rumors of insolvency dogged his bank and, on the Saturday before Christmas, frightened depositors began a run on the twenty-year-old Neal Bank. The bank withstood the immediate challenge and kept its doors open for fifteen minutes beyond its customary one o'clock closing hour, but the onslaught left it staggering. Its officers requested that the Atlanta Clearing House Association investigate its books before business opened again on Monday. The Neal's management expected that the Clearing House or one of its member banks might see the Neal Bank through its crisis. Representatives of the Clearing House worked until after midnight on Saturday and resumed their task on Sunday morning. The Sunday newspaper reported the "general opinion" that the bank could return all deposits "dollar for dollar."[13]

In fact, the Clearing House investigators found that the Neal Bank's combined checking, savings, and deposit certificate obligations amounted to about two million dollars, while about $700,000 of its assets were tied up in questionable investments. On Sunday afternoon they concluded, "the investments and loans of this bank...can not be readily converted [to cash]." On the following day the state treasurer placed the bank under supervision and appointed special examiners to investigate its affairs more fully.[14] The morning newspapers of Christmas Eve brought rumors of an impending receivership for the Neal bank, but Governor Hoke Smith issued reassuring statements to the press urging depositors to "sit steady in the boat." The worried depositors might have received this advice with some skepticism if they understood that the State of Georgia, one of the Neal Bank's largest depositors, would enjoy a first lien on the bank's limited assets. The Governor knew that lawyers for other interested parties were preparing to file suits against the bank. He "feared complications" and he wished to protect the interests of the state by acting first. By the end of the day lawyers for the state applied for the appointment of a receiver. Their application quoted the opinion of the bank examiner that "said bank was not in a position to resume business or liquidate its indebtedness." The Neal bank could offer no effective rebuttal, so the court agreed to the state's request. It appointed Asa Candler's Central Bank and Trust as receiver of the Neal Bank.[15]

On Christmas day, the *Atlanta Journal* featured a two-column photo of Asa Candler—solemn and bankerly in his wing collar—and printed his reassuring statement in a box on the front page: "...every depositor in the Neal bank will receive every dollar of his money...when the affairs of that institution are wound up there will be something left for the stockholders....The people will get a square deal." The standard fee for this service was five percent, but Central Bank and Trust would ask only two-and-a-half.[16] As befitted a good steward, Candler saw that his own bank would receive compensation for its services, but his acceptance of a fee of only half the permissible amount underlined the public spirit of this undertaking. Candler set "a large and competent clerical force" to work on Christmas morning and promised a 10 per cent payment to depositors in about thirty days.[17] The public, reassured by his statements, expected that he would protect the interests of the Neal Bank's depositors.

Shortly before the problems of the Neal Bank brought Candler increased public attention, the businessmen of Atlanta had elected him president of the Chamber of Commerce. He made his first presidential address about a week after the failure of the bank. In it he praised the social usefulness of capitalism, but he also asserted the important link between "righteousness and fair dealing" and business: "[N]o sort of progress can justify the abandonment of the first principles in morality and the sound maxims of economics." His next words stand as a vivid insight into the mentality of the Christian steward: "Men cannot take short cuts on the decalogue nor can they afford to set aside the natural laws of trade to appease the clamor of the unthinking multitude."[18] He asserted that in its highest form, commerce was "human brotherliness organized for the supply of human wants and the promotion of human well-being. In its best estate it disdains rewards without services rendered, and despises gains gotten without 'value received.'"[19] With this view of an ennobled commerce as a quasi-religious pursuit, Candler could see the Neal receivership as a Christian service as well as a business opportunity, and experience no sense of contradiction.

However, not every Atlantan—and in particular, the smaller depositors of the Neal bank—could accept Candler's perception of himself as a disinterested and reliable guardian of the public welfare. Those who lost access to their bank accounts when the Neal went into receivership soon discovered that all depositors did not enjoy equal claims against the assets of the failed bank. Certain Neal depositors sued to assert prior claims—that is, they asked to be paid in full before the ordinary depositors received their share of whatever remained. One of the largest of these was the State of Georgia, which had deposited about $200,000 of state funds in various accounts; State law protected this money from the claims of other depositors.[20] Preferred status also went to certain private interests, for example the Hamilton National Bank of Chattanooga. According to the Hamilton's petition, the two banks sometimes acted as collection agencies for one another, and at the time of its failure Neal bank held certain funds collected on behalf of the Chattanooga bank that were about to be forwarded there. The Hamilton successfully argued that their money, although located in the Neal bank, was not any part of the Neal's own assets.[21]

Many individual depositors also tried to press claims for prior status. (One can only imagine Asa Candler's reaction to the unsuccessful attempt by the Koca-Nola company to settle a claim, given his passionate resentment of those who attempted to infringe on the Coca-Cola trademark.)[22] In fact, the courts denied the petitions of most depositors who sought preferred status. The intervention of S. Booth, for example, failed to recover the desired $257; however, unlike most of those whose petitions failed, Booth did not give up the effort. He next appeared at the head of a list of petitioners asking for the appointment of an additional receiver. Booth, et al., complained that a conflict of interest existed because a third bank (the Trust Company) that had claims against the Neal also belonged to the Atlanta clearing house, as did Candler's Central Bank and Trust. In effect, Booth and his four friends believed that the members of the Clearing house were conspiring to collect funds at the expense of the small depositors. The court refused their petition. The litigious quintet returned to court repeatedly with absolutely no success.[23] Certain other depositors objected to the state's first lien on the Neal assets, on the grounds that Georgia had itself violated the law by depositing such a large amount of money in a single bank. Furthermore, they pointed to the fact that the state had made one large deposit in December, at a time when officials should have known of the bank's weakened condition. This challenge also failed.[24]

By late January, when the Central Bank filed its first report, some assets had already been liquidated. Judge John Candler, attorney for the Central Bank, repeated the prospect of a "dollar-for-dollar" payment to Neal's creditors, but depositors, now aware that the state had first call on the bank's remaining assets, were not reassured by the statement. One group called a mass meeting to consider organizing to defend their interests. They vented their dissatisfaction, but in the end, they took no actions.[25] The editor of the city's only black newspaper, although he expressed confidence in Candler, thought that the state of Georgia should be last, not first, to collect from the Neal funds.[26] About a month later another reassuring statement from Central Bank suggested that a twenty per cent payment might be forthcoming in about thirty to fifty days, depending on legal red tape.[27]

Candler labored on, selling property and collecting debts owed to the defunct bank. The index to the court records of the Neal Bank receivership offers mute testimony to the size of the responsibility he faced. Over five hundred entries, most involving the sale of small parcels of real estate, represent individual transactions related to the liquidation of the failed bank.[28] One of the Neal Bank's few large assets was a loan secured by a parcel of land in Cuba. During this period Candler visited the island, but what he actually did there is not known. Family support of missionary activity and a Methodist college occasionally took one of the Candlers to the island, but Asa also may have made this trip in connection with the bank's property. In late January, Candler arranged for the sale of the Cuban acreage in a 1.5 million dollar deal that cleared its owners' debt to the bank.[29]

In some cases Candler himself purchased downtown Atlanta real estate that was under obligation to the Neal Bank. Thus, he infused the bank's depleted coffers with funds from his own pockets. In the true spirit of stewardship, which should not be confused with charity or largess, Candler frankly acknowledged that he expected to reap a profit from these transactions when the property values increased. There is no evidence that the idea of a conflict of interest ever occurred to him. His purchase of downtown property moved the *Atlanta Journal's* cartoonist to portray him as a giant in the streets of the city, his pockets stuffed with "titles" to Marietta Street and Decatur Street, pensively studying buildings festooned with "Not for Sale" signs. The caption reads, "ANYTHING ELSE ON THE MAR-KET?"[30]

Settlements sometimes required compromise. The Atlanta Utility Company could not immediately raise the $31,000 it owed to the Neal bank, so Candler agreed to accept payment of fifty cents on the dollar. He made this arrangement because the Neal also held a significant amount of stock in the utility company; a demand for full payment would have bankrupted the utility company and rendered the stock worthless. Candler took the long view that the full value of the $31,000 loan eventually would be recovered as the value of the utility company's stock increased; however this decision reduced the amount of cash immediately available to settle the claims of the depositors.[31]

While these activities continued, Judge John Candler, the attorney for the receiver, urged Neal depositors to hold fast and not sell their accounts at a discount. On Friday night, March twentieth, the receiver mailed checks totaling $342,388 to the rank-and-file depositors. Judge John Candler, attorney for the Central Bank, stated that nine thousand persons "would be directly touched by the dividend." He added that the total dollar amount represented about one fifth of the bank's indebtedness, with the exception of certain preferred claims. The front page of the *Journal* presented a cartoon on the subject, depicting a "GOOD BEGINNING" in the form of a hand representing "9,000 DEPOSITORS" reaching out to accept from "RECEIVER" a chunk of bread sliced from the end of a "NEAL BANK" loaf. Two days later the paper described the effect of the payment on the city's commerce as a "golden flood."[32]

To the Neal bank's small depositors this golden flood may have been less than reassuring. If wildly optimistic, they might hope to recover all of their deposits, but the most reasonable expected to receive a portion. In the mean time, depositors had lost all access to their money, while bankers, businessmen and government officials seemed to be handling it quite freely. Inevitably, business connections of Asa Candler took part in the liquidation of the Neal debt. Unless he had sold everything to out-of-town investors nothing else could have been possible. None the less, when property across from the Candler Building sold for $65,000 and then plans were announced to build a hotel on the site, the ordinary Neal Bank depositor might have had second thoughts about Candler's disinterested management of the matter. They had already seen legally favored interests pass them in the "line" to receive payment from the failed bank. Although they lacked financial sophistication, these people understood all too well the effects of the bank's failure on their personal lives. This awareness, coupled with early promises of dollar-for-dollar reimbursement that had raised hopes beyond reasonable expectations, must have left a residue of resentment with many of the nine thousand ordinary Neal depositors.

The receivership process ground slowly on and depositors from time to time received small portions of the money that had been in their accounts at Christmas time in 1907. A decade after the failure of the Neal bank, in June 1917, the receiver announced an eight per cent dividend, bringing the total repayment to seventy-six and a half cents on the dollar. Unidentified sources at the courthouse expressed the belief that the liquidation of the last of the Neal assets would raise the total recovery to eighty or eighty-five per cent.[33] As late as 1920, the Fulton County Tax Digest shows a property tax payment of $25,825 by Central Bank and Trust still acting as trustee for the Neal Bank. Shortly after this time the Citizens and Southern Bank absorbed the Central Bank and Trust, ending any Candler involvement in the matter.[34]

As the process of winding down the affairs of the Neal Bank went on for years, Candler acted responsibly, but as a good steward he also continued to acquire profits. By the time Candler left the banking business, more than a decade had passed and the small accounts of Neal Bank's thrifty, working-class customers had been partly and slowly salvaged by his careful work. However, this must have been small comfort to those who had saved for some large purchase or to provide a cushion against unforeseen trouble, only to lose the comfort and protection that a little money put aside can provide.

Another economically vulnerable segment of Atlanta's population suffered as a result of the panic. A collapse in real estate values hit small homeowners hard as their homes lost much of their value. According to Howard Candler, his father instructed the realtor George Adair to purchase the homes of small property owners at pre-panic prices, thus protecting the sellers from loss. This was not charity. He bought with the expectation that the market would right itself. Candler's agent later sold some 250 houses to persons of moderate means on a simple plan of ten per cent down with the balance divided into one hundred equal payments. One family member estimated that Candler put about a million dollars into this activity.[35] If the terms of his buying and selling are correctly reported by Howard Candler, the profits on these transactions could not have been large.

This sort of business dealing, not quite philanthropy, but demonstrating an awareness of the needs of the ordinary Atlantan, helped build Candler's reputation.

Asa Candler again combined private investment with public service, in the spring of 1915, when he purchased over three million dollars in State of Georgia bonds. The state needed money to cover a number of obligations, including an earlier bond issue. Hoping to refinance this debt, Georgia floated a new group of bonds. This plan to borrow from Peter and pay Paul faced defeat when the second bond issue failed to attract investors. Candler came to the rescue in March, 1915, by offering the highest bid of $1,017.82 for each thousand-dollar bond. His personal check for $70,500—the amount required to guarantee the bid—accompanied his offer. The *Journal* adorned its front-page story of the sale with a three-column photograph of the millionaire banker, reporting that the other bidders "were profoundly impressed not only by the large financial resources of Mr. Candler, but by his magnificent confidence in his state's securities…."[36] Every Atlanta citizen could not follow the technicalities of this transaction, but the words "personal check" were plain enough, as was the dollar amount on the check's face. The next day's *Journal* attempted to explain, in a small front-page box, how it was that "State Saves $372,000 By Bid of Mr. Candler." Candler told the newspaper that the time had come to demonstrate that Georgia could finance her own enterprises. He declared that local businessmen gave too much attention to, "enterprises yielding quick returns" and advised "more self-reliance and … a nobler commercial courage."[37] He added that he hoped to sell the bonds to small investors within the state.

Governor Slaton issued a statement that expanded on Candler as a "splendid citizen, broad of vision, munificent in charity, capable in business" who had helped render Georgia independent of "foreign" capital. He pointed out that if Georgians did buy the bonds from Candler, the interest paid would remain within the state's economy.[38] Candler's call for "nobler commercial courage" might be interpreted as a bit of a sales pitch to those small Georgia investors who he hoped would buy the bonds. However, in the final analysis, Candler intended to sell the bonds somewhere and recoup his $3.5 million investment with a modest profit. An *Arkansas Gazette* editor reported on the purchase by "a Georgia man who made his money out of a well-known soft drink," declaring that "soda fountain patrons may never have proposed toasts to this Georgian's health, but they have drunk to his wealth." The general public of Georgia would later remember Candler simply as a man who wrote large personal checks and thus saved the taxpayers even larger sums of money.[39]

In addition to acting as a careful steward of his personal wealth, Asa Candler was a family man, a civic booster, and a realistic business man; all of these aspects of his life came into play in his dealings with the Atlanta Automobile Association (A. A. A.) and their aftermath. Candler himself had come of age in horse-and-buggy days but his son Asa, Jr., was one of the first generation of Americans that became devoted to the automobile. As early as 1905 he owned a car and shortly after this he became one of the founders of the Atlanta Automobile Association, Incorporated. Most likely it was this family connection that first moved the elder Candler to provide significant support to his son's organization, although he followed his usual custom of charging interest and requiring collateral for loans. (His sons repaid their college loans—with interest.) He agreed to sell the Association a piece of property that was the site of a small race track, near Hapeville, south of the city of Atlanta. He accepted a note for $130,000 at seven percent. On this property, the Association developed an automobile racing facility with a smooth, two-mile track that drivers pronounced one of the best in the nation.[40]

In November 1909, the A. A. A. sponsored an "Automobile Week" that included auto shows and races. Participants from all over the United States came to Atlanta. To prepare the city for these visitors, downtown merchants donated funds to illuminate the area of Peachtree and Whitehall streets; the "Arc Avenue" plan called for electric arc lights to burn at the top of every trolley pole in the designated area for a period of thirty days. Candler, always in favor of boosting Atlanta's reputation, supported the plan publicly: "It will go far toward making an impression for good…. It will give me great pleasure to make [a] substantial contribution to cover the expense of this work." He actually gave sixty dollars toward the estimated cost of $2500, while four other donors gave $100 or more. Although he regularly gave money to all sorts of "worthy causes," he did so moderately, saving sumptuous donations for church related projects.[41]

Demonstrating his support of the Association and the Automobile Week events, Asa Candler officially opened the auto show at a banquet, where Asa, Jr. presented him a loving cup. The races constituted the highlight of the week. Georgians paid ten cents to ride a special train to the racetrack, where they cheered famous drivers, including the legendary Barney Oldfield. Louis Chevrolet won the Coca-Cola trophy by driving his "Buick No. 10" at speeds of seventy miles per hour in a two-hundred mile race.[42]

When Automobile Week ended, the A. A. A. still owed Asa Candler a total $130,000 for real estate and improvements. He had a lien on all their future gate receipts and control of the title to the Hapeville property until the debt was paid.[43] The Association continued to conduct races at the track, but in spite of the brilliant success of Automobile Week, the A. A. A. never succeeded in meeting its financial obligations. In August 1909 Candler loaned the group $5000 in a demand note secured by fifty shares of A. A. A. stock; several other notes of this nature followed. In 1910, Candler loaned the association $31,000 at six percent. Later that year another small loan—$500—added to the burden of debt. By 1913, with no significant repayment in sight, Candler asked his lawyers for their opinion. They advised foreclosure. His patience worn out, Candler agreed. The Association was willing to surrender the property in exchange for forgiveness of the debt, an arrangement acceptable to Candler. He closed down the racetrack, salvaging what he could. He demolished the fences, grandstands, and other facilities and sold the used construction materials.[44]

A new use for the actual racetrack soon developed. The age of aviation had dawned and pilots needed a place to land their planes. The track served nicely, and evidently had unofficial use as a landing field as early as 1918, when two Army aviators stationed in

Montgomery flew their plane to Atlanta to spend the weekend. These two, along with another pilot and his craft, landed at the former race track. Later, after taking off for the return flight, the plane carrying the two aviators flew low over the field, waving to a group of admiring Atlanta girls. Their engine died and they crashed nose down, demolishing their aircraft. Both survived, although Lieutenant Lincoln Weaver suffered some head injuries and two broken ankles.[45]

At almost the same time, aviation promised to play a more serious role in Atlanta's future. Representatives of the postal service, locating nodes in the new US air mail system, came to the city. Civic leaders took pains to charm the delegation, which sought "three or four acres of fairly level ground as a landing place" that could be used as a part of an air mail route.[46] The former speedway soon took on a new life as an airport called Candler Field.

By 1925 the future of aviation seemed assured, and the city of Atlanta began negotiations to acquire Candler Field for a Municipal Aviation Field. The city took a five year lease on the property with an option to purchase at the end of that time for $100,000. Candler asked no profit on the lease to the city, only that he be paid an amount to equal the taxes due on the property during the period of the lease. The city of Atlanta ultimately purchased Candler Field, and the country racetrack once owned by Asa Candler became the genesis of the future Hartsfield International Airport, one of the major air transportation centers in the United States.[47] This series of dealings demonstrates that although he seldom threw good money after bad, Asa Candler would at times minimize profits for the sake of some civic benefit.

About seven years after Candler undertook the effort to mitigate the effects on Atlanta's economy of the 1907 panic he made the greatest of his investments in the spirit of stewardship. He once again applied his personal assets to the relief of distress in the Atlanta economy.

In a curious parallel to the events of 1907, Candler went on vacation shortly before the advent of a national calamity. Under the urging of their children Mr. and Mrs. Candler sailed to Europe in the summer of 1913. As is often the case with such journeys, they raced to complete an exhausting schedule. Candler confided in a letter to his sister, "Wife enjoys being here. I do not but will tough it through."[48] The entire tour did not bore him, however. Even as he had once been moved by the sight of the Grand Canyon, the mountains at Interlaken, Switzerland moved him, in his letters home, to rhapsodize on God's greatness. John Wesley's carefully preserved possessions whispered to him the unspoken message, "Go do something" for the betterment of the world. In a letter to his son he resolved, "I must try to do it."[49]

The opportunity to *go do something*—if not for the world, at least for his fellow Georgians—soon came. It began to develop in the summer of 1914, as the cotton bolls swelled to bursting in Georgia while the nations of Europe moved toward world war.

Even before the official outbreak of hostilities, the assassination of the Austrian archduke in the last days of June began to threaten the established trade relations between the United States and Europe. On the continent, buyers canceled orders because ships could no longer reliably carry goods to their ports. As a result, on 31 July 1914, exchange officials in New York suspended trading in both stocks and commodities. By the end of summer, blockades and battles cut the normal lines of trade. Even as they harvested a record sixteen-million-bale crop, southern cotton growers faced ruin. Credit dried up and the price of cotton fell to six cents a pound. About half the anticipated value of the crop was lost. The exchanges resumed trading on 16 November but after three and a half months this was of little use to the cotton growers of the South.[50] This disaster struck at a region that was already economically vulnerable. The hopes and fears of Georgia farmers, as always, rose and fell with the price of cotton.[51]

Over the years, city folk always had plenty of unsolicited advice to offer to the farmers. Newspapers and the Georgia Chamber of Commerce admonished them to adopt progressive business methods and scientific farming, while labor union spokesmen urged farmers to organize after the fashion of his "city brother-worker." These city dwellers simply did not grasp the full reality of the small farmers' condition. Although farmers supposedly operated independently, in reality a system of perpetual indebtedness entangled many of them. Each year the small farmer borrowed against his next crop in order to finance the present year. At harvest time these debts would be settled, only to be renewed in the ensuing months. Any disruption in this precarious pattern could bring financial disaster. Furthermore, the entire cotton crop came into the market at the same time. The resulting glut always led to a fall in price, further limiting the prospects for high profit. Those who could wait to sell could expect a higher price, but only the comparatively wealthy had the resources to ride out the post-harvest glut.[52]

The sudden downward turn in the cotton market that resulted from the outbreak of the World War aroused new interest in programs intended to ease the effects of swings in the price of cotton. One naive response to the immediate problem, the "Buy-a-Bale" scheme, put actual bales of cotton for sale in hotel lobbies and other public places. A hardware merchant in Erie, Pennsylvania, bought a bale to display on the floor of his store, for the interest of his customers who had never seen raw cotton. However, the Buy-a-Bale plan was really a charitable activity rather than a realistic effort to adjust the staggering cotton market. The ultimate solution would lie with bankers, brokers, and government officials.

Members of Congress advised farmers "to hold cotton as long as possible, pending a settlement of the present disturbed condition of the cotton trade incident to the war in Europe," but law-making processes moved too slowly to provide immediate help.[53] Anxious cotton producers bombarded the government with calls for aid. Secretary of the Treasury William G. McAdoo reassured representatives of the cotton (and tobacco) producers that national banks in affected areas could receive $170 million in emergency funds. He said that this would be sufficient to deal with the situation.[54]

The Federal Reserve Board, perhaps the most powerful economic institution involved in the cotton crisis, also responded to the financial needs of agriculture. Its member banks could offer loans on easy terms for the purchase of fertilizer, tractors, and implements.

Farmers were allowed to use some portion of the money originally assigned as an agricultural loan to support household expenses.[55]

A group of bankers in St. Louis responded to the willingness of the Federal Reserve to assist farmers and gained national attention in late August 1914, by organizing warehouse facilities for 250,000 bales of cotton; they would lend $35 a bale on cotton to be stored in their warehouses. President Wilson rejected suggestions that the government lend directly to the troubled farmers but endorsed the St. Louis plan. At the same time, a delegation of southern bankers threw their support behind the program. As the plan moved toward final approval by the Federal Reserve Board, the St. Louis plan gained support from banks in New York City, which agreed to put in $50 million.[56]

Apparently, Asa Candler intended to sign on to the St. Louis Plan. The Georgia Bankers' Association made a $10 million commitment to the plan in a meeting in Atlanta on Wednesday, 14 October. One of the delegates, A. P. Coles, vice-president of Candler's Central Bank and Trust, endorsed the program enthusiastically. Taking a long view of the plan's probable good effect on the market, he predicted a strong rise in the price of cotton in the coming months.[57]

Asa Candler watched all of these activities with the informed interest of a southern banker who had, in his youth, helped harvest his father's cotton crops. As usual, he had kept his head in the crisis. On the same day that the Georgia bankers endorsed the St. Louis plan, he wrote a letter that included a passing comment on the commodities situation. "The European war has almost scared the life out of business in this part of the world. It's no more than scare. We have great crops."[58] Nor was Candler alone in his perception that the crisis offered an opportunity to those with nerve. A. Barton Hepburn, a New York financier wrote to Atlanta banker Robert Maddox in a similar vein, declaring that "This is not our trouble, it is our opportunity."[59]

"Opportunity" is a key word. Candler's confidence moved him to a decision, some time in the following few days, not to participate in the St. Louis plan. Instead, he decided to act on his own to make the most of the situation. The following Sunday, a banner headline on the front page of the *Atlanta Journal* proclaimed, "Asa G. Candler to Lend $30,000,000 on Cotton." A three-column photograph accompanied the story that announced his proposal: calm and confident, lips pressed firmly together, Candler gazed with level eyes through rimless glasses. His bank's formal statement, blandly disregarding the efforts of the St. Louis bankers, announced: "We have waited patiently hoping that some practical, safe plan would be suggested and adopted by some source to relieve the cotton situation in the south. Nothing so far having appeared, we feel it our duty to the patrons of this bank to offer them the following proposal."[60]

Candler's "exceedingly large" personal resources, as well as those of the Central Bank and Trust Company would back the loans to cotton farmers all over Georgia. The bank would lend money on cotton at the prevailing market price (six cents). The cotton would then be stored in bank warehouses until 1 July 1915, "or longer if necessary," until the price recovered. When the market price went up, a farmer who received a loan could redeem his cotton at "an extremely low interest rate" and take his profit. However, if the worst happened, and the borrower defaulted because the price did not rise, the farmer had at least obtained the cash he would have made by selling at harvest time. The plan included construction of a mammoth 40-acre warehouse to store the cotton. To this end, the Atlanta Warehouse Company issued 5,000 shares of stock, of which Candler retained 4,325.[61]

At the end of that week, on Saturday, 24 October the Federal Reserve Board approved the St. Louis plan, with minor modifications. The pool made $135 million available "for the relief of cotton producers who must be tided over the period during which there is no adequate market for the staple." The participating southern banks (without the aid of Candler's Central Bank and Trust) contributed $35 million of the total. Terms were to be set based on 6 cents a pound at 6 percent interest, for a term of one year, with an option for a six-month extension.[62]

Meanwhile, Candler's plan had brought an avalanche of applications. Nearly 3,000, by mail and telegraph, arrived on the first business day. A. P. Coles estimated that he received twice as many on the next day.[63] Wednesday, 21 October, the *Journal* carried a statement from Coles emphasizing that loans were to be offered only through Central Bank and its correspondent banks throughout the state. He reported that several loans, one for $25,000, had already been arranged and he added, "Our plan is one of business and co-operation with our customers....We are not out with a charity proposition."[64]

Even though Coles declared that the loan program was strictly a business proposition, the people of Georgia thought otherwise. Clippings preserved in the Asa Candler papers testify to the enthusiasm for Candler and his program expressed by editorial writers throughout the state and beyond. Praise came from such unlikely sources as the *Journal of Labor*, which editorialized that "Mr. Candler has always been at the forefront of any movement which looked to the aid of the whole people."[65] Some writers seem to have been swept away with a notion of Candler as savior of the cotton business. The original *Atlanta Journal* story on the Candler program stated that although other "cotton plans" existed in the fall of 1914, none had "got beyond the preparatory stage." The paper had to backtrack a few days later (24 October, the same day that the St. Louis plan received federal approval), writing that they had "developed the fact...that the national banks of Georgia have already loaned several millions on cotton" by accepting warehouse receipts in payment for debts and by making new loans. The story included a statement from local banks in the National Currency Association of Georgia, a part of the Federal Reserve system, that "ever since the present cotton crop began to move" they had been making such arrangements."[66] The only negative press comment came from the black-owned *Atlanta Independent*, which found the publicity objectionable and pointed out that "Candler will make money at interest and will also get storage in the warehouse."[67] Of course, making money was exactly what Candler intended to do. He never claimed otherwise.

Howard Candler, writing the story of his father's life, called this plan "revolutionary" and said that it "burst upon the business world of the South like a bombshell."[68] However, earlier precedents for Candler's action existed. On more than one occasion, for example, J. P. Morgan, the financier, used his resources to stabilize the national economy. In Atlanta, the business and banking community responded to the panic of 1893 and its aftereffects by combining their resources to back a special issue of clearing house certificates that served as temporary currency. This facilitated the sale of that year's cotton crop in spite of a limited supply of currency due to the deepening depression.[69] Another precedent was Candler's own smaller project to purchase real estate at above-market prices in the aftermath of the panic of 1907. The market strategy of Candler's 1914 program also compares the earlier plans of populist farmers' groups to organize cooperatives to hold cotton for a better market.[70]

Against the background of other contemporary programs such as the St. Louis plan, Asa Candler's willingness to use his wealth to ride out turbulent market conditions on behalf of less wealthy men seems less than a revolutionary bombshell. Rather, Candler's actions show his ability to move swiftly and marshal his resources effectively in order to capture a significant share of a rapidly developing business opportunity. He simply beat the banks of St. Louis to the draw. Part of his plan included construction of a gigantic warehouse to store all the cotton he held.[71]

This warehouse, as Howard Candler wrote, "was a miracle of its time," expensively constructed to "get lower insurance rates for the farmers." The largest structure of its type in the region, it enclosed about forty acres under one roof. Low and massive, it could store 250,000 bales and was equipped with the most modern compresses, machines capable of pressing loose cotton into bales weighing hundreds of pounds. Located on Stewart Avenue, south of the Atlanta business district, the warehouse owned railroad tracks that connected it to the nearby Georgia Railroad lines. A tall, cylindrical masonry tower contained the water supply for its sprinkler system. Construction of the Candler Warehouse cost $1.8 million.[72]

Two pamphlets advertising the services of the warehouse reflect an attempt to reach two classes of customers. The shorter of the two pamphlets, straightforward and dry, targeted large participants in the cotton business: "banks, merchants and supply men of Georgia, ... those of other States and particularly ... the farmer, whether large or small, who wishes to store his cotton and to borrow money on the same at a low rate of interest and reasonable charge."[73] It briskly outlines the services and terms offered by the Atlanta Warehouse. The intended readers of this material required no explanations of banking and credit mechanisms, but Candler also wanted the business of the small farmer.

The second pamphlet appeals to this unsophisticated class of potential customer. Written in the tradition of the local color literary genre, "Old Bill Bobbin's Say-So on Cotton, recorded by Atlanta Warehouse Co. Asa G. Candler Pres." pretended to be the account of a country storekeeper's experience with the cotton market. Plagued by falling prices, fire, insurance problems, and unsympathetic loan officers, Bill Bobbin was near despair, until he visited Atlanta's Harvest Festival in November of 1915 and went to see the newly opened warehouse:

> Got out there and it a-rainin'.
> But that warehouse!
> Man, it was a sight!
> Still buildin' it then, but it looked like all outdoors covered over....Watchmen walkin' around, totin' more o' them little fire-extinguishers in their hip pockets. Some buck niggers pickin' banjos and singin'. An' that there compress workin' right befo' my eyes all the time. Just couldn't help watchin' it. [74]

Particularly impressed by the strong emphasis on fire prevention he saw at the warehouse, Bill promptly put his twenty bales in Candler's warehouse. The charges were "Ten cents for handlin' in and out, twenty-five cents a month for storage, and two cents a month for insurance." He received a negotiable receipt that could serve as collateral for a loan of up to 10 cents a pound for middling cotton, at 6 percent "ef the money market stays like it is." Cotton was to be accepted for storage if it arrived in good condition with a prepaid freight receipt.[75]

Bill's experience with the warehouse allowed him to earn top dollar when his cotton finally was sold, while his neighbors lost their uninsured cotton in a fire. The folksy sixteen-page pamphlet ended with Bill Bobbin's explanation of the commodities market and its relation to credit: "[B]ein' as how holdin' is the only way to stay out of a heavy market, and bein' as how a man can't hold without he's got money, its got to kind of seep in on a man that he's got to take care of the borrowin' end….a receipt's got to be what they call negotiable. It's got to stand for something in black and white. It's got to show they ain't no liens on the cotton. Then he can sign it on the back, and it's the same as money."[76]

Evidently many real-life counterparts of Bill Bobbin also found Candler's warehouse impressive. For the first two weeks after it opened, the average business day saw 1,000 bales of cotton placed in storage for a daily total of about $100,000 in loans. Nonetheless, although records of the actual utilization of the warehouse are scattered and incomplete, it seems clear that it was never filled with cotton. As a practical matter transportation and handling costs would have limited its usefulness for smaller and more distant growers, and growers had the option to choose other warehousing plans.[77]

Candler's financial stewardship in the cotton crisis contributed to the myth that was growing around his name. According to contemporary observers, his action gave others the courage to act. Some believed that "Nothing was done to help the farmers until Asa G. Candler agreed to loan money on cotton at six percent. When Asa Candler did this, other bankers followed his example…."[78] In fact, although Candler was among the first to act, he was not the only one to attempt to control the situation. He offered a reasonable service at a fair price and made no personal claims that his plan was anything but business. Its terms were competitive with those suggested by the

Federal Reserve and the organizers of the St. Louis Plan. Furthermore, his risk was minimal; Candler had made secured loans based on a cotton price that had fallen to a nearly record low. An increase was sure to come sooner or later, and on that happy day either the farmer or Candler himself could take the profit from a sale. In spite of these considerations, his plan was singled out to be treated then and since as a species of philanthropy. Obituary writers, eulogizers, and Asa Candler's son Howard present the cotton warehouse plan as a great undertaking in which the millionaire staked his personal fortune to save the cotton planters from financial ruin and the state economy from collapse. In Howard Candler's view, it was an act of "sheer personal courage...unsurpassed in the annals of American business." He shared the opinion of a number of editorialists that the decision of "a shrewd, level-headed businessman...to stake every dollar of his resources upon cotton" restored confidence in the future of that commodity.[79] In fact, the greatest public benefit of Candler's scheme does seem to have been psychological. According to a contemporary newspaper account: "The effect of the announcement was electrical. It may be pointed to as the turning point in the tide. It was not so much the number of bales of cotton which were pledged for loans made under this plan as it was the influence of Mr. Candler's bold stroke on other less courageous financiers."[80]

Candler's expectation that cotton would rise was correct; the price of cotton soared in the year following the crisis.[81] In addition, the new cotton concentration activity in Atlanta provided increased employment and banking activity to the city.[82]

Early in October 1914, when Asa Candler had the problem of the collapsing cotton market in the forefront of his thoughts, he spoke to the Bible class of the First Christian Church. His subject was "Christianity and Wealth." He presented the principle that great wealth brings great responsibilities to its holder. Even the nation has a duty of stewardship. Speaking of the national wealth of the United States, he said, "It is too great to be without great effects. Either good or bad—with it we must save the world or destroy ourselves."[83]

Perhaps the motivations of the millionaire banker mattered little to the cotton grower in need of ready cash, but for Candler, duty was clear. Feeling justified in adding to the fortune that he believed divine providence had entrusted to him, he understood that the good steward does not simply give handouts to the needy. Therefore, he often chose a course intended to improve the general economic conditions of the community. He made a profit, but he did not profiteer. He served his church while he also devoted himself to building a sizable personal fortune. For Asa Candler the two interests, linked by the concept of Christian stewardship, were as one.

[1]AGC to CHC, 7 March 1909, folder 7, box 1, AGC Papers.

[2]Ibid.

[3]Winthrop S. Hudson, *Religion in America: An Historical Account of the Development of American Religious Life*, 2nd ed. (New York: Charles Scribner's Sons, 1965, 1973) 306; see also pp. 303-305 for a discussion of stewardship in relation to Andrew Carnegie's gospel of wealth and (in a note on page 304) a sketch of John Wesley's view that those who "gain all they can" must "give all they can" in order "to grow in grace." See Doyle, *New Men*, 98-99, for another example of stewardship in the person of Edmund "King" Cole (d. 1899), a Nashville railroad magnate and supporter of various Methodist charities. Cole said, "I suppose I have been able to do more good by giving to the church from the store I have been allowed to collect than I could have done as a minister of the gospel."

[4]Ibid.

[5]Ibid.

[6]"Newly Rich All Asses Says Bishop Candler," unidentified clipping in Candler Family Papers, The Archives, The Coca-Cola Company.

[7]WAC to AGC with attached "Memoranda of Principles About Making and Using Money," 13 January 1912, folder 7, box 1, AGC papers, Emory.

[8]Ibid. The "Memoranda" includes some specific advice about how much attention Asa should give to various causes: Inman Park Church and Wesley Memorial Church need less, while Wesley Memorial Hospital needs a new building; conditional gifts will provoke others to give as well. Emory College needs a dormitory and funds for faculty salaries. Finally: "[T]he Druid Hills Church building is vitally related to John's salvation, and, it may be, to the salvation of his family....[H]e thinks now that he has done all he can do. His heart needs expanding and his vision of things religious extended."

[9]Paul Studenski and Herman E. Krooss, *Financial History of the United States: Fiscal, Monetary, Banking, and Tariff, Including Financial Administration and State and Local Finance*, second edition (New York: McGraw Hill Book Company, Inc., 1952, 1963), 252-54; Louis D. Brandeis, *Other People's Money and How the Bankers Use It*, new edition with foreword by Norman Hapgood (New York: Frederick A. Stokes Company, 1914, 1932), 17, 41.

[10]For example, the *Atlanta Journal*'s coverage included: "Copper Crash Cuts Down Heinz," 17 October 1907, 1; "New York Banks Under Close Scrutiny," 18 October 1907. 1; "Banks

Resume Normal State" and "No Banks Suffer Outside of N.Y." 21 October 1907, 1.

[11]"$552,293 Increase in Clearings for the Week," *Atlanta Journal*, 26 October 1907, 5.

[12]"Neal Bank in Hands of State," and "Names of Stockholders of the Neal Bank and Extent of Liability," *Atlanta Journal*, 23 December 1907, 1; "Big Reduction in Neal Debt," *Atlanta Constitution*, 31 January 1908, 2.

[13]"Neal Bank in Hands of State," *Atlanta Journal*, 23 December 1907, 1; "Neal Bank Asks Clearing House to Investigate," *Atlanta Journal*, 22 December 1907, 1.

[14]"Neal Bank in Hands of State," *Atlanta Journal*, 23 December 1907, 1.

[15]J. C. Hart, Attorney General v. Neal Bank, et al., Fulton County Superior Court Writ Book 100, p. 28, 30, and Fulton County Superior Court Minute Book 57, 313; "Receivership for the Neal Bank," *Atlanta Journal*, 24 December 1907, 1; "Central Bank Receiver of Neal," *Atlanta Journal*, 25 December 1907. Central Bank and Trust posted a half-million dollar bond.

[16]"Central Bank Receiver of Neal," *Atlanta Journal*, 25 December 1907, 1.

[17]Ibid.

[18]"Notable Address Delivered by Mr. Candler," *Atlanta Journal*, 31 December 1907, 5.

[19]Ibid.

[20]J. C. Hart, Attorney General v. Neal Bank, et al., Fulton County Superior Court Minute Books 61, p. 97 and 68, p. 124 and Minute Book 133, pp. 457, 458..

[21]*J. C. Hart, Attorney General v. Neal Bank, et al.*, Fulton County Superior Court Writ Book 100, 351, 366.

[22]*J. C. Hart, Attorney General v. Neal Bank, et al.*, Fulton County Superior Court Writ Book 100, 348, 363.

[23]"Say Receiver Is Preferred," *Atlanta Constitution*, 19 January 1907, n.p.; J. C. Hart, Attorney General v. Neal Bank, et al., [Intervention of S. Booth], Fulton County Superior Court Writ Book 100, p. 227, [Denial of Petition] Minute Book 57, p. 507; Writs Book 100 contains 15 items pertaining to actions filed by S. Booth, et al. The parties that joined Booth in these cases were J. S. Lester, Rob't Hughes, A. P. Lincoln, and E. H. Osborn.

[24]"Big Reduction in Neal Debt," *Atlanta Constitution*, 21 January 1908, 2; "Bank Hearing Before Court," *Atlanta Constitution*, 28 January 1908, 7.

[25]"Big Reduction in Neal Debt," *Atlanta Constitution*, 21 January 1908, 2. See also, "Mass Meeting of Depositors," *Atlanta Constitution*, 30 January 1908, 7.

[26]"The Atlanta Banks are Sound and Confidence Restored" [editorial], *Atlanta Independent*, 28 December 1907; "The Neal Bank and Depositors" [commentary], *Atlanta Independent*, 25 January 1908, 4.

[27]"Twenty Per Cent for Depositors," *Atlanta Constitution*, 19 February 1908, 7.

[28]Neal Bank *adv.* J. C. Hart, Attorney General, Index to Land Suits, 1854-1914, vol. N-R, Office of the Clerk of the Superior Court, Fulton County, Atlanta, Georgia. Fragments of the documentary materials related to these cases may be seen in the Manry Pittman Family Papers, MS450, Atlanta Historical Center Library Archives, Atlanta.

[29]"Cuban Company Sells Property for $1,500,000," *Atlanta Constitution*, 9 January 1908, 1; Candler's trip to Cuba is mentioned in passing in "Investigation of Big Bond Issue Is Begun," *Atlanta Journal*, 16 March 1908, 5, in which he spoke in favor of a bond issue to improve the city's water system and used the Havana waterworks as an example of a model system.

[30]Candler's purchases of city real estate may be seen in $100,000 Paid for Property on Marietta," *Atlanta Constitution*, 24 February 1908, 1; "$80,000 Paid for Property on Decatur St," *Atlanta Constitution*, 27 February 1908; "Moore-Marsh Building is Sold," *Atlanta Journal*,

2 March 1908, 1 (mentions AGC's purchase of the Orpheum Theater); "Mr. Candler Considers a Department Store," *Atlanta Journal*, 19 March 1908; at this time, as discussed in another chapter, he also purchased the Lowndes Building as an annex to the Candler Building. The cartoon appeared in *Atlanta Journal*, 3 March 1908, 1. For some other examples of the efforts to liquidate the bank's assets see: "Says Neal Bank Gave Up Right to Push Claim," *Atlanta Constitution*, 25 February 1908, 1; "Lots Are Sold For Neal Bank," *Atlanta Constitution*, 27 February 1908, 9; "Neal Receivers to Accept Half," *Atlanta Constitution*, 29 February 1908.

[31] J. C. Hart, Attorney General v. Neal Bank, et al., Fulton County Superior Court Writ Book 100, 359; "Neal Receivers to Accept Half," *Atlanta Constitution*, 29 February 1908, 7.

[32] J. C. Hart, Attorney General v. Neal Bank, et al., Fulton County Writ Book 100, 386; "Tells Depositors Not To Sell for 50 Per Cent," *Atlanta Journal*, 4 March 1908, 8; "$342,388 Dividend of Neal Bank To Be Paid Friday," *Atlanta Journal*, 18 March 1908, 11; "A 'Fifth' of a Loaf is a Good Beginning" [cartoon], *Atlanta Journal*, 20 March 1908, 1; "Neal Bank Money Floods the City Saturday," *Atlanta Journal*, 22 March 1908, 1.

[33] "Neal Bank Depositors To Get another Dividend," *Atlanta Journal*, 16 June 1917, 3.

[34] "Neal Bank Receivers Sell Sawtell Property on Saturday for $65,000," *Atlanta Journal* 30 October 1909, 1; "Atlanta Will Have Another Big Hotel Near Candler Building," *Atlanta Journal* 24 December 1909, 5; "Sawtell Deal Will Be Closed Shortly," *Atlanta Journal* 30 December 1909, 7. In 1908, a candidate attempted to raise the receivership of the Neal Bank as a political issue; this aspect of the case will be discussed in the context of city politics in another chapter.

[35] Candler, *Asa Candler*, 269-70.

[36] Candler, *Asa Griggs Candler*, 320-21; AGC to Hon. John M. Slaton, Governor of Georgia, 13 March 1915, fol. 10, box 18, AGC papers, Emory; "Candler Buys $3,525,000 Bond Issue of Georgia," *Atlanta Journal*, 15 March 1915, 1; "Asa Candler's Bid for Georgia Bonds Accepted by State," *Atlanta Constitution*, 16 March 1915, 1. The guarantee was actually a cashier's check; the *Journal* called it a "personal check" apparently to indicate that the funds came from Candler's personal holdings and not those of Central Bank and Trust.

[37] "Candler to Give Georgians First Call on Bonds," *Atlanta Journal*, 16 March 1915, 1.

[38] Ibid. See also, miscellaneous materials associated with the sale in fol. 10, box 18, AGC papers, Emory. The Atlanta firm of Robinson-Humphrey-Wardlaw acted as Candler's agent in selling the bonds.

[39] Comptroller-General's receipt, 1 July 1915, and clipping (n.d.) marked "Ark. Gazette," fol. 10, box 18, AGC papers, Emory. The receipt indicates that Candler paid $3,524,710.66 for 3463 bonds; an attached schedule showed their maturity spread over the years from 1935 through 1945.

[40] For Candler's dealings with the A.A.A., see box 18, AGC papers, Emory. See also: Garrett, *Atlanta and Environs*, vol.2. 552. "Journal Cup Won by Inman," *Atlanta Journal*, 29 March 1908, Sports Section, 1, records a typical A.A.A. event; AGC, Jr. was an official, judging events that included a hill climb.

[41] "'Arc Avenue' Is Assured; Merchants Respond Promptly," *Atlanta Journal*, 5 October 1909, 6; "Heart of Atlanta Will Be a Blaze of Myriad Lights," *Atlanta Journal*, 11 October 1909, 1.

[42] F. J. Robinson, Assistant General Passenger Agent, Central of Georgia Railway to Brooks Morgan, Atlanta Automobile Association, 23 September 1909, box 18, AGC papers, Emory; *Coca-Cola Bottler*, December 1909, 12; Lt. Col. Lowell E. Whitlaw, "Buick No. 10," *The Horseless Carriage* (January-February 1957): 21. The *Coca-Cola Bottler*, February 1910, 24, carries a photograph of AGC with "daredevil Chevrolet."

[43] Agreement, 2 December 1909, box 18, AGC papers, Emory.

[44] Candler, Thompson and Hirsch to AGC, "In Re: Atlanta Automobile Association," 22 May 1913, box 18, AGC papers, Emory. Various memoranda in this portion of Candler's papers record the progress of the sale of the salvage materials. At some point he also had become the largest shareholder in the association, according to an undated list in box 18 of his papers; he had 300 shares, Asa, Jr. had 100, three other persons had fifty, a few had twenty or thirty, and most members had one or two.

[45] "Two Aviators Are hurt in Fall at Speedway and Sent to Hospital," Atlanta Journal, 10 December 1918, 2.

[46] "Plans for Air Mail Route between Atlanta and N. O. Outlined," Atlanta Journal, 11 December 1918, 1; "Atlanta in Line for Aerial Mail, Declares Prager," Atlanta Journal, 1 April 1919, 1.

[47] Candler Field was renamed in honor of another Atlanta mayor of note, William B. Hartsfield.

[48] Transcription of letter, AGC to "Sissie" from Élysée Palace Hotel, Paris, 22 June 1913, folder 8, box 1, AGC papers, Emory.

[49] AGC [to CHC], Edinburgh, 23 July 1913, folder 8, box 1, AGC papers, Emory.

[50] The New York Stock Exchange. "Cotton and Cotton Futures" [pamphlet] (1952) 30; James H. Street, The New Revolution in the Cotton Economy: Mechanization and its Consequences (Chapel Hill: The University of North Carolina Press, 1957) 40; Candler, Asa Griggs Candler, 308; George Brown Tindall, The Emergence of the New South, 1913-1945, A History of the South, vol. X, Wendell Holmes Stephenson and E. Merton Coulter, eds. (Baton Rouge: Louisiana State University Press and The Littlefield Fund for Southern History of the University of Texas, 1967) 33-34. According to Street (p. 41), "The war reduced the net world consumption of American cotton about 12 per cent, on an average, below such consumption in the three years preceding the war."

[51] Gavin Wright, Old South, New South: Revolutions in the Southern Economy Since the Civil War (New York: Basic Books, Inc., Publishers, 1986) 116-119, including Fig. 4.8 and Table 4.6 shows the fluctuations in the condition of postbellum and early twentieth-century cotton growers.

[52] Steven Wayne Wrigley, "The Triumph of Provincialism: Public Life in Georgia, 1898-1917" (PhD diss., Northwestern University, 1986) 38-39, 182; "The Farmers' Lesson in the European War," Journal of Labor, 11 September 1914, 4.

[53] "Urged to Hold Cotton," New York Times, 8 August 1914, 5.

[54] "Discuss Cotton Problem," New York Times, 25 September 1914, 8. McAdoo repeated these reassurances many times. See "M'Adoo Draws Plan for Moving Cotton," New York Times, 28 August 1914, 11, an account including the Treasury Department's plan to accept notes from national banks, if they were secured by warehouse receipts, having not more than four months to run, at 75percent of their face value; and "M'Adoo Points Way to Finance Cotton," New York Times, 26 August 1914, 11.

[55] A. E. Nielsen. Production Credit for Southern Cotton Growers (Morningside Heights NY: King's Crown Press, 1946) 100-07. On p. 103 Nielson writes, "[I]t appeared that the Board was willing to accept for discount practically any kind of agricultural paper except paper representing a fixed investment, such as land and buildings."

[56] "Plan to Store Cotton," New York Times, 29 August 1914, 10; "President Opposes Valorizing Cotton," 8 October 1914, 15; "Ratify Cotton Pool," New York Times, 6 October 1914, 15; "Cotton Pool Plan to Reserve Board," New York Times, 15 October 1914, 15.

[57]"$150,000,000 Cotton Pool is Indorsed [SIC] by Georgia Bankers," *Atlanta Journal*, 14 October 1914, 1.

[58]AGC to "My dear Joe," 14 October 1914, box 1, AGC papers, Emory..

[59]Hepburn to Robert F. Maddox, 10 August 1914, Alonzo Barton Hepburn Papers, Columbia University in Robert H. Wiebe, *Businessmen and Reform* (Chicago: Quadrangle Paperbacks, Quadrangle Books, 1962) 145.

[60]"Asa G. Candler to Lend $30,000,000 on Cotton," *Atlanta Journal* 18 November 1914, 1.

[61]Candler, *Asa Griggs Candler*, 309-312. See p. 310 for an aerial photograph of the warehouse; "Asa G. Candler to Lend $30,000,000 on Cotton" *Atlanta Journal*, 18 November 1914, 1. In 1916 and 1917, Candler transferred ownership of his shares in the warehouse company to his children.

[62]"Reserve Board Puts O. K. on Cotton Pool," *New York Times*, 25 October 1914, II:13.

[63]"Candler Cotton Loan Plan Spreads Rapidly," *Atlanta Journal*, 20 October 1914, 14.

[64]"Central Bank and Trust Corporation Will Make Loans Only to Customers," *Atlanta Journal*, 21 October 1914, 3.

[65]"Asa Candler, Southerner" [editorial], *Journal of Labor*, 23 October 1914, 4. The editor did not lose his head entirely; on the same page "A Plea for Others," pointed out that the "poor fellow in town" could not "call on the government for material aid," and added that "it is the duty of the cotton farmer to work out his own salvation."

[66]"Georgia National Banks Lending Millions on Cotton," *Atlanta Journal*, 24 October 1914, 1.

[67]"Asa G. Candler and the Cotton Situation," *Atlanta Independent*, 24 October 1914, 4. The paper later praised one of its advertisers who allowed customers to settle their accounts with cotton at ten cents per pound, making invidious comparisons to Candler. See "Mr. Randolph Rose, Chattanooga, Tenn." 7 November 1914, 1; for one of Rose's advertisements see "Rose-O That's My New Soft Drink," 25 November 1916, 7. Rose-O supposedly put "pep" into people without any harmful after-effects.

[68]Candler, *Asa Griggs Candler*, 308.

[69]Cooper, *Fulton County*, 344.

[70]The state of Georgia also took an interest in easing the crisis by using warehousing plans. In 1915, J. O. Adams introduced a bill in the Georgia legislature providing for the creation of a state sponsored cotton warehouse commission and a publicly financed compress plant. Some legislators wanted to treat receipts for stored cotton as legal tender, but this drew the opposition of small banks and the bill failed. In 1918, a new version required farmers who wanted to use warehouses to submit a property lien, a provision that reassured bankers and business men. The bill passed, ostensibly as a benefit to small farmers. In fact, many small farmers had already used their crops as security for loans before it was harvested, and so were unable to put up the lien required to use the warehouses. See Wrigley, "The Triumph of Provincialism," 204-205.

[71]Wrigley, "The Triumph of Provincialism," 225-28; Candler, *Asa Griggs Candler*, 311.

[72]Candler, *Asa Griggs Candler*, 313; Lyon, "Business Buildings," 338. A "birdman's view" (aerial photograph) of the facility may be seen in *The City Builder*, July 1922, 11. The water tower (now painted a garish aquamarine, trimmed with yellow bands, and occasionally sporting red flags) is still visible from the north-south MARTA rapid transit line.

[73]"Atlanta Warehouse Company, Atlanta, Georgia" [pamphlet], fol. 7, box 7, AGC papers, Emory.

[74]"Old Bill Bobbin's Say-So on Cotton, Recorded by Atlanta Warehouse Co. Asa G. Candler Pres., Atlanta, Georgia" [16 page pamphlet], fol. 7, box 7, AGC papers, Emory.

[75]"Old Bill Bobbin . . ." Most of these terms were described on pages 10-12 of the text; the back cover summarized them in plain English, and added the handling charge for less than carload lots that Old Bill neglected to include in his enthusiastic account.

[76]Ibid.

[77]Candler, *Asa Griggs Candler*, 313. For one example of other options available to growers, see "Fourth National Bank Will Loan Money on Cotton," *Atlanta Journal*, 25 August 1915, 1. Fourth National announced its intention to lend up to three-fourths of the market value of lots of cotton, at six per cent, for up to six months. The cotton was to be stored in designated warehouses and could be sold at any time during the six-month term of the loan.

[78]"Taking Care of the Farmers," *The Jackson Herald*, (Jefferson GA) 2 September 1915.

[79]Candler, *Asa Griggs Candler*, 308-309.

[80]"Atlanta Warehouse Co.'s Enormous Plant Opened, *Albany* [Georgia] *Herald*, 20 November 1915, 1; Candler, *Asa Griggs Candler*, 311-12.

[81]Gavin Wright, *Old South, New South*, 117, Figure 4.8.

[82]Candler, *Asa Griggs Candler*, 315.

[83]"Christianity and Wealth Topic of Asa G. Candler," *Atlanta Journal*, 5 October 1914, 9.

CHAPTER SIX

Philanthropist

Sealed in the cornerstone of the Candler Building, along with newspaper clippings, floor plans, business papers, and a bottle of Coca-Cola, rests a "Copy of the Holy Bible, presented to Mr. Asa G. Candler by his Sunday School and read by him for nearly ten years."[1] Candler put a Bible in the cornerstone of his namesake building because the cornerstone of his life was his religion. He never failed the practice of church going instilled in him during his Villa Rica childhood. As a young bachelor, new to the city of Atlanta, he immediately became a church member and Sunday school teacher. After he moved to the "miniature farm" near the village of Edgewood, Candler became one of the founders, in 1897, of the nearby Inman Park Methodist Church. He was its first secretary and he later supervised its Sunday school; he continued his active interest to the end of his life.[2]

Candler's friendly interest in protestant Christianity in general led him to take part in a citywide organization of superintendents of Atlanta Sunday schools. In minutes kept during the years 1889 and 1900, Candler's name appears prominently as a member of the executive committee. The superintendents met to share their mutual concerns and swap teaching tips. On one occasion Candler told his colleagues that the home was the "greatest opportunity for good work" in Christian education and urged a program of home visitations to promote that end. On another day he discussed the usefulness of the blackboard as a teaching device. This group, which chose Candler as its secretary in June 1900, included Hoke Smith, a businessman who was to become a leading figure in Georgia politics and governor of the state, and W. S. Witham, the banker who had a long association with Asa Candler. Their amiable meetings often included "a goodly feast of edibles prepared for them by the ladies."[3]

When his old family church building in Villa Rica was demolished, Asa Candler took the trouble to have its bell moved to the grounds of the Methodist Children's Home in DeKalb County. This bell symbolizes a concern for Methodist children that extended beyond those in his own congregation. He did not content himself with writing checks for the children's home, but also took part in managing its affairs. He joined its board of trustees in 1894 and served as secretary of the board for fifteen years. Any organization fortunate enough to have Candler as an officer could count on first-rate management advice and a sound financial position. The president of the executive board of the children's home expressed its indebtedness to Candler "for his wisdom and counsel as well as large financial aid."[4] For Candler, such service was a religious duty. Speaking of the children's home, he called for an explicitly Christian philanthropy to care for those he called "the unfit and unfortunate." As this language suggests, he accepted some of the current progressive social ideas about the existence of "unfit" persons, but he rejected the social Darwinism that was fashionable in some circles: "We may not rely on men whose philosophy pursues a paradise produced by the survival of the fittest...." Meeting solely the physical needs of young people was not enough. The moral development provided to the children was paramount: "[T]he characters made here and polished after the similitude of a palace will be the heritage of the ages." Secular charity could not, in his view, achieve this goal: "We may not depend upon the unchristian wealth which deifies gold and dethrones God...."[5]

Over his lifetime Candler made some donations of spectacular size; indeed, the designation "philanthropist" became attached to Asa Candler's name as naturally as the phrase "founder of the Coca-Cola Company." However, even before he achieved great prosperity, Candler gave freely, beyond the routine deposits in the collection plate expected of any regular churchgoer. As his wealth grew, Candler consistently accepted the responsibility to disburse a generous portion of it. In 1890, while struggling to launch the Coca-Cola enterprise, he gave $500 to Emory College. The first of what proved to be a cornucopia of gifts to the college or its university successor.[6] He regularly made small or individual gifts in connection with his religious affiliation. In 1899, when a poverty-stricken preacher with five children "decided to write to ten of my brethren & beg for a loan of $10.00 from each," Candler sent money and a sympathetic note. In 1906 he evidently matched several collections made for the Inman Park Methodist Church's parsonage fund. He also made regular gifts to the Candler College in Cuba, part of his brother's missionary program for Latin America.[7] Furthermore his gifts of time and expertise were as valuable—or more so—as his gifts of money.

Although their faith obliges both rich and poor Christians to practice charity, the widow's mite presents fewer problems of allocation than the Christian capitalist's millions. Large-scale giving needed a systematic approach. Candler worked through a useful vehicle for giving, working through the Wesley Memorial Enterprises, a complex Methodist philanthropy centered in Atlanta. Although its formal existence began a bit later, this organization had its genesis in the 1902 decision of Atlanta's First Methodist Church to sell its Peachtree Street building and relocate away from the center of the city. Methodist leaders, notably Bishop Warren Candler, feared that this move would leave a vacuum in the city's religious life; the Atlanta Methodists' district conference passed a resolution to that effect. To counteract this threat, Bishop Candler proposed the establishment of a "People's Church" to serve the spiritual needs of office workers, newcomers and transients of the business district. The proposed church would also provide a reading room, classrooms, and other facilities for wholesome activities for the young working population of the central district of the city. So it was that Wesley Memorial Church, the heart of the proposed complex of services, began its life in a rented building in November 1902. The following year Wesley Memorial purchased the southeast corner of the intersection of Auburn Avenue and Ivy Street and erected a temporary structure, known as Wesley Tabernacle, that could hold two thousand souls.[8]

Medical care also concerned the Methodists. In 1903, the Southern Methodist North Georgia Conference adopted a resolution in support of spending as much as $200,000 to build a hospital, and shortly afterward Wesley Memorial Hospital received its charter in Fulton County. It aimed to provide medical and surgical care, but also proclaimed its mission to promote Christian education and charity. However, none of this amounted to more than paper and good intentions. Fund raising efforts fell far short of the conference's goal. To advance the project, Asa Candler purchased a substantial antebellum residence, known as the "Calico House," which was close to the Wesley Memorial Tabernacle. He handed it over for use as Wesley Memorial Hospital. Bishop Warren Candler then designated Christmas Day of 1904 as an "Ingathering Day," that is, a day for making charitable contributions. He encouraged donors by revealing that his brother Asa would match as much as $12,500, if the city's Methodists would give it. They met the challenge and the resulting $25,000 paid the cost of converting the Calico house into a fifty-bed hospital. Soon the hospital expanded into some adjoining structures and added a nurses' home next door to the church.[9]

Georgia's Methodists determined in 1907 to provide the Wesley Memorial Church with a more suitable facility and launched another huge fund-raising campaign. They contemplated not just a house of worship, but the social service project that came to be known as Wesley Memorial Enterprises. It would include an auditorium and church that would be part of a complex also encompassing the hospital and nurses' residence, and additional separate boarding facilities for young men and women. They hoped for a gymnasium, baths, and a roof garden where "suitable entertainments under the proper surroundings and environment" could be held. The *Wesleyan Advocate* could locate its editorial offices there.[10]

The executive committee for this undertaking included Asa Candler. In the early newspaper stories his name is modestly tucked away among those of his fellow committee members, but his personal role proved critical to the project. To stimulate giving, he promised a donation of $50,000 if his fellow churchmen would gather $150,000 for the cause. The campaign climaxed on a Sunday in June 1907. The members of Georgia's Methodist College of Bishops each preached at one of Atlanta's Methodist Churches. Bishop Candler, for example, warned the congregation of Grace Church of the dangers awaiting the innocent young men and women constantly arriving in the city. He also told them that wealth without spirituality would lead to moral decay. He urged the church not to neglect the spiritually needy and allow them to fall "into the hands of...enemies." Moved by his plea, the congregation of Grace church collected $5,000.[11]

At 4 P.M., the bishops presided together over a mass service at Wesley Memorial Tabernacle. Prominent Methodists from all over the area arrived by train—taking advantage of a special rate to attend the event. Both Methodists and other Christians who supported the project packed the Tabernacle and the newspaper reported that "thousands" were turned away. The gifts poured in. The *Constitution* noted both large and small, including $25 from a recently converted "Chinaman." Yet in spite of all efforts, as the day wore on the Methodists began to realize that they had fallen short of their goal; only about $125,000 had been pledged. Once more Asa Candler came to the rescue. He decided to make up the needed balance by increasing his gift to $75,000. Bishop Galloway's announcement of the increase left the crowd in the Tabernacle amazed and silent; then a voice called out, "Do you mean it?" Candler and Bishop Galloway both answered, "Yes," and the crowd broke into an explosion of joy.

Cheering and applause spontaneously gave way to song. Candler, a nearly "beatific" look on his face, joined the congregation to sing, "Praise God From Whom All Blessings Flow."[12]

In the mind of the public, such open-handedness combined with obvious financial success to create the mistaken idea that Candler's resources were without limit. In 1908 Asa wrote to Warren, one person whose advice he respected deeply. In his letter Candler lamented, "Alas—how some do magnify this poor wiggling worm." He had been talking with the president of Emory College, James E. Dickey, who wanted a $100,000 contribution. Dickey argued that a generous endowment would "spur others to follow" and give to the college. In fact, Candler lacked the liquid assets to oblige, since he had only recently completed the construction of the Candler Building and launched himself in the banking business. He estimated his personal net worth at about $700,000, with only about $5,000 in cash available. Although Candler hoped, if he continued successful, to be worth a million dollars in about five years, he now faced the necessity to refuse to make the donation. He did not wish to air his financial affairs in public and he begged for his brother's advice: "You will have to stand close beside me my dear brother. Moses did not need Joshua, nor Jonathan, David, as I need you. Except you my friends too often are very envious. Don't talk of this letter except to God."[13] Exactly how the Candler brothers worked out of this embarrassing impasse remains unclear, but in later years Emory received many greater gifts from Asa Candler. Furthermore, when five years had passed, Asa Candler had considerably more than one million dollars at his disposal. His gifts, largely made through the Wesley Enterprises, established and supported institutions that sustained protestant Christianity in the South.

The Enterprises passed a major developmental milestone when Wesley Memorial Church opened in the spring of 1910, to replace the old Tabernacle. Asa Candler presided over a Sunday afternoon mass meeting that included hymns, prayers, and sixteen three-minute speeches by an assortment of Atlanta clergy, including Rabbi David Marx.[14]

The ecumenical character of this meeting demonstrates the importance of the Enterprises in the larger Atlanta community and reflects a national trend in church-community relations. As churches in other cities moved to the new suburbs, abandoning their center-city locations, they sometimes undertook the support of mission chapels in their old neighborhoods. The resulting "institutional church" became a prominent aspect of the Progressive era.[15] Historians take interest in the place of the South in the larger Progressive movement. However, in spite of the fact that the programs of the Wesley Memorial Enterprises resemble the social programs of progressive-era social improvement projects, Asa Candler and his associates did not identify themselves as "Progressives." Asa Candler did not trouble himself over philosophical or theological questions, but he frequently insisted on his absolute trust in his brother's judgment in such matters. For example, in 1913 he expressed this faith in a letter to Warren: "I am weak. You are strong. I have nothing but a little money to pledge, but I pledge it…I ought to have better prepared myself to [provide] help for my strong & noble brother."[16]

This close attachment to Warren, coupled with both brothers' objection to secular education and modernist theology ultimately led to Candler's most well known philanthropy—his million-dollar donation for the establishment of Emory University in Atlanta. It was his largest single outright gift of money. This grand gesture came as the climax of a long series of events involving three millionaires, two universities, and one religious denomination. Coincidentally, the story began in the same year that Asa Candler first came to Atlanta to seek his fortune. In 1873, when the New York capitalist, "Commodore" Vanderbilt endowed a new university to be built in Nashville, Tennessee.

Vanderbilt University came into existence because of the influence of the former Miss Frank Crawford, the Methodist wife of the elderly Cornelius Vanderbilt. Before their 1869 marriage, she had come from her native South to earn her living as a music teacher in New York City. After the marriage, she introduced a new element of gentility into the life of the rough and profane capitalist and introduced him to the Methodist Church. Although he did not undergo a dramatic conversion, he attended services occasionally and was friendly to the institution. Vanderbilt made generous gifts to a New York City congregation, the Church of the Strangers, composed largely of displaced southerners such as his wife. Its members preferred the Methodist Episcopal Church, South, a faction of the church that had split away during the regional disputes over slavery that preceded the outbreak of the Civil War. The Southern Methodists remained unreconciled to their northern co-religionists after the end of the war. To assure a continuing supply of clergy they found suitable, the southerners hoped to establish an institution of higher learning sensitive to their peculiar concerns. No concrete actions had been possible in the impoverished days of reconstruction, but Southern Methodism's fortunes soon would change. In the early 1870s, Commodore Vanderbilt supposedly remarked to his wife's pastor Charles F. Deems, "I'd give a million dollars today if I had your education." Deems followed up on this thought and urged Vanderbilt to show his respect for education by making some sort of financial gift. At about this same time, another Methodist clergyman, Bishop Holland McTyeire, a distant relation of Mrs. Vanderbilt's family, came to New York for medical treatment. He spent some weeks with the Commodore's household. In conversations with the elderly millionaire, he described the Southern Methodists' hopes to found a central university in their region. This goal—and its representative— so impressed Vanderbilt that he made a proposal for an endowment shortly thereafter. As a result, the Methodist Episcopal Church, South, built its Central University in Nashville, and gratefully named it "Vanderbilt."[17]

Over the ensuing years the institution grew but remained under the control of the church. Its school of theology trained clergymen while its other departments developed as well. In the new century it became the scene of a decade-long power struggle that changed its fundamental character. Asa Candler's brother Warren, as a bishop in the Methodist Episcopal Church, South, played an important role in this drama.[18]

Vanderbilt had both attracted and produced its share of scholars. As its various academic departments matured they naturally recruited faculty from beyond the boundaries of the Methodist denomination, and some of these choices displeased certain members of the General Conference of the church. In 1904 Bishop Candler, an ex-officio member of the university's Board of Trust and chairman of the committee on faculty nominations, submitted a report complaining that the numbers of non-Methodists in various departments "…is out of all proportion and must necessarily tend to estrange the University from the Church and the Church from the University."[19] The chancellor of the university, James H. Kirkland, protested that while he regarded Vanderbilt as a Methodist institution and filled vacancies with qualified Methodists whenever possible, a rigidly sectarian hiring policy would damage university interests. The war was on. The university party fought for academic freedom, while the church party, led by Bishop E. E. Hoss, Warren Candler, and others, asserted that as a Methodist institution, Vanderbilt must defer to their authority as representatives of the General Conference. Unwilling to surrender, the Board of Trust reorganized itself in 1905 and excluded from its membership Bishop Candler and his allies. Uncertainty surrounded the question of who should govern the institution, and neither the founding documents nor the customs established over the years, provided any clear answer. Attempts to negotiate failed, and the parties became ever more estranged. In 1910 the College of Bishops sued for the right to fill certain positions on the Vanderbilt Board of Trust. In this spirit, the Southern Methodists, in their sixteenth annual conference in 1910, notified church-affiliated colleges that three-fourths of their trustees must be Methodists, giving them until July 1912 to meet the requirement.[20]

In 1913, while the lawsuit still was in the appeals process, a second millionaire philanthropist entered the scene. Andrew Carnegie offered a large gift to Vanderbilt. Carnegie believed that successful individuals should use their wealth for the benefit of humankind, but social Darwinism influenced him rather than ideas of Christian charity. Carnegie was not conventionally religious and his arguments for philanthropy were entirely secular. His philosophy—and the strings he attached to his gift—heated up the controversies surrounding the Vanderbilt Board of Trust.[21]

Andrew Carnegie's involvement in American colleges had begun with his sympathy for the poverty of the average college professor. He created a ten million dollar pension fund for retired professors. He wanted to make the profession more attractive, but he did not wish to extend benefits to scholars associated with religious colleges. The administrators of Carnegie's fund applied his limitations rigorously although they later dropped another restriction against the faculty of state-operated colleges. By 1910 only two southern colleges appeared on the accepted list of seventy-one institutions. However, some colleges quietly accepted Carnegie's view that only secular schools could be serious centers of professional teaching and scholarship. They began to distance themselves from their denominational origins, in order to entitle their faculty members to the benefits of the Carnegie pension plan.[22]

Andrew Carnegie demonstrated his anti-sectarian views when he offered Vanderbilt University Medical School a total of a million dollars in conditional gifts: $200,000 for a laboratory and an $800,000 endowment. In return, Carnegie demanded that Vanderbilt's endowment be administered by a secular governing board. The university needed the funds to bring its medical school up to standard and Carnegie's terms did not offend the majority of the university's Board of Trust, so they accepted the gift. The Methodist bishops, led by Bishop Hoss and including an infuriated Warren Candler, condemned what they saw as a subversive effort on Carnegie's part. Still claiming authority over the university, they voted to refuse the gift. Candler denounced the impudence of the "aggressive and agnostic steel-monger" who made it.[23]

Such controversies did not disrupt all church supported southern colleges, however. Trinity College (now Duke University) offers an interesting point for comparison. Although generally considered a Methodist school, Trinity's founding documents left its precise relationship to the church unclear. Furthermore, its presidents in the early twentieth century resisted the notion that their college might become a "connectional" school, directly controlled by the church. However, the presidents all had impeccable credentials as loyal churchmen, and furthermore, a goodly number of Methodist laymen served as Trinity's trustees and executives.[24] While the Candlers and their allies battled grimly for control of Vanderbilt, they felt no need to put pressure on Trinity College. Carnegie's worldly influence could hardly affect an institution generously supported by the reliably Methodist Duke family and administered by presidents who were personal friends of the Candler family. The spirit of their defense of Methodist education, and not its letter, determined their choice of battles.

In any case, the bishops' attempt to veto the Carnegie gift to Vanderbilt proved to be an empty gesture. Their suit for control of Vanderbilt's Board of Trust moved through the courts until March 1914, when the Supreme Court of Tennessee denied most of their claims. The ruling also stated that if the General Conference of the Methodist Episcopal Church, South, must cooperate with the university's administration or its limited rights to representation on the board would end. Unwilling to accept a half-loaf, the Conference convened in Oklahoma City where delegates—including the Candlers—voted 151–140 to sever the church's connection with Vanderbilt University.[25]

Without Vanderbilt, the conservative Methodists had no institution to offer what they considered suitable preparation for new clergymen. Therefore, the conference created an Educational Commission and instructed it to investigate the establishment of two institutions of higher learning that could be kept firmly within control of the denomination. The Conference recommended that one of these, Southern Methodist University, be located in Dallas, but the site of the second, to be established somewhere east of the Mississippi river, remained unspecified. Bishop Candler chaired the commission and his brother Asa was its treasurer.[26]

In his account of his father's life, Charles Howard Candler speculates that the actions of the Conference, as well as later developments, were prearranged. Asa and Warren had made their plans in advance and rumors had it that Asa Candler might use his resources to establish the second new university in Georgia. Two locations entered into the speculation: Candler's home city of Atlanta seemed likely, as did the village of Oxford which was the site of Bishop Candler's *alma mater*, Emory College.[27]

The creation of Southern Methodist University in Dallas got under way promptly, while the Candler brothers, as Howard Candler put it, "were busy making their arrangements" for the second university. These arrangements in fact revolved around Emory College in Oxford, Georgia. Old and deep ties connected the Candler family to that school. In his youth, the family patriarch, Samuel Candler, had made his home with his relative and Emory's founder, the clergyman and lawyer Ignatius Few. Warren and John Candler studied at Emory, as did most of the next generation of young Candler men. Warren served as Emory's president in the last decade of the nineteenth century. Although Asa never went to any college, his association with Emory already had included several large gifts of money. After service as a member of its finance committee he became committee chairman in 1900, a position he held for the rest of his life. In 1906 he also accepted election as president of the Board of Trustees.[28]

In his involvement with Emory College, as in his other philanthropic interests, Asa Candler took an energetic interest in its operations. Something of the tone of the meetings of the college trustees (and most likely that of any enterprise involving Asa Candler) may be sensed from its minutes. For example, in the discussion of a resolution offered in 1909, half a dozen members ventilated their views before, as the minutes dryly record, "President Candler also spoke and told the board some wholesome truths." The matter at hand was then briskly concluded. Candler's subscription, at this same meeting, of $50,000 to an endowment fund may well have influenced his fellow board members to listen carefully to their president's "wholesome truths."[29]

Assessing the state of higher education in the South, Candler admitted that state colleges offered increasingly sharp competition to small religious schools, but he invoked the "high mission" of institutions such as Emory. He urged the trustees, "Let us not swerve from its unworldly policy, nor lower its standards, nor depart from its sacred traditions."[30] Candler also called upon his own business experience as a guide to the continuation of Emory's success: "[S]peaking in terms of the commercial world, we must preserve [Emory's] own trademarks and keep its products up to the grade which they have always stood for. The demand for such goods was never greater than now. The world wants men of high moral character, unfaltering faith, calm courage, clear heads, and of undiluted integrity."[31]

Until the time of the Vanderbilt controversy, Candler had opposed suggestions to move Emory from Oxford to the city. He resisted an Atlanta alumni petition for such a move in 1908, and on another occasion expressed his view that Emory was an "influence for good" because it was "a quiet place, separated from unwholesome distractions."[32] However, the loss of Vanderbilt led Candler to reconsider. Most immediately, while the new schools were being organized and built, the need to continue training clergymen in an appropriate atmosphere pressed upon them. The Education Commission created by the General Conference—with Warren as chairman and Asa as treasurer—immediately arranged for the opening of a School of Theology, to be housed temporarily in Atlanta's Wesley Memorial Church.

Up to this time, at least two cities seriously hoped to acquire the new university. The citizens of Birmingham, Alabama, organized in the hope of collecting $700,000 to be added to the estimated $300,000 value of Birmingham College. They hoped that this package could form the nucleus of the new institution. In Atlanta, real estate developer Edwin P. Ansley offered a seventy-five acre site near Oglethorpe College.[33] The decision to place the School of Theology in Atlanta suggested that the winds of change already had begun to blow in Atlanta's direction.

No question of any conflict of interest seems to have concerned the southern Methodists. The Candlers' positions on the Education Commission and on the Board of Trustees of Emory College moved the creation of Emory University rapidly and smoothly forward. The trustees of Emory College, with Asa Candler as their president, voted in early June 1914 to "do whatever they can in furtherance of the work" of the Commission. They had recently amended the Emory charter to assure that "all trustees of said college, however elected, shall be confirmed by the Annual Conference of the Methodist Episcopal Church, South." Obviously this measure was to prevent another Vanderbilt-style loss of control.[34] The trustees continued their session on the following day and Asa Candler again reached into his pockets to cover the college's $30,000 deficit and put the institution in the best possible financial condition.[35]

Correspondence in Asa Candler's papers provides a few glimpses of the maneuvering behind the scenes. On 26 June, Mell Wilkinson, president of the Atlanta Chamber of Commerce, offered unspecified assistance in acquiring the university for Atlanta. A few days later, Candler wrote from New York City to "My Dear Brother" about the Chamber's possible role and added comments on his own involvement: "[B]eing on the commission to locate the institution, I could not take the initiative publicly.…I have made to you a frank definite statement as to what I will be able to promise." He wanted the plan to remain secret for as long as possible, because "I am certain to be annoyed [by the press] whenever the arrangement is made."[36]

A letter written a few days later to an associate, Walker White, remains somewhat obscure in its precise meanings but clearly was part of the effort to win the university for Atlanta. It originally included two enclosures (now missing) one to be handed to Mell Wilkinson and the other to "the Bishop." The bishop in question was not Bishop Candler, because the letter also instructed Walker to return the documents to Warren after carrying out the instructions. Along with these instructions, Candler fretted that, "If Atlanta does not wake up she's going to lose the biggest & best thing ever possible for her to get....I do not want to personally force this thing on Atlanta as I am one of the Commission but maybe I'll have to."[37]

On the same day, Asa wrote directly to Warren. They already had begun to consider possibilities beyond merely capturing the Methodist university for Atlanta: "It had not occurred to me that the university should be down town, nor yet as far out as Ansley offers. If it were not my own property, I would unhesitatingly place it on 50 acres in the Druid Hills, where there are several magnificent locations."[38] Still, Candler never failed to keep his priorities firmly in order: "[To] locate in Atlanta is the main consideration." He worried "...that the men who wanted the Hospital Bond Issue and the School of Technology subscription, to neither of which I gave my support, are now disposed to punish me by seeing to it that Atlanta does not make an offer...."[39]

A third letter written on that busy July day went to Mell Wilkinson, to let him know that Atlanta's chances of victory would be enhanced by a "dignified and earnest" campaign of support by the Chamber of Commerce. Candler added the private information that Atlanta was in the front running.[40]

Ten days later Candler wrote a last letter, this one intended for public consumption. Asa Candler, acting as a private individual and a member of "our Southern Methodist connection," addressed the long letter to the Chairman of the Educational Commission, his "Dear Brother" Bishop Warren Candler. He began by declaring himself to be, "Impelled by a deep sense of duty to God and an earnest desire to do good to my fellow men...to take in hand the repairing of the loss inflicted upon the Church by the decision in the case of Vanderbilt University."[41] The body of the letter reiterated the position of the Candlers and their allies in the Vanderbilt controversy: Education of the intellect without attention to moral and religious development is a curse "creating dangerous ambitions and arousing selfish passions faster than it supplies restraints upon these lawless tendencies..."[42] He went on to praise Christianity in general but stated that he saw no reason not to entrust his contribution to the particular denomination that had provided him with life-long guidance. Here he made the nature of the gift plain; he offered to the Methodist Episcopal Church South, "the Sum of One Million ($1,000,000.00) Dollars, for the endowment of [a university, east of the Mississippi River], the plans and methods of which are to be definitely directed to the advancement of sound learning and pure religion."[43]

Asa Candler's gift matched the total of the fund proposed by citizens of Birmingham, Alabama, but more significantly, it matched the amount of Andrew Carnegie's donation to Vanderbilt University. Whether this was a conscious decision, the result of an unconscious influence, or simple coincidence remains unclear, but the latter possibility seems to be the least likely of these three. Editorial writers all over the South praised his gift, and some took the occasion to argue that Candler's million, intended to promote religious education, excelled over Carnegie's million, given in support of academic freedom. Candler's son wrote that his father "had pledged practically his entire personal fortune to secure the payment of the money."[44] In fact, Candler may have extended himself, but he still had sufficient resources a few months later, in October, to establish the program for the support of the price of cotton. In any case, Candler's devotion to the creation of the new university did represent a considerable personal sacrifice, when compared with the resources of Carnegie's foundation.

Candler had not been so crude as to place any conditions of location in his offer, but nonetheless this cash-on-the-barrel-head offer from an Atlanta donor removed any possible obstacles to a location in his home city. Furthermore, he used his influence in the Atlanta business community to develop a community base of support. Candler's fear that some members of the city leadership might bear him a grudge because he did not support certain earlier fund-raising projects proved groundless.

The first edition of the Chamber of Commerce publication *The City Builder*, in March 1916, promoted the acquisition of the new University. Georgia Railway and Power President Preston W.

Arkwright, head of the Chamber's fund-raising committee, argued that Emory would contribute not only to the city's prestige, but also to its economy, and that the university would tend to attract desirable citizens to the city and uplift its cultural atmosphere. Other prominent Atlantans expressed similar ideas. The campaign raised an additional half-million dollars for Emory University.[45]

The success of the campaign aroused Candler's passionate religious sentiments, which he expressed in a private letter to Warren about ten days after his million dollar offer: "I write only a line of (I steadfastly believe) humble but earnest gratitude to our Great Father, who has so mercifully spared us to see this day. He is so good. Pray that he give me virtue, not vanity. I beg Him to guide you who are under his guidance…to do still greater things for his glory."[46]

In August the Emory College trustees again met; on this occasion, Candler arranged to lend almost $67,000 to relieve a debt incurred in the construction of a dormitory.[47] This put the finances of the college in perfect order, eliminating any obstacle to the formalities that followed. Warren Candler, Asa Candler and W. D. Thomson (John Candler's law partner) acting in their capacity as a committee from the General Conference, formally proposed to the Emory College trustees that the new Methodist university to be built east of the Mississippi might incorporate their college. These men then figuratively changed their hats and joined the other Emory trustees to resolve, "that the Trustees of Emory College co-operate with the Educational Commission of the Methodist Episcopal Church, South." The new university would bear the name Emory, "so as to preserve and conserve the assets, history and traditions of Emory College and enlarge its field of usefulness to the…Church.…and at the same time promote the success of the new University."[48]

Emory University received its charter on 25 January 1915. Its trustees came from all over the South, but of course included Asa and Warren Candler and W. D. Thomson. The trustees selected Asa Candler as their president. The first pages of the minute book of the trustees included a solemn reminder of the crisis that had led to the creation of the new university. Immediately after a copy of the charter, the trustees entered extracts from the resolutions of the General Conference, requiring that if the new university be founded, the Educational Commission should "take such steps as are necessary...to secure to the Methodist Episcopal Church, South, the ownership and control of the same in perpetuity."[49]

After completing these arrangements, the trustees of the new university turned to the practical problem of relocating to Atlanta. Meeting in August 1915, they decided that the site must be no more than five miles from the center of the city. A trustee moved that "the property known as the 'Guess Place,' located in Druid Hills, be selected...provided it could be secured." After this motion carried, Asa Candler stated—a bit coyly—that Druid Hills had not offered to donate the site, but as president of the Druid Hills Corporation, he would submit the matter to the stockholders. All forms were observed scrupulously, but of course, Candler himself held almost all of the stock in Druid Hills. Construction of theology and law buildings—designed by architect Henry Hornbostel—began almost at once.[50]

In September 1917, dignitaries and students, sheltered by a large tent, assembled for Emory's official opening. Newly constructed buildings testified that the Methodist Episcopal Church, South, once again could offer a college education in accordance with its most conservative principles.[51] In the ceremony Bishop Candler expanded on a religious theme while a Chamber of Commerce official praised the connection between Emory and the business community. The two speakers reflected, as the writer David Levine has pointed out, the dual nature of Emory University: "its deep sectarian roots and its modern entrepreneurial spirit." The new institution had its beginnings in a denominational dispute, but Candler and his supporters also persuaded their community to recognize the economic and social benefits Emory might provide to the city and the region.[52]

Building a new university, virtually from scratch, is no easy task. One student remembered the early campus: "Before the days of pavement one of the chief accomplishments was to get up a steep muddy bank in order to get to the dining hall. We were really pioneers."[53] As always, the Candlers kept a close eye on costs and on student demeanor. As chancellor, Warren required students to attend chapel services, disapproved a request to form a Dramatics Club, and squashed student efforts to participate in intercollegiate athletics. The brothers shared these views, but some differences began to arise between them over the university's handsome new buildings. Designed by New York architect Henry Hornbostel after the style of a high renaissance Italian villa, they face a green quadrangle.[54] Construction proved costly, and Warren believed that the contractor, Arthur Tufts, was to blame.[55] A draft of a three page letter to Tufts is filled with complaints; near its end the chancellor lectures Tufts: "Perhaps it may not be amiss for me to say that the money my brother has given goes exclusively to endowment, and that the money for buildings is raised by myself and the various agents of the University....we do not have an unlimited amount of money to draw on."[56]

Warren's high-handed approach to Tufts led to a rare quarrel between the two brothers that is revealed in a long letter from Warren to his brother. He begins by reminding Asa that he had originally disapproved of the contract with Arthur Tufts for the erection of buildings at Emory but had given in to his brother concerning the matter. None the less, he said that he had protected the interests of the university—probably a reference to his letter to Tufts. Therefore, he was, "surprised and grieved" that when the interested parties met to discuss the matter, "...you rebuked me in their presence for the manner in which I had endeavored to meet my responsibility." The chancellor, although "smarting naturally under the rebuke...and feeling more keenly the humiliation of the rebuke in the presence of Mr. Tufts and Mr. Adams," had repressed his desire to offer his resignation on the spot. Thinking about the confrontation afterward, however, he decided that "my efficiency as chancellor has been impaired and that I ought to retire...."[57] Heart-felt pain fills the letter ("I can not contemplate for a moment the possibility of an estrangement from you, the dearest of brothers...) but it fails to show empathy for Asa Candler's own preoccupations. In 1917 he had just retired from several of his most absorbing business interests in order to take on new responsibilities as mayor of the city, and furthermore his wife was seriously ill. The patronizing tone of the chancellor's letter to Tufts suggests that Warren Candler felt a proprietary interest in his brother's fortune. He seemed to resent Asa's insistence on independent authority in the hiring of Tufts and to feel absolutely shocked that his brother would, under any circumstances, fail to show deference to him. Decades of affection could not easily be cast away, but he poured out his hurt feelings for five pages. He emotionally proclaimed his intention to resign from Emory. "I am convinced that it is my duty to take a course which will make impossible the repetition of such a painful incident...."[58]

Warren's letter is remarkable not simply for its strong emotions, but because the brothers had so few open disagreements in their lifetime. Changes in the relative status of the brothers probably had much to do with the quarrel. Warren (and John) had found their names in *Who's Who* while Asa was just another small businessman, but by the late 'teens Asa had gained a national reputation as a capitalist and philanthropist. His brothers' position, meanwhile, remained relatively unchanged. Warren's reaction to Asa's brusque behavior in the matter of the Emory contractor suggests that Asa had usually showed deference to Warren that he gave to few other persons. This rare exception had shaken Warren to his foundation.

Somehow the brothers made up their differences but their reconciliation must have been face-to-face; they left no record in writing. The Bishop continued at Emory. By April 1917, Asa was again in friendly communication with his brother on the subject of the university. He was still concerned with education and wanted Emory to train teachers, which he considered to be more important than the running of law or medical schools: "The Medical was forced upon us, and if we had not taken it at the time it was offered, permanent dwarfing of our entire system I believe would have occurred."[59]

This passage hints that Asa Candler was somewhat more flexible than the bishop; he understood that even he could not always have the last word on the development of the university. In a few short years, Emory included schools of theology, medicine, law, and appropriate libraries and laboratories. The faculty and curriculum of Emory College became the heart of the university's undergraduate department, while the Oxford campus became an adjunct institution, first a prep school and then a two-year college.

In addition to its foundation upon the bedrock of Emory College, much of the university's institutional structure can be traced back to the Wesley Memorial Enterprises, begun early in the century. The School of Theology that had met in the Wesley Memorial Church moved to the Emory campus as soon as possible; Wesley Memorial Hospital became connected to Emory's medical school and relocated to the campus. The Candlers' involvement bound these institutions together for all time. Asa Candler told his "wholesome truths" to their boards of trustees in those years, giving them the benefit of his judgment as well as his pocketbook. As Emory moved into a new decade, Bishop Candler continued as chancellor for a short period, although for part of that time the creation of a new office, the presidency of the university, lightened his burden of responsibilities. Asa Candler remained active as president of the Board of Trustees until his last illness.[60]

[1]"This Box Contains the Following Articles:" typed list pasted in "Record Book of Candler Investment Company, 1903-1910," box 18, AGC papers, Emory.

[2]"Twenty-first Anniversary Service" [program], and "Golden Anniversary Service" [program], Inman Park Methodist Church, fol. 3, box 4, AGC papers, Emory. Historical sketches in these two items suffer a kind of institutional amnesia about Candler's support of church activity: "A few members of Inman park launched the Wesley Memorial Institutional Church with all of its attendant enterprises. Emory University…has her corner stone in Inman Park Church and much of her financial aid and encouragement came from the [unnamed] members."

[3]"Sunday School" bound volume, box 4, AGC Papers; "The HOW Convention, the twenty-fourth annual meeting of the Georgia State Sunday-School Association" [program] held at Newnan GA, 13-15 April 1897, fol. 4, box 4, AGC papers, Emory.

[4]Mrs. Alva G. Maxwell, "Story of the Methodist Children's Home, Decatur, Georgia," pamphlet, c. 1938, in Georgia Collection, Atlanta-Fulton Public Library, Atlanta, 18, *passim*. Candler's mother had raised money to buy a bell for the Methodist Church in Villa Rica; when the church building was sold, Candler bought the bell and gave it to the Methodist Children's Home. Mrs. Maxwell's account of the home's history includes a photograph of a group of children posed around the bell.

[5]"Decatur Orphans' Home" manuscript of speech, fol. 8, box 2, AGC papers, Emory. A similar, slight-

ly shorter version of this talk, delivered at the observance of the thirtieth anniversary of the home is found in folder 9 of the AGC papers; folder 18 contains his "Historic Statement of the Orphans' Home."

[6]WAC, "The Epochal Gift of William P. Patillo" in "Reminiscences of Emory, Dictated 1938-39" manuscript, fol. 22, box 93, series III, WAC papers, Emory. Patillo gave Emory College $25,000 on the condition that the alumni, the Board of Trustees, and the Methodists at large each match his gift.

[7]Account book, fol. 3, box 4; 1899 letter in fol. 5, box 4; AGC to WAC [re: Candler College], 13 January 1913, fol. 8, box 1; all in AGC papers, Emory.

[8]Garrett, *Atlanta and Environs*, 2 vols., 2: 443-45. The original church site mentioned in this paragraph was the same one that became the site of the Candler building.

[9]Garrett, *Atlanta and Environs*, 2: 482.

[10]"Leaders of Methodism Launch Big Enterprise in City This Morning," *Atlanta Constitution*, 16 June 1907, 1.

[11]Ibid.; Garrett, *Atlanta and Environs*, 2: 445; "Seven Bishops Fill Pulpits of Methodists," *Atlanta Constitution*, 17 June 1907, 6; see also scrapbook clippings in box 4, AGC papers, Emory. The headquarters of the fund drive, supervised by Walker White, had offices in the Candler Building.

[12]"Seven Bishops Fill Pulpits of Methodists;" "$201,450 Is Subscribed By the Methodists of Atlanta;" "Rise of Asa G. Candler from Poverty to Wealth," *Atlanta Constitution*, 17 June 1907, 6, 1, and 6.

[13]AGC to "My dear Brother," 16 June 1908, box 1, AGC papers, Emory.

[14]"Opening Exercises of Wesley Memorial Church, Atlanta Georgia, April 6th—May 1st, 1910" program, box 4, AGC papers Emory.

[15]Edward Judson, "The Church in Its Social Aspect," *The Annals of the American Academy of Political and Social Science* 30 (November 1908): 486, offers a contemporary discussion of the term. See also Hudson, *Religion in America*, 301. Thomas K. Beecher (pastor of Park Congregational Church of Elmira, New York, he was one of the famous family of clergymen and writers and also the son-in-law of Mark Twain) led the construction of what probably was the first such institution, located in a block-long structure erected in 1872. By 1900 over 170 similar churches could be identified, and many other churches had adopted some programs of a similar type.

[16]AGC to WAC, 29 June 1913, AGC papers, Emory. This passage comes from a discussion of the struggle to keep Emory out of intercollegiate athletics. Asa wrote to Warren during a European tour that he and Mrs. Candler took at the urging of their children. Several letters written during this time expressed Asa's devotion to Warren and his desire to be of service to his fellow man and a better Christian, but they also exhibit a saltier side of his personality. He summarized the service at St. Boniface Victoria, the Anglican Church in Frankfurt, Germany: "High church. Low preach. Much program." It had been the only English language service he could find.

[17]Edwin Mims, *History of Vanderbilt University*, (Nashville: Vanderbilt University Press, 1946) repr. Arno Press Collection, The Academic Profession, Walter P. Metzger, ed. (New York: Arno Press, A New York Times Company, 1977) 13-32.

[18]The Vanderbilt controversy is treated in: Mims, *History of Vanderbilt*, 291-314; Norwood, *The Story of American Methodism*, 303; Bauman, *Warren Akin Candler*, 101-103;

[19]Mims, *Vanderbilt University*, 295.

[20]Earl W. Porter, *Trinity and Duke, 1892-1924: Foundations of Duke University* (Durham NC: Duke University Press, 1964) 196. According to Porter, the three-fourths Methodist requirement is reported in the *Journal of the Sixteenth Annual Conference of the Methodist Episcopal Church, South*, (Nashville: 1910).

[21]Frederick Rudolph, *The American College and University: A History* (New York: Alfred A. Knopf, 1962) 424-25; John H. Brubacher and Willis Rudy, *Higher Education in Transition, An American History: 1636-1956* (New York: Harper & Brothers Publishers, 1958) 360.

[22]Brubacher and Rudy, *Higher Education*, 192, 205, 342, 347, 368; David O. Levine, *The American College and the Culture of Aspiration, 1915-1940* (Ithaca: Cornell University Press, 1986) 15-16, 79-80; Porter, *Trinity and Duke*, 162-64. The latter provided the 1910 statistic.

[23]"Carnegie's Gift to Vanderbilt is Scored by Bishop" *Atlanta Journal*, 18 June 1913, 1; see also, untitled holographic draft version of a statement on this subject in fol. 9, box 12, WAC papers, Emory. Of course, this collection contains considerable other material on this matter.

[24]Porter, *Trinity and Duke*, 196. According to Porter, the three-fourths Methodist requirement is reported in the *Journal of the Sixteenth Annual Conference of the Methodist Episcopal Church, South* (Nashville: n. p., 1910). One of the Trinity presidents, Alonso Few, was a distant cousin of the Candlers.

[25]Mims, *Vanderbilt University*, 291-314; Candler, *Asa G. Candler*, 391-93.

[26]Candler, *Asa G. Candler*, 391-93; see pages 390-409 for Candler's full account of the founding of Emory University in Atlanta.

[27]Ibid., 393.

[28]Candler, *Asa Griggs Candler*, 382-387.

[29]Microfilm of Minutes of the Board of Trustees of Emory College, vol. 5, 1 July 1909, Emory University Archives.

[30]Ibid., [President's Annual Address] 10 June 1912.

[31]Ibid.

[32]Ibid., 6 June 1908; [President's Annual Address] 3 June 1910.

[33]"Big Plans Ready for Fight to Win Methodist School," *Atlanta Journal*, 28 June 1914, 1. Scholars of urban history who perceive cities as being in combat with one another will enjoy the imagery used by the writer of the cited newspaper story: Ansley's offer is a "big gun" signaling Atlanta's "advance;" other "big guns" were expected to be heard soon, because, "Never has there smoldered in Atlanta a greater force...."

[34]Microfilm of the Minutes of the Emory College Board of Trustees, 8 June 1914.

[35]Ibid., 9 June 1914.

[36]AGC to "My Dear Bro." [WAC], 30 June 1914, folder 8, box 1, AGC papers, Emory.

[37]AGC to "My Dear Walker [White]," 6 July 1914, folder 8, box 1, AGC papers, Emory. Walker White had supervised the fund drive for the Wesley Memorial Enterprises.

[38]AGC to WAC, 6 July 1914, box 1, AGC papers, Emory.

[39]Ibid.

[40]AGC to Mell Wilkinson, 6 July 1914, box 1, AGC papers, Emory.

[41]AGC to WAC, 16 July 1914, box 1, AGC papers, Emory. This letter has been widely reproduced. See also, Minutes of the Board of Trustees of Emory College, 14 August 1914; "'For the Blessing of Man and the Glory of God' A Letter From Asa Griggs Candler, July 16, 1914" (Atlanta: Emory University, 1951) 11, a pamphlet issued in connection with Emory's centennial. Copies may be found in the "Asa Candler" folder, "Personality File," Atlanta Historical Society Library/Archives or in folder 1, box 6, AGC papers, Emory; the letter also is printed in Charles Howard Candler's *Asa Candler*.

[42]Ibid.

[43]Ibid.

[44]Candler, *Asa G. Candler*, 407; Walker White to W. D. Thomson, 6 April 1915, folder 1, box 3, Series I, Board of Trustees, Emory University Archives, refers to Candler's collateral to secure a note of $980,000, including 2502 shares in the Atlanta National Bank, 3500 shares in Central Bank and Trust, and 391 shares in the Coca-Cola Company.

[45]Charles Paul Garofalo, "Business Ideas in Atlanta, 1916-1935" (Ph.D. diss., Emory University, 1972) 158-160.

[46]AGC to "My Dear Bro" [WAC], 25 July 1914, box 1, AGC papers, Emory.

[47]Microfilm of the Minutes of the Board of Trustees of Emory College, 5 August 1914, Emory University Archives. Candler had made several short-term loans to cover various construction costs; this was essentially a refinancing, on terms of 6 percent for five years.

[48]Ibid.

[49]"Charter of Emory University"; "Extracts from resolutions…"; and minutes of the meeting of 31 March 1915, all in "Minutes of Emory University" [microfilm copy of bound volume], Emory University Archives. Counsel for the petitioners for the charter was the firm of Thomson, Candler, and Hirsch. Note that between the founding of Emory University in 1915 and reorganization in 1919, Emory College continued to have a separate board of trustees (and therefore continued to keep a separate set of minutes). They were chosen by the University's trustees and included Asa Candler, president, W. D. Thomson, secretary, and Warren Candler, trustee.

[50]Ibid.; "Emory Buildings Draw Great Architect's Praise," *Atlanta Journal*, 8 October 1916. The "great architect" was none other than Hornbostel, himself.

[51]"Emory University is Given Great Opening," *Atlanta Journal*, 16 September 1917, 1.

[52]Levine, *The American College*, 80-81. Levine offers as evidence of the secularization of Emory's mission statements that higher education must prepare not only "gentlemen" but business and professional men. However, Emory's institutional values can also be seen as an attempt to defend old values in a changing society; otherwise the founders of Emory would have been satisfied to let their young men go to Vanderbilt. Emory did indeed promote Southern economic and social progress and went on to take a place in the development of "new" Southerners, but this undertaking does not necessarily contradict the spiritual goals of the Candlers. Of course both men would have put the goal of advancing Christian values above any attainment of professional skill.

[53]Clifford M. Kuhn, Harlon E. Joye, and E. Bernard West, *Living Atlanta: An Oral History of the City, 1914-1948* (Atlanta: The Atlanta Historical Society; Athens: The University of Georgia Press, 1990) 7. The student was Hunter Bell, who also remembered that the first automobile arrived on campus in 1920.

[54]Isabelle Gournay, "Area 15, Emory University (EU) *AIA Guide to the Architecture of Atlanta* (Athens: University of Georgia Press, 1993) 217.

[55]See *American Institute of Architects Guide to Atlanta*, Kermit B. Marsh, ed., (Atlanta Chapter of the AIA, 1975) 131: "In an unusual agreement" Tufts had responsibility for the completion of the first two buildings, although the design was the work of architect Henry Hornbostel of New York.

[56]Draft of letter, WAC to Arthur Tufts, [1917], folder 6, box 3, Series I, Board of Trustees, Emory University Archives. Chancellor Candler's views on student activities are found throughout his papers; for one example see: Minutes of Emory University, 30 December 1919, Emory University Archives.

[57]WAC to AGC, 13 February 1917, box 1, AGC papers, Emory.

[58]Ibid.

[59]AGC to WAC, 27 April 1917, box 1, AGC papers, Emory.

[60]The Chancellor did initiate a move to retire in 1918 but the trustees did not accept his offer; when he again expressed the wish to leave in 1919 they voted "to pray daily" for his "strength to carry on the work during the coming year" but later accepted his resignation. A few months later he again assumed the title of chancellor, but the new office of the president of the university took on some duties that had formerly been attached to the office of chancellor. See: Minute Book of Emory University, 8 June 1918; 7 and 9 June 1919; 30 December 1919, Emory University Archives, all of which contain matter pertaining to Candler's various attempts to resign. See also, Thomas W. English, *Emory University, 1915-1965*, (Atlanta: Emory University, 1966) 24-25.

CHAPTER SEVEN

Elitist

As a boy growing up in Carroll county, Asa Candler saw the men in his family buy and sell valuable property, including land and slaves, and he saw them supervise the labor of their human chattels. From time to time, his relatives held public offices. As a rule, these men gave orders rather than receiving them. Asa's experiences as a child of Georgia's rural gentry shaped his personality and social ideas, effectively preparing him to take a place in Atlanta's leadership. When he became part of his city's elite, his background, his social and religious conservatism, and his energetic personality gave him the assurance to hold strong, public positions on a number of important issues.[1]

Atlanta's leaders usually (but not inevitably) shared his views. They joined a few exclusive organizations where, along with purely social activities, they could swap ideas and information and coordinate business and civic activities. Asa Candler also joined the Capital City Club, Piedmont Driving Club, and Atlanta Athletic Club. He took an active part in them, but he seems not to have over-emphasized this social aspect of life, nor was Mrs. Candler unusually prominent in the society sections of the newspapers.[2] Church life and business, rather than "society," occupied the couple, probably because Candler did not become truly wealthy until he was in his middle age. Still, the indefatigable Candler spent many evenings in organizational meetings or dinners after days engaged in business, civic, and church work. His capacity for activity seemed limitless.

Among the most influential civic groups was the Atlanta Chamber of Commerce. Candler's rise as an important member of the Chamber parallels his increasing prominence in Atlanta affairs in general. As a young manufacturer of patent medicines, he supported Chamber activities for many years. He was an ordinary member, who occasionally served on committees.[3] The Chamber's influence increased in the early twentieth century, and Candler's influence within the organization grew during the same period. Effective service on various committees led to his election to the board of directors in 1905; he was Chamber president for the 1908–1909 term.[4]

Atlanta's commercial leaders took a deep interest in public policy. They saw public and private business as forming the two sides of the coin of prosperity and progress. Representing the interests of the business elite, the Chamber of Commerce often acted to promote city policies that it deemed desirable. At times, it functioned as an unofficial branch of city government. When the Chamber chose Candler as its president for the 1908–1909 term he was fully prepared to pursue such tandem activity, if it seemed appropriate to the city's business leadership.

Such an occasion arose in that spring, when a member of the Atlanta City Council proposed a million-dollar bond issue for a number of city improvements.[5] A Chamber investigation revealed that the lack of proper water and sewage facilities threatened the health of the city; that three-quarters of the city's streets remained unpaved; and that many children attended school in dark, poorly equipped "wooden death traps." Therefore, in June, the Chamber committee appeared before the City Council. President Candler presented their findings and urged the adoption of a Chamber proposal for a $1.5 million bond issue.[6] (As the campaign continued, it became evident that the city needed even more improvements; the amount of the proposed bond issue increased to three million dollars in early 1910.[7])

The convoluted legal procedure necessary to arrange a bond election dragged on for over a year. As time went on, further city needs became known. To persuade the public, the bond issue supporters concentrated on the threat to public health represented by impure water and primitive sanitary facilities. In his presidential address at the beginning of 1909, Candler reiterated the point that poor water and sewerage services caused Atlanta's high mortality rate and demanded that the city spend the money necessary to improve them: "Can we save money by destroying life? And if we could, should a civilized community consider for a moment such a policy?"[8]

Candler's high-minded statements passed over one of the planners' reasons for improvements in certain black residential areas; they feared that Negro servants might bring diseases from their unhealthy neighborhoods into the homes of the white families who employed them. In fact, the runoff of contamination from white neighborhoods, which typically occupied the higher ground, contributed to the sordid sanitary conditions in low-lying black residential areas.[9] In a letter to Chamber members, Candler declared, "The health of Atlanta is at stake...."[10]

Candler's term as Chamber president ended in 1909, so he took a place on the Campaign Committee, and wrote to business owners urging each of them to designate an employee who would work to get out the vote.[11] The Chamber blitzed the city with circulars, letters, and pledge cards in support of the plan. The newspapers endorsed the project.[12] On election day, 15 February, a bank of telephone operators called throughout the city, urging last-minute support. The backing of the city's elite—its business and political leadership—swept away all opposition, and the bond issue passed. The efforts of Candler's Chamber of Commerce had contributed greatly to the victory that brought Atlanta improvements that included new sewage disposal plants, expanded water service, improved school buildings and hospital facilities.[13] In the 1910 bond election, as in many other instances, the Chamber acted as a kind of shadow branch of government unencumbered by a restrictive city charter. Men such as Asa Candler, working through the Chamber, got things done and left the political technicalities to be cleared away after the fact.

Atlanta City Council did not always receive the advice of the city's business elite with unqualified enthusiasm. In the years between 1901 and 1913, businessmen-reformers who desired a more efficient city, made three attempts to change the form of Atlanta's municipal government. Modern business methods inspired their new ideas. Such reformers wanted professional city managers instead of elected executive officers; others wanted to reorganize the city into departments in the same way that large commercial enterprises organize their various functions into separate divisions. Asa Candler figured prominently in the first two revisionist movements (1908 and 1909), but was out of the country during the 1913 campaign. In each case, the political element of the city's elite, with some difficulty, succeeded in using a combination of parliamentary strategy and appeals for public support to fend off the revision attempts and maintain the status quo.[14]

Candler's public health-based arguments for the bond issue and his support of charter revision suggest that he was more reform-minded than he actually was. In matters of gender, labor relations, and race, his traditional, paternalistic views become plain.

In the age of the woman suffragist, few women in Candler's circle stepped out of the bounds of convention to challenge his stereotypical views of their sex. In contrast to his treatment of his sons, Candler never initiated his daughter into the family business concerns. When his children had grown, Candler consulted his sons on important decisions; he merely informed his daughter. Candler always preferred the homely virtues of Christian domesticity that characterized his own wife, whose cheerful acceptance of her traditional role probably reinforced her husband's views on the proper place of women. Late in his life, when he did come to know one woman who thought of herself as a suffragist, he expressed his opposition to the movement, ridiculing its supporters as "them things."[15]

Her response, coy and flirtatious, presented no serious answer to his offhand dismissal, but it was as close as anyone in his circle ever came to directly contradicting his ideas on the subject of women's rights.

Candler expressed this view in at least two speeches. The 1918 graduates of Martha Berry School for Girls were, by implication, gently admonished to keep their places in a speech whose title—Pegs and Holes—exhibits total innocence of the Freudian theories that were soon to infect public discourse. He admonished the girls "to live a life of service and not of selfishness." Although he was too polite to be explicit, he clearly thought that the natural abilities of women narrowed the field where this life of service might take place: "[N]o life ought to be spent trying to do what it cannot do well...."[16] Candler used this natural aptitude theme in talks given to young men as well, but the roles he foresaw for the two sexes differed. He expressed his expectations more directly in another talk, given at about the same time to another class of women graduates. His theme was the virtue of "Home!" as the foundation of civilization: "The home is nothing less than a divine institution taking rank with the church and with the state, antedating both." As such, it "should be made both holy and happy." This preservation of the home, he asserted, is the highest duty of Christian womanhood.[17]

As an employer, Candler had no large or public conflicts with organized labor, perhaps because his manufacturing interests were not labor-intensive and therefore fewer occasions for confrontation arose. One minor controversy actually involved a disagreement between an Atlanta printer's union local and the Atlanta Coca-Cola Bottling company, a concern not directly under Candler's control. Indifferent to these fine distinctions, the union called for a boycott of the beverage in 1907. The *Journal of Labor* story on the settlement of the dispute said, "All differences existing between the Coca-Cola company and the union have been settled satisfactorily to all parties concerned and the printers are again at liberty to drink coca-cola [sic]." More information emerged in the next issue of the paper, which carried a letter from an executive of the bottling company purportedly sent to St. Elmo Massengale, head of one of the Coca-

Cola Company's advertising agencies, to be passed on to the press. It declared, "It has been our disposition and policy in every department of our business to patronize union concerns wherever it was possible. We have always felt very kindly towards them...." The letter included several specific examples of union-made goods such as bottles and crown corks used in packaging Coca-Cola. The *Journal of Labor* went on to praise the bottling company and Massengale's advertising agency: "Mr. S. C. Dobbs, general sales manager of the Coca-Cola Company, has also proven his friendship to the organized laboring classes by giving them preference if in his power to do so." The article ended by requesting "the labor press" to pass along the information in the article and urged, "Let's all take a Coca-Cola!" A few months later the paper carried an enthusiastic feature article on the virtues of the bottling company as a user of union-made goods and the virtues of Coca-Cola as "the most popular soft drink in the land."[18]

Candler seems to have been willing to deal realistically with organized labor, but his treatment of his employees at all levels also demonstrates a decidedly patriarchal approach to administration. The "Chief," sometimes called "Uncle Asa," might give out gold coins for Christmas gifts, but he could also dictate private behavior. For example, he took it upon himself to prohibit the use of alcohol by his subordinates. While Howard traveled through the Midwest selling Coca-Cola, his father instructed him to visit the Dallas office to "carefully though discreetly investigate that Branch...I am afraid he is intemperate." Such an employee might receive a stern letter advising him to mend his ways; one such individual gratefully credited a letter from Candler with persuading him to give up drinking. Another long-time Coca-Cola employee remembered that "in the old days...the entire manufacturing and selling force could then sit on one Sunday school bench, and often they did that very thing." No doubt this brought joy to their Sunday school-teaching employer. In this, Candler resembled other successful men of his time who also imposed their personal Christian beliefs on their employees; a few required church attendance and others strongly encouraged it. These men of affairs had complex motives that extended beyond the desire to spread the Good News; they believed Sabbath-keeping employees to be more reliable and they rewarded the more pious workers with greater job security. Incidentally, Candler's close interest in the lives of his personnel extended beyond moral supervision. He visited and dosed with medicine those who were ill and kept infirm elderly employees on the payroll when they no longer could work.[19]

We can easily understand that Asa Candler's paternalistic attitudes toward his employees were typical of a man of his time and social position. However, his ideas and actions on the subject of child labor are more difficult to sort out. His actions and his words do not paint an unclouded picture of his point of view, and in the end all we can know for certain is that human behavior can be too complicated to classify into simple categories.

In the spring of 1908 the National Child Labor Committee, which fought for legislation to protect child laborers throughout the United States, held its annual convention in Atlanta. Both Asa and Warren Candler were members of the Georgia branch of the committee, which provided arrangements for the four-day meeting. The extent of Asa's involvement with the child labor issue remains unclear but may be connected to the fact that his brother Warren, in 1901, was one of the founders (and more active members) of the Child Labor Committee of Georgia.

Delegates to the convention assembled at the Piedmont Hotel for the opening banquet. They paused outside of the palm-decorated dining room to examine a photographic exhibit of the dreary factory districts of the urban northeast and to browse through educational materials and pamphlets circulated by the committee. Many prominent Georgians who supported the cause were among the 150 guests.[20] Less than two years earlier, the Georgia contingent had achieved their first limited political success: Governor Joseph M. Terrell had signed the first Georgia child labor law on 1 August 1906, establishing a twelve year minimum age for most jobs and an absolute prohibition of the employment of children under age 10 in factory work. The law required that child workers under fourteen must be literate and that children would not be permitted to work at night. However, there remained a great deal of work to do. Attempts to establish an eight-hour day for workers under age sixteen had failed, and the bill was, in fact, toothless, in that it offered little mechanism for the enforcement of its requirements.[21]

Delegates to the national convention were keenly aware of the tasks they still faced in Georgia and elsewhere, but this did nothing to dampen their spirits; all reports of the opening banquet in the brilliantly illuminated main dining room of the hotel describe it as highly enjoyable. The *Atlanta Journal* reporter, who had evidently seen his share of such events, wrote, "The entire occasion was marked with that informal heartiness and ease which now and then lift the word banquet from the slough of despond in which it is commonly sunk. The menu was long and palatable. The speeches were short and witty."[22]

Among these witty speakers was Asa G. Candler, then president of the Atlanta Chamber of Commerce, whose talk was titled "The Business World and Child Labor." According to the *Journal* correspondent, Candler welcomed the visitors to his city with the modest assertion that although Atlanta was "a child in many things" she was open-minded and "welcomed all visitors who could teach her."[23] The *Atlanta Constitution* writer said that Candler's talk "showed how business and the care of the children went arm in arm in this enlightened day of civilization and charity."[24]

Candler's dry, ironic wit evidently leavened his talk. The official *Proceedings* of the meeting quote him extensively, with the crucial introductory phrase, "With subtle humor he defended child labor..." Alas for those who indulge in subtle humor, they are in danger of being taken literally. A few sentences, evidently delivered in an ironic tone that was lost when they were transcribed to the printed page, have dogged Candler's reputation ever since: "Child labor properly conducted, properly surrounded, properly conditioned, is calculated to bring the highest measure of success to any country on the face of the earth. The most beautiful sight that we see is the child at labor; as early as he may get at labor, the more beautiful, the more useful does his life get to be."[25]

Unfortunately for Candler's reputation, no complete text of his talk remains and this tidbit has been served up ever since as an example of the mentality of the cruel exploiter of child labor. One writer does take the trouble to mention that the editor of the *Proceedings* characterized Candler's tone as one of "subtle humor" but then goes on to take Candler's words literally anyway, dismissing the opinion of those who actually heard the talk. Other writers, evidently unable to resist the opportunity to caricature him as a heartless capitalist, do not trouble themselves to report the fact that Candler spoke his "incriminating" words at a meeting held by opponents of child labor. They also fail to mention the fact that Candler was an active member of that group.[26]

To be fair, it is possible that Candler did not entirely reject the idea of employing youthful workers. Candler himself, as most rural children, had done his share of the farm work and evidently harbored no ill feeling about the experience in later years. In his talk Candler said that he understood the function of the committee was "solely to tell us how to surround the child that his labor may develop him into a noble, useful competent person." He also told the delegates that they labored "in the richest field in all this universe."[27] Evidently, Candler distinguished between child labor and child exploitation. Whatever his precise opinions on the subject may have been, one point is certain: Candler was not so stupid as to praise the exploitation of children before an audience that would find the idea entirely odious.

If this painstaking examination of a few words in one after-dinner talk leads a reasonable person to conclude that Asa Candler did not claim to find beauty in the suffering of children, one shadow yet remains, cast by the efforts Candler made for the future of his own child, Asa, Jr. The Witham Mills undertaking, discussed in a previous chapter, was one of Candler's rare business failures. An absence of evidence to the contrary opens the possibility that it may have been an ethical failure as well. Although Candler publicly opposed child labor a decade later, Witham Mills already employed large numbers of child laborers when Candler acquired it. The 1900 manuscript census returns for the town of Hartwell, taken in the year when Asa, Jr., arrived to begin his new career as mill manager, include at least one cluster of residences occupied by families employed in the textile mills. They are listed together on three pages that identify sixty-two persons whose occupations (spinner, weaver, carder, spooler hand) clearly indicate mill employment. A third of these mill hands were children of fourteen years or less; a dozen of the children were twelve or younger; half of these were ten years old. None of these children had ever attended school and only twelve were listed as literate.[28]

Ruby Tolbert, a ten-year-old spinner in 1900, worked along with her widowed father, two of her brothers, and a sister in the mill. If Asa Candler had taken any steps to end the exploitation of such a family, it could hardly have passed without notice. The very absence of any record may thus provide circumstantial evidence of a sin of omission. By the time of the next census the mill had closed and its employees scattered, but it may be that while he dined at the gala opening of the child labor convention, Asa Candler had forgotten that he himself once employed children in factory labor.

If the conditions of women and labor improved somewhat during the early years of the century that are customarily labeled "Progressive," this era can hardly be regarded as progressive for African-Americans. In the South, repressive laws reinforced the customs of racial separation that already were widespread throughout the United States. Beginning after the Compromise of 1877 (while Asa Candler was selling patent medicines on Peachtree Street), such laws became pervasive throughout the region. Within a quarter century "Jim Crow" had spread its shadow over Southern life, imposing formal separation of the races and legally limiting access by blacks to most public accommodations. Both in Atlanta and throughout the South, those who desired the rigorous separation of the races seemed never to be satisfied, as regulation piled upon regulation. Separate seating on streetcars came early and eventually segregation even applied to the Bibles used for court oaths. Poll taxes and literacy tests were the first steps in a movement for the sweeping disfranchisement of all African-Americans. The Republican party nearly vanished and Georgia's Democratic party excluded all black voters from its primary elections, but the issues of segregation still provided the state's politicians with clubs that they might beat each other in punch-and-judy campaigns of racist posturing. In the 1906 governor's race, Hoke Smith (who in former times had known Asa Candler as a fellow Sunday school superintendent) attacked the "ignorant, illiterate, savage, vicious, inhuman, unendurable, venal, arrogant, brutish, venomous" Negro voter. Clark Howell, his opponent, also promised the complete disfranchisement of blacks if he were elected.[29]

A cursory examination of Atlanta newspapers of the day reveals race-based stories as routine features. The stories tend to fall in two broad categories, representing the Negro as either ridiculous or vicious. The white elite had no patent on bigotry; the *Journal of Labor* attacked the "slant-eyed Celestial…Chinaman," while the black-owned *Independent* had hard words for "the motley dago" and foreigners in general.[30] However, African-Americans remained the principal target of the mainstream press. Atlanta newspapers (they were not unique in this) never tired of reporting tales of "outrages" against white women, committed by black "brutes." With equal enthusiasm, they reported on the frequent instances of vengeance by whites who lynched the Negroes accused of these crimes. These ideas had such power that even an African-American editor, while condemning mob law and scare headlines, wrote: "The law-abiding colored people of this community have no patience with that element of our race who seems bent upon destroying the virtue of the white women of our community."[31] Anyone who read a daily newspaper—as Asa Candler must have done—could not avoid the stories of rape and retribution and most probably accepted their validity. Bishop Candler certainly did so, and on several occasions he wrote on the subject of lynching. His essays, published in church newspapers and the *Atlanta Journal,* followed a pattern. He condemned lynching as an abuse of due process, but he seemed always to presume that most of the victims of lynch mobs were, in fact, guilty. In opposing lynching, the Bishop and his ilk opposed the social disorder that it represented, more than the actual incident of violence, itself— a real, if subtle difference.[32] Asa probably shared Warren's belief that southern racial relations would remain untroubled if "outside agitators…will leave them alone to work out their problem."[33]

Upper-class whites imagined that they had gained, through a long and close association that began with the institution of slavery, a special understanding of the black population. Furthermore, they had no patience with vulgar race-baiters. As was typical of persons of their class, they exhibited a kind of *noblesse* in their kindly demeanor toward those blacks whom they regarded as appropriately deferential, but they despised others, such as the Negro bishops of the Methodist churches of the North, who attempted to rise above their station. Warren Candler, a spokesman for this point of view, defended a segregated "White Man's Church," inveighing against the northern Methodists who ordained Negro bishops on the same basis as whites.[34] To those African-Americans who did not challenge the white elite's conception of the proper order of society, they were generous with cash and kind words. When a group of Atlanta blacks held a mass meeting to raise money for Morris Brown College, Asa Candler doubled the fund they raised and in his talk spoke approvingly of the "elevation of the colored people of the South." Addressing the meeting, he mentioned the names of some "useful colored men," and paid the race what he must have intended as a high compliment: "I have never sold a Negro a home that he did not pay for it according to the terms of our agreement."[35]

The Candlers' attitudes toward the education of African-Americans demonstrate their paternalistic viewpoint. Atticus Haygood, president of Emory College when young Warren Candler studied there, helped shape their ideas on the subject. Haygood supported Negro education, but only in the trades and not in the classical curriculum offered to whites. He promoted the founding of Paine College to advance such a program and Warren Candler later served as a trustee of the school. Haygood assured critics that the school would not arouse any claims of social equality from its students.

Candler defended the school's biracial faculty, but this could be interpreted as a defense of the paternalistic principle that whites should be in charge, since the black faculty members of this school occupied lower ranking positions than the whites.[36] As kindly-intentioned paternalists, racial elitists like the Candlers favored the full development of blacks but presumed that such development had naturally low limits.

Once again, the editor of a black newspaper demonstrates the power of such ideas to persuade even those who suffered from them. Although Benjamin Davis, the editor of the *Atlanta Independent*, did insist that "We do not believe that God created us inferior," he was willing to accept as fact "a difference in racial achievement:"[T]here are fundamental differences existing between the races, whether they be inherent or artificial, and argument cannot permanently hide the fact. These differences are...broad and discernible...Wisdom suggests that each race be equipped and provided the blessings of Christian civilization as it develops capacity to digest and utilize."[37] Davis followed with a plea for white assistance to develop his "child race":

> We are largely a charge upon our white neighbors hands and he cannot escape his responsibility. The protectorate held over us...whether civil, moral, political, educational or industrial, should be administered in the same spirit with which the parent restricts the personal liberty of the child, with a view of strengthening our racial character and equipping us for the duties and responsibilities of citizenship.... [W]e implore you to give us the same opportunities for improvement you give the dago and other illiterate foreigners.[38]

The Candlers would have found little to dispute in Davis' editorial, except for the editor's goal of equality in some indefinite future time. The Candlers had little or nothing to say about the prominent or successful blacks of their day, but Asa and Warren each have left revealing comments about black individuals of humble callings. Warren, in a reminiscence of Emory College, cited "Robert Hammond, Faithful Janitor" for his thirty years of service and his Christian character. Asa took the trouble to send a postcard to Lucy to notify her that "William Curtright died this P.M....He has faithfully served us...."[39] Curtright and his brother George had delivered Coca-Cola from a one-horse dray in the early days of the company. In spite of their genuinely felt affection for faithful servants, a barrier of separation between the races seemed important and natural to the Candlers.

If Asa Candler had no criticism for the racial arrangements that prevailed in the South of his day, others were less complacent. Some of these were southerners, and one was a member by marriage of the Candler family. Andrew Sledd, son-in-law of Bishop Candler and an Emory College classics professor, wrote an article for the July 1902 issue of *Atlantic Monthly*, which demonstrated his comparatively moderate racial views. He expressly accepted the principle of Negro inferiority, but advocated equal treatment for blacks, particularly before the law. He denounced lynching.

As a result of this publication, Rebecca Felton, a writer with great influence in some segments of Georgia politics, led an outcry against its author. Felton, a journalistic harpy who combined the qualities of a racist, a feminist, and a populist, never forgave nor forgot anyone who crossed her. Her opposition to all things Candler began when Milton, the eldest of the Candler brothers, failed to support her husband's reelection to Congress in the early 1890s. Warren's support of a modest program of industrial education for blacks also drew her ire, and several other petty controversies followed.[40] Felton's longstanding dislike of the Candler family, coupled with her negrophobia, fueled a vitriolic campaign of letter writing and comment in the public press. Within two weeks of the initial attack, Sledd offered to resign. Emory president J. E. Dickey, new in his position, had received the weight of the complaints against Professor Sledd and accepted the resignation with relief. He wrote to Bishop Candler that two of the bishop's own brothers—almost certainly Asa and John—strongly opposed Sledd's views.[41]

This generation of the Candlers, with some recollections of childhood in a slave-owning household, shared the ideal of a firmly stratified social structure, with themselves in its top tier and blacks at the bottom. A man like Asa Candler did not hate Negroes, he simply assumed that they were beneath him. When demagogues threatened the lives and limbs of blacks, Candler and his ilk perceived the violence as an undesirable interference with the orderly conduct of society—a society that they alone were suited to lead. This was the case in Atlanta, in 1906, as well-brought-up folk like the Candlers looked on with genuine horror while their city suddenly writhed in the paroxysms of a race riot. In the confused scenes of those bloody days, a glimpse of Asa Candler occasionally appears.[42]

The Atlanta race riot of September 1906 began on the twenty-second day of the month, a Saturday night. From the "low dives" of the Negro section of downtown Decatur Street, odors of beer and frying mullet filled the air. A man with his weekly pay envelope in his pocket could find corn whiskey and a fifteen-cent steak; in some places he could rent a bed for the night for the same price. Prostitution flourished. Although considered a Negro district, this area of Decatur Street (including some of its neighboring thoroughfares) saw plenty of white faces as well, both as proprietors of some of the businesses and occasionally as customers. Establishments that served both races did so in separated areas. Scandalized investigators thought that some of the "dives," located in dark basements or alleys, seemed almost subterranean. Committees of reform-minded citizens reported that many of these "holes in the wall" displayed advertising posters that included suggestive images of white women. The African-American editor Davis decried the conditions in the district, condemning the "club rooms, dives, and pool rooms" as "cess pools that breed criminals."[43]

At about nine o'clock, the riot began at the edge of this district.[44] Some eyewitness accounts described a knife fight between a black man and a white man, and others told of a race-baiting street orator, inspired by the day's newspaper hearsay tales of outrages by "black brutes" against innocent white womanhood.[45] Perhaps both of these served as a spark; but however it began, rowdy mobs of drunken whites began to attack any Negro who strayed, unaware, into their reach. Rioters broke into hardware stores to steal guns and ammunition. They attacked perfectly respectable persons—passengers of street cars, employees of downtown businesses, or Pullman porters—maiming or killing them. The *Atlanta Journal*, a newspaper that had no special fondness for the Negro, expressed the shock of respectable Atlanta in a headline describing the mob's "Mad Spirit of Vengeance." The Sunday morning front page prominently reported the night's horrors. For example: "[T]he cry went up that a Negro was in sight and with one mad rush the crowd began to swarm around him. Those who had sticks began to pound him in an unmerciful manner and he began running up the street....those who were armed began to fire upon him and he was literally torn to pieces."[46]

The violence spread. Although a riot call brought the entire police force to the downtown area, they lacked sufficient numbers to control the bloodthirsty crowds. City authorities called out firemen to use hoses to drench groups of rioters who were beyond the control of the police. When this strategy failed, units of the state militia entered the struggle and brought a degree of order to the streets in the early hours of Sunday morning.

Periodic outbreaks of violence disturbed the city over the next days. Unwilling to be passive victims, black Atlantans armed themselves; snipers on rooftops deflected mobs from certain of their neighborhoods. Between Saturday night and the following Tuesday three factions struggled for control of the situation: white rioters, driven by a pathological combination of fear and hate; black Atlantans, who not only suffered and died, but also armed themselves and fought back; and the established municipal authorities, who used police, firemen and militia to restore control over the city. The police took white rioters into custody and charged them with various crimes, although those whites arrested seemed to be perceived as individual, exceptional evil-doers. Meanwhile, the authorities treated the black population, as a whole, as a serious threat to the public peace. On the twenty-fifth, the city council "condemned and repudiated the terrible wrong done on the streets of our city," but before calling for law and order they went on to condemn "outrageous assaults upon innocent white women" allegedly committed by blacks. Mayor Woodward sent a communication to the council that likewise blamed "beastly crimes attempted by black brutes" along with "inflammatory, sensational newspaper extras," for the troubles.[47] After the initial night of bloodshed, some incidents of violence followed when the white authorities, which perceived the Negroes to be the source of the disorder, moved systematically to disarm the black population. In response to the shooting death of a police officer near the African-American neighborhood known as Brownsville, the authorities launched a military style assault on the area, searching house to house for weapons and herding the populace into an open area in the range of a Gatling gun that was "prepared to rake the country if any serious trouble followed."[48]

Even before order could be restored, the voice of the city's white establishment decried the situation and sought to discover remedies. Their statements also seldom failed to mention the supposed "outrages" against white women that had enlivened the newspapers of recent date. While they condemned violence against faultless individual blacks, many of the most respectable voices in the city called for the elimination of the Negro slum district along Decatur Street to forestall future riots. This was the burden of a resolution adopted on Tuesday morning at a mass meeting called by the Chamber of Commerce. The meeting rang with denunciations of the disorders of the past days.[49] During the discussion, Asa Candler rose to express his views; an *Atlanta Journal* writer paraphrased the first portion of his statement: "Asa G. Candler said that people were talking too much and were carrying too many pistols…He said that all the blame for crime should not be placed upon the members of a weak race."[50] The writer then quoted Candler directly: "We are trustees of this great nation; there's never a time in our life when we should not try to govern ourselves with Christian righteousness." The reporter added that

Candler "heartily favored the cessation of wild rumors."[51] He seemed to imply that the trustees of the society's well being (that is, the white leadership) needed to pull themselves together and do a better job of managing the "weak race." In his view, had the "trustees" been more Christian and righteous, the troubles never would have occurred. When he briskly asserted that "people" should stop talking wildly and packing guns, Candler spoke as a man accustomed to telling other "people" what to do.

Those who attended this mass meeting heard a number of speeches "in the interest of law and order" and established a fund for the relief of riot victims, although Asa Candler's name does not appear among the ninety-four original subscribers. Those who attended resolved that "every man should be asked to work" but also approved of the principle that "it was the duty of every white man to protect the good Negroes." They adopted a resolution including the words, "We deplore the crime of both races…[and] call upon the authorities…to crush anarchy with an iron hand."[52] Led by the Chamber of Commerce, the mass meeting rejected the disorders without recognizing the racism that had fostered them. Although meetings such as this heard numerous heartfelt denunciations of violence, they also continued the theme of rape. The resolutions adopted that day called for the authorities to "crush anarchy," but also included the "demand that the authorities spare no effort to put a stop to the assaults on our women.…Our womanhood must and shall be protected."[53]

The violence done both to persons and property dismayed whites of the Candlers' class but they also deplored the riot's disruption of the city's economic routine. The *Atlanta Journal* had reported with premature relief on Monday that normal commercial activity had resumed and that "The Negroes Are Back at Work"—plenty of waiters had reported for duty in the city's hotels and restaurants. When order finally returned on Wednesday, the *Constitution* expressed its satisfaction that "every plant in the city that has been closed down will resume work." The writer of this editorial alluded to the fears of "the authorities" that the closing of industrial plants by the disorders had the effect of "throwing out of employment a large number of men and furnishing material for mobs should an outbreak occur." The slippery language of this phrase does not suggest that the mass of Atlanta working men actually engaged in rioting; rather, "the authorities" feared that they might. Evidently, the *Constitution* and the vaguely identified "authorities" thought that the working class (of either race) might easily become violent.[54]

As the victims of the riot were laid to rest, Atlanta set about the task of restoring the relations between the races to a more peaceful footing. The president of the Chamber of Commerce addressed the congregations of Negro churches to reassure them. Moneys were distributed to the needy and the inevitable committees formed.

In the aftermath, even the most well-intentioned whites seemed to believe that the blacks bore the ultimate responsibility for the riot. Like the citizens at the meeting where Candler spoke, newspapers, magazines, and even a master's thesis prepared a quarter-century later, pointed to the licentious conditions on Decatur Street, the scene of much of the violence, and to the supposed wholesale sexual transgressions of the black population as the root causes of the riots.[55] The role racial and sexual fears of the white population, inflamed by irresponsible newspapers and the racial rhetoric of the recent gubernatorial race, remained largely unrecognized until much later. At the time, only one organized group did not denounce "brutes" while condemning the rioters: the report of "the committee to dispense funds for the relief of the riot victims" frankly stated that the perpetrators of murderous assaults against "honest, industrious and law-abiding citizens" had largely gone unpunished and as a result "several hundred murderers or would-be murderers are at large in this community."[56] This forthright statement seems to have had scant effect on the generally held opinion that the origins of the riot lay in "the Negro problem" and not in white attitudes or behavior. Only a few individuals took any note of the race prejudice and sexual paranoia that fed the riot—individuals such as the scholar W. E. B. Du Bois, who probably did not fall in Asa Candler's category of "useful colored man."

Candler was among those who thought that religion would lead the way out of the disorders of 1906. He joined his fellow members of the Atlanta Business Men's Gospel Union to lay the groundwork for the formation of a Christian League, through which they expected to solve what they perceived as "the Negro problem" with "the power of the Christian religion." The League included prestigious figures such as the former Governor William Northen; Candler and his old friend William Witham were among the members of the executive committee. The League was to be open to members of both races who would promote peace and good will, "under the direction of the gospel." A "representative body of colored ministers and laymen" met at the "colored" Young Men's Christian Association and heard the proposal for the organization approvingly. However, in a statement to the public, the executive committee explicitly restated the elitist view of the proper social order with the African-American in a subordinate position: "It was proper that the initiative in this movement...should be undertaken by the white people, not only because of their greater numbers and superior wealth and intelligence, but for the reason that they constitute the ruling class and are therefore chiefly responsible for our present social, industrial, moral and political conditions."[57]

Although the Christian League received some favorable attention in the black community, another group also found approval. Begun only a few days after the organization of the Christian League, the Civic League held its organizational meeting at the Temple, the city's principal synagogue. This Civic League also hoped to cope with the "Negro problem," but they employed a secular rhetoric, quite different from that of the Christian League. They sought to put forward the "sentiment of the real Atlanta—Atlanta the law-abiding, Atlanta the God-fearing, Atlanta the progressive and prosperous..."[58] Charles T. Hopkins, the attorney for Atlanta University, hoped to attract as many as five thousand of the "better white people in Atlanta" into the group, which would work with a similar, parallel group of black Atlantans.[59]

An established organization, the Atlanta Chamber of Commerce, took a central part in the city's reaction in the aftermath of the riots.

Unlike the two leagues, its response had an immediate and tangible result. Walter G. Cooper, once the Secretary of the Chamber of Commerce, later wrote, in a history of that group, that in 1906: "The urgent need of an armory for the National Guard troops of Atlanta developed…and out of this grew the big Auditorium-Armory." He added that the Armory was intended to serve the Fifth Georgia Regiment of Infantry, the Atlanta Artillery, and the Governor's Horse Guard.[60] The unnamed "urgent need" was, of course, the riot that was quelled partly through the exertions of the Atlanta troops that Cooper named. In the days immediately after the riot another member of the Chamber, Captain James English—a prominent manufacturer who also served on the police board—spoke more plainly when he called for construction of an armory: "We would save the cost of the building in the protection of property alone."[61]

Before the riots of September 1906, Asa Candler had been involved in a Chamber of Commerce-sponsored plan to build an auditorium with a projected cost of over $200,000. Discussions had begun in 1904. In the following year Candler presented a report, "The City of Atlanta Needs a Great Auditorium," to the Chamber, stating that "[W]e need a place more dignified than a play house and less restricted than a church" where Atlantans could gratify "aesthetic tastes" and cultivate their "intellectual faculties."[62] No further action had taken place on this project, which was to have been under the control of the Chamber, by the time of the 1906 riot. Within days after the violence ended, a committee of seven citizens, including Candler, met to devise ways and means for the construction of the building, but with the functions of an armory added to its previous "aesthetic" and "intellectual" goals. Over the next days, the plan developed to an estimated cost of a quarter million dollars.[63] Next, Mayor Woodward met with the Chamber, which appointed a committee of twenty-five (again including Candler). It set out to urge the city council to approve the armory project and to devise a plan to finance it. The *Journal* reported that committee spokesman Candler delivered "a ringing speech" in favor of an auditorium-armory.[64] State law severely limited the amount of debt a city might incur, but

Candler offered a plan to avoid these restrictions, so that construction might begin immediately. Chamber leaders, including Candler, would form an Auditorium-Armory Company, capitalized at a half-million dollars, to acquire the land and erect the building. At the conclusion of the project the company was to convey the entire property to the city, subject to reimbursement with money to be raised by a municipal bond issue.[65]

After some early difficulties, the Atlanta Auditorium-Armory Company sold its bonds. Candler had invested $1,500 in the stock of the company and he purchased $3,500 of the bonds, thus becoming one of the larger individual investors in the project.[66] As the plan went forward, the Chamber put its considerable resources into the marshaling of public support. Discussion emphasized the usefulness of the auditorium to a city that attracted a great many conventions, while only passing public mention went to the military function of the new building. Having ended the riot and having agreed that its cause was some vaguely defined "Negro problem," none of the Atlanta elite chose to make further public comment about it. The secretary of the Chamber of Commerce, for example, wrote both a history of the Chamber and an *Official History of Fulton County* that avoided the subject of the riot.[67]

The Auditorium-Armory opened in 1909 with a splendid banquet in honor of US President-elect Taft. Asa Candler, as Chamber of Commerce president, served as toastmaster. He thought the occasion one of the high points of his life and ever afterward the event was part of his entry in *Who's Who in America*. Atlanta's leading citizens joined the visiting dignitaries to dine on "'possum and 'taters," a culinary eccentricity that was served at Candler's insistence.[68] G. H. Mumm's Extra Dry Champagne appeared on the dinner menu, but "drys" were able to lift a glass of persimmon beer or a cup of "Merry Widow Punch, a la Candler." After dinner, the guests heard sentimental speeches on the theme of sectional brotherhood and joined their voices to sing "Way Down Upon the Suwanee River" and "My Country 'tis of Thee."

On the following day, Taft addressed a meeting of the city's black population, a group that included most of the president's fellow Republicans living in the Gate City of the South. Some controversy preceded the inclusion of this event in Taft's itinerary. Two factions of the African-American community quarreled over the arrangements. One "harmony meeting" intended to work out these differences opened with an announcement by Bishop Wesley John Gaines of Big Bethel Church: "I have a message from the Chamber of Commerce to the colored people which says the colored people must not take any action as to place of entertaining Mr. Taft until they hear from the Chamber of Commerce." A group of persons associated with the black Republicans of the city objected to this and the meeting ended in a shouting match. The Republicans preferred that Taft appear in Turner's Tabernacle, a structure with four times the capacity of Big Bethel. A "delegation from the colored people" appealed to the Chamber committee that planned the presidential visit, requesting that Taft speak at Turner's Tabernacle, but the Chamber committee rejected their request and chose Big Bethel on the grounds that it was in a better state of repair. Black Atlanta ultimately bowed to the authority of the Chamber.[69]

Soon Taft returned to Washington to assume his new office, petty controversies ended, and the remains of 'possum dinners were cleared away. The Atlanta-based militia units now met to drill at the new facility situated at the corner of Courtland and Gilmer Streets, a block away from the "Negro dives" of Decatur Street. The memory of the violence of 1906 that had moved the city's leaders to implement the Auditorium-Armory plans vanished from public sight like a wisp of smoke from an extinguished fire.[70]

Up to this point most of the major controversies in which Asa Candler played a part—such as the response to the violence of 1906 or the struggles over charter revision—took place entirely within the arena of public policy. Only rarely did the participants raise issues of moral reform. Given this context, Asa Candler would seem to be the perfect representative of Atlanta's business elite. However, Candler's intensely religious upbringing had instilled in him a sense of moral responsibility that left him unable to accept policies in conflict with these beliefs. He never hesitated to make his opinions known and to advocate what he saw as the right, even when faced with powerful opposition. The principles of Candler's Christianity informed his judgments, and his conviction of the truth of these large principles tended, for him, to confer an unshakable sense of the righteousness of his various individual decisions. The strength of his beliefs would become evident in the years between 1912 and 1915, when Asa Candler came to differ with much of Atlanta's business and political elite in a few dramatic ways.

[1]Some examples of treatments of Atlanta's elite include: David F. Bonislawski, "Business Leadership in Atlanta During World War I," (Master's thesis, Georgia State University, 1984); Deaton, "Atlanta During the Progressive Era"; Doyle, *New Men, New Cities, New South*; Garofalo, "Business Ideas in Atlanta"; and a classic study of Atlanta in the 1950s, Floyd Hunter, *Community Power Structure: A Study of Decision Makers* (Chapel Hill: The University of North Carolina Press, 1953). Although Hunter protected his informants with pseudonyms and called their community "Regional City," the fact that he studied Atlanta is now generally known.

[2]See Garofalo, "Business Ideas," 29-32, for a discussion of these three major clubs as well as several other important social organizations in Atlanta.

[3]Atlanta Chamber of Commerce, Minutes of the Board of Directors, 1890-1903; Cooper, *Fulton County*, 353. Extensive discussion of the Chamber may be found in Doyle, *New Men, New Cities, New South*, 139-144 and in Deaton, "Atlanta During the Progressive Era," 99-102. See also, Candler, *Asa Griggs Candler*, 89, 317-18. Charles Howard Candler's memoir of his father's life, however, overstates Candler's role in the nineteenth-century Chamber: "Asa G. Candler had been one of the founders of the predecessor of the present Atlanta Chamber of Commerce in 1883." (p. 89) Atlanta's original Chamber, organized in 1860, was followed by a series of related groups formed and disbanded throughout the seventies and early eighties. A Chamber of Commerce formed in 1871; in 1883 it reorganized and expanded its membership as part of an effort to acquire funds for the construction of its own building. If Candler joined the Chamber at this point in its existence, he was a "founder" only of the reorganized Chamber and one of about two hundred Atlanta businessmen who contributed a $100 initiation fee to fund the construction of a four-story brick building at the corner of Pryor and Hunter streets.

[4]Atlanta Chamber of Commerce, Minutes of the Board of Directors and Minutes and Reports of various committees, 1904-1908. As a member of the 1904 Committee on Manufactures, he organized local arrangements for the Atlanta meeting of the National Association of Manufacturers scheduled to be held the following year. Perhaps in recognition of his services to the organization or perhaps because of his increasing prominence on the Atlanta economic stage, the Chamber elected him to serve on its board of directors in 1905. For more than a decade after this date he held important offices and committee posts including the presidency of the Chamber.

[5]According to Walter G. Cooper, "Seventh Chapter in History of Atlanta Chamber of Commerce—Asa G Candler's Administration," *City Builder*, 16, the original proposal had been made at an unspecified earlier time by Dr. T. D. Longino; it received new support from Harry L.

Schlesinger and other persons who hoped that a program of public works might provide employment to persons suffering the effects of the panic of 1907.

[6]"Report of the Bond Committee," [1908], in Minutes of the Board of Directors, Atlanta Chamber of Commerce. See Candler, *Asa Griggs Candler*, 89, 317-18 for a detailed discussion of this bond issue.

[7]AGC form letter to Chamber of Commerce members, 29 August 1909, in Minutes of the Board of Directors, Atlanta Chamber of Commerce.

[8]AGC, "President's Address" in "Annual Report of the Atlanta Chamber of Commerce...." 7 January 1909, fol. 2, box 2, AGC papers, Emory.

[9]Stuart Galishoff, "Germs Know No Color Line: Black Health and Public Policy in Atlanta, 1900-1918," *Journal of the History of Medicine and Allied Sciences* (January 1985): 33-39; Stuart Galishoff, "Atlanta's Water supply, 1865-1918" *The Maryland Historian* (Spring 1977): 16-18.

[10] AGC form letter to Chamber of Commerce members, 29 August 1909, in Minutes of the Board of Directors, Atlanta Chamber of Commerce.

[11]Various campaign materials are found in the January and February pages of the Minutes of the Board of Directors, Atlanta Chamber of Commerce.

[12]Galishoff, "Germs...," 38-39; in addition to the support of the mainstream press, positive comment included: "Only He That Rules Justly Has the Right to Rule," *Atlanta Independent*, 14 March 1908, 4; "Racial Prejudice Much Responsible For Death Rate in the City," 25 July 1908, 4; "Vote for the Bond Issue" *Journal of Labor*, 14 August 1908, 4.

[13]Deaton, "Atlanta During the Progressive Era," 103-104. Substantially the same account is in Deaton, "The Chamber of Commerce in the Economic and Political Development of Atlanta from 1900 to 1916, *Atlanta Historical Bulletin*, 19/3 (1975): 24. See also, Cooper, *Official History of Fulton County*, 362, which asserts that these measures lowered the city's mortality rate "within a few years." Deaton, in "The Chamber of Commerce in the Economic and Political Development of Atlanta from 1900 to 1916," discusses the Chamber as a political force in Atlanta.

[14]Willie Miller Bolden, "The Political Structure of Charter Revision Movements in Atlanta During the Progressive Era," (Ph.D. diss., Emory University, 1978) *passim*, treats in detail the various issues, factions, and personalities in the charter revision campaigns of 1901–1903, 1911, and 1913. In a series of appendices, Bolden includes lists of the membership of every committee organized to promote some aspect of the revisions; Asa Candler's name appears on committees both in 1908, 1909, and 1911.

[15]Onezima de Bouchel to AGC, 23 November 1919, see Appendix. The de Bouchel letter makes reference to an earlier Candler letter, in which he called suffragists as "them things." De Bouchel responded that all progressive women were suffragists. The Candler-de Bouchel association receives full attention in the final chapter below.

[16]AGC, "Pegs and Holes" manuscript of speech at Martha Berry School, 30 April 1918, fol. 26, box 2, AGC papers, Emory.

[17]AGC, "Home!" manuscript of speech [internal evidence dates it during US involvement in WW I], fol. 29, box 2, AGC papers, Emory. Bishop Warren Candler's public utterances can illuminate the views of his brother, since Asa regularly looked to Warren for advice; Asa probably thought, as Warren did, that "both reason and revelation alike teach us that the father is the head of the house." [WAC, "Enemies of the Home," fol. 31, box 85, WAC papers, Emory.] Furthermore, "No career offers a woman such an honorable and useful position as that of being the queen of a Christian home." [WAC, "Keepers of the Home and Home Keepers, fol. 25, box 87, WAC papers, Emory.]

[18]"Coca-Cola," *Journal of Labor*, 7 February 1908, 3; "Coca-Cola," *Journal of Labor*, 14 February 1908, 1; "Coca Cola—Its Great Bottling Works," *Journal of Labor*, 31 July 1908, 8. Coca-Cola advertised regularly in this newspaper.

[19]Candler, *Asa Griggs Candler*, 167-170; AGC to CHC, 14 August 1899, box 1, AGC papers, Emory; J. J. Willard, "The Early History of Coca-Cola as I Know It," part 5, in *The Coca-Cola Bottler*, (May 1930): 45; Irvin G. Wyllie, *The Self Made Man in America: the Myth of Rags to Riches*, (New Brunswick NJ: Rutgers University Press, 1954) 68-69.

[20]Alton DuMar Jones, "The Child Labor Reform Movement in Georgia," *Georgia Historical Quarterly* 48 (1965): 401; "Child Labor and Social Progress: Proceedings of the Fourth Annual Meeting of the National Child Labor Committee," supplement to *Annals of the American Academy of Political and Social Science*, no. 22 (July 1908) (1908; reprint, New York: Kraus Reprint Co., 1970) passim [cited below as "Child Labor Proceedings"]; "Delegates Attend Child Labor Meet," *Atlanta Journal*, 2 April 1908, 9. The National Child Labor Committee, a subdivision of the American Academy of Political and Social Science, carried out its activities by means of state and local Child Labor Committees.

[21]Ibid., 405-406.

[22]"Banquet for Child Labor Delegates," *Atlanta Journal*, 3 April 1908, 16.

[23]Ibid.

[24]"For the Child Plea is Made," *Atlanta Constitution*, 3 April 1908, 7.

[25]"Child Labor Proceedings," 159.

[26]Jones, "The Child Labor Reform Movement in Georgia," 407; C. Vann Woodward, *Origins of the New South, 1877-1913*, vol. 4 of 4 vols. in *A History of the South*, Wendell Holmes Stephenson and E. Merton Coulter, eds., 1st ed. (Louisiana State University Press and The Littlefield Fund for Southern History of the University of Texas, 1951) 418; Elizabeth H. Davidson, *Child Labor Legislation in the Southern Textile States* (Chapel Hill: University of North Carolina Press, 1939) 204-205. Jones and Woodward characterize Candler as a "capitalist;" Davidson commented, "The speech was open to more than one interpretation. The committee chose to interpret it as subtle humor." Another mangled fragment of the "original and convincing" after-dinner talk, preserved in the *Atlanta Georgian*, 1 April 1908, 12, reads, "The most valuable asset of our country is the children, and recognizing that the country abounds in children."

[27]"Child labor Proceedings," 159.

[28]Microfilm copies of manuscript census returns, Hart County, 1900, 220-222, US Bureau of Census, Federal Records Center, Atlanta.

[29]Doyle, *New Men*, 261-62; Deaton, "Atlanta During the Progressive Era," 186-87. Hoke Smith on p. 170.

[30]"The Chinese Laundry" *Journal of Labor*, 12 February 1915, 4; "More of the Chinese Laundries" *Journal of Labor*, 26 March 1915, 5; "Labor Problem Takes a New Turn" *Atlanta Independent*, 3 November 1906, 4. Both papers denounced foreign workers who had entered the American job market. In one interesting exception to this pervasive race prejudice, Benjamin Davis's *Independent* (6 April 1918, 4) praised "the great example of the little Japs" who had acquired "high, modern civilization" in just sixty years. No single newspaper can speak for an entire race, but Davis's paper is a particularly limited source of information on the opinions of Atlanta's African-American community during the progressive period. Davis supported Booker T. Washington and his approach to the place of the Negro in American life; he violently rejected W. E. B. Du Bois and those who agreed with him. [See "Washington and Du Bois, the Products of Different Educational Processes, 23 November 1908, 4; and an untitled discussion of *The Crisis*, an NAACP publication, 15 February 1913, 1.] Davis did, however, condemn the most bla-

tant racial injustices of his day, such as lynching, unfair wage scales, poor schools, and the white primary. However, the *Independent* spent most of its column inches on the internal politics of the various fraternal organizations, particularly the Odd Fellows, which obsessed its editor. Aside from his propensity to portray his opponents as speaking an illiterate dialect, his willingness to call them "coons," and his editorials on the "Lack of Character" of many blacks (30 May 1908) the fact that the *Independent*'s advertising revenue came almost entirely from white sources casts a shadow over this paper's reputation. [See "Misunderstandings Always Cause Confusion and Friction," 14 November 1908, 4.]

[31]"Lynching Does Not Prevent Rape" [editorial], *Atlanta Independent*, 25 August 1906, 4, probably written by Benjamin Davis, the chief editor of the paper.

[32]For examples, see "Is the South a Sinner Above All Others?" folder 18, box 87; "Lynchings and the Like," folder 34, box 90; "Lynchings in the South and Murders in the North," folder 35, box 90, all in WAC papers, Emory.

[33]"Southern Whites and Southern Blacks," fol. 31, box 94, WAC papers, Emory. This essay also includes an apology for lynching along the lines discussed above.

[34]Horace Calvin Wingo, "Race Relations in Georgia, 1872-1908," (Ph.D. diss., University of Georgia, 1969) 191-98; for examples of the attitudes discussed here, see WAC, "White Man's Church," manuscript, fol. 8, box 96; and "'The Colored Troops Fought Nobly,'" fol. 13, box 85, both in WAC papers, Emory.

[35]"Asa Candler Addresses Negro Mass Meeting," *Atlanta Constitution*, 11 September 1916, 7.

[36]Wingo, "Race Relations," 150, 191; Bauman, 43-44.

[37]"Let Us Admit Our Inferiority" *Atlanta Independent*, 20 October 1906, 4.

[38]Ibid.

[39]WAC, "Robert Hammond" in "Reminiscences of Emory, Dictated 1938-39," typed manuscript, fol. 22, box 93, WAC papers, Emory; AGC to Miss Lucy Beall Candler, 20 March [?], The Archives, The Coca-Cola Company; Candler, *Asa G. Candler*, 110.

[40]Bauman, *Warren Akin Candler*, 72-74; John E. Talmadge, *Rebecca Latimer Felton: Nine Stormy Decades* (Athens: University of Georgia Press, 1960) 109-110.

[41]Henry Y. Warnock, "Andrew Sledd, Southern Methodists, and the Negro: A Case History" *Journal of Southern History* 31/3 (August 1865): 251-271. The letter to Bishop Candler is cited on p. 262. In spite of these difficult events, Sledd received a loan from "Uncle Asa" when his finances became hopelessly tangled; see the previous chapter.

[42]Among the more useful accounts of the rioting are: Deaton, "Atlanta During the Progressive Era," 187-203; Dittmer, *Black Georgia in the Progressive Era*, 123-31; Gregory Lamont Mixon, "The Atlanta Riot of 1906" (Ph.D. diss., University of Cincinnati, 1989); and Charles Crowe, "Racial Violence and Social Reform—origins of the Atlanta Riot of 1906," *Journal of Negro History* 53 (July 1968): 234-56. Glen Weddington Rainey, "The Race Riot of 1906 in Atlanta,"(M.A. thesis, Emory University, 1929) is tainted by the racial presumptions of its author and must be consulted with caution.

[43]For example, see "2,455 Negroes in Barrooms in Decatur St." *Atlanta Georgian*, 18 September 1906, 1; "Negro Clubs the Cause of Assaults?" *Atlanta Georgian*, 22 September 1906, 1; "Let Us Be Practical" [editorial], and "The 2,500 Negroes in Barrooms Saturday Night" [commentary], *Atlanta Independent*, 22 September 1906, 4.

[44]"Exterior View of Typical Decatur Street Dive" [photo feature], and "Decatur Street Was Undismayed until 9 O'Clock when Threatened Riot Cleared the Whole Street," *Atlanta Journal*, 23 September 1906, 1 and 2. Other examples are found in the *Atlanta Georgian* for the same period.

[45]In addition to the longer accounts listed in note 42, the following account of the riot synthesizes material from the following sources: Eye-witness accounts include: Thomas Gibson, "The Anti-Negro Riots in Atlanta," *Harper's Weekly* (13 October 1906): 1457-59; John Temple Graves, "The Tragedy at Atlanta, from the Point of View of the Whites," and W. E. Burghardt Du Bois, "The Tragedy at Atlanta, from the Point of View of the Negroes," *The World To-Day*, (November 1906): 1169-1174; and newspaper accounts, 23-29 September 1906 in the *Constitution, Journal*, and *Georgian*; the latter featured particularly lurid "evidence" of "outrages" in its many Saturday street editions.

[46]"Peters Street Raided by Mob After Negroes; Many Volleys Are Fired," *Atlanta Journal*, 24 September 1906, 1. Although the account breaks off with the wounded man guarded by a policeman while waiting for medical assistance. Evidently the man died; the subhead introducing this item reads, "Tore Negro to Death."

[47]Minutes of the Atlanta City Council, vol. 21, Records of the City of Atlanta on deposit at the Atlanta History Center Library/Archives.

[48]For example, see Dittmer, *Black Georgia*, 128-29; "Officer Heard Killed; Four Others Hurt in Brownsville Raid," and "Town of Brownsville Is Taken By Militia," *Atlanta Journal*, 25 September 1906, 3.

[49]Atlanta Chamber of Commerce, "Law and Order Meeting," 25 September 1906, Minutes of the Board of Directors, Atlanta Chamber of Commerce; "Closing of Low Dives Urged by Citizens," *Atlanta Journal*, 25 September 1906, 1; "Citizens in Mass Meeting Condemn Mob Law and Favor Punishment of the Rioters," *Atlanta Journal*, 26 September 1906, 2; "The Men who Made and Make Atlanta Speak—All is Peace and Business Resumed," *Atlanta Independent*, 29 September 1906, 1.

[50]"Closing of Low Dives Urged by Citizens," *Atlanta Journal*, 25 September 1906, 1.

[51]Ibid.

[52]Atlanta Chamber of Commerce, "Law and Order Meeting," 25 September 1906, Minutes of the Board of Directors, Atlanta Chamber of Commerce.

[53]"The Men who Made and Make Atlanta Speak—All is Peace and Business Resumed," *Atlanta Independent*, 29 September 1906, 1.

[54][editorial], *Atlanta Constitution*, 26 September 1906, quoted in Garrett, *Atlanta and Environs*, 2 vols., 2: 503.

[55]The black-owned *Independent*, although it also identified "dives" as the underlying source of the disorders did assert that rape is not a "race crime." See "Let Us Strike at the Root," *Atlanta Independent*, 29 September 1906, 4. Unfortunately the latter point lies buried on a page filled with denunciations of vice and admonitions that Negroes should comply with the law and perform their duties. Furthermore, an editorial advises "Let us keep cool and convince the white man by our demeanor that we are not the only barbarians in the city." The editorial also testifies to the good character of most whites as contrasted to those in the mob, while another item on the page characterizes the "dives" of Decatur Street as "owned and operated by dagoes." One can only wonder what proportion of the African-American community shared such self-defeating notions.

[56]"Facts About Riot Told by Committee," *Atlanta Independent*, 5 January 1907, 8. The committee also concluded that two white and ten "colored" persons had died as a result of the riot. The report added, "Wild rumors of a larger number killed have no foundation that we can discover. As the city was paying the funeral expenses of victims, and relief was given their families, they had every motive to make known their loss." Nonetheless, the statistic continues to be the subject of dispute. For example, W. E. B. Du Bois (who was out of the city at the time of the riot) claimed that at least a hundred persons died. See Dittmer, *Black Georgia*, 129-30.

[57]"Christian League Formed to Solve the Race Problem," *Atlanta Constitution*, 22 November 1906, clipping in "1906 Riot" subject file, Special Collections Department, Woodruff Library, Atlanta University Center.

[58]"Civic League Planned by Committee of Ten," *Atlanta Constitution*, 30 November 1906, clipping in "Atlanta Riot" subject file, Special Collections Department, Woodruff Library, Atlanta University Center.

[59]"The 'Riot' in Atlanta and Reconstruction," *Atlanta Independent*, 15 December 1906, 6; "The Civic League and Its Scope and Purpose," *Atlanta Independent*, 19 January 1907, 4.

[60]Cooper, *Official History*, 355-56.

[61]"Big Armory Wanted in Atlanta," *Atlanta Journal*, 27 September 1906, 3.

[62]"Monthly Meeting of the Chamber of Commerce," 11 July 1905, Minutes of the Board of Directors, Records of the Atlanta Chamber of Commerce, Atlanta, Georgia; Cooper, "Fifth Chapter in the History of the Atlanta Chamber of Commerce—Sam D. Jones' Administration," *City Builder* (April 1929): 16, 33; Cooper, "Sixth Chapter…J. Wylie Pope's Administration," *City Builder* (May 1929): 16.

[63]"Around Banquet Board Brains and Money are Pledged," *Atlanta Journal*, 29 November 1905, 1; "25 Representative Citizens Are Named to Provide Ways and Means for Great Atlanta Exposition," *Atlanta Journal*, 6 December 1905, 1; "Committee Will Plan for Big Auditorium," *Atlanta Journal*, 7 October 1906, 9; "Auditorium and Armory Favored by Committee," *Atlanta Journal*, 9 October 1906; "Plans Perfected for Auditorium Building," *Atlanta Journal*, 12 October 1906, 3. At the first meeting the suggestion arose that $350,000 previously subscribed for another Chamber project, a commercial exhibition scheduled for 1910, might be diverted to the Auditorium-Armory project.

[64]"Plan Is Adopted to Finance Auditorium," *Atlanta Journal*, 18 October 1906, 1.

[65]Ibid.; Minutes of the Atlanta City Council, vol. 21, Records of the City of Atlanta on deposit at the Atlanta History Center Library/Archives; Minutes of the Board of Directors, Auditorium Armory Committee Records, *passim*, Records of the Atlanta Chamber of Commerce, Atlanta, Georgia.

[66]Auditorium Armory Committee Records, *passim*, in Minutes of the Board of Directors, Records of the Atlanta Chamber of Commerce, Atlanta, Georgia. These records include lists of stockholders and bond purchases and correspondence concerning the sale of the larger part of the bonds to Fidelity Mutual Life Insurance Company of Philadelphia.

[67]Cooper, *Official History of Fulton County*, *passim*: 356-364; Walter G. Cooper, "Seventh Chapter in History of Atlanta Chamber of Commerce—Asa G. Candler's Administration," *City Builder* (June 1920): 32, 41; "Magnificent Auditorium-Armory for the City of Atlanta Will Cost $250,000, Seat 8,500, and House Ten Companies," *Atlanta Constitution*, 23 June 1907, 3.

[68]Minutes of the Board of Directors of the Atlanta Chamber of Commerce, Committee of Arrangements for Taft Banquet, 29, 30, and 31 December 1907, 1 and 2 January 1909, Records of the Atlanta Chamber of Commerce, Atlanta, Georgia. On 2 January, "Mr. C. E. Claverly, Chairman of the 'Possum Committee, reported that 100 fat 'possums had been tendered free of charge by Hon. Frank Park of Sylvester…."

[69]"The Arrogance and Naked Impudence of Downright Ignorance," *Atlanta Independent*, 9 January 1909, 4; "Atlanta Negroes at War over Taft's Entertainment," *Atlanta Constitution*, reprinted in *Atlanta Independent*, 9 January 1909, 4; Minutes of the Board of Directors, Minutes of Committee of Arrangements for Taft Banquet, 30 December 1908 and 1 January 1909, Atlanta Chamber of Commerce. The *Independent's* description (almost certainly written by its editor, B. J. Davis) of the "harmony meeting" may not be entirely accurate, since Davis was

"Howard's Old Stand" on Peachtree Street
Candler is probably third from the left.

Bishop Warren Candler was his brother Asa's closest advisor.

Mrs. Candler (far right) visited the New York City offices of Coca-Cola.

From its earliest days Coca-Cola advertised heavily.

DE-LEC-TA-LAVE

MAKES TEETH══════

══════WHITE AS SNOW.

A FEW IMPORTANT QUESTIONS ASKED AND ANSWERED.

1—What will whiten my teeth? Delectalave.
2—What will clense my mouth? Delectalave.
3—What will harden and beautify my gums? Delectalave.
4—What will purify my breath? Delectalave.
5—What will aid me in preserving my teeth? Delectalave.
6—What will prevent the formation of tartar? Delectalave.
7—What will neutralize any acidity of the saliva? Delectalave.
8—What will cure tender and bleeding gums? Delectalave.

Dr. Calhoun Indorses Delectalave

ATLANTA, GA., October 17, 1885.

DR. C. T. BROCKETT:

My Dear Sir—It affords me pleasure after a careful examination of the formula of your Delectalave, to bear testimony to its value, and to state that its curative qualities are beyond question. I regard it as the name implies a delightful wash, and can confidently recommend it to the public.

Yours truly, A. W. CALHOUN, M. D.

If your Teeth you wish to save,
Use DELECTALAVE.

ASA G. CANDLER & CO., GEN'L AGENTS,

47 PEACHTREE STREET,

ATLANTA, GA

Price 50 cts. per bottle.
Sold by Druggists.

Before Coca-Cola, Asa Candler dealt in a variety of patent medicine and toiletries.

A skilled rider, Candler (center) was a member of the Governor's Horse Guard.

CHAPTER EIGHT

Moralist

An attitude of moral elitism marked Asa Candler and his brothers, a sense that they knew what was best for everyone around them. This sense of entitlement sprang from a belief in the superiority of their Anglo-Saxon ancestry and their protestant religion. Bishop Candler claimed the superior quality, not merely for the white race, but for the protestant, Anglo-Saxon element within it. He wrote that England's imperial success derived from the influence of Protestants such as John Wesley: "...when England and France were struggling for supremacy in the eighteenth century, it was a contest between Wesley and Voltaire—and Voltaire lost."[1] His brother Asa asserted that Christianity would bestow success on the believer: "the Americans are richer than the Chinese because the Chinese are pagans."[2] By Christianity, he meant only its protestant segment; "Romanism" was barely better than paganism in the Candlers' estimate. Asa held up South America as a negative example of "what Romanism can do in the matter of nation-building."[3]

The Candlers also rejected the newer trends in Protestant theology. The movement known as the "social gospel," which resulted from the influence of modern social reform ideas on Christian thought, was anathema to both Candler and his brother, the bishop. Indeed, all of the newer theological interpretations fell beyond the pale. "Our Only Hope Is That Which Has Been Our Security in the Past," the title of one of Bishop Candler's essays on the value of evangelical Christianity, neatly summarizes the Candler brothers philosophy.[4]

If no other faith could compare to protestant Christianity in Asa Candler's mind, it is only fair to note that he seemed less denigrating of Judaism than of the others. In part, this reflects the attitudes of his class and time. Although anti-Semitism is hardly unknown in the South, it has never been a central feature of southern culture. Atlanta newspapers, for example, usually treated news of Jewish cultural and religious activities respectfully.[5] Candler vetoed a proposal for restrictive covenants against Jews in Druid Hills, and, as mayor, he spoke at a meeting of Atlanta's Jewish citizens that celebrated the British government's promise to support a Jewish homeland in Palestine. His brother John had a Jewish law partner. The notorious case of Leo Frank might offer further insight into Asa Candler's opinion of Jews, but unfortunately, no such direct evidence of his views has emerged.[6]

As a man who tried to place himself on the side of morality, Candler occasionally found that he agreed with the urban social reformers of his day who called themselves "progressives." However, Candler preferred to invoke old-time traditional values. In a speech that condemned "communistic ideas" on one hand and "corporate greed" on the other, he also warned against "pseudo-progress" that might lead to departures from "well-established principles of righteousness and fair-dealing."[7] In the final analysis, Candler believed that good works should be carried out in the hopes of gaining the world to come, not to improve this present world. He said, "The way in which one uses his talents here is an index to character and a forecast of eternal destiny."[8]

Convinced that he belonged to a superior race, and that within that race, his ethnic and religious connections conferred additional high status, Candler believed that God had attached serious responsibilities to his honored position. These he dutifully sought to fulfill.

He wanted to sustain an orderly society. To trample on social order verged on blasphemy because God had arranged human society: "Every human life is made to fit some place, and there is a place for every life. The lives and the places…are made for each other that they may serve the purposes of the God who made them."[9]

In Asa Candler's view, city life tended to foster not only disorderly conduct but downright indecent behavior. Although the large population of a city gives it "influence and carrying power," individuals may find that life in the urban crowd also can "enfeeble the power of individual conviction." He told a rural Sunday school meeting that cities needed continual infusions of country folk if they were to thrive. In his view, the rural upbringing of most of Atlanta's leaders in business and the professions accounted for the city's unusually high standard of morals. However, in spite of this good influence, his city still was at risk: "Wherein Atlanta's standard of life has been lowered, it has been [lowered by] the breaking away from the sweet and wholesome influences of rural christianity and the imbibing of mephitic influences of urban expediency." Men such as himself, he believed, had the responsibility to defend Atlanta against the "mephitic influences" eating away at its moral center.[10]

He felt a duty as a Christian steward and civic leader not only to advocate order, but also to act as a moral guide to his community, and he had no misgivings about using government authority to impose moral discipline on the public. According to the records of the regular Chamber of Commerce director's meeting of September 1908, "President Candler stated that in his opinion the failure to enforce the prohibition law had brought about a deplorable state of affairs…." He wanted the chamber to act, "in the interest of law and order." After discussion, the directors voted to endorse the platform of the "Good Government League," which hoped to produce such reforms.[11]

Some Atlantans shared Candler's standards of public morality, but of course, some did not. Mayor James L. Woodward, a regular—and often successful—candidate in various Atlanta elections since the mid-nineties, seems almost a mirror image of Candler's respectable moralism. Woodward was not, however, a cardboard villain, but rather a refreshingly human individual who often found himself at odds with the ostentatiously virtuous element of the city's leadership. He began his career as a printer and a trade-union member and then entered politics. He presented himself as a working man's candidate and received strong labor support. He was first elected Mayor of Atlanta for the 1899-1900 term. When again eligible for office in 1904 he benefited from a five-man race that resulted in his election by a 168-vote plurality. His overjoyed supporters carried him through the streets on their shoulders; the *Journal of Labor* savored the fact that "a man with a [union] card in his pocket" would soon address the National Association of Manufacturers meeting in Atlanta.[12] As a blue-collar candidate Woodward represented a mild challenge to the established elite, in which business and professional interests dominated. However, even though he did continue to speak on behalf of the interests of labor, Woodward was by no means radical. He forged an alliance with one of the city's most powerful capitalists, H. M. Atkinson, president of the Georgia Electric Company, and generally cooperated with the city's business leaders.[13]

A perennial candidate, Woodward again won the mayoral contest in the Democratic primary of 1908. As the Democratic nominee in a virtually one-party state, he certainly should have taken the general election in December. However, events did not follow expectations. Late in November, Woodward was arrested for public intoxication. Nor was this the first time he had suffered this sort of embarrassment. In the previous year, his supporters at the *Journal of Labor* accepted the fact that he "may have his faults" and "weaknesses" and may have "made mistakes," but they asked, "Who of us are infallible?"[14] Unfortunately for Woodward, his moment of weakness had come at a critical moment in the electoral process, less than a month before the formality of the December general election, which would have made him officially the mayor of Atlanta. Although he claimed he had been drinking a rock-and-rye concoction to cure a cold, his transgression received wide condemnation. His troubles increased when additional accusations surfaced to the effect that his drinking had taken place on the premises of a disorderly house under the Washington Street viaduct. The situation offered an irresistible opportunity to those who might have opposed Woodward for purely political reasons, but Asa Candler, who had already expressed concern over the existence of drinking establishments in the city, also sincerely despised the mayor-elect's social habits. Under Candler's presidency, the Chamber of Commerce organized a mass meeting to protest Woodward's conduct. Following the pattern of such events, which well and truly demonstrate one technique by which Atlanta's elite could steer public opinion, the mass meeting selected a committee of twenty-five leading citizens—one of whom was Candler—to find a suitable challenger to oppose Woodward in the upcoming general election. The committee then nominated one of their own respectable sort, a banker named Robert F. Maddox.[15]

Asa Candler made the first donation—$600—to Maddox's campaign fund.[16] The campaign appealed to "the Voters of Atlanta": "A city should be as jealous of its good name and obligations as either man or woman. You cannot reflect upon its name without, in turn, injuriously affecting the interests of every man within its limits. When the pall of national criticism is cast upon a city, each citizen must feel it and carry his part of the misfortune."[17]

Woodward fought back by calling for the support of the laboring classes of the city. He accused Maddox's supporters of manipulating the election with money. A political broadside struck directly at Candler, suggesting that his receivership of the Neal Bank had unfairly benefited preferred creditors, one of whom was the banker, Maddox.[18] The flyer depicted Candler, clad in morning coat and striped trousers, perched on the roof of his namesake building, handing a bulging sack labeled "$40,000 (PREFERRED)" to the "BANKER CANDIDATE" Robert F. Maddox. While a regiment of well-dressed preferred creditors marched away with sacks of money, proclaiming, "We got ours!" Candler fended off the "9,000 NEAL BANK DEPOSITORS." To the appeal of a ragged widow and a weeping orphan, not to mention a Negro workman and other common folks, the plutocratic receiver replied, "Nothin doin."[19]

Woodward's appeal failed to move even his traditional support-ers. The editor of *Journal of Labor*, who had praised Woodward effusively at the time of the primary, could not bring himself to con-demn the errant candidate but neither could he support him. The paper advised each citizen to vote according to his personal princi-ples. The African-American *Independent*, which also had spoken kindly of "Jim" Woodward earlier in the year, at first urged toleration for Woodward, but on second thought gave its support to Maddox because its editor believed that his independent candidacy would weaken the grip of the Democratic white primary on local political life.[20] His newspaper printed photographs of the two candidates on its front page on the twenty-first of November: A crisply tailored and youthful Maddox struck a jaunty pose leaning on his tightly furled umbrella, while Woodward, with drooping moustache and advancing belly, wore a shapeless dark suit and straggly necktie. In spite of all Woodward could do, Maddox offered an acceptable alternative for the Atlanta voter. He won the election, and the ordinary citizenry of Atlanta seemed satisfied. The *Independent* claimed "The combination of money, corporation, white republicans, Negroes, and the press was too formidable for Uncle Jim....But the old man made a gallant fight." The *Journal of Labor* thought Maddox would make a good and impartial mayor and that no "classes" versus "masses" issues entered into the voting.[21]

Of course, Woodward was not the only consumer of alcohol in the city of Atlanta. To avoid anti-saloon laws, the more affluent Atlanta drinkers in the early decades of the century frequented pri-vate "locker clubs" that served drinks from separate bottles owned by each individual member. Others resorted to "blind tigers" that simply flouted the law. Nor was alcohol the city's only vice; Atlanta also had an active compliment of prostitutes. Decatur Street remained notori-ous; one small red-light district developed in the area of Mechanic and Hulsey streets, near the city incinerator; other areas and individ-ual locations contained houses of ill repute. Such conditions alarmed and outraged Atlanta's more moralistic citizens and moved some to action.

One such group of reformers, the Men and Religion Forward Committee, undertook a controversial campaign to uplift the moral condition of the city of Atlanta. The founders of the committee, inspired by attendance at a national "Men and Religion" conference in May 1911, determined to expose and eradicate the city's moral shortcomings. They received strong support from the city's evangelical Christian ministers, and Asa Candler became the ally of Atlanta's Men and Religion Forward group. He had known Marion Jackson and John Eagan, the Atlanta organizers, at least since 1906 when they had served with Candler on the executive committee of the Christian League that had been organized to "solve the race problems" that had created that year's riot. Under Jackson and Eagan, the Men and Religion committee attempted to marshal public opinion by publishing descriptions of Atlanta's vice conditions, using paid advertisements that appeared frequently although irregularly in the *Constitution.* The first of these, "The Houses in Our Midst," demonstrated their preoccupation with prostitution.[22] The Men and Religion crusaders condemned prostitution for the harm it brings to the community, speaking in veiled terms of spread of venereal disease: "The mother is asking God and man: 'Why is my child blind at his birth? Why is he a weakling physically and mentally?' The wife asks: 'Why is my body racked with pain—my health gone?' Cold Science without emotion answers, 'The Public Prostitute.'"[23]

Although they condemned prostitution, the Men and Religion Forward committee did not attack prostitutes. Their first bulletin declared, "None would hurt the pitiful inmates. Help in the name of Jesus Christ is offered those who will leave the life!" Rather, the men hoped to rescue the "fallen" women by exposing the conditions that led them to undertake their pathetic trade.[24] Seeking the underlying causes of the problem, they condemned the operators of the houses, the profiteering property owners who collected their rent, and the greedy employers who refused to pay a living wage to young female employees.

The latter theme repeatedly found expression in the newspaper bulletins and led the committee to offer some support to the laborers of Atlanta. They naively attempted to interject the principles of Christian forbearance into the conflicts between employers and employees. Although their efforts received praise from some representatives of both sides, all Atlantans did not share their optimism. At a mass meeting convened in the summer of 1914 at the Baptist Tabernacle, held with the aim of discussing the issues of a bitter strike against the Fulton Bag and Cotton mill, the representative of the Men and Religion group urged the application of Christian principles to labor problems. A working man in the audience declared that "We have been waiting for nineteen hundred years for Christ to solve our problems and they have yet to be solved; it is time for us to get busy ourselves."[25] Another sort of misunderstanding between the Men and Religion and the working people of Atlanta came from the effort to reform prostitutes. While the representatives of the unions accepted the premise that low wages might force a girl into a life of sin, they objected when the Men and Religion supplied two of these unfortunates with a rented house and a job in East Point. The women soon abandoned their new mill jobs and resumed their old trade in the new neighborhood. The *Journal of Labor* demanded to know by what right the reformers had put "these wayward women in contact with a helpless industrial class in the long chance of their honest reformation in one week's time."[26]

Men and Religion Forward also applied its passionate energies to the already ongoing struggle for the suppression of the liquor trade. Statewide, prohibition had its greatest support in rural areas, which saw the urban liquor trade as proof of their worst suspicions about city life. In town or country, the strongest opposition to alcohol came from religious sources, most particularly evangelical Protestants. Methodist clergy, including Warren Candler, regularly spoke out against drinking.[27] On the other hand, urban business leaders first tended to oppose prohibition as bad for business, and urban political leaders saw the taxes on the sale of alcohol as a reliable source of revenue. A smaller proportion of urban progressives and other reformers deplored the social evils they saw emanating from the use of alcohol. Eventually, elements of the nation's business elite began to perceive other dimensions of the question, as they sought to control the lives of their employees in order to make them more productive. Obviously, a hangover from a night of drinking might reduce efficiency on the job, but employers had other reservations about saloons, which became informal "working-man's clubs." If they offered amusement and comradeship, they also could provide an arena for the development of social solidarity and labor organizing activity. Anti-saloon agitation thus became a special category of the larger prohibition movement. This particular aspect of "reform" activity aimed at the saloons, but did not necessarily seek to prevent the use of alcohol entirely.

In spite of such ulterior motives among its advocates, the abstinence movement gained support. Atlanta's *Journal of Labor* agreed with the *Constitution* "Whiskey makes against efficiency," but countered that unions deserved credit for fostering sobriety. Georgia adopted a state prohibition law in 1907, but in the following year, the state allowed an exception. Locker clubs, where private individuals could store their own liquor for consumption in a social atmosphere, became legal. Only in 1915 did a special session of the legislature succeed in tightening the Georgia laws to establish "bone dry" as the rule. This law stood until the national amendment took its place.[28]

Although Asa Candler probably shared the concerns of the business progressives regarding the effects of alcohol on the productivity of workers and of saloons on their organized activity, his opposition to drink had its deepest roots in his religious beliefs. Regardless of the effects of alcohol on the productivity of the workers, he would have deplored its use. The Men and Religion Forward activists shared this view. They condemned locker clubs in a bulletin in July 1915, and complained that the police committee continued to issue licenses in spite of wholesale violations of the law. The bulletins reported that these clubs sold whiskey at forty cents the half-pint; they challenged the mayor and council to enforce the laws. Further scandalizing the city, the moral reformers charged that their investigations showed that many respectable "Christian men" had at least indirect interests in the town's bordellos, because they owned the properties where the disorderly boarding houses were located and they collected rent from them.[29]

In their opposition to prostitution and the sale of liquor, the Men and Religion Forward committee found a ready ally in Chief of Police James L. Beavers, who took office in August 1911. However, the Men and Religion canvassed the red-light districts offering to aid women who wanted to reform their lives, Beavers gave the women five days to vacate. He then attacked all the disorderly boarding houses with "flying squads" of Atlanta police. Those women who did not choose to accept the offer of the reformers or take the chief's threats found themselves in jail. The operators of the "blind tigers" received similar treatment.[30]

Backed by the Men and Religion movement, Beavers continued to defend public morality. Police kept former prostitutes under surveillance. They closed locker clubs and arrested lovers who became publicly amorous. Many Atlantans approved of the morality campaign, but others had doubts because some people believed that Beavers activity damaged the city's public image. Members of the Men and Religion committee, having received information that Beavers would "get the ax" on this account, set out to protect him. In the mayoral election of 1912, they asked for statements of support from the two candidates. One candidate, Aldine Chambers, flatly refused. However, the perennial James Woodward had, in the years between 1908 and 1912, managed to restore his blasted reputation and was back in the game. Woodward was too canny a politician to say "no" outright, so the Men and Religion found themselves awkwardly leaning toward the old sinner. However, all possibility of the reformers support for Woodward evaporated after it became clear that he planned to establish a segregated red-light district, a tactic that he considered to be more realistic than an attempt to wipe out all vestiges of vice. Chambers, somewhat belatedly, issued a statement opposing segregated vice, but was too late. Woodward, who campaigned with the delightfully ambiguous slogan "The Man Who Does Things," once again sat in the mayor's office.[31]

The temperaments of the new mayor and the chief of police could hardly have been more different. Woodward attempted to work with Beavers for a short time, but in the end, he attempted to curb Chief Beavers' zeal for reform. The relentless "flying squads" had alarmed not only the patrons of disorderly establishments, but also began to distress elements of the commercial elite who felt increasing resentment against actions that caused the city to be seen as "a hot bed of thievery and thuggery." James English, an important brick manufacturer, supported a plan for a regulated red-light district, and favored locker clubs and gambling at the Southeastern Fair. Furthermore, his position as a member of the police board made him a dangerous opponent. Of course, the Men and Religion condemned the idea of segregated vice and published impassioned bulletins to that effect.[32]

Meanwhile, ordinary crime in the city increased. The chief's opponents charged that he needed to give more attention to this problem. In 1913, Beavers did order the force to concentrate on the more serious offenses, and the total number of arrests dropped off while the proportion of felony arrests increased dramatically. Unfortunately for the chief, the crime rate continued to climb, and the criticism continued unabated.[33] Meanwhile, the shrill cries of the Men and Religion continued. Their bulletins insulted by name prominent persons and their associations:

> More than 15% of a million dollars, or $154,712.14, is the gross profit for the year shown to have been made in liquor dealing by nine of the clubs licensed by Council... THE CAPITAL CITY CLUB [earned] a gross profit of $21,218.30 from the liquor business. Mr. Edwin Johnson, a member of the Board of Governors of the Capital City Club, is Chairman of the Police Committee.... Mr. E. H.Inman is President of the Capital City Club. He is also a member of the Council.[34]

The bulletin accused the Athletic Club of soliciting written liquor purchase orders from its membership, implying an intention to falsify records. It also attacked by name all members of the council who voted to repeal an ordinance requiring clubs to reveal their business methods. The bulletin vilified those who voted to reinstate any club that had lost a license, and those who voted to permit the sale of 3.999 alcohol in the city.[35]

At the outset, those who opposed the Men and Religion campaign had been understandably reticent, lest they be seen a supporters of illicit behavior. However, the African-American *Independent* offered the interesting argument that the cooperation between Beavers and the Men and Religion movement, coupled with the movement's increasingly political outspokenness, resulted in an unconstitutional mixture of church and state.[36] As time went by, other objections began to be heard. Opponents of the clean up complained that Atlanta had become "a damn unpleasant town," and again raised the complaint that national publicity brought by Beavers activity damaged the city's reputation.[37]

In response to the growing outcry against Beavers, the police board appointed a special investigating committee to look into his actions. While this ninety-day probe continued, Beavers also kept up his usual pursuit of sin and sinners. When directly ordered to reduce his numerous vice charges, Beavers began closing the clubs on the grounds of other violations. The reformers held a mass meeting in July 1915, calling for an end to the locker clubs, but the council ignored their demands. At the end of the month, the police board received the report of the investigating committee, and formally charged Beavers with gross inefficiency and incompetence. Among the specific charges, the board alleged that Beavers "failed to suppress a vast number of felonies," had lost the confidence of his men, and accepted policy advice from private citizens while disregarding the authority of the police board.[38]

Although this list of charges begins with accusations of mismanagement, the great weight of the document goes to Beavers failure to follow the policies of the constituted authority while accepting advice from individuals outside the chain of command. The moral-reform campaign had failed to show proper deference for those in power, and the city's elite had struck back smartly. Another sign of the reform movement's loss of favor came now when the *Constitution* announced that it had stopped accepting the Men and Religion bulletins for publication. Judge Jesse Wood, who had been clerk for the council during the trial, when interviewed more than forty years after the event, declared that the charges against Beavers were trumped up because he had offended powerful interests.[39]

Responding to the charges, Beavers displayed his self-righteous and politically intemperate manner: "It is appalling to contemplate that a chief of police who unflinchingly fights vice and crime where ever it shows its head should lose his head at the demands of the beneficiaries of this same vice and crime." He charged that an unnamed, powerful individual on the police board had "close relations to those interested in the closed [prostitution] district," and he singled out Mayor Woodward as catering to "the vicious and criminal through personal tastes and for political reasons. My overthrow is a political triumph for him." Beavers presented himself as the champion of law and order, "I expect those who are opposed to these things to be against me. I welcome their opposition from whatever source it may come."[40]

When he received a preliminary hearing, Beavers accused members of the police board of illegal liquor purchases, insulted the board generally, and declared his own innocence of any wrongdoing. When James English called him a "bull in a china shop," Beavers retorted, "You're as much an old bully as I am!" The exchange becomes more personal and insulting until English had to be prevented from physically attacking Beavers. The board suspended the chief and ordered him to appear before them for a trial.[41]

The crusading police chief's trial began on the last day of July. The crowded hearing room echoed with the mutual denunciations of pro- and anti-Beavers factions. At times, testimony could not be heard over the tumult. The Chief attempted to interject charges of governmental corruption into the trial, while his opponents pressed the original charges against him. Violence erupted when Beavers's lawyer, James Key, assaulted a newspaper reporter who had criticized his client in print. Near the end of the trial, when order finally prevailed, Beavers was able to control himself and testify calmly: "All I ask is justice."[42] The police board demoted Atlanta's guardian of public virtue to captain, and he resigned, vowing to fight for his job. He wrote to the Board of Police Commissioners: "I am advised by the newspapers that I have been removed as Chief of Police, and have been made a Captain." Stating that he refused the new position, he declared, "I am not willing to consent to a reversal of the moral policies of the City at the price of a Captain's job. I did not do it for a Chief's job."[43]

To defend Beavers position, the Men and Religion and several city ministers began a campaign to seek the recall of Mayor Woodward and the seven police board members who pushed Beavers out. A series of advertisements in the *Journal of Labor* demanded the recall of the mayor and commissioners, continued the defense of Beavers, and condemned ward politics and "Woodwardism." Several quoted Asa Candler's statement, "To approve the removal of James L. Beavers would be to penalize virtue and eulogize vice."[44]

Defending the mayor and police board, anti-recallers used newspaper advertisements to present "Some Facts Against the Recall." Working from a headquarters (complete with a bank of telephones) at the Chamber of Commerce, the recall opponents included James English, whose advocacy of a red-light district, locker clubs, and gambling cast him as the arch-villain in the eyes of the pro-Beavers recallers. Those who sided with English and Woodward repeated the argument that support of Beavers actions implied that Atlanta was a vice-ridden city in need of reform. To them, opposition to Beavers and the recallers was defense of the city's honor.[45]

Clearly, feelings ran high, but the city had not divided predictably along traditional lines. In spite of the long association between Mayor Woodward and the city's labor movement, the *Journal of Labor* defended Beavers and the recallers and asserted that "the people" desired that the city council, not the police board, appoint the chief of police.[46] Although out of the mainstream debate, the African-American *Atlanta Independent* opposed recall on the principle that it could undermine the integrity of courts and orderly government.[47] These parallel campaigns—Beavers attempt to reclaim his office and the movement to recall Mayor Woodward and the other opponents of Beavers—opened a year of charges and counter-charges, law suits and public debate that ultimately involved Asa Candler more deeply in the political life of the city than ever before.

In December 1915, Candler spoke to a pro-Beavers mass meeting at the Lyric Theater. The audience filled the orchestra and the balcony boxes and an overflow of thirty or forty persons had seats on the sides of the stage. H. Y. McCord, the presiding officer, introduced Candler as "a tower of moral strength" and this was the tone of Candler's oratory in defense of Chief Beavers. He also included an extended, pessimistic analysis of the nature of cities. Although "mankind seems to have an invincible disposition towards urban life," it is a life fraught with difficulties: "In the cities the worship of mammon is the ever prevalent tendency to which thousands succumb. The sins incident to luxurious living more easily abound in urban communities than in rural sections and the vices which flourish in secret burrow like moral rodents in places convenient for hiding."[48]

He warned that societies begin to fail when city dwellers neglect their moral responsibilities and commercial diligence, becoming corrupt and lazy. Candler's intense feelings then moved him to a startling choice of language: in this environment "a vicious social life secretes putrid politics as pus exudes from a purulent wound."[49]

As the recall campaign against Beavers opponents reached its climax, Candler was unable to speak publicly because of a sore throat, but he still came down firmly on the side of Beavers as a defender of public morals. He placed a "card" or advertisement in the *Atlanta Journal* on the 4 January 1916; it reproduced a letter from Candler to the chairman of the recall campaign in which he repudiated those who had attacked Beavers. He denied the claim that "all moneyed interests" opposed the effort to recall Beavers opponents; furthermore, the Chief's supporters were "...as good and noble a constituency as ever undertook to repel attacks on homes of righteousness and virtue."[50] He failed to win wide support for his view, but his consistent support of Beavers and the recall testifies to his willingness to pursue the course he considered morally justified, in spite of the fact that the consensus of both the political and business leaders of the city opposed him.

The *Constitution* defended the morality of the mayor and police board and condemned the leaders of the Men and Religion movement as puritanical power-seekers. The moralistic recallers then resorted to the shabby tactic of claiming that the anti-recallers hoped to get Negro votes for their cause.[51] The relative merits of their tactics aside, the business and political elite of Atlanta successfully persuaded the public that they should vote against the recall of the police jurors responsible for firing the crusading police chief, because recall would amount to a shameful admission of Atlanta's "vice-ridden" condition. The view that a recall vote would harm Atlanta's business reputation prevailed, and the recall attempt failed, two-to-one.[52] The city's leadership and a majority of its electorate had rejected Candler's rigorous moralism.

Some will always prefer leadership that is strongly principled, while others want flexibility and tolerance. Whatever may seem better in theory, practical considerations seem to have ruled in Atlanta. In the aftermath of the recall election, the opposing parties avoided public recriminations and many of the vice outlets remained closed, so both factions could claim a sort of victory. Beavers, however, continued to campaign for his old job, taking his case to the courts where he battled on for about two years. Throughout Beavers ordeal, Asa Candler supported his position, and this support was to have effects on his own life as well as the life of the city.[53]

---

[1]WAC, "Methodism and Anglo-Saxonism," fol. 31, box 91, WAC papers, Emory. Tindall, in *Emergence of the New South*, 196-97, discusses these ideas that mixed patriotism and religion and cites another Warren Candler effort, *Great Revivals and the Great Republic* (1904) as "One of the classic tributes to the newest Chosen Race...."

[2]AGC, "Do Missions Pay?" manuscript of speech, fol. 10, box 2, AGC papers, Emory.

[3]"The Worth of the Sunday School Teacher to the Community," manuscript of speech, fol. 44, box 2, AGC papers, Emory. Warren made similar invidious comparisons; both supported Methodist missionary efforts to proselytize Latin American Catholics.

[4]Folder 43, box 92, WAC papers, Emory.

[5]One specific example: "A Jewish Philanthropy in Atlanta," *Journal of Labor*, 10 January 1913, 4, lauds a Jewish plan to provide for indigent widows: "The Jews teach us a valuable lesson in their new philanthropy—which is so practical and so filled with a sentiment as delicate as it is revolutionary."

[6] Frank, the Jewish manager of a pencil factory, was accused of the murder of a young female employee. Convicted in a trial that received national criticism, Frank received a commutation of his death sentence. Before his supporters could arrange for a new trial, Frank was abducted and lynched. When questioned on the issue of the quality of the trial, Warren expressed irritation and flatly refused to comment on a matter before the courts.

[7]AGC, untitled manuscript of speech, fol. 1, box 2, AGC papers, Emory. For another example of the link between commerce and progress, see "Introduction of Speakers at Taft Banquet," manuscript of speech, 15 January 1909, fol. 38, box 2, AGC papers, Emory.

[8]AGC, "Stewardship" manuscript of speech, fol. 34 or 35 [two versions, the second dated 13 May 1917], box 2, AGC papers, Emory. These issues received more detailed discussion above, in connection with the founding of the Wesley Enterprises and Emory University.

[9]"Pegs and Holes," manuscript of speech, 30 April 1918, fol. 26, box 2, AGC papers, Emory. Similar themes and language also occur in "How Shall We Make Our Boys Successful Business Men?" reprinted in *Coca-Cola Bottler*, August 1915, 21-22.

[10] AGC, "Rural Sunday School Celebration" typed manuscript for speech, n .d., fol 28, box 2, AGC papers, Emory. Mephitic means poisonous or foul-smelling.

[11]Minutes of the Board of Directors, 2 September 1908, Atlanta Chamber of Commerce.

[12]"Mayor Elect J. G. Woodward," *Journal of Labor*, 7 October 1904, 2; "Mayor Woodward s Address," *Journal of Labor*, 19 May 1905, 2.

[13]Deaton, *Atlanta During the Progressive Era*, 342-44 and Thomas M. Deaton, "James G. Woodward: The Working Man's Mayor, *Atlanta History* (Fall 1987): 11-23 delineate Woodward's political career.

[14]"The Retiring Mayor," *Journal of Labor*, 11 January 1907, 4.

[15]Deaton, "James G. Woodward," 16-17.

[16]"Robert F. Maddox Campaign Fund, November 1908," Robert F. Maddox Papers [MSS 143], box 1, Atlanta History Center Library/Archives. Candler's was the first entry and showed the largest single donation on this list.

[17]"To the Voters of Atlanta" [broadside], 28 November 1908, Robert F. Maddox Papers [MSS 143], box 1, Atlanta History Center Library/Archives.

[18]As explained in the chapter "Steward" above, preferred status came through a court proceeding called an intervention, and the receiver had no prerogative either to give or withhold such preference.

[19]Deaton, *Atlanta During the Progressive Era*, 342-44; Deaton, "James G. Woodward," 16-17. The original handbill, "Vote for James G. Woodward" [ca. 1 December 1908], folder 12, box 3, AGC papers, Emory, is reproduced on p. 18 of the Atlanta History article.

[20]"Let Him That Is Innocent Cast a Stone," *Atlanta Independent*, 14 November 1908, 4; "Disintegration of the White Primary Sets In," *Atlanta Independent*, 21 November 1908, 4;

"Maddox the Embodiment of Independentism," *Atlanta Independent*, 28 November 1908, 4.

[21] "Independent Candidate Sweeps City," *Atlanta Independent*, 5 December 1908, 1; "Mayoralty Race Over—Thanks," *Journal of Labor*, 4 December 1908, 4.

[22] "Christian League Formed to Solve the Race Problem," *Atlanta Constitution*, 22 November 1906, clipping in "1906 Riot" subject file, Special Collections Department, Woodruff Library, Atlanta University Center; Martha Tovill Nesbitt, "The Social Gospel in Atlanta: 1900-1920" (Ph.D. diss., Georgia State University, 1975) 79-91; "*Men and Religion Bulletin*: The Houses in Our Midst, " *Atlanta Constitution*, 15 June 1912, 3. A second bulletin with the same title but different text appeared in the Constitution, 22 June 1912, 3.

[23] "*Men and Religion Bulletin*: "The Houses in Our Midst, " 22 June 1912, 3.

[24] Nesbitt, "Social Gospel," 92-3; "$30,000 Voted Home for Wayward Girls," *Atlanta Constitution*, 6 August 1913, 4; and a series of *Men and Religion Bulletins* in the Constitution on 7, 8, 10, 12, 14, and 15 August 1913, demonstrate the forceful campaigning methods of the group as they fought for a facility that they believed would save girls from the dangers of life in the streets.

[25] Harry G. Lefever, "The Involvement of the Men and Religion Forward Movement in the Cause of Labor Justice," *Labor History* (Fall 1973): 521-35, passim; quotation on 530-31.

[26] "Bearing Witness with Us," *Journal of Labor*, 4 October 1912, 4; "Raise Wage Standards," *Journal of Labor*, 11 October 1912, 4; "An Unwarranted Liberty," *Journal of Labor*, 18 October 1912, 4.

[27] Wrigley, "Triumph of Provincialism," 123-27; John Allen Krout, *The Origins of Prohibition* (New York: Alfred A. Knopf, 1925) 297-304; James H. Timberlake, *Prohibition and the Progressive Movement, 1900-1920* (Cambridge MA: Harvard University Press, 1963) 1-7; Paul E. Isaac, Prohibition and Politics: Turbulent Decades in Tennessee, 1885-1920(University of Tennessee Press, 1965) 45, 48. Candler expressed his opposition both from the pulpit and as editor of the Christian Advocate, published in Nashville. Wets in that city complained that "Methodist rabbis" were trying to take over the government of the state. For more on Methodist prohibition activity, see also Sean Dennis Cashman, *Prohibition, the Law of the Land* (New York: The Free Press, 1981) 196-97.

[28] James H. Timberlake, *Prohibition*, 67-68; John J. Rumbarger, *Profits, Power, and Prohibition: Alcohol Reform and the Industrializing of America, 1800-1930, SUNY Series in New Social Studies on Alcohol and Drugs*, Harry G. Levine and Craig Reinarman, eds. (Albany: State University of New York Press, 1989) passim: 108-190; Ernest H. Cherrington, *The Evolution of Prohibition in the United States of America: A Chronological History of the Liquor Problem and the Temperance Reform in the United States and from the Earliest Settlements to the Consummation of Nation Prohibition* (1920; reprint). Publication No. 40: Patterson Smith Reprint Series in Criminology, Law Enforcement, and Social Problems (Montclair, NJ: Patterson Smith, 1969) 281-81, 293, 345-46, 356, 360, 374, 382; Nesbitt, "Social Gospel," 98-99; "The Unions and the Drunkard," *Journal of Labor*, 11 October 1912, 4.

[29] Nesbitt, "Social Gospel," 89-90; "Truth Will End Law-Breaking Locker-Clubs," *Men and Religion Bulletin* No. 181, *Atlanta Constitution*, 3 July 1915, 7; William J. Mathias and Stuart Anderson, *Horse to Helicopter: First Century of the Atlanta Police Department, Community Life Publications: Criminal Justice Series* (n.p.: School of Urban Life, Georgia State University, 1973) 70-71.

[30] Deaton, *Atlanta During the Progressive Era*, 387-88; Nesbitt, "Social Gospel," 92-94.

[31] Deaton, *Atlanta During the Progressive Era*, 400-402; Nesbitt, "Social Gospel," 94. An advertisement that listed 156 Chambers supporters (Candler headed the list) could serve as a roll call of the reform-minded members of the Atlanta elite. See "Prominent Citizens Indorse

Candidacy of Aldine Chambers for Mayor," *Journal of Labor*, 20 September 1912, 12. Woodward's slogan appears in an ad in the *Journal of Labor*, 27 September 27 1912, 6.

32"The Houses in Our Midst," *Men and Religion Bulletin* No. 3, *Atlanta Constitution*, 29 June 1912, 3. The bulletin cited the experience of various cities that had found that vice could not successfully be contained in a district.

33Mathias and Anderson, *Horse to Helicopter*, 72.

34"Why the Clubs and Saloons Must Cease law-Breaking in Atlanta," *Men and Religion Bulletin*, n. 182, 8 July 1915, 9.

35Ibid. The figure 3.999 refers to a low percentage of alcohol content.

36"The Men s Religion and Forward [SIC] Movement," *Atlanta Independent*, 19 October 1912, 4.

37Deaton, "*Atlanta During the Progressive Era*," 400-01; Howard B. Woolston, *Prostitution in the United States, Prior to the Entrance of The United States into the World War* (1921; reprint) Publication No. 29: *Patterson Smith Reprint Series in Criminology, Law Enforcement, and Social Problems* (Montclair NJ: Patterson Smith, 1969) vii. In fact, many American cities of that day experienced anti-vice campaigns; by 1917, for example, the American Social Hygiene Society had investigated prostitution in forty U. S. cities, including Atlanta.

38Nesbitt, "Social Gospel," 99; Mathias and Anderson, *Horse to Helicopter*, 74; "Specifications of Charges Against James L. Beavers, Chief of Police," fol. 10, box 3, AGC papers, Emory.

39Deaton, "*Atlanta During the Progressive Era*," 401.

40"Police Chief Beavers Will Be Tried Tonight," *Atlanta Constitution*, 29 July 1915, 1.

41Nesbitt, "Social Gospel," 100; Mathias and Anderson, *Horse to Helicopter*, 74.

42Mathias and Anderson, *Horse to Helicopter*, 75-76.

43Deaton, *Atlanta During the Progressive Era*, 401; Nesbitt, "Social Gospel," 99-100; J. L. Beavers to Hon. Board of Police Commissioners, 4 August 1915, fol. 10, box 3, AGC papers, Emory.

44Nesbitt, "Social Gospel," 100; in the *Journal of Labor*: "Be On Your Guard Woodwardism's the Issue," 8 October 1915, 3; "Why You Should Sign the Recall," 5 November 1915, 3; "the Harvest Festival, The Recall," 12 November 1915, 3; "Only a Policeman," 26 November 1915, 3; "The Recall Will vindicate Atlanta and Bring Peace," 10 December 1915, 3; "Recall Will vindicate Atlanta," 24 December 1915, 3; "Recall So Simple Impossible to Cloud the Issue," 17 December 1915, 6; "Recall News," 31 December 1915, 3.

45Nesbitt, "Social Gospel," 100-101; "Some Facts Against the Recall," *Journal of Labor*, 254 December 1915, 6; "To All Atlantans," *Journal of Labor*, 7 January 1916, 3.

46"Let the People Rule," *Journal of Labor*, 6 August 1915, 4.

47Deaton, *Atlanta During the Progressive Era*, 402; "Recall," *Atlanta Independent*, 1 January 1916, 2. The *Independent* had long supported Mayor Woodward and police board member James English.

48AGC, "The City is the Nerve Center of Civilization, 1916," manuscript of speech, fol. 5, box 2, AGC papers, Emory.

49Ibid.

50"Asa Candler and the Recall," *Atlanta Journal*, 4 January 1916, 11.

51"Recall," *Atlanta Independent*, 1 January 1916, 2. The editor characterized the recallers as "religious fanatics and Negro haters" but also opposed the recall because duly elected officials should be free to use their own judgment. In a typically nasty attack on those it opposed, this newspaper called Negro supporters of recall "coons [who want] a little bread they have not worked for."

[52] Deaton, "*Atlanta During the Progressive Era*," 402-405; Nesbitt, "Social Gospel," 100-101; "A Glorious Day's Work" [editorial], *Atlanta Independent*, 7 January 1916, 4.

[53] Deaton, *Atlanta During the Progressive Era*, 401-405. The outcome of the Beavers case will be discussed in a subsequent chapter as will Beavers' support of Candler during a personal crisis late in his life.

CHAPTER NINE

Candidate

Long before the controversies surrounding the Men and Religion and Chief Beavers arose, Asa Candler told the Chamber of Commerce that Atlanta should "remedy with all haste what can not be mentioned without shame..." But he also declared: "I love Atlanta. I pledge to you, for her, my chiefest concern."[1] By 1916, there was a good deal to be concerned about.

Mayor Woodward and his friends on the police board withstood the challenge of the recall, and Woodward's administration had brought about a number of improvements, but other problems assailed the city's government. The effects of the World War on the national economy meant that anticipated tax revenues failed to materialize, so the budget became a football for various factions. A large debt demanded attention. Furthermore, the school system (at that time administered by the city government) also had been upset by factional disputes.[2] Finally, after the anti-vice crusades, opponents would condemn any sort of government shortcoming as "Woodwardism." Atlanta's business elite, a group that had never been particularly comfortable with a nominally pro-labor mayor, wanted a change in leadership. Their task was to find some candidate also acceptable to the general citizenry of Atlanta. The right person could restore unity among reformers, the members of the business elite, and members of the city government.

A few mayoral candidates emerged over the spring and early summer of 1916. I. N. Ragsdale, who had made his fortune in the stock yards and played a part in making Atlanta the second largest mule market in the world, announced his candidacy in May. Shortly after, Mell Wilkinson, a prominent member of the Chamber of Commerce, tentatively put himself forward as a representative of the city's business leadership. A year earlier, the *Journal of Labor* had already put the question "Why Not Armistead?" suggesting that Linotype operator Jesse W. Armistead, a past president of the typographical union and seventh ward alderman, might make a suitable candidate for mayor. Now Armistead also entered the mayoral contest, advocating school improvements and supporting modernization of the fire and police departments. The labor newspaper endorsed him as "a man of the people."[3]

The business elite of Atlanta evidently found none of these candidates satisfactory. The possibility of a Candler candidacy, however, was also in the air. At a pro-Beavers mass meeting the previous winter, before beginning his prepared text, Asa Candler had said, "If I love any one thing above another, it is Atlanta's good name. If there is anything which I can do to keep the city on a high plane, give it to me. Nothing else do I want, except your esteem."[4] At the time, some hearers inferred from these remarks that "Mr. Candler might make the race for mayor," although he had never shown any interest in public office, evidently preferring the role of the concerned citizen.

In the middle of the summer Atlanta's commercial leadership decided that Candler was their man. How they concluded remains unclear, but the choice had much to recommend it. Although Candler's defense of Chief Beavers may have made some uneasy, he possessed a generally positive public image. Only a few months earlier, he had launched his plan to save Georgia's cotton growers. As a citizen and philanthropist, no scandal had been attached to his name. Issues of personal character aside, Candler's business success demonstrated his executive abilities and he also had served as president of the Chamber of Commerce, and on various committees and advisory boards. Public affairs occupied a good part of his attention, but he remained unstained by the grubby striving of elective politics. The city's commercial leaders threw their support behind Asa Candler so unequivocally that the two other business-oriented candidates, Ragsdale and Wilkinson, immediately withdrew.

Candler's entry into the race had the qualities of a coronation rather than the kickoff of a political campaign. On 19 July, five Atlanta civic leaders, representing a larger group of 200 citizens, called upon him at his office. Evidently he expected the visit. Candler's secretary, Walker White, handed them a letter "just written by Mr. Candler," declining the nomination, because of Mrs. Candler's ill health. The committee then insisted on seeing him personally and overcame his reservations. That night he issued a statement reluctantly accepting the new responsibility "on the one condition that the people of Atlanta want me to do so, expressing this desire by electing me without any importunity on my part." He would stand for election, but would not personally campaign.[5] If this little drama seems a bit pat, no evidence has emerged to cast doubt on it. Candler's private letters make clear his sincere concern over his wife's health. On her account, they had already made plans to visit a spa in August.

On the day following Candler's acceptance, his supporters invited their candidate to meet them at the Piedmont Hotel for "a rousing send-off" for the mayoral campaign. They planned to hang a huge— if somewhat wordy—banner on the Peachtree side of the Piedmont hotel: "Asa B. Candler will be formally notified at noon today that he is the choice of Atlanta's business men for mayor of Atlanta."[6]

According to the *Constitution*, about 500 of Atlanta's "most representative citizens, men from all classes and sections" appeared at the Piedmont Hotel luncheon meeting. Candler arrived late, but a series of prominent citizens, including Mell Wilkinson, who had recently withdrawn his name from the race, and former Mayor Robert F. Maddox, rose to testify to the candidate's good qualities. Clark Howell, editor of the *Atlanta Constitution*, had just called him

"God-given" and "a great man" when Candler finally entered the room. He made slow progress through the admiring crowd toward the podium. In his extemporaneous opening remarks, he coyly suggested, "This committee may be making a serious blunder." The audience broke in with shouts of "No!" and answered his 30-minute talk with cheers and applause. For his prepared speech, Candler chose the topic "cities as the nerve centers of civilization." Characteristically, he forged a link between prosperity and morality, proclaiming, "Material prosperity can not long prevail in the absence of popular virtue." Near the end of his talk he repeated his intention not to solicit votes for himself. He seemed to think that campaigning would be unnecessary, confidently telling his audience, "You know just who I am and what I am."[7]

The newspapers glowed with enthusiasm for Candler's candidacy. Congratulatory letters and adulatory interviews abounded. Stories recounted his gifts to Emory and Oglethorpe universities, his actions to stabilize the real estate market in 1908, and his numerous business interests. Interviewing one of Candler's friends, who remained anonymous, the *Constitution* concluded that "only his sense of duty to the city persuaded him to enter the race…he is one of the most sensitive men in the city to the call of duty."[8]

Setting to work at once, the citizens' committee presented Candler as a candidate for mayor "drafted for public service" at the request of "a large group of earnest citizens, representing all departments of business and every political faction," who sought an end to "the bickering and strife characterizing [Atlanta's] municipal administration for the past few months." Voter registration closed on 24 July, when more than 16,000 of a possible 18,000 voters were enrolled.[9] Only at this point did the first criticism of Candler reach the pages of the *Constitution*; Councilman Edwin F. Johnson (who had ties to the labor movement) issued a statement in support of Armistead and said, "Mr. Candler was allied with a minority faction which polled one third of the votes cast in the recall election. He is now the candidate for mayor of that one-third faction."[10] However, statements of support for Candler filled the pages of the newspaper and swamped the small voice of opposition.

Although he had agreed to be a candidate for mayor, Candler held to his resolve not to campaign. This task, he insisted, was to be carried out by that group of "the city's most prominent business leaders" who had persuaded him to run. Conflicting loyalties pulled at him: he wanted to serve his city but had promised to accompany his wife Lucy, who had become seriously ill, to a Mt. Clemons, Michigan, spa. He wrote of his plans to his son, Howard, revealing a certain innocence of the ways of politics: "The Mayoralty race into which I was induced to go, is as I might have known, becoming unpleasant. Those opposed to the election of such a man as I am said to be, do not fail to use unfair means, and untruthful statements . . ." He remained determined to go with Mrs. Candler, "as I am satisfied it is my duty to do for both her and myself."[11]

Candidate Jesse Armistead, a union Linotype operator and seventh ward alderman, attacked immediately.[12] At a rally at Sentell's Store in the Tenth Ward, he "challenged the patriotism and disparaged the benevolence" of Asa Candler. He charged that Candler's real estate activities had brought him huge profits and that he was personally aloof: "His friends say that Mr. Candler is a friend of the people...I say to you...He has friends in the moneyed class but he has not made himself friendly with the people as a whole." Armistead continued in this vein and also accused Candler of using a speech writer. He attacked Candler's own statement that he did not desire the office of mayor, frankly admitting his own desire to serve: "Mr. Candler also wants the office but is unwilling to go among the people and ask for their support...But he is no greater than any other man, and like any other man, he wants the office." Armistead also claimed that an unidentified "citizen of Decatur" had offered him a position as Candler's secretary, if he would retire from the contest.[13]

The committee of distinguished citizens responsible for calling Candler to serve also failed to impress Armistead. He claimed that Candler was himself a member of the very committee that selected him to run. "The members of this committee were men who fought for the recent recall which split this city asunder. This is the class of people who are behind this movement." On the other hand, Armistead claimed, he wanted to serve the city as a whole. He continued on the issue of class and politics: "I have been a working man all my life and a member of the union. I have worked and talked for the union and all that it represents. I have consistently labored for the good of the people as a whole and not for any selfish interest."[14]

Disregarding this opening volley, Mr. and Mrs. Candler boarded the northbound train on the afternoon of the last day in July and arrived in Detroit the following night. Coca-Cola's "advertising man" in Detroit, a Mr. Walker, drove the couple to the spa at Mt. Clemons. Throughout Candler's stay in Michigan, the useful Mr. Walker provided Atlanta newspapers, so that the candidate could follow the progress of his campaign against his opponent, Armistead.

Meanwhile, Candler tried to take advantage of the spa's health-improving facilities. A day in the baths did nothing for his jaundiced view of the election, however. On 2 August, he wrote to his son, Howard, "It was nothing less than calamity that befell me when Atlanta men forced the mayoralty candidacy on me, but I'll go through with it if they keep up their effort. I'll be mayor, with my city financially and morally bankrupt." In any case, he expressed his determination to do his best and added that he needed "my 4 strong sons" to act "as guy ropes to keep me perpendicular" through the strains to come.[15]

Armistead continued his campaign, attacking Candler as an exploiter of the working man who "took advantage of hard times" by paying unemployed men half of their accustomed wage rate when he built the cotton warehouse in 1915. Armistead declared that the warehouse was "a purely business proposition and had nothing to do with any philanthropic or patriotic ideas." If Candler had made large gifts to Emory, they only tended to enhance the value of the "thousands of acres" that he and his friends owned in the vicinity of the school: "Will he not in the next few years get back his gift with interest and a good profit for his own pocket?" He went in for the kill with a classic weapon of southern politics, telling his listeners that the recall movement, in which Candler and others sought to defend Chief Beavers, "employed Negroes for the first time in many years. They brought into the contest the Negro voters."[16]

While in Michigan, Candler apparently had trouble in keeping up with events in Atlanta. His letter to his son on 8 August complained that he had not seen a paper more recent than 4 August. In spite of this disadvantage, he analyzed the political situation: "Armistead's public utterances are weak. The Woodwardites are not under any circumstances going to vote for me. The danger I see is that those men who desire my election may not be careful to vote. If they'll vote, it will be for me."[17]

According to his son Howard, Asa Candler believed that because of his own economically advantaged position, any "recriminations and personal charges against his opponent" might backfire. Therefore he avoided answering Armistead's campaign in a similar personal tone.[18] As he said he would do, he left the struggle to his supporters, and his committee worked diligently. They sent out "Candler Club for Atlanta" lapel buttons bearing the candidate's likeness and mailed letters urging the recipients to sign and return a card declaring support for the candidate. Each member of the Atlanta Athletic Club received a button attached to a letter on Athletic Club stationery: "We herewith enclose a Candler button, which we earnestly request you to wear until the election is over." At noon each day, the committee held "Candler meetings" and urged supporters, "Please attend…as often as possible, thereby exhibiting your interest in this Campaign."[19]

In spite of his reluctance to campaign openly, the energetic Candler chafed at being so far away from the center of activity. The spa routine had little attraction for him. For the first week of their stay in Michigan, a heat wave left them drenched with perspiration and made sleep nearly impossible. Mrs. Candler showed little improvement after a week, although she dutifully followed the prescribed regimen. Candler remained optimistic that a thirty-day stay would benefit her, but the mayoral campaign was irresistible. He returned to Atlanta before she did.[20]

Back in the city, Candler continued to hold himself aloof from the public campaign struggles while the committee soldiered onward in his behalf. Armistead, as a laboring man, pressed his claim to be a people's candidate and characterized Candler as "capitalism personified."[21] Still, he dared not go too far in assaulting the venerable capitalist; in a statement "to the Citizens of Atlanta," he wrote, "Against the private character of the gentleman opposing me, I have no word of criticism or censure, but every man's public and political record is a proper subject of comment whenever he appears before the people for their suffrage." In the same statement he advocated "the happy medium" between a "wide-open town" and a "strait-laced Blue-law town."[22]

The national magazine *Leslie's Weekly* found the race interesting enough to send their man Raymond Everett White to Atlanta. White reported that although Candler already had the backing of the city's elite, he needed to acquire the support of laborers, small businessmen, and small home-owners. Eight days before the primary vote, Candler finally accepted the fact that he must campaign openly if he hoped to win. He at last condescended to meet the electorate face-to-face. The *Constitution* relished the "unique spectacle of a multi-millionaire speaking to ward audiences," as did the writer for *Leslie's*. Although Candler had spoken on religious and civic occasions throughout his life, it must have been difficult for this dignified man, clad in his customary morning coat and wing collar, to feel entirely at ease while appealing, in his somewhat reedy, high-pitched voice, to a crowd assembled by a ward politician.[23] However, as always, he did what he saw as his duty. He asked for votes based on his personal ability and character, ignoring Armistead's continued condemnation of "money-rule" and "plutocracy."[24]

By the end of the eight days, open-air orations had nearly cost Candler his voice, but he found the resources for one last speech. "I have never faltered or hesitated to do my duty toward [Atlanta] as God has given me to see it... I have tried to promote its interest— materially, intellectually and morally." He told his listeners that the city administration needed to be business-like, devoted to public service, and free of petty personal politics. Pledging to lay his strength, energy, and ability "upon the altar of service" he declared, "Such a city as Atlanta ought never to be committed to incompetent or impure hands… Atlanta is too big and too good to be the stake in the game for which petty politicians play."[25]

With 7,821 votes to his opponent's 3,712, Candler carried every ward in the Democratic primary but the Fifth, where Armistead won by a margin of about 200. Members of the city government cheered his victory. The *Constitution* expressed the belief that Candler's election marked the end of petty ward politics in Atlanta. Georgia editorialists called his election a case of "the office seeking the man" and a recognition of Candler's personal qualities, but Howard Candler also attributed his father's victory to "the energy and foresight and the hard work of the hundreds of businessmen who supported his campaign."[26] Even the *Journal of Labor*, the official publication of the Atlanta Association of Trades and Allied Unions, cautiously extended "the right hand of fellowship to the distinguished fellow citizen" whose promise to represent all the classes of the city "whatever his private belief" they accepted.[27] One less solemn observer, the editor of the Jacksonville, Florida, *Metropolis* took the occasion, to twit Georgia's prohibitionist tendencies: "It appears eminently fit that Atlanta being in the arid center of the Desert of Georgia, should have elected the Coca-Cola king for burgomaster."[28]

Although the Armistead-Candler race might be seen in terms of a labor-*versus*-capital contest, Atlanta's electorate was not so clearly polarized. Most of Atlanta's working class citizens were first-generation city dwellers, still under the influence of traditional rural values rather than the newer notions of worker solidarity. This segment of the laboring community identified strongly with the values and goals advocated by the business elite.[29] This was true of the typographers union, the group that produced Armistead and the colorful Jim Woodward. According to Gary Fink, who wrote on the Atlanta typographers as "city boosters," these skilled craftsmen valued "independence, freedom, equality, and the dignity of labor." They recognized that, as laborers, they had certain group interests, but they

also took pains to project "an image of harmonious industrial relations" between labor and capital. In their desire to be seen as civic
patriots, the typographers did not necessarily speak for all laboring
people of Atlanta; some unions took strong steps in these early years
to assert their interests. The mill hands who struck the Fulton Bag
and Cotton Mill and lived in a tent city when expelled from their
company-owned houses probably did not lose sleep over their status
as city boosters. To be fair, the typographers did not turn their backs
on fellow union members, but their ambivalent attitudes meant that
on many occasions they could easily be persuaded to support goals
formulated by the business elite of Atlanta. Although Atlanta's working people occasionally found their political voice, particularly in the
first decades of the twentieth century, in the long run they failed to
develop a cohesive and effective political movement.

Georgians assumed that Candler's success in the Democratic primary settled the question of who Atlanta's next mayor would be. In
1900 the Democratic party had adopted the rule that only whites
could participate in their primary elections. Because the Democrats
controlled Georgia politics, the winner of the primary could expect
that the December general election would be merely a formality.
Furthermore, state poll taxes and literacy tests had eliminated most
blacks and many lower-class whites from the general voting rolls.
These provisions had gutted opposition to the Democratic party and
the business and political elite that directed it. The Democrats had
long since absorbed the remnants of their only serious antebellum
challengers, the small farmers of the populist Farmers' Alliance. The
state's remaining Republicans (almost entirely black) might rail
against the white primary, but his opponents for undermining white
solidarity would condemn any challenger to the Democratic candidate in the general election.[30] Indeed, the only instance in recent
memory when a Democratic nominee had failed to win his office had
been Robert Maddox's defeat of Jim Woodward in 1908. That unique
development had come as a result of the reaction of the city's leadership to Woodward's indiscretions, not as a result of a political
challenge to white Democratic control.

The cliché that a Democratic nomination was "tantamount to election" certainly expressed Asa Candler's expectations as autumn came to Atlanta in 1916. Candler pursued his usual round of public activities, for example speaking to retail merchants on how best to keep good relations with their bankers. At a ceremony held in a large tent pitched between the law and theology buildings, Asa Candler saw his brother Warren preside over the opening of Emory University; the Bishop was now Chancellor of the new school.[31] However, events already in motion were about to alienate the laboring segment of the city's electorate from the man the newspapers blithely called the "mayor-elect" of Atlanta.

In the summer of 1916, even before Asa Candler's candidacy for mayor had been proposed, disgruntled linemen employed by the Georgia Railway and Electrical Company began attempts to organize a union. Another group employed by the same company, the streetcar motormen and conductors, also sought to organize. The issues surrounding the streetcar service soon came to eclipse those of the linemen in the public's attention. Conductor I. H. Mehaffey recalled that "They had meetings at different homes and talked about the union and how it would be favorable…. There had been a lot of discussion, and several men were fired for meeting."[32] The streetcar company implacably refused to recognize the complaints of its workers, even when they threatened a strike. On 29 September, dissatisfied streetcar men threatened to walk off the job. Company President Preston W. Arkwright issued a bullheaded statement, refusing to recognize their position: "There will be no strike…There is no dissatisfaction….There is no dispute nor question nor difference nor difficulty of any kind…." He blamed the unrest on W. M. Pollard, "a paid organizer of the Brotherhood of Electrical Workers of Springfield, Ill." who, he said, had no interest in the street railway employees or the city of Atlanta. Arkwright's lengthy statement admitted that Pollard had "succeeded in misleading a small number" but added that the company had discharged them immediately. Pollard answered that unless the company immediately recognized the right of the union to organize, "a strike will positively occur."[33]

The next day, 30 September, Mayor Woodward called Pollard to his office for a conference. The union organizer had already been before the Police Board, where he told various police and sheriff's authorities that he intended no violence, but asserted, "I didn't come to Atlanta to be intimidated." Later accounts of his meeting with the Mayor reveal that feelings ran very high. Testifying under oath in late November, Councilman Ashley described their meeting: Woodward told Pollard that if he called a strike he "would be landed behind bars." Pollard expressed surprise at Woodward claiming that he had been a union man for forty years. According to Ashley, as the exchange continued, Woodward became enraged and picked up a paper weight from his desk while calling Pollard a "d—- infernal scoundrel." In Pollard's version of the encounter, Woodward called him a "contemptible scoundrel" while brandishing an inkwell, threatening to knock his brains out. In addition, Ashley and Pollard both reported that Georgia Railway and Power Company President Preston Arkwright stood at his office window, which was across the alley from the mayor's open windows, and observed the entire drama. After the meeting, however, the mayor simply announced that he had told Pollard that in the event of a strike, no violence would be tolerated. Pollard reported that he had assured the mayor that "the streetcar men under no conditions would resort to violence." Although he declared the meeting satisfactory, Pollard also warned, "I regard the situation, with regards to the prospects of strike, as critical."[34]

At 6 o'clock that evening the streetcar men struck. Strikers first abandoned their cars in front of the Red Men's Wigwam, a fraternal meeting hall at 86 Central Avenue where the union made its strike headquarters. Crowds of stranded commuters and strike supporters collected at several important intersections in the center of the city and at the ends of certain routes where some motormen and conductors abandoned their posts. As each new car rolled onto the scene strikers urged its operators to join them. Sympathizers in the crowds cheered new converts to their cause and heckled those who resisted. The *Constitution* characterized the crowd as "boisterously good-natured" but with a "tinge" of ugliness. As the strike gathered momentum, strikers shouted abuse at motormen and conductors who stayed on their cars: "Take off that badge, you d—- scab! Come on, join us, fellow. Be a man! You scab! You scab!" Supporters attempted to snatch away the badges and caps that identified employees of the streetcar company, while others stalled some cars by pulling down the trolley arm that connected the car to the power line above the tracks. In other cases, tracks were greased or soaped. A few rocks and bottles flew. Police made some arrests and assisted men who remained loyal to the company in reaching the streetcar company's center of operations at the starter's office at 2 1/2 Walton Street. The company attempted to re-man abandoned cars and protested inadequate police protection, but at 10:30 they called in all the cars and suspended service until the following morning. Within an hour of the suspension of streetcar service, Judge George Bell of the Fulton County superior court signed a temporary restraining order against two unions and several individual leaders of the strike.[35]

The strikers voiced their complaints in a series of mass meetings. Because the men were paid to operate the streetcars during separate intervals in each work day, they put in a total of thirteen to sixteen hours interspersed with periods when they received no pay. This schedule left the men with insufficient time for a good night's sleep, let alone any other free time. "We go to work from two to three times a day. In other words, we have no time we can call our own from 4 o'clock A. M. to 2 o'clock A. M. the following morning." For these long, irregular hours, they received low pay, from seventeen to twenty-five cents an hour depending on seniority, and were required to join a "benevolent" association at a cost of fifty cents a month. The worker lost this money if he left the company.[36]

Another complaint of the strikers might cast some doubt on the supposedly universal enthusiasm for "Mayor-elect" Asa Candler, although he was not mentioned by name: "We have been denied political freedom by the company. Whenever we dared express ourselves upon a question of a political nature, where a man was running for public office who was a friend to the company, we dared not criticize him, or it meant discharge."[37]

On Sunday "a large number of the leading business men and public-spirited citizens" of Atlanta, including Asa Candler, appeared before the police board in the afternoon to protest the performance of the police on the previous night. These citizens were decidedly not friends of the strike. The delegation complained that "certain members of the police force not only appeared indifferent but really seemed to be in sympathy with those creating the disorder." Asa Candler, balancing his roles as the future Mayor of the city and as a director of the Georgia Railway and Power Company, suggested that the police had merely misunderstood their responsibilities in the situation. Nonetheless, he proclaimed, the strikers had no right to snatch official badges and caps away from the street car employees— any more than they would have the right to snatch a badge from his own hat if he should choose to wear one.[38]

At almost the same time, Pollard, the organizer, was speaking to a union meeting. According to the *Journal*, he charged that Candler and Forrest Adair, Candler's business associate and campaign manager, "two of the heaviest stockholders in the Georgia Railway and Power company, had used their influence in making the police act unjustly and beyond their rights." The paper then quoted Pollard directly: "These two men dictated to Andy King, chairman of the police board, just what he was to do... The police can't help it now, for they know that Mr. Candler is soon to [be] in power in Atlanta and a lot of people would lose their jobs."[39]

As the struggle continued, the company expended great effort and money to thwart the strike. It hired large numbers of replacements for the strikers and paid double wages to non-striking employees.[40] It also involved itself in the prosecution of those who interfered with the free movement of the cars or otherwise took part in the disorders. For example, on Tuesday morning, 3 October, streetcar company attorneys joined the official prosecutors to insist that 17-year-old Robert Neal's use of the word "scab" constituted profanity. The defendant's lawyer responded that it simply signified "strike-breaker," but the court found that the word was offensive, and fined Neal $5.75.[41]

Young Neal had plenty of company in the courts of Atlanta. Pulling a trolley from the wire, greasing a track, or heaving a rock at a streetcar might have seemed merely mischievous at the time of the act, but Judge Benjamin H. Hill took a stern view. He charged the grand jury that was about to consider indictments of some strikers, first explaining that any interference with the progress of business was a misdemeanor under the law. Then he told the jurors that any attempt to wreck a streetcar, and thus endanger life, constituted a felony punishable by life in prison: "[The] man who shoots a pistol or throws a rock or greases a track has murder in his heart and is attempting assassination ...unless the jury shall recommend him to mercy." He went on to describe the strike as a "fight between law and lawlessness" and an attack on "the right of free contract."[42]

On Monday, less than forty-eight hours after the walkout, one hundred persons, described in the daily press as "leading Atlantans," turned to a perennial standby of Atlanta civic life by organizing a Citizens' Committee that began to play its part in the controversy. (The *Journal of Labor* called them "merchants of the city.") The Citizens' Committee on Public Safety first convened at 11:30 Monday morning, at the Chamber of Commerce. They elected Asa Candler their president and selected an executive committee of seven "to keep in touch with the situation and, if necessary, swear in the entire membership as deputies to assist the police department."[43] In the view of the labor newspaper these merchants made "veiled threats of arming themselves and rushing to the defense of a city that was as peaceful as a camp meeting."[44] Like the members of the previous day's delegation to the police board, those who addressed the committee hardly represented a cross-section of the community; they included Candler; Henry S. Johnson, a merchant and member of the police committee of the city council; Georgia Railway and Power President Arkwright; and Chamber of Commerce president Victor H. Kreigshaber. The *Atlanta Journal* paraphrased and quoted Candler, who spoke of the danger to the well-being of the city's businesses and the need for law and order: "The situation must be met and it must be met now. For it will expand if something is not done. And the remedy is action." He called on his audience "to show visitors to the city and outsiders that this is not a town of foreigners who will countenance any kind of disorder." Finally, he expressed confidence in the police and urged his listeners to "get on the firing line" to support them.[45]

Early in October the leading opponents of the strike decided to take over control of the Citizens' Committee. Exactly how the decision came about can only be surmised. Its shape appears like the shadows on the wall of the philosopher's cave, an indirect image of reality. The first clue came on 5 October, shortly before the daily noontime meeting of the citizens' public safety committee. An unidentified member of the committee leaked information to a reporter for a new publication known as *The Way*. This paper had been founded by Marion Jackson, one of the leaders of the Young Men and Religion Forward movement, after the *Constitution* had ended publication of their controversial "Bulletins." *The Way* continued the support of labor begun by the Men and Religion, and so, took a close interest in the strike.[46] The inside source revealed that a plan had been made in advance of the meeting to dissolve the larger public safety committee. In the new arrangement, "all matters pertaining to the strike would be left to the executive committee, a majority of whom are directors of the street railway company."

Events followed the pattern that the inside source had predicted. Asa Candler opened the meeting with the announcement that the situation was in hand and that "there was nothing more for the Citizens' Committee to do." Somewhere in the room, a voice immediately offered a resolution to dissolve and several seconds immediately followed. Pro-labor members of the committee refused to go along with this obviously prearranged scenario. Before a vote could be taken, someone suggested that Jerome Jones, editor of the *Journal of Labor* and president of the Southern Labor Conference, should address the meeting "relative to the strike and its principles." Numerous objections were heard. Jones, evidently unready to play such a part on short notice, immediately left the room. W. S. Wardlaw, a leader of the typographical union, then attempted to move that the committee designate a group to meet with representatives of "conservative" labor groups in an effort to settle the strike.[47] Appealing to be heard, Wardlaw reminded the committee that he had participated along with Preston Arkwright in fund raising efforts for Emory University. He reiterated his love for the city and the need to mitigate the hostilities that divided it, lamenting that "We are getting farther apart every day." Even this feeble attempt to gain a hearing for the strikers' grievances received no sympathy from chairman Candler, who cut Wardlaw off: "I don't hear a second to that motion. This is no place to discuss unionism. We have nothing to do with it and any such motion is all out of order." The plan was carried out: the Citizen's Committee had been replaced by its own executive committee, under the chairmanship of Mayor-elect Asa Candler. The meeting adjourned.[48]

Outside, the strikers, aiming to advance their image as responsible citizens, staged a parade through the downtown streets. The procession moved in good order as 401 marchers wearing carman's caps, and their sympathizers, passed through the city streets with the lively encouragement of a marching band. Since the final meeting of the "Citizens' Committee on Public Safety" had lasted only about thirteen minutes, its members had plenty of time to see the parade.

Evidently the executive committee reconsidered the wisdom of their brutal rejection of a plea for community peace. After the fact, they did agree to hear three representatives of the Georgia labor movement present the strikers' position on Friday, 6 October. They listened but they took no action. The following day Candler and the executive committee held a closed session but had no comment, other than to describe their meeting as "highly satisfactory."[49] Finally, on 8 October, the *Journal* trumpeted his committee's "Plan to Bring Trolly Company and Employes [sic] Together," which was published on the front page over Asa Candler's signature. In this plan, the senior judge of the Fulton County Superior Court would appoint a mediation committee of nine members: three from the union, three from the company, and three from the Presidents' Club, which was the same group of civic leaders that had offered to underwrite the costs of extra policemen on the day after the strike began. The committee's proposal insisted that "the cessation of all acts of violence, no matter who may be …responsible" must precede any effort at reconciliation. Labor interests believed that the judge in question did not understand the issues and that the proposed mediation committee lacked balance. These factors combined to guarantee the prompt and complete failure of the project.[50]

Throughout the autumn of 1916, city life went on. A minor earthquake that rattled Atlanta's dishes; the distant rumble of the World War, the cheers of baseball fans at the World Series, and even a visit of the Ballets Russes, sometimes pushed strike news from the front pages—but the strike continued. The union scheduled regular meetings aimed to support strike morale; the *Journal of Labor* claimed that 8,500 persons attended one rally on 13 October at the Auditorium-Armory. The first speaker contrasted his audience, "bent upon hearing the truth," to another class of auditorium users that came "its taxi-cabbing way" in "grand opera regalia." (The Metropolitan Opera performed there each spring. The event was a high point of Atlanta's social season.)[51] On the other hand, another speaker could still call Georgia Railway and Power president Preston Arkwright "my personal friend" and "a valuable citizen" whose attitude toward the union was merely misguided. But he also called his audience, a "representative gathering …of consecrated men and women who have Atlanta's interest at heart and who will not hesitate to right a wrong," and compared them to the Citizens' Committee led by Asa Candler, who were "only 150 citizens, largely stockholders of the Georgia Railway and Power company, hastily drummed up over the telephone to consider conspiracies that have never had the slightest basis of foundation."[52]

Trade-unionism may have preoccupied Asa Candler when he told Atlanta's credit men in mid-October that "Every man should rely upon his own individual effort for success, for within him are the elements of success if he will apply himself."[53] Perhaps he measured all mankind against himself, but he certainly failed to understand that for the ordinary laborer "individual effort" might not guarantee success. As a man who wielded great power, he did not grasp the realities of life for those on the receiving end of authority.

Daily strike meetings at the Wigwam and weekly mass meetings at the Armory continued, while the company refused to yield. As they had done on the first night of the strike, the adherents to both sides occasionally lost self-control. Arrests occurred regularly. Newspaper stories on the strike reported not only mischief such as greasing tracks or pulling down of trolley arms, but also more threatening actions, such as flying rocks, gunfire, and attempts to derail the cars. Years later a motorman remembered, "There was some shenanigans from both sides. There was a school on English Avenue, a streetcar came up through there and they opened up and shot all the windows out of it and everything."[54] The contemporary *Journal of Labor* offers a more detailed account of what was probably the same incident: A motorman, operating a car with no passengers, had stopped to allow a special deputy to remove a plank from the tracks when some forty masked men opened fire. In addition to the damage to the car, the motorman sustained a wound in the leg and a "shattered" left hand. By the time the police arrived the gunmen had escaped.[55] The "shenanigans" were taking a decidedly ominous turn. Beginning in early October and through the month of November, small quantities of dynamite placed on the streetcar tracks exploded under the cars on several occasions. At times injuries to passengers occurred, although no reports of fatalities appeared in the *Atlanta Journal* accounts. The strike leaders issued statements disavowing the violence.[56] (These incidents provide an odd testimonial to the sturdy quality of the streetcars. On many occasions they were immediately returned to the tracks and continued to run.)

As the struggle continued, Atlanta's labor supporters had quite sensibly rejected the claims of the restructured Citizens' Committee to be neutral. Labor also expressed growing resentment of the Committee chairman, Asa Candler. In early November, they determined to challenge his position as "mayor-elect" by fielding another mayoral candidate in the upcoming general election. A meeting of citizens held at the Red Men's Wigwam, the fraternal hall that was strike headquarters, nominated a businessman named C. W. McClure. They sent a telegram to inform the nominee, who was on a business trip in New York. The meeting formed itself into an "Anti-Asa Candler Club" and asserted that it was not a labor organization as such but was composed of "bona fide citizens of Atlanta from every walk of life" and welcomed all classes and creeds. Its announcement of McClure's nomination pointed to "Mr. Candler's activities as chairman of the citizens' committee, so-called …which was very active in seeking to protect only the interests of the corporation, ignoring the fact that personal rights of many citizens were also involved."[57]

While McClure, still in New York, mulled over his decision, the anti-Candler campaign progressed. About 2,500 persons attended a mass meeting held on 10 November where several speakers claimed that Candler had failed to do his part to end the strike. Reporting this event, the *Journal* began to identify Candler as the "choice of the Democratic white primary."[58] Meanwhile, McClure dithered; the headlines for the next few days told the story. He was "not certain" and then he said "he may run"; he promised to "give answer" but a few days later he had "not made decision." On 14 November, however, he had definitely "decided not to run."[59]

The anti-Candler forces now turned to a railroad engineer and union member, Arthur Corrie, who accepted the nomination to appear on the 5 December ballot. Corrie campaigned against the utilities, announcing his intention to "relieve the oppression that is now being put upon the people of the city, and tax payers of the city by the Georgia Railway and Power Company." The people, he said, were paying more for gas, power, and streetcar fares "than the citizens should pay" while receiving "less for our franchise privileges" than proper. Corrie condemned Candler because he "never made mention of these facts to the citizens of Atlanta, neither has he said that he would even try to relieve the people of the burden and oppressions of the said Georgia Railway and Power company." He accused Candler of intending to raise the tax rate unnecessarily when the city's deficit could be cured by better management of the funds on hand. He also promised to do everything in his power to "correct the evil of irregularities with both electric and gas meters." He called for the usual improvements in sanitary, hospital, fire, and police services, and expressed his good intentions toward the city and its citizens.

Meanwhile, police arrested the union organizer Pollard and charged him with one felony and one misdemeanor, claiming that he circulated "incendiary papers." While the general election campaign for mayor proceeded, Pollard's trial ran a parallel course. As in the earlier court proceedings, attorneys employed by the power company assisted the prosecution, and James L. Key led the defense.[60]

In testimony, Forrest Adair, the manager of Candler's mayoral campaign denied earlier charges that he had publicly advocated putting Pollard behind bars or running him out of town. Key tried to ask Adair, "How much stock do you own in the Georgia Railway and Power Company?" but Judge Hill sustained the prosecution's objection.[61] The case ended in a mistrial on 6 December, and was pushed off the front page by the climax of the general election contest for mayor. Judge Hill postponed any decision on a retrial until after the Christmas vacation.[62]

In the general election campaign, the pro-Candler forces finally played the racial trump card that has served a multitude of southern politicians when faced with an electoral crisis. They represented the general election candidacy of Arthur Corrie as a threat to the white race in Atlanta. White southern laborers set great store in their racial identity, providing a convenient lever for those who sought to control both black and white workers.[63] Candler's supporters vowed to arouse the voters "to the imperative necessity of upholding the city white primary …. Control of Atlanta's municipal affairs by the white voters of the city is absolutely dependent upon the supremacy of the city white primary."[64]

Even Armistead, the labor candidate defeated by Candler in the September white primary, rallied to the cause of his former opponent when Candler's men invoked a threat to racial solidarity. After former

Armistead supporters met at the Candler headquarters on the first day of December to express their sense of "moral obligation" to the white primary nominee, the *Atlanta Journal* of 30 November announced that "Jesse W. Armistead Works for Asa Candler In General Election." Other segments of Atlanta's organized labor also rallied to Candler's support. Tull C. Waters, identified in the *Atlanta Journal* as "chairman of the committee of citizens appointed by the labor organizations of Atlanta and the mass meeting of Atlanta's citizens to adjust the differences" between the strikers and the company, signed a statement on behalf of his committee of union groups in support of "the nominee of the white primary." Front page editorials kept up the drumbeat and reiterated the argument that anyone who had voted in the white primary, indeed "Every White Citizen," had a moral obligation to turn out for Candler in the general election.[65] The *Atlanta Journal* story, written on election day before the polls closed, included a confessional letter from a certain painter, W. B. Russell, who claimed that he had "drifted into the Corrie movement" but had been dismayed to discover that "Tom Blodgett, a leader of the black portion of the Republican party …proposed to deliver to Mr. Corrie the solid Negro vote …" This "self-respecting, loyal Democrat" realized, he said, that he was with "the wrong crowd" and wrote his letter to warn the city of its peril.[66]

As it happened, the overall vote was light, although a high percentage of Corrie's voters turned out, in the estimation of Candler's own campaign manager, Forrest Adair.[67] Yet in spite of these possible difficulties, Candler was elected, 6,168 to 3,524. The total of Candler votes had dropped by over 1,500, while Corrie's vote totals came close to those taken by Armistead in the primary, which suggests that this was the absolute political strength of the Atlanta labor movement in 1916.[68] If, as Adair believed, ninety percent of Corrie support turned out against sixty percent of Candler support, then Candler's supporters must not have felt terribly threatened by the Negro vote, which was not large in any case.

Benjamin Davis, editor of the weekly *Atlanta Independent,* the only newspaper that served the city's black community, saw the election in terms of the white primary. He wrote that "the race of Mr. Corrie …was a great victory for independent thought and freedom of action. The white primary must go." In making this argument, Davis disregarded the fact that Corrie had not run against the white primary, but as a supporter of organized labor. Davis correctly pointed out the influence of Candler's overwhelmingly superior resources in the race. However, his claim that Corrie's supporters were "tired of political slavery and sought to free themselves at the ballot box," thus beginning "the disintegration of the white primary" was more wishful thinking than acute political analysis.[69]

In the end, those who led Candler's campaign may have overestimated the threat of the general election to white supremacy, but they did not hesitate to invoke racial solidarity in the service of his candidacy. Furthermore, they must have realized that this particular white man's victory would also be a defeat for organized labor. The ordinary voters of Atlanta evidently chose race over class unity and thus accepted the leadership of one of the more paternalistic representatives of the city's elite. Candler and his friends turned to the task of smoothing over, as much as possible, the divisions within the white citizenship of Atlanta. On 7 December, Ivan Allen announced his intention to enlist every member of the new administration in the Chamber of Commerce, including every city and county official and employee. He lauded cooperation and invoked the clumsy Candler slogan, "Let's all get together again for Atlanta."[70]

Meanwhile, proceedings against the dynamiters brought convictions. The strike ended with a pay raise for car men, but the settlement did not include recognition of the union or the rehiring of strikers. The "compromise" amounted to a defeat of the strikers, with a reward for those hired as strike-breakers as well as for workers who stayed with the company. Authorities pursued Pollard, the labor organizer, through years of criminal prosecutions. However, after further incidents of strike activity in Atlanta, the company later recognized the local chapter of the Amalgamated Association of Street and Electric Railway Employees of America, under some pressure from the National War Labor Board, a federal regulatory agency created to meet the crises of the World War. It became "one of the largest and strongest unions in the city" but did not strike again until 1949.[71]

During the challenge of the general election, Asa Candler's public statements passed over the issues of the strike and continued their customary moralistic tone, while he also continued to insist on his old-fashioned stance as a citizen who was responding to the will of the public. He avoided endorsing candidates in other races: "In the gubernatorial contest, with which my status as prospective mayor of Atlanta has nothing to do, I ask the privilege of recording my ballot as unobtrusively as any other citizen."[72] Always unwilling to assume any hint of the political, he expressed his resolve to apply the same effort and business judgment to the administration of Atlanta as he had to "every other corporation over which I have been called to preside."[73]

A few days after the election, in a newspaper interview, the mayor-elect explained that he proposed to conduct city business without a tax increase. From his examination of the assets of the city, he had concluded "that her greatest assets are her people." He planned, through careful economy, to confine the city's expenditures to its current income. The interviewer reported that "Mr. Candler's eyes sparkled when he referred to his campaign promises and he rapped his hand heavily on his desk to emphasize the statement that he intended now to truthfully carry out every pledge he made before his nomination." He further expressed the desire that Atlantans recognize him as "just an ordinary man, striving to serve them." He said, "I am not such an awfully smart man. There are a whole lot of men in Atlanta who are smarter than I am, but there is not one who is any more honest. I intend to be the people's candidate and I believe if we all pull together we can make Atlanta even a greater city."[74]

The duties of a public servant now largely eclipsed the role of the capitalist in Asa Candler's life. He withdrew from active involvement in most of his commercial enterprises, ostensibly to devote himself to his responsibilities as mayor and to show his impartiality in office.[75] At Christmas, scarcely a week before he assumed the office of mayor, he divided most of his shares in The Coca-Cola Company among his wife and five children. He did, however, continue to serve on the Coca-Cola board of directors and its minutes show that he still made himself heard in their consultations, in spite of the fact that he owned only seven shares in the company. Howard Candler—nominated by his father—became the new president of Coca-Cola.[76]

Candler also wound up his active interest in Asa Candler, Incorporated, the real estate firm, leaving it under the supervision of Asa, Junior. On 15 March 1917, he completed his withdrawal from private real estate investment in Atlanta. He transferred the titles of a large number of parcels of property that he owned individually over to Asa G. Candler, Incorporated. Surviving indentures show that the corporation paid nominal sums, from ten to one hundred dollars for at least a million dollars worth of Atlanta real estate.[77] Several other parcels of property that show early ownership by Candler as an individual, at some point after 1917 appear as property of Asa G. Candler, Incorporated, indicating that they too may have changed hands on the Ides of March, 1917. From this day onward, Asa Candler, Junior, managed these properties, and evidence of his careful attention to detail abounds in the Asa Candler papers.

Candler did not withdraw completely from the world of commerce. He maintained his active connection to Central Bank and Trust and the Atlanta Warehouse Company.[78]

Having passed his sixty-fifth birthday, the new Mayor planned to divide his day equally between City Hall and the Candler Building. He briskly faced the large and challenging task ahead, ready for hard work, but his constituents expected that he would apply a Midas touch to solve the city's fiscal problems quickly and painlessly.

[1]AGC, "President's Address" in "Annual Report of the Atlanta Chamber of Commerce..." 7 January 1909, fol. 2, box 2, AGC papers, Emory.

[2]Deaton, "Atlanta During the Progressive Era," 409; "The City Hall Mess," *Journal of Labor*, 12 February 1915, 4.

[3]"Present President and Past," *Journal of Labor*, 10 January 1913. 4; "Why Not Armistead?" *Journal of Labor*, 21 May 1915, 4; "Armistead in Race for Mayor," *Journal of Labor*, 19 May 1916, 5; "Jesse W. Armistead," *Journal of Labor*, 28 July 1916, 4.

[4]"Asa Candler Addresses Recall Mass Meeting," *Atlanta Journal* 4 December 1915, 2

[5]"Asa Candler Urges Atlantans To Name Good Men to Serve City in the General Council," *Atlanta Constitution*, 20 July 1916, 1. According to the page one story, the five-man committee included H. S. Johnson, a merchant; Charles T. Hopkins, lawyer; T. K. Glenn, manufacturer; Nym McCollough, wholesale producer; and J. K. Orr, manufacturer.

[6]"Candler Will Be Formally Notified Today He Is Choice of Business Men for Mayor," *Atlanta Constitution* 20 July 1916, 1.

[7]"Pledge Hearty Co-Operation To Candler in Mayor's Race," *Atlanta Constitution*, 21 July 1916, 5.

[8]"Candler Will Be Formally Notified Today He Is Choice of Business Men for Mayor," *Atlanta Constitution*, 20 July 1916, 1.

[9]"Support Pledged to Asa Candler," *Atlanta Constitution*, 23 July 1916, 6A; Henry S. Johnson, Chairman Citizens Committee, to "Dear Sir", 29 July 1916, in Atlanta Historical Society Library/Archives personality file "Candler, Asa G." This form letter is written on stationery bearing the letterhead "Campaign Headquarters, Asa G. Candler for Mayor of Atlanta, the slogan "Let's all get together again for Atlanta," and a prominently displayed printer's union "bug."

[10]"Support Pledged to Asa Candler," *Atlanta Constitution*, 23 July 1916, 6A.

[11]AGC to CHC, 29 July 1916, box 1, AGC papers, Emory.

[12]Garrett, *Atlanta and Environs*, 2: 697.

[13]"Armistead Challenges Patriotism of Candler," *Atlanta Journal*, 29 August 1916, 3.

[14]Ibid.

[15]AGC to CHC, 2 August 1916, box 1, AGC papers, Emory.

[16]"Clique Backs Candler, Says Jesse Armistead," *Atlanta Journal*, 2 August 1916, 3.

[17]"Papa" [AGC] to "My dear man" [probably CHC], 8 August 1916, box 1, AGC papers, Emory.

[18]Charles Howard Candler, *Asa Griggs Candler* (Atlanta: Emory University, 1950) 321-23.

[19]Unsigned to "Dear Sir" August 10, 1916, on letterhead of The Atlanta Athletic Club, Atlanta Georgia, in Atlanta Historical Society Library/Archives personality file "Candler, Asa G."

[20]AGC to CHC, one letter written the day before the departure, and two letters written at Mt. Clemons, box 1, AGC papers, Emory. Candler observed that those who came to soak in the inky mineral waters were "not society folk" but "mostly plain people from every quarter of the globe. … As is usual, many are Jews."

[21]Raymond Everett White, *Leslie's Weekly* (September 1916; reprint) as "Writer in Leslie's Weekly Tells of Election of Asa G. Candler," *Atlanta Constitution*, 21 September 1916, 8.

[22]"Armistead's Direct Appeal to People of Atlanta," *Journal of Labor*, 18 August 1916, 8.

[23]Franklin M. Garrett, personal communication. Mr. Garret saw then-Mayor Candler speak at a school assembly. He remembered his dress and the quality of his voice, but says that the content of the speech made little impression on the mind of a schoolboy.

[24]White, *Leslie's Weekly* article, repr. *Atlanta Constitution*, 21 September 1916, 8.

[25]AGC, untitled manuscript of speech, fol. 20, box 2, AGC papers, Emory. A note on the manuscript mentions his bad throat.

[26]Garret, *Atlanta and Environs*, 2: 698 (voting statistics); "Council Solid Behind Candler," *Atlanta Constitution*, 3 September 1916, 1F; Candler, *Asa Griggs Candler* 321-23.

[27]"Atlanta's Next Mayor," *Journal of Labor*, 1 September 1916, 4.

[28]Quoted in the *Coca-Cola Bottler*, October 1916, 15, along with a great many adulatory excerpts form editorials throughout the country. "Prohi" was a slang term for prohibitionists or their movement.

[29]Gary W. Fink, "We Are City Builders," 44-43, 52.

[30]Numan V. Bartley, *The Creation of Modern Georgia* (Athens GA: University of Georgia Press, 1983) 149; "The Lily White Abomination," *Atlanta Independent*, 29 January 1916, 4; "A Democratic Negro A Political Anomaly," *Atlanta Independent*, 15 July 1916, 4.

[31]"Emory University is Given Great Opening" *Atlanta Journal*, 27 September 1916, 1; "Candler Urges Closer Relation with Bankers" *Atlanta Journal*, 27 September 1916, 23.

[32]Kuhn, *Living Atlanta*, 14. The *Atlanta Journal*, the *Atlanta Constitution*, and the *Journal of Labor*, carried accounts of the streetcar strike of 1916 and related events, beginning in September, Newspaper accounts beginning in December and continuing through the spring of 1917 cover various court actions involving Pollard and others and sometimes fill in details missing from the earlier accounts. For example, "Pollard's Statement to Jury," *Journal of Labor*, 23 June 1917, 1, included the union organizer's account of the beginnings of the strike.

[33]"Labor Chiefs Call on Arkwright and Ask for a Hearing," *Atlanta Journal*, 29 September 1916, 1. The union was the Atlanta division 732 of the Amalgamated Association of Street and Electric Railway Employes [SIC] of America.

[34]"Mayor Tells Union Men There Must Be No Violence In Strike," *Atlanta Journal*, 30 September 1916, 1; "Two Dynamiters Star Witnesses in Trial of Pollard," *Atlanta Journal,* 28 November 1916, 1; "Pollard's Statement to Jury," *Journal of Labor*, 23 June 1917, 1.

[35]"Great Crowds Witness Beginning of Trolley Strike; Cars Continue Running Despite 'Walkout' of Men," "Street Car Service Halted At 11 Saturday Night; Company Scores Police," and "Injunction Against Strikers Sought By Power Company," *Atlanta Constitution*, 1 October 1916, 1; "Union Men and Company Differ as to Number on Strike," "Judge Bell Enjoins Interference with Street Car Service," "Street Car Officials Promise Regular Schedule Today" [all on p. 1], "Emotion Sways Throngs Which Cheer on Streets; Crowds Thick and Noisy," and several small sidebar stories [p. 2], *Atlanta Journal*, 1 October 1916. The *Atlanta Journal* and the *Constitution* have similar material, although the *Journal* accounts, written for a later deadline, seem a bit more complete and well-organized. The two unions were Local 84 of the International Brotherhood of Electrical Workers and the Atlanta Division 732 of the Amalgamated Association of Street and Electric Railway Employes of America. The officers of the "Chippewa Tribe" of the "Red Men" who met at the Wigwam on Central Avenue included a Sagamore and Junior Sagamore, a Collector of Wampum and a Keeper of Wampum, a Chief of Records, a Property Director and several Directors; see "Red Men Hold Their Election of Officers," *Atlanta Journal*, 6 December 1916, 9.

[36]"Union Men Differ With Company on Number Striking," *Atlanta Journal*, 1 October 1916,1; "Loyal Employes [SIC] Hold 'Experience Meeting,'" *Atlanta Journal*, 2 October 1916, 3; "Sunday Meeting Held by Strikers and Friends," *Atlanta Journal*, 2 October 1916, 3; "Reasons for Streetcar Strike," *Journal of Labor*, 6 October 1916, 4.

[37]"Reasons for Street Car Strike," *Journal of Labor*, 6 October 1916, 4; see also, "Car Men's Union Issues Statement to Public," *Atlanta Journal*, 3 October 1916, 3.

[38]Members of the citizens' delegation listed in the newspaper were "Mayor-elect" Asa G. Candler, Forrest Adair, Mell R. Wilkinson, Alex C. King, Ivan E. Allen, George P. Howard, Albert S. Adams, C. W. Bernhardt, F. J. Paxon, Victor H. Kreigshaber (president of the Atlanta Chamber of Commerce) Mayor Woodward, R. R. Otis, H. S. Johnson, J. J. Haverty, Bolling H. Jones, J. J. Spalding, J. K. Orr, L. J. Daniel, P. C. Alson, C. J. Kelley, W. W. Orr, Nym McCollough, W. M. Dixon, Edward Inman, John E. Murphy, W. O. Foote, W. L. Peel, and E.

P. McBurney.

[39]"Few Arrests Made of Pedestrians Who Refuse to Move On," *Atlanta Journal*, 2 October 1916, 1.

[40]"Federation of Trades Pledges Aid to Strikers," *Atlanta Journal*, 3 October 1916, 3; "Citizens' Committee Takes Up Contention of Striking Car Men," *Atlanta Journal*, 7 October 1916, 1. After one week of the strike the company announced that double pay for loyal workers would continue for at least another week.

[41]"Fined $5.75 for Calling Car Employe a 'Scab,'" *Atlanta Journal*, 3 October 1916, 2.

[42]"Grand Jury Charged to Indict Offenders in Strike Disorders," *Atlanta Journal*, 6 October 1916, 1.

[43]"Law and Order Demanded by Citizens" *Atlanta Journal*, 2 October 1916, 1. The committee included Mell R. Wilkinson, Forrest Adair, F. J. Paxon, Ivan E. Allen, W. W. Orr, W. H. White, Jr., and E. V. Carter; Candler was chairman.

[44]"What Atlanta Should Know," *Journal of Labor*, 6 October 1916, 1.

[45]"Law and Order Demanded by Citizens," *Atlanta Journal*, 2 October 1916, 1.

[46]"The Way" [advertisement], *Journal of Labor*, 29 October 1915, 3; Marion M. Jackson, "An Appeal to Reason," *The Way*, [other publication data unknown] repr. in *Journal of Labor*, 6 October 1916, 1; "Citizens Committee Tries To End Strike In 13 Minutes," *The Way* [other publication data unknown], repr. *Journal of Labor* 14 October 1916, 4. Billed by Marion Jackson as "A Journal of Co-operation," the first issue of *The Way* appeared December. Jackson pledged that it would "fight every evil" and "oppose every compromise with wrong." He expressed his opinion that "PUBLICITY means the cure of every civic disease" and claimed as his paper's creed the words of Jesus, "You shall know the truth, and the truth shall make you free."

[47]"'Billy' Wardlaw," *Journal of Labor*, 21 May 1915, 4, sketches his twenty-year record of union activity.

[48]Ibid.; "Grand Jury Expected to Find Indictments On Charge of Rioting," *Atlanta Journal*, 5 October 1916, 1. The *Atlanta Journal* account paraphrases Candler's parliamentary proceedings, but essentially corroborates the version from *The Way* that was quoted in the *Journal of Labor*. Some years later Floyd Hunter, in *Community Power Structure*, 93, commented that Atlantans are connoisseurs of meetings and admire those who can skillfully conduct one.

[49]"Citizens' Committee Takes Up Contention of Striking Car Men," *Atlanta Journal*, 7 October 1916, 1. The representative of the labor movement were Jerome Jones, president of the Southern Labor Congress; R. E. Gann, president of the Atlanta Federation of Trades; and L. P. Marquardt, president of the Georgia Federation of Labor.

[50]"Citizens' Committee Presents Plan to Bring Trolley Company and Employes Together," *Atlanta Journal*, 8 October 1916, 1

[51]T. Eldin Burton, "The Music Festival of 1909," *The Atlanta Historical Bulletin* (9 July 1939): 199-202.

[52]"Five Splendid Speeches Heard at Auditorium," *Journal of Labor*, 14 October 1916, 1. The first quoted speaker was Marion M. Jackson, editor of *The Way*.

[53]"Mayor-elect Addresses Credit Men," *Atlanta Journal*, 11 October 1916, 2. He also "felicitated" credit men on the modern capabilities for sharing information that they enjoyed. In the old days credit merchants had to depend on private memoranda, circulated privately; on the other hand, modern efficiency did eliminate elements of personal responsibility and personal association from business.

[54]Kuhn, *Living Atlanta*, 17.

[55]"Battle Fought Between Company Agents and Forty Masked Men," *Journal of Labor*, 21 October 1916, 1.

[56]Stories dealing with dynamite incidents, or comments on the incidents, appeared in the *Atlanta Journal* on 8, 18, 24, 26, 28, and 29 October and 2, 3, 4, 5, 6, 9, 16, 18, 27, and 28 November,. In the 18 October edition, a possibly related story on page 6 reported the theft of dynamite from a toolshed in a cemetery; on the same day a dynamite cap exploded under one of the cars on the English Avenue line. The report of a serious injury appeared in the 2 November *Journal*, on page 3. During the aftermath of the strike, Pollard again denied knowledge of the violence: see "Pollard's Statement to Jury," *Journal of Labor*, 23 June 1917, 1.

[57]"Labor Paper Announces M'Clure for Mayor," *Atlanta Journal*, 4 November 1916, 2.

[58]"M'Clure Will Give Answer by Monday" *Atlanta Journal* 10 November 1916, 6.

[59]Respectively, these stories from the *Atlanta Journal* ran on 5, 9, 10, 13 and 14 November.

[60]Newspapers carried detailed accounts of the trial of Pollard. For example, see the *Atlanta Journal* for November and December 1916: "Five Panels Are Exhausted During Pollard's Trial" 24 November, 1; "Arkwright Testifies at Trial of Pollard," 27 November, 1; "Confessions Clear Up Dynamiting of Cars, Say Officers," 27 November, 1; "Seventeen Indicted on dynamiting Charges" and "Two Dynamiters Star Witnesses in Trial of Pollard," 28 November, 1; "Judge Hill Declares A Riot Prevailed on Night of Car Strike," 5 December, 1; "Pollard Takes Stand in His Own Defense," 2 December, 3; "Pollard Jury Unable to Reach Agreement on Question of Fact," 5 December, 1; "Unable to Agree, Jury in Pollard Case Dismissed," 6 December, 3.

[61]"Pollard Takes Stand In His Own Defense," *Atlanta Journal*, 2 December 1916, 3.

[62]"Unable to Agree, Jury in Pollard Case Dismissed," *Atlanta Journal*, 6 December 1916, 3.

[63]Dittmer, *Black Georgia*, 28, 30-34; Doyle, *New Men*, 264-65.

[64]"Atlanta Will Give Candler Big Majority," *Atlanta Journal*, 25 November 1916, 1.

[65]"Jesse W. Armistead Works for Asa Candler In General Election," *Atlanta Journal*, 30 November 1916, 5; "Former Armistead Men Now Candler Supporters," *Atlanta Journal*, 1 December 1916, 7; "Organized Labor Support Asa Candler," *Atlanta Journal*, 3 December 1916, 1; "Every White Citizen Should Go To The Polls Wednesday and Vote For Asa Candler," *Atlanta Journal*, 4 and 5 December 1916, 1. The Armistead men included Councilman J. N. Renfroe, Councilman A. W. Farlinger, Alderman J. R. Seawright, Councilman Carl Dolvin (Armistead's manager) J. P. Wall, and others. The labor organizations represented by the statement included the Brotherhood of Railway Trainmen, Brotherhood of Locomotive Firemen and Enginemen, the Brotherhood of Locomotive Engineers and the Order of Railway Conductors. This announcement, dated December 2, also decried violence and stated that the committee had hired an attorney, Thomas B. Felder, to offer assistance to the solicitor general in prosecuting those accused of dynamite offenses.

[66]"Says Blodgett Planned to Deliver Negro Vote," *Atlanta Journal*, 6 December 1916.

[67]"Light Vote in City Election Indicated by Ballot at Noon," *Atlanta Journal* 6 December 1916, 1.

[68]Garrett, *Atlanta and Environs*, 2: 698-99. In the primary, Candler received 7,821 and Armistead 3,712; the general election totals were: Candler, 6,168 to Corrie, 3,524. In the general election, Candler's vote had dropped by 1,653; anti-Candler votes dropped by 188.

[69]B. J. Davis, "The Signs of Political Emancipation," *Atlanta Independent*, 9 December 1916, 1.

[70]"Every Member of City Administration in Chamber of Commerce," *Atlanta Journal*, 7 December 1916, 2.

[71]Minutes of the Atlanta City Council, vol. 26, 10 December 1918, City of Atlanta Records on deposit at Atlanta History Center Library/Archives; Deaton, *Atlanta During the Progressive Era*, 131-32; Garrett, *Atlanta and Environs*, 2: 688-89.

[72]"Candler Decries Misuse of Name," *Atlanta Constitution*, 11 September 1916, 2. His intention to vote for Nathaniel E. Harris in the coming governor's race became an issue, since Harris's opponent was H. M. Dorsey of Fulton County, the son of Candler's friend Judge R. T. Dorsey. The political career of the younger Dorsey evidently benefited from his successful prosecution, in 1913, of the Leo Frank case.

[73]White, *Leslie's Weekly* article, repr. in *Atlanta Constitution*, 21 September 1916, 8.

[74]"Mayor-elect Outlines Aims of Administration," *Atlanta Journal*, 8 December 1916, 3.

[75]"Candler Resigns from Various Officerships," *Atlanta Journal*, 22 December 1916, 1; Candler, *Asa Griggs Candler*, 324-25.

[76]Minutes of the Coca-Cola Company, vol. 2, The Archives, The Coca-Cola Company; Watters, *Coca-Cola*, 89.

[77]The indentures, all found in the AGC papers, Emory (along with other documents indicating the possible monetary value of the properties in question) transferred the following: 86 Hood street (later sold for $1500) fol. 2, box 14; Krog Street coal lot (later sold for $15,000) fol. 3, box 14; a portion of the old Exposition Cotton Mill property (later sold for $203,800; Coca-Cola acquired the balance of this parcel) fol. 1, box 15; 115-19 Auburn Avenue, near Edgewood Avenue (mortgaged at one time for $26,000) fol. 3, box 15; property in 200 block of Peachtree Street near Harris (later sold for $250,000) fols. 4 and 5, box 15; Forsyth Building, also called Realty Trust Building, at 74-78 Forsyth Street (involved in several large transactions, once mortgaged for $200,000, it was a valuable property in the business district) fols. 1-3, box 17; Point Peachtree property, near Peachtree Road and Dunwoody Road (parts of a residential development acquired by AGC after its developers defaulted on a loans from AGC totaling $103,500) see box 17.

[78]Candler, *Asa Griggs Candler*, 324-25.

CHAPTER TEN

Mayor

On the evening of New Year's Day 1917, Atlanta's council chamber filled with dignitaries who had come to see the new mayor take up his responsibilities as "chief executive of this corporation."[1] Candler had rejected proposals for an elaborate inauguration, and the *Journal* praised the occasion for its "genuine democratic simplicity." Although the outgoing Mayor, Jim Woodward, took the occasion to fire a few final barbs at his critics, he inflicted no serious wounds. The event remained congenial, providing a symbolic opportunity to set aside differences exposed during the recent election. Alderman Armistead, Candler's opponent in the summer primary, received a silver loving cup from grateful constituents; Mayor Woodward accepted a silver service from the hands of an old opponent, Alderman Albert Thomson. These pleasantries completed, onlookers stood to cheer Candler as he took the podium, where he was handed a basket of white roses. After reading and signing the oath, the new mayor asked his pastor, R. C. Cleckler of Inman Park Methodist Church, to lead a prayer.[2]

The ceremonies ended with an address by the new mayor. Candler again cautioned the city that belt-tightening would be necessary. He estimated the city deficit to be $150,000, and furthermore, revenues were low and likely to stay that way. The city charter strictly limited Atlanta's capacity to go into debt and could not be changed without the approval of the Georgia legislature. Even if the citizens agreed to a bond issue, final action had to await the next legislative session. For these reasons, Candler cautioned the city that "any great undertaking" would not be possible in the near future.[3] He promised to conserve the city's resources "by a harmonious, economical and businesslike administration of its affairs...neither parsimonious nor prodigal...neither niggardly nor wasteful." He also assured his listeners that he would serve Atlanta impartially, "as God gives me vision to see and strength to discharge my duty."[4]

Candler planned to be at work by ten o'clock each morning and to spend most of his day on the city's business, but during the first few days well-wishers paraded through his office and adorned his desk with bouquets of flowers. Enthusiasm ran so high that the mayor expressed the concern that "they expect great things of my administration—too much, I am afraid."[5] Nonetheless, he went to work with his usual zeal, demanding of others as much as he demanded of himself.

Fiscal matters took most of his attention in the early months of his term, when he demonstrated the money managing skills that had played an important part in his election. For example, he determined that Atlanta was selling its water below cost, in spite of the popular opinion that water service was priced high. He based his position on the sort of sophisticated accounting that was more common in business than in government:

If the waterworks department were charged with interest on the money spent in building it, and were charged with interest on the old abandoned system of waterworks at Lakewood, and were charged with depreciation of machinery and equipment, and were charged with a sinking fund to enlarge and renew equipment in the future, my opinion is that the department would show a loss at the present water rate.[6]

This analysis of the finances of the waterworks laid the groundwork for a proposed increase in the tax rates (in spite of his campaign promises), but first Candler insisted that Atlanta must cut expenses. A scant week after his inauguration he informed the chairman of the finance committee that "the city should live within its income." He insisted that the city's financial plans be realistic, based on future revenues "that they know or have every probable reason to suppose will be received during the year."[7] In another week he pounded the point home, telling the council's finance committee: "[You] gentlemen will simply have to make an apportionment sheet that stays within the city's income…. If the people will not give you the money to…do all the other things for which they are clamoring, then you are under no obligation to attempt those things." He added that they had a responsibility to protect public health, and life and property, but "you will have to apply the knife pretty deep…. You will have to cut out thousands of dollars."[8] The following day he again asserted the hard truth: Atlanta already was overspending its income, while at the same time, a growing population had increased demands for services. As a result, education, public health and recreation services suffered: "[The] city hasn't got the money, and it cannot give the people things until it gets the money…. I am merely stating a fact which must be perfectly obvious."[9]

The council accepted the mayor's admonitions, beginning by reducing the number of city employees. The construction department removed 112 jobs while the streets department slashed its work force from 297 to 64. The finance committee gave the Mayor a dose of his own medicine, proposing to reduce his salary by $500—although the final version of the budget restored it to $4,000 a year. Candler's son later said that the Mayor himself attempted unsuccessfully to reduce his annual salary to $2,000. In any case Candler donated the entire sum to various charitable causes. Over all, the committee cut department expenses by more than $80,000 and still was able to provide for modest improvements to some schools, streets, the water system and other city facilities.[10]

Expenses having been well cut, revenue increases became the next order of business. Candler urged property owners to fulfill their responsibility to pay fair taxes, invoking the support of a number of civic groups in the effort. He told the Atlanta Ad Men's Club, "With reasonable assessments and honest tax returns, Atlanta won't need any bond issue and we can do all that ought to be done...."[11] Meanwhile, the council began the process of putting a tax rate increase into effect, which needed approval by both the city and by the state legislature. In the interim, Candler relentlessly resisted all outlays of city funds that he considered unnecessary— a pattern that was familiar to all who had served with Candler on numerous boards of directors.[12]

Candler operated on a stated principle of "no politics and good service." He patterned his management of city affairs on modern business methods, delegating more responsibility to department heads. He sought to employ professional managers, not merely men with political connections.[13] The *Atlanta Journal* reported "Mayor Candler believes [in]...placing full power in the head of the department and holding him strictly accountable for good service."[14] The one-time prescriptionist could dose Atlanta with the strong medicine of careful management and fiscal conservatism precisely because he was not worried about reelection.

Candler's careful management paid off within the year; by December 1917 the city was debt free and able to grant modest salary increases to the remaining city employees.[15] The *Atlanta Journal* reported that "A balance of $296.17 remained in the city treasury of Atlanta on the first day of the New Year, after all current indebtedness had been paid" and attributed this "splendid financial showing" to the "efficient work of Mayor Candler and the members of the 1917 finance committee."[16] City workers, it should be noted, did not always share this enthusiasm for thrift. At least once in March 1918 a group of skilled construction department employees became frustrated enough to threaten a strike unless they received a half-dollar per day raise in pay.[17] The Mayor, however, continued to counsel rigorous economizing.[18]

Wealth and prominence begets enmity, and Asa Candler had his share of foes. During his term in city government, one such enemy, Mrs. Bessie Linn Smith, briefly published a tabloid newspaper devoted almost entirely to assaulting the character of Mayor Candler. Two 1917 issues of her *Atlanta Civics* equate Candler with the German Kaiser. She accused him of stiffing a newsboy of his three-cent sale and of denying the widow of the inventor of the original Coca-Cola formula a much-deserved pension. He supposedly told a delegation of women appealing on behalf of the widow Pemberton that "he was under no obligation in any way, shape, or form, morally, or otherwise, to provide for her....His conscience was clear and he dismissed the angry committee." In another edition of her paper, Smith directly accused Candler of swindling Mrs. Permberton out of the Coca-Cola formula. In this story, Smith reported that Mrs. Pemberton, now riddled with cancer, attempted to sell a homemade "set of table mats" to Candler, who "exclaimed over their beauty but firmly said, 'No, I can't afford it.'"

In spite of Smith's sympathy for the widow Pemberton's supposed loss of the rights to Coca-Cola, she also condemned Candler as the purveyor of a drink rendered habit-forming by the presence of cocaine—"...debauching almost an entire nation." Furthermore, according to Smith, Candler masterminded numerous plots to raid the public treasury and simultaneously evaded paying his fair share of taxes. She reminded her readers that the Neal Bank depositors never received a full return on their deposits.[19]

Who was Bessie Linn Smith and why did she hate Asa Candler? Her frequent references to his activities as mayor and to statements made during the mayoral campaign suggest that she filled her pen with a political venom brewed in a crucible of social struggle. Her loathing of Candler seems focused on his wealth, while her pathetic account of the lives of Atlanta's newsboys and a brief remark on the long-term results of the streetcar strike show her attachment to the city's laboring classes. In the November issue, the "Statement of the Ownership" required by the Post Office identifies Mrs. Smith, 100 North Moreland Avenue, as the publisher, editor, manager, and owner of the paper. The 1918 city directory also carries this information; after that she disappears. One possibility does exist. During this same period, a certain Ola Delight Smith (who was generally known as Mrs. E. B. Smith) played an active part in the Fulton Bag and Cotton Mill strike of 1914-1915, the most important organized labor action of this period in Atlanta, but one to which Asa Candler had no apparent connection. Ola Delight was as outspoken and combative as Bessie Linn and both avidly supported the interests of the working class. Ola left Atlanta at about the same time that Bessie disappears from the records. Could Ola and Bessie have been the same person, flamboyantly seeking public attention? Or, were they sisters? The mystery of Bessie Smith's identity remains unsolved.[20]

Smith's surly criticism aside, Asa Candler was generally well received by most Atlantans, who accepted his leadership as he imposed fiscal discipline on the city government. Indeed, Candler's administration experienced very little open opposition. The quarrels over public morality and the rights of labor, which had recently divided the city, began to fade from view as the Mayor played his customary fatherly role on this most public stage.

As Mayor, Candler had more to do than to pinch pennies and moralize. Cheerful and energetic, he provided plenty of light material for the newspapers. Shortly after taking office, he took part in a PTA-sponsored spelling bee at Grant Park School. Evidently he was a good speller, because he was one of the final three contestants when he finally missed a word. The Mayor "was so tired of standing up [that] he was mighty glad to miss." Perhaps some gallantry was also a factor, since the remaining two contestants were women. A Miss Ora Stamps was the winner of the contest; the identity of Candler's misspelled word is lost to history.

During a two-month period in early 1917, in addition to taking part in two spelling bees, he joined fire fighters at a rabbit dinner in honor of Fire Chief Cody. He also attended the annual Chamber of

Commerce banquet, an unusual occasion because members' wives for the first time were invited. This departed from the traditional practice of Atlanta civic organizations where all-male dinners were the norm.[21]

Candler's participation in public events as mayor also demonstrates once again his knack for public relations that was first apparent when he marketed Coca-Cola so effectively. If he acted as a tough administrator, he also had time to listen to any number of persons who sought his ear. Single tax advocates, prison reformers, lonely soldiers looking for wives, and sponsors of a "Better Babies Week" received friendly attention. When a "well-known charity worker," Martha W. Hogan, inscribed a Bible verse on a "tastily [SIC] decorated cardboard, enclosed in a glass frame," Candler "suspended" it over his desk.[22] He took time to reassure Mrs. E. Rumble of the Women's Christian Temperance Union that he would "do anything in my power to induce proper Sabbath observance in army circles as well as in civil life."[23]

His contemporaries saw him as powerful, wealthy, and pious, but he never played the stuffed shirt. Asked if he preferred to ride in an automobile or in a carriage in the 1917 Memorial Day parade he replied, " . . . speaking for myself I want neither one. Hundreds of schoolchildren are going to walk in the parade...certainly a man with the health and vigor I possess can march on foot, too."[24]

On one occasion, Asa Candler's service as mayor allowed him to demonstrate real qualities of leadership and physical courage. All cities, until late in the second half of the twentieth century, were terribly vulnerable to fire. In Atlanta, wooden shingles covered the roofs of many houses and the fire department still used horse-drawn pumps. Although the city had already begun the mechanization of the fire department and had recently passed laws to require the use of fireproof roofing materials, lumber dealers resisted the shingle change and persuaded the council to delay full implementation of the shingle ordinance. The *Journal* attempted a bit of humor when it headlined the story, "Anti-Shingle Roof Law of City is Under Fire."[25]

The joke soon ceased to amuse. On 21 May, a fire went out of control, consuming a seventy-three square block swath of homes and businesses in eastern Atlanta.[26] The great fire of 1917 began in a crowded district of warehouses and African-American homes near Decatur Street, traveled northward up Jackson and Boulevard streets, and crossed Ponce de Leon Avenue. As the flames spread from roof to roof, residents desperately tried to drag belongings out of danger and searched for missing family members. Streetcar conductors gave free rides to persons escaping the advancing fire. Atlanta's antiquated fire fighting apparatus could not keep up with the spreading destruction. By early afternoon Fire Chief W. B. Cody asked the mayor to appeal to neighboring communities for additional fire fighters. At least a dozen towns responded and local military forces also joined in the effort. In spite of their exertions, fires continued to break out. Chief Cody finally concluded that only a fire break could stop the wave of destruction. To create this strip of barren land, the firefighters dynamited several groups of houses, including some along Ponce de Leon Avenue, near a popular amusement park that was situated in the area of the present City Hall East.[27] Throughout the struggle, mayor Candler was on the scene. News stories credited him with going to the DuPont powder storehouse to get the dynamite to create the firebreak. The newspaper dramatically recounted his activities: "Throughout the sweep of flames…he directed efforts to check the river of fire. Always he showed utter disregard for his own safety. Up and down Ponce de Leon avenue where hot flames scorched the cheeks and blasts of dynamite threw fragments of brick and shafts of wood for distances of a hundred yards, he passed a dozen times to see what assistance firemen and soldiers needed…proving himself in every sense 'city father.'"[28]

Surprisingly, only one life was lost, that of a woman who died "of shock." The destruction covered a strip of land two miles long and half a mile wide, leaving some 10,000 people without homes. Many families camped out in Piedmont Park until they could find better shelter. Included in the losses were 1537 dwellings, 42 stores, 351 garages and outhouses, and 8 other structures, including churches, schools, and warehouses, a loss of $5.5 million. Some eighty percent of the burned structures had wood shingle roofs.[29]

The Mayor appointed a Committee on Rehabilitation made up of "carefully selected businessmen and three negro citizens." The city council appropriated $15,000 for the relief of fire victims; citizens of Atlanta donated money, goods, and services. Asa Candler made a personal gift of a thousand dollars and each of the Candler-connected firms, such as Central Bank and Trust and Coca-Cola, gave similar amounts. However, if generosity prevailed, the Jim Crow customs of the day never lagged. The Red Cross relief station in the Auditorium-Armory distributed relief supplies to whites through the main entrance, while Negroes were sent up the side alley to a freight entrance to obtain their help. Rehabilitation Committee General Chairman Lee Ashcroft organized a canvassing subcommittee to raise money for a general relief fund that included "twelve leading negro preachers of Atlanta." The chairman of the committee, Colonel F. J. Paxon complacently informed the newspaper "This relief campaign has recognized no race or color..." and congratulated the "colored pastors" for their performance of their duties. After about a month, the wood-shingle ordinance was belatedly put into full force and the story disappeared from the daily news.[30] A retrospective article written a year later boasted, "Within another year, if the rebuilding goes on as planned, there will be small trace of the burned district left."[31]

Financial problems, managerial responsibilities and even disasters did not occupy all of Asa Candler's concerns as mayor of Atlanta. Public morality still worried him. In his inaugural address, Candler had told the City Council, "Human history had its beginning in a garden—it will have its consummation in a city....Evidently God meant men to come together and work out their salvation under the conditions of the mass."[32] However, if cities were both unavoidable and full of dangers, his own city seemed to be a special case. In the spirit of moral guardianship, he asserted that Atlanta's position as a commercial center was both a "great advantage and solemn responsibility," because "if evil things prevail in our midst, they quickly spread all over Georgia and surrounding territory."[33]

Controversies over the morality of the city had sparked the dismissal of former Police Chief James L. Beavers, but the chief refused to go quietly. He took the city to court. Therefore, the issue continued through the first year of Candler's service. The Mayor had made his personal position clear in 1916, at a mass meeting in support of Beavers' cause, when he declared, "The good people of Atlanta cannot approve the demoting of a faithful officer until they are ready to penalize virtue and eulogize vice; and surely they are not yet ready for that."[34] Beavers now had a friend in city hall; his case symbolized the mayor's view of the need to uplift public morality as it struggled against the obstacles imposed by urban life.

When Beavers first went to court, he won a ruling that ordered the police board to give him a new hearing. The board then amended their charges against him and added some new ones. The ex-chief again turned to the courts for relief. In April 1917 the court once again ruled in Beavers' favor, although various delays postponed the final board hearing until the end of October.[35]

With the Beavers controversy in the background, it follows that Mayor Candler took an active interest in the proceedings of the police board. By the time he assumed office, the membership of this group had entirely changed and those who had originally voted to remove Beavers were out of office. However, at the board's first 1917 meeting, Mayor Candler made a point to reiterate his support for public virtue. At this meeting, the board suspended for thirty days an officer who had been found drunk. They took this action even though the officer was off duty at the time of the offense. Candler declined to vote on the matter, because "I do not want to force my opinions down your throats." However, he could not resist the opportunity to express his opposition to drinking: "A policeman and a drunk man are incompatible. My idea is that a man carrying a pistol should not take a drink under any circumstances....If I were chief of police I would want every drinking man fired." Remembering his original intention to refrain from interference, he then added: "It has been said by many persons that when I became mayor I would 'tear up' the police department and make many changes. I do not intend doing any such thing...but we must have good discipline."[36]

By the end of the month the *Journal* reported that Candler "let it be understood...from his knowledge of the police department already gained, he is not very favorably impressed with its discipline." Not only did Candler think that the police department needed more discipline, he objected to the casual atmosphere of police board meetings. Board members smoked while they carried on business with their feet propped on the table; police officers and other spectators came and went, gawking through the open doors.[37]

While the litigation in Beavers's case continued, Candler, the ever-attentive manager, continued to watch police conduct closely. When a policeman, A. S. Brannen, petitioned to be paid for two days he had taken off to nurse a "mashed" thumb, the mayor waved his own nailless thumb (smashed in a limousine door) and declared, "I didn't lose a minute from work." The officer lost his petition.[38] From time to time, but particularly during the period while the Beavers case remained unresolved, the newspapers carried stories of police misconduct: contraband liquor stored as evidence vanished mysteriously, officers abused prisoners, and some accepted so-called "rewards" for recovering stolen property or otherwise performing their regular duties. Clergy accused police of winking at disorderly houses, while police defenders countered with the feeble claim that "white slavery" (prostitution) was no worse than it had been during Chief Beavers' administration.[39]

As Beavers' final hearing approached, the rumor mills of city hall provided plentiful grist for consumption by the daily press. Some members of the police board apparently hoped that Beavers would agree to a prearranged outcome: he would be exonerated and reinstated but would immediately resign. Some versions of the "understanding" went on to have Captain Lamar Poole elevated to the position of chief, replacing Chief Mayo. Some even hinted that "some place of subordinate rank" might be found for Beavers. None of this took into account Beavers' desire for complete vindication.

Although he agreed to accept the board's evaluation of his perform-ance as chief, he understood that any "deal" would undermine his claim to be a victim of injustice. The contest went forward.[40]

With a new police board and a powerful ally in Mayor Candler, Beavers' position had greatly improved, although doubts about his competence remained strong. Off-the-record hallway conferences had marked the final hearing, which lasted until two o'clock in the morning. The board cleared him of all charges, except a count of incompetency based on "instances of friction" in the department. Beavers was reinstated as chief while former Chief Mayo resumed his rank of captain. Two conditions attached to the reinstatement. Beavers waived any claims to back pay and promised to resign after ninety days, if requested to do so by the board.[41]

Although he had won, Beavers' enjoyment of his victory must have been diluted by the faint public praise offered by his support-ers—even Mayor Candler. Commissioner E. H. Inman, one of those who voted for him because the conditions of his dismissal had been irregular, told a reporter, "Beavers...possesses neither the executive ability nor the proper temperament to make a satisfactory head of the Atlanta police department." Former Mayor Woodward denounced the conclusion of the controversy as "a dirty piece of pol-itics."[42] Nonetheless, within three days Beavers resumed his relentless pursuit of vice. Although he did not always receive enthusiastic sup-port from Atlanta's leaders, neither was he asked to resign when his ninety days trial period had passed. He held his position for several years and in the future was to prove loyal to Asa Candler in a time of intense personal trial.

Although Candler went against the tide of popular opinion in his support of Beavers, he usually found himself in accord with his peers. A faithful Democrat as well as a civic leader, Candler organized and led the "Loyal Legion" of Atlantans that attended Woodrow Wilson's second inauguration. On a gray, drizzly Saturday morning about sixty "leading citizens" gathered at the station where a special train, ten Pullman cars long, waited to carry them to Washington, D.C. Representatives of the police and fire departments, and a drum and bugle corps joined the party. Mayor Candler posed for a newspaper photographer at the throttle of the red, white, and blue locomotive. The 12-year-old daughter of the leader of the drum and bugle corps—a sort of mascot for the music group—also posed for the camera; she the only female to make the trip to Washington.

As the train rolled toward the capital city, Candler received constant attention all along the way. A reporter observed, "At every station, the people swarm forward asking for Mayor Candler, anxious to shake the hand of the south's foremost capitalist and the mayor of the south's foremost city." When they reached Washington, the Loyal Legion marched in the inaugural parade, dressed in business suits and black derby hats; they carried white hickory walking canes, and wore "Atlanta" arm bands. An over-sized flag that bore the city seal on a field of blue preceded them. The new president had spent a brief year in their city, in the days when Asa Candler had been an ambitious young entrepreneur selling pharmaceuticals only a few blocks away from the future president's law office. Now he smiled and bowed as Candler and the "venerable" Judge George Hillyer led the Atlanta contingent past the reviewing stand.[43]

On another occasion, Mayor Candler, as a retired member of the Governor's Horse Guard, took particular pleasure in helping to plan—and participating in—a celebration to honor the return of local members of the National Guard from the Texas-Mexico border where they had stood guard against raids by the forces of the legendary revolutionary, Pancho Villa. Two trainloads of men arrived late on the night of 28 March, to be met by joyful and weeping families and well-wishers. The next day the citizens of Atlanta treated them to a celebration dinner, "a plain meal for plain men," in the Auditorium-Armory. Patriotic ceremonies marked the occasion, which ended in a dance.[44] The Mayor, as he prepared to present medals to the four senior officers of the Guard, praised the guardsmen and told them that he hoped their camp would be located in Atlanta. "We will feel safer to have you here, for we know that the Germans will never get to Atlanta while you are with us."[45]

Candler's reference to the German "threat" to Atlanta points to the fact that when he spoke to the Georgia guardsmen, a formal U.S. declaration of war against the Central Powers was scarcely a week away. The nation's blood was up; preparation for the apparently inevitable conflict stirred both civilians and the military into action.

Candler's position as leader of the city put him in the forefront of the Atlanta war effort, where he filled both practical and symbolic roles. He now had the responsibility to keep the city in compliance with various federal regulations on consumption of fuel and food-stuffs. He also appointed the Exemption Boards that drafted young men for military service.[46]

However, Mayor Candler understood that leadership went beyond grimly regulating the city to do its duty in the war effort. When President Wilson proclaimed a day of prayer for an American victory, thousands of Atlantans met at Five Points. There, beneath "Old Glory," representative clergy (including Bishop Candler) offered their prayers. Then Mayor Candler "strode to the edge of the plat-form."

> "Three cheers for General John J. Pershing!" he shouted
> "Whee! Whee! Whee!" the crowd echoed.
> "Three cheers for General Petain of the French army!" Mr. Candler cried and the crowd again yelled.
> "And let us not forget Marshal Haig." said the mayor.
> "Again three cheers!"
> "And General Foch!"
> "Cheer again."
> "And now for our great president, who has called us togeth-er...."
> The cheers were redoubled and the military band first played "Dixie" and "The Marseilles."[47]

To promote interest in the planting of victory gardens, the Mayor challenged Governor Hugh Dorsey to a plowing contest. "I've plowed before in the old days on the farm and I am confident that I can plow the better furrow," Candler boasted to a reporter. Before the contest, city gardeners shouldered their rakes and hoes and paraded through the city streets to military tunes provided by a volunteer band of Atlanta Federation of Musicians members. The victorious plowman was to receive "a special bouquet of carrots, onions, cabbage and other popular vegetables," but tactful judges ruled the contest to be a draw.[48]

Another symbolic gesture by Candler reflects a subtle shift in Atlanta customs that had begun during the Spanish-American War. Late in March 1917, he made an exception to his rule against advertising displays or "private cards" in the windows of the Candler Building to give his tenants permission to hang American flags there.[49] Throughout the city, increasing use of the national flag and anthem demonstrated the return to the display of symbols of national patriotism in the territory of the old Confederacy. The process had begun when sons of the South—including Asa's brother John, who suffered a serious wound—fought under the stars and stripes during the Spanish-American war. Now, international conflict made national patriotism increasingly popular, and the mayor's sentiments matched those of the general public. Atlanta schools began to open each day with patriotic observances. Mayor Candler and members of the Board of Education attended some of these ceremonies. The newspaper reported that "[They] have come away feeling a new pride and a new enthusiasm, and they are glad to know that the exercises will be continued."[50] At the same time, the mayor ordered the flag to be flown daily from nine to five at City Hall and, in a similar spirit, led a public subscription campaign to purchase regimental and national colors for Atlanta's 125th (formerly the Fifth) regiment. In less than a year after the country entered the World War, the decorations and patriotic *tableaux vivants* presented at the annual Chamber of Commerce dinner prominently included American flags.[51]

As soon as war became likely, Candler and other leaders of Atlanta's business community combined patriotic concerns with the furtherance of Atlanta's economic interests in a campaign to bring a military training camp to the city.[52] For many years the military outposts of the United States had been scattered and relatively small, but the prospect of a major war inspired the military to reorganize and to establish a number of large training camps dedicated to the production of the mass armies that soon would do battle in Europe. These "cantonments" were to be scattered across the country in locations that met certain qualifications. They must be inland and away from borders, to protect against invasion. They must be close to centers of rail transportation. They must be large and on well drained sites to permit mass maneuver exercises. They must have adequate supplies of water and power. As a final point, the price of the land had to be acceptable.[53]

The Chamber of Commerce, with Candler's full cooperation, launched a campaign to acquire real estate where a cantonment might be located. Candler announced that, "I am convinced…that Atlanta, if she goes after this in the proper manner, can get it. It will mean so much to Atlanta."[54] Patriotism, both national and local, certainly played some part in their enthusiasm for the project, but practical considerations came into play as well. Such a camp could be expected to bring large numbers of men—potential consumers—into the area; estimates put their aggregate pay at about $400,000 a month. Furthermore the camp itself would be a large purchaser of local goods and services.[55]

If Atlanta fit the criteria established for the selection of a cantonment location, it also enjoyed an added advantage. Major General Leonard A. Wood, the hero of the Spanish–American War who was in charge of the site selection process, had formerly been stationed at Fort McPherson, on the southern outskirts of the city. During that time he had coached Georgia Tech's first football team. His return to the city to inspect possible sites for a cantonment was a reunion with old friends. The general enjoyed a Sunday breakfast at the Capital City Club as the guest of the Chamber of Commerce. There he regaled his hosts with stories of the first Georgia Tech-University of Georgia football game.[56]

While awaiting a final decision, the Chamber again acted as an unofficial branch of government taking responsibility for sorting out the various tracts of land put forth as possible sites. They raised money to cover the expenses of their campaign and sent delegations to Washington to press the city's interests. A gift to the federal government by Mayor Candler furthered the case for an Atlanta cantonment. Ivan Allen, then president of the Chamber of Commerce wrote his recollection of this early contribution to the war effort, referring to himself in the third person: "Early one morning young [Ivan] Allen rushed into the Mayor's office in the old City Hall with the idea of locating the Quartermaster's Depot in the Candler Warehouse, which was the largest modern fire-proof building in the South.…Before Allen could finish with the suggestion, the Mayor said, 'What are you doing about it? Get on the first train to Washington!'"

"Young Allen" inquired what terms might be offered to the government.

Candler replied, "Terms! Terms! Ivan. We are in war. Nothing counts now except to win the war. The Government can have the Warehouse and use it free."[57]

Making some allowance for literary license, this exchange still seems to represent Candler's enthusiastic approach to the war effort fairly. On the other hand, it may not convey the entire picture. The crisis in the cotton market had passed as wartime demand had brought about a quick recovery in cotton prices. The amount of cotton stored for the long term in the mammoth warehouse probably no longer filled its acres of space. Cotton growers did not need to hold their crops and wait for a better price. In fact, Charles Howard Candler, in his account of his father's life, commented: "Its purpose accomplished, Father was no longer interested in owning the warehouse and the company.…"[58] On the other hand, the mammoth warehouse was well-suited to be a depot for the Quartermaster's Corps—and where better to locate a new training camp than close to a supply depot? The committee that put Atlanta's proposal for the cantonment before General Wood also presented him with Mayor Candler's offer of the warehouse. No one seems to have questioned the propriety of the Chamber's acting as the agent of the city.[59]

On 18 May 1917, the citizens of Atlanta read the official announcement that the city would be the site of one of thirty-two divisional cantonments to be constructed around the country. Camp Gordon, named for the Confederate hero and Georgia politician John B. Gordon, was to be located adjacent to the Oglethorpe University campus, on Peachtree Road. To secure the final arrangements, the Chamber of Commerce, still speaking for the city government, made the crucial promise that 2.5 million gallons of water a day could be supplied to the site.[60]

Mayor Candler summoned the city council to a special meeting to appropriate the $197,500 needed to pay for the water main that would link Camp Gordon to the Atlanta water system. A special tax provided the funding for this outlay. Furthermore, after receiving the approval of the city attorney, the city reimbursed the Chamber of Commerce the $13,050 it had paid out to compensate tenant farmers who had lost their crops when they had to move off the land where the camp was to be built. Convicts went to work on the ditch where city water department employees would lay cast iron and wooden pipes. By the end of August, Camp Gordon had water.[61]

This expansion of the Atlanta water service imposed a heavy load on an already stressed system. As a result of this and other city needs, the following summer the city faced an emergency bond election. The largest portion of the bond issue, $500,000, was to be spent to improve the water works, where old and patched pumps threatened to fail at any moment. Other proposed expenditures were complete motorization of the fire department, construction of a fireproof building to house properly the giant Cyclorama painting of the Battle of Atlanta, and the purchase of an electric generating plant to be operated by steam produced by the heat of the city incinerator. The pumps and other proposed water department improvements would benefit all city water users, but the supporters of the bond issue centered their public emphasis on the patriotic need to support the further development of Camp Gordon. Future expansion of the cantonment depended on improved water service.[62]

To pass a city bond issue, the state law required the approval of a two-thirds majority of all registered voters. Therefore, if a small number of voters turned out, the bond issue could not pass, even if it received all of the votes cast. Since many registrants were away in the military, city leaders began an energetic campaign to get out enough votes. They went so far as to encourage even the small number of registered Negro voters to participate. The *Atlanta Journal* cartoonist implored a figure representing the "VOTERS," sleeping in a "BED OF APATHY" to "WAKE UP" before "THE BURNING NEED OF CITY BONDS"—tongues of flame—consumed him in his sleep. The bond issue did receive a majority, but the total number of votes cast failed to meet the rigorous requirement of the law. This failure blocked the city's funding of the water project, so the commander of Camp Gordon immediately informed Washington and halted all plans for further expansion.[63]

On the day after the bond election, Mayor Candler issued a statement condemning the state law, asserting that the situation showed "the necessity of amending the state constitutional requirements governing bond issues if cities are to progress and prosper." However, he stated, "Our citizens may rest assured that the governing authorities will find some means whereby the water supply will be protected without needless delay."[64] A representative of the city council bond committee announced that the council was willing to spend the necessary amount, but the fact remained that they simply did not have the money.[65]

When the council met the following day, Candler, with what the *Journal* called "characteristic civic loyalty," presented a solution to the crisis. He believed that the next year's council would be able to push through a bond issue to raise the $250,000 expense, so, in the mean time, Candler would personally pay for the immediate purchase of the needed pumps. Reordering of other budgeted expenditures provided the balance of the funds needed to complete the planned improvements to the water system. The newspaper said that to the council, this plan was "manna from heaven."[66] Of course it was not manna—an unencumbered gift from above—but rather, Candler had once again loaned his economic strength to assist Atlanta through a crisis. Of course, the good steward expected repayment, as this also was his responsibility. Its water supply assured, the cantonment continued its activities for the duration of the war.

Asa Candler received little but positive publicity during the years of his service as Mayor, but on Valentine's Day 1918, a minor scandal and subsequent legal proceedings touched his name. Newspapers reported that the Mayor had charged two persons, J. W. Cook and a Mrs. H. H. Hirsch, with attempted blackmail; they had threatened to reveal improper advances allegedly made by the elderly mayor toward Margaret Hirsch, an attractive, dark-eyed brunette in her late thirties. In the following weeks, the scandal regularly pushed war news out of the lead position in the *Atlanta Journal's* front pages and received prominent play in the *Constitution*. The latter primly characterized much of the testimony as "morbid and obscene" and then enthusiastically reprinted the transcripts at length.[67]

Mrs. Hirsch claimed innocence and refused to seek bail. She brought a few items from home to decorate her special quarters in the hospital section of the Fulton County jail—an institution known, with a touch of the gothic, as the Tower. There she knitted a sweater for the Red Cross and gave interviews to reporters who took note of her chic clothing. Her friend Cook, in a nearby part of the prison, paced, chain-smoked, and met with attorneys. Mrs. Hirsch's husband, an insurance man described as having a worried look in his eyes, returned from a business trip and consulted with his tearful wife and their clergyman. He waffled when asked if he would stand by her: "I can't answer that now. She has always been a good wife. Wait until I learn something about the matter."[68]

The superficially delicious testimony in these trials still has the interest that any scandal offers to those of us who are merely human. Atlantans loved it at the time, lining up early for seats at the trials and bringing box lunches so as not to lose their places. On the other hand, we can find in this petty scandal a demonstration of the steely character of Asa Candler and his closest associates and an example of the way they worked together when challenged by a crisis.

Mrs. Hirsch had first met Candler at a Red Cross charity event, and she evidently pursued the association thereafter. According to Candler's testimony, she had come to his third floor office on the afternoon in question, ostensibly to discuss issues of animal cruelty. Saying that she was tired and hot, she took off her coat before sitting down. As they were talking, she "suddenly exclaimed" that there was a man on the ledge outside of the window. When Candler reassured her that it was probably a window washer, she objected, "it was a well-dressed white man." Candler went to the window, looked out, but saw nothing; turned back into the room, and saw that Mrs. Hirsch had removed her hat and opened the door to the hallway.

A man, standing in the doorway, said, "Our Honorable Mayor! This is nice!"[69]

The man in the door proved to be the second defendant, J. W. Cook. Candler recognized the potential danger of the situation at once and left the room, returning in a few moments with his son Asa, Jr., whose office was on the next floor. Cook had already gone and Mrs. Hirsch then left as well. Candler immediately called his friend and business associate Forrest Adair and asked him to come to his office. Candler's brother, Judge John Candler also joined them. While the men discussed the incident, Mrs. Hirsch telephoned to ask for "a conference." Over the next few days, there followed a complicated series of meetings between Candler's associates and either Mrs. Hirsch or Cook.

At one of these conferences, Forrest Adair asked Cook, "Cook, what is it you want? What is this we're up against?" Adair testified that Cook answered, "I am a great friend of Mr. Hirsch, and I am very much shocked by what has been going on. Asa Candler is an old hypocrite, and I will talk with him and nobody else. I will tell him what he has got to do."[70] After some maneuvering, Adair did set up such a meeting. Cook then claimed to be a friend of Mrs. Hirsch's husband and said that he only wanted to protect his friend from "this woman." But Cook also made a point of his own shady and violent past and claimed that a recent Billy Sunday crusade had made him a changed man. He told Candler that he had seen him in a compromising position with Mrs. Hirsch. Candler told Cook flatly that he had seen "no such thing." Cook insisted that they should force Mrs. Hirsch to sign a written agreement to get out of town.

Adair's trial testimony continues the story. He reported Cook's statements to Mrs. Hirsch in a meeting that included the three of them. After a nice display of weeping, Mrs. Hirsch told Adair, "If I do have to leave my husband and leave the city I ought to be well provided for." She was ready with the figures this would require—bonds and securities yielding at least $3,000 a year. An annuity would not be acceptable, because it might end with Candler's death: "she wanted the principal in her own hands." At this point the negotiations broke off because the lady had a card party to attend. Later in the day she returned to Adair's office to add another proviso to the negotiations, that her husband's debts also be paid off. She thought that about $5,000 would cover everything. She also took the occasion to warn Adair that her husband was "a cool, nervy man" who might have shot both her and Candler, had he known about their supposed relationship.

A few days later, Adair again conferred with Cook, sitting on a retaining wall somewhere on Alabama Street. Adair testified that Cook threw an arm over his shoulders and told him: "Now, Forrest, you tell old man Candler to do the things I have told him to do, then eat a hearty supper and go to bed, and I'll never breathe it to a soul."[71]

In the midst of these developments, the inconvenient Mr. Hirsch came back to Atlanta for a weekend visit, delaying the blackmailers' progress. When he again left town, Cook met with Adair. He reiterated his own criminal past and said—according to Adair—"I am getting damn tired of all this talking....I have told Candler what to do, and if he don't do it I will tell my friend." He claimed that it "was all that he could do" to resist the urge to tell Hirsch the awful truth during the previous weekend's visit. Another meeting was arranged with Mrs. Hirsch.

The Mayor did not attend this conference, but Asa, Jr. and Forrest Adair represented him. Mrs. Hirsch preferred to speak with the elder Candler, but she soon settled down to the task at hand, describing her formerly happy marriage, weeping and wringing her hands. Adair's testimony continued: "Then she said she had been thinking the matter over and she had in her possession a newspaper clipping telling of Mayor Candler's gift of $1,000,000 to Emory University, and she thought he would be getting off light if he gave her one-half that amount."[72] The husband's debts would still be part of any appropriate settlement. She did a bit of figuring on the margin of a newspaper; the exact sum of his indebtedness was $4,250. Adair made no promises, but stated that he would confer with Candler and communicate with her later.

Cook and Mrs. Hirsch had no idea what a dangerous game they played, perhaps because they only knew the kindly public persona that Candler had so carefully cultivated over the years, not the iron will that it concealed. He would not be intimidated. Candler promptly took the incriminating evidence—Mrs. Hirsch's jottings in the margin of the newspaper—to the grand jury, which indicted the two blackmailers.

By the end of the month Cook's trial took place, and Mrs. Hirsch's trial followed in the middle of March. Neither defendant was able to present a credible case. Other than the newspaper, the only physical evidence produced was an article of woman's underwear that Cook claimed to have picked up when Candler left his office to get his son. These silk panties provided a good deal of peek-a-boo fun for the lawyers who "accidentally" dropped them in front of the jury well before introducing them into evidence, but Cook could not prove his claim as to their origins.

On the other hand, prosecution witnesses linked the two accused blackmailers on a number of occasions. They often shared drinks at Al Martin's soda fountain and on one occasion took alternate bites from a piece of pie at a fair. He had made daily visits to her during a time when she was in the hospital. Furthermore, she had consulted both a lawyer and a banker days before the incident at the Candler building, evidently planning the investment of the anticipated windfall. Mrs. Hirsch's claim of social "respectability" lost ground when testimony revealed two former husbands (one attended her trial) and an early career as a manicurist. Most damning was the newspaper with her estimate of her husband's debts figured in the margin. In the end, both juries found their respective defendants guilty, and Judge Ben Hill meted out the maximum penalty to each offender: a $1,000 fine and one year in jail. The luckless Mr. Hirsch sued for divorce. Judge Hill then reduced Mrs. Hirsch's sentence and she promptly left town.

In both trials Candler and Adair recounted their version of events and stood up to some fairly aggressive and insinuating cross-examination. If it cast little light on the facts of the case, it did air some interesting bits of information about the two men and their relationship. They revealed that Forrest Adair had helped Candler with half a dozen other shakedown attempts. As a result of this experience, they had become adept at playing the extortionists along, as in this case where he let them "develop the plot," to the point that physical evidence was created. Adair testified to a long and close association with Candler and revealed that "in some years we [the Adair brothers firm] realize as much as $100,000 from him in commissions and in business transactions generally."[73] Candler, asked on cross examination if he were "a normal man," tartly replied, "I am as normal as any 66-year-old man can be." He also directly denied making any improper advances to Mrs. Hirsch and answered simply "No," when asked if he were "worth fifty million dollars."[74]

In the course of this episode, several men, including two of Asa Candler's sons and his brother, and his business associate Forrest Adair, worked together to trap the blackmailers in a way that demonstrated mutual trust and long experience at cooperative undertakings. Asa Candler proved to be the "cool, nervy man" in this little drama. His personal reputation remained unblemished, as editorial support testified.[75] The two schemers, plotting as they sipped their sodas on the mezzanine of Al Martin's fountain, never had a chance.

At the end of his two-year term, Candler had sorted out the city's fiscal problems and although all the needed city improvements had not been accomplished, he had seen Atlanta through fire, war, and other, lesser crises. In part he succeeded because he had no political aspirations and thus had no particular need to cater to any interest group in order to be reelected. In this sense the city had enjoyed the services of a professional manager not unlike the city managers advocated by some progressive reformers. He left office with a plea for a more efficient system of city administration, because Atlanta's government was "too scattered and disconnected in its operations" to be effective.[76] At the end, he still worried that the mass character of urban society would erode the sense of individual morality and that democracy might degenerate into mob rule.[77] Like the Puritans of old Boston, he saw a larger role for his city: "Ours is indeed a city set on a hill, which we cannot hide. This fact imposes upon Atlanta people a responsibility as sacred as a trust. Its life must be pure or it will be poisonous to communities outside. Wherefore, let us stand firmly, immovably, for the things that are good."[78]

As Candler observed his sixty-seventh birthday, the *Coca-Cola Bottler* of December 1918 announced: "Mr. Candler Retires from Active Business." The story outlined the new roles his sons would take in the various Candler enterprises.[79] His term as mayor completed, Asa Candler neared the end of his career as a public servant.

---

[1]Charles Howard Candler, *Asa Griggs Candler* (Atlanta: Emory University, 1950) 145, 324. In the following pages, the descriptions of AGC's routine activities as mayor draw largely on a detailed examination of the daily *Atlanta Journal* for the years 1917-1918.

[2]"Candler Resigns from Various Officerships," *Atlanta Journal*, 22 December 1916, 1; "Candler Inaugurated Amid Prolonged Cheers," *Atlanta Journal*, 2 January 1917, 5.

[3]Deaton, "Atlanta During the Progressive Era," 409; "Economy is Urged by mayor Candler in His Inaugural," *Atlanta Journal*, 2 January 1917, 5. A second version of Candler's inaugural address, virtually identical to that reported in the *Journal*, may be found in fol. 21, box 2 of AGC papers, Emory.

[4]Ibid.; "Asa G. Candler Will Take Charge Today of Affairs of City," *Atlanta Constitution*, 2 January 1917, 1.

[5]"Scores of Atlantians [SIC] Throng City Hall to Greet Mayor Candler," *Atlanta Journal*, 2 January 1917, 4. See also: "With Candler as Mayor Feeling of Confidence Sweeps All of Atlanta," *Atlanta Journal*, 3 January 1917, 1.

[6]"$175,000 Is Needed to Pay the City's Operating Expenses," *Atlanta Journal*, 7 January 1917, 5.

[7]"Economical Sheet Urged by Candler," *Atlanta Constitution*, 7 January 1917, 4.

[8]"Finance Committee, Hopelessly at Sea, Calls in the Mayor," *Atlanta Journal*, 11 January 1917,

1. See also, "Economical Sheet Urged by Candler," *Atlanta Constitution*, 7 January 1917, 4.

[9]"City Must Have More Revenue, Says Mayor," *Atlanta Journal*, 12 January 1917, 1.

[10]"Must Discharge 112 Men, Says Collier," *Atlanta Journal*, 17 January 1917, 9; "Only 64 Employes [SIC] Out of 297 Left for Street Work," *Atlanta Journal*, 19 January 1917, 1; "Salary of Dixie's Biggest Financier Is Reduced by City," *Atlanta Journal*, 18 January 1917, 1; "Finance Sheet Passed with But Few Changes," *Atlanta Journal*, 19 January 1917, 4; "New Money Sheet Passed by Council with Few Changes," *Atlanta Constitution* 19 January 1917, 1; and "January Finance Sheet Provides for $226,567 Improvements in City," *Atlanta Constitution*, 13 January 1917, 1. See also, "Many City Departments Must Reduce Employes [SIC]," 13 January 1917, 1; and "$107,000 Needed to Meet Expenses," *Atlanta Constitution*, 11 January 1917, 1; Candler, *Asa Candler*, 327-28; "Mayor Candler Gives Away a Year's Salary," *Atlanta Journal*, 22 December 1917, 1.

[11]"With Tax Returns We Won't Need Bonds,'" *The City Builder* 1/12 (10 February 1917): 32; the same event is treated in "Candler Urges Proper Return of City Taxes," *Atlanta Journal*, 9 February 1917, 4. This story quoted Candler: "I don't know when I have seen so many organizations that are ready and willing to help."

[12]"Mayor Leaves Initiative in Tax Rate Increase in Hands of Council," *Atlanta Journal*, 13 February 1917, 5. Some examples of Candler's economizing may be seen in: "Mayor, in First Veto, Kills Resolution to Align Power Co.'s Building," *Atlanta Journal*, 9 February 1917, 3; "500 Citizens Demand Paving of Peachtree St.," *Atlanta Journal*, 14 February 1917, 5 (and a related story on p. 9 of the next day's paper); "Mayor Vetoes Measures, and Then Explains Why," *Atlanta Journal*, 28 February 1917, 8; "Man Who Improves Street Must Pay For It," 12 June 1917, 12; "Mayor Vetoes Increase of Firemen's Benefits," *Atlanta Journal*, 7 July 1917, 2; "Mayor's Veto Expected on Fireman's Increase," *Atlanta Journal*, 24 September 1917, 5.

[13]Ibid.; "Death Knell of Politics in Departments of City Sounded by New Mayor," *Atlanta Constitution*, 5 January 1917, 1.

[14]"Death Knell of Politics in Departments of City Sounded by Mayor," *Atlanta Constitution*, 5 January 1917, 1; "Chief Cody Given Full Control over Firemen," *Atlanta Journal*, 5 January 1917, 9.

[15]"Mayor Expected Soon to Sign Salary Ordinances," *Atlanta Journal*, 18 December 1917, 10; "Atlanta Ends Business Year Entirely Free of Debts," *Atlanta Journal*, 23 December 1917, 3.

[16]"Atlanta Had Balance of $296.17 January 1 after All Debts Paid," *Atlanta Journal*, 6 January 1918, 4.

[17]"City Workmen Threaten to Strike for More Pay," *Atlanta Journal*, 20 March 1918, 2.

[18]AGC, untitled, 6 January 1918, "Mayor's speeches and Reports, 1918," fol. 22, box 2, AGC papers, Emory. This report also can be seen in "'Who Serves His Country Well Serves His City Best,' Mayor Candler's Message for Year 1918 to City Council," *Atlanta Journal*, 8 January 1918, 4.

[19]*Atlanta Civics* (November and December 1917), in AGC papers, Emory. These may be the only copies of Smith's publication extant. Inquiries have failed to discover any others.

[20]Ibid.; Atlanta city directory, 1918. No Atlanta city directory was published in 1917. For further information on Ola Delight (Mrs. E. B.) Smith see Gary Fink, *The Fulton Bag and Cotton Mills Strike of 1914-1915: Espionage, Labor Conflict, and New South Industrial Relations* (Ithaca NY: ILR Press, 1993); this volume also provides a helpful insight into the labor movement in Atlanta during the first decades of the century.

[21]Stories in the *Atlanta Journal* demonstrate these activities: "Candler Returns to Boyhood Days in Spelling Bee," 25 January 1917, 1; "Mayor Candler Will Attend Spelling Bee," 20 February 1917, 5; "Mayor Is Honor Guest at Fire Chief's Dinner," 22 February, 1917, 18;

"Presence of Ladies to Feature Chamber Dinner," 3 January 1917, 4.

[22]"Single Tax Advocates Seek Aid of Candler," *Atlanta Journal*, 26 February 1917, 2; "Prison Reform Workers Call on Mayor Candler," *Atlanta Journal*, 16 November 1917, 7; "Ask Mayor Candler to Add Marriage Bureau to Office," *Atlanta Journal*, 13 March 1917, 5; "Mayor Behind Success of Better Babies Week," *Atlanta Journal*, 3 May 1917, 5; "Mayor Hangs Favorite Psalm Over His Desk, *Atlanta Journal*, 12 August 1917, 8. The motto, Psalms 127:1, read, "Except the Lord keep the city, the watchman waketh but in vain."

[23]Mrs. E. Rumble to Mayor Asa Chandler [SIC], 2 February 1918; and Mayor Candler to Mrs. E. Rumble, Supt., 4 February 1918, both in fol. 6, box 4, AGC papers, Emory.

[24]"Mayor Scorns Ride; To Walk in Parade" *Atlanta Journal*, 22 April 1917, L-10.

[25]"Anti-Shingle Roof Law of City Is Under Fire," *Atlanta Journal*, 15 January 1917, 14.

[26]In addition to newspaper coverage from 21-30 May 1917, the following account of Atlanta's great fire of 1917 rests on Steve B. Campbell, "The Great Fire of Atlanta, May 21, 1917" *Atlanta Historical Journal* 13/2 (1968): 9-14 passim; Kuhn, *Living Atlanta*, 20-28; Candler, *Asa Griggs Candler*, 330-331; WPA, *Atlanta*, 36.

[27]Minutes of the Atlanta City Council, 21 May 1917, Records of the City of Atlanta, on deposit at the Atlanta History Center Library/Archives; "Four States Make Quick Response to City's Call," *Atlanta Journal*, 22 May 1917, 19. Cities that helped on the first day included Newnan, East Point, Griffin, Kirkwood, Decatur, Marietta, Macon, and Augusta; on the following day men and equipment came from Nashville, Knoxville, Savannah and Jacksonville.

[28]"Leading Citizens Fight in Battle with Flames," *Atlanta Journal*, 22 May 1917, 10. Most of this story praised the mayor, but it also named Ivan Allen, Frederic J. Paxon, Forrest Adair, Lee Ashcraft, Reuben Arnold, and John Y. Smith as prominent citizens who personally took part in the struggle.

[29]"Conflagration of May 21, 1917," Annual Report of the Chief and Board of Fire Masters of the Atlanta Fire Department for the Year 1917, 17, City of Atlanta records on deposit at Atlanta History Center Library/Archives; "New and Better Houses to Replace Burned Ones," *Atlanta Journal*, 22 May 1917, 1; "Few Serious Injuries as Result of the Fire," *Atlanta Journal*, 22 May 1917, 9. Page 6 of the 22 May *Atlanta Journal* carries a map of the burned area. The fire department's annual report identified the total number of structures destroyed as 1,938.

[30]Minutes of the Atlanta City Council, vol. 25, 22 and 30 May 1917, Records of the City of Atlanta on deposit at the Atlanta History Center Library/Archives; "Grass at Piedmont Park Only Bed That Hundreds Could Find Monday Night," *Atlanta Journal*, 22 May 1917, 8; "$50,000 Is Raised for Fire Relief in typical Meeting," *Atlanta Journal*, 22 May 1917, 1; "Restoring Families to Housekeeping is Now the Main Task," and "More Money Now Necessary for Aid of Fire Sufferers," *Atlanta Journal*, 24 May 1917, 1; "The Great Conflagration," *Atlanta Independent*, 26 May 1917, 1; "Rebuilding Committees Will Meet Every Day," *Atlanta Journal*, 30 May 1917, 4; "Many Victims of Fire Accept Relief," "Not Even in Our Hour of Distress and Sorrow," and "The Rehabilitation of Atlanta Marks Some Progressive Tendencies," *Atlanta Independent*, 2 June 1917, 4; "Rebuilding Plan to be Submitted to Owners," and "Anti-Shingle Ordinance Is Passed by Council," *Atlanta Journal*, 31 May 1917, 3; "Relief Offices are Closed Temporarily," *Atlanta Journal*, 1 June 1917, 5. Many other examples of such coverage can be found in Atlanta newspapers for the period. One of the three "negro citizens" was A. F. Herndon, the founder of Atlanta Metropolitan Life Insurance Company, a man whose rise from barber to millionaire compares interestingly with Candler's own career (see "Restoring Families..." above).

[31]"A Year Ago and Today in Atlanta's Burned District," *Atlanta Journal*, 19 May 1918, magazine section, 1.

[32] AGC, "Mayor's comments to the first meeting of the City Council after he assumed office" [inaugural address], 1 January 1917, fol. 21, box 2, AGC papers, Emory; or see: "Economy Is Urged By Mayor Candler in His Inaugural," *Atlanta Journal*, 2 January 1917, 5.

[33] "The City is the Nerve Center of Civilization," fol. 5, 6, or 7, box 2, AGC Papers. Three virtually identical versions of this talk are in the three folders; the version in folder 6 is marked "Lyric Theatre—Recall Mass Meeting—1916," which was the meeting that was held to protest Chief Beavers' demotion and dismissal.

[34] Ibid. The Young Men and Religion Forward had delighted in reproducing a version of this comment in their bulletins.

[35] "Beavers Case To Be Retried By Commission, Belief," *Atlanta Journal*, 15 March 1917, 1; "Beavers Granted New Trial Before Board," *Atlanta Journal*, 30 April 1917, 1; "Third Beavers' Trial To Be Held Tuesday Week," *Atlanta Journal*, 7 October 1917, L-5.

[36] "To Investigate Boarding and Rooming Houses," *Atlanta Journal*, 10 January 1917, 8.

[37] "Talk of Army Man As Police Department Head" *Atlanta Journal* 30 January 1917, 4.

[38] "Policeman's Mashed Thumbnail No Worse Than Poor Millionaire," *Atlanta Journal*, 11 July 1917, 6.

[39] For some examples, see: "Mayor Will Probe Taking of Rewards by the Police Force," *Atlanta Journal*, 18 February 1917, 3; "Ministers' Letters Will Not Hurry Beavers' Trial," *Atlanta Journal*, 14 September 1917, 8, in which Councilman C. L. Barnwell asserted that "Chief Mayo has done more to eliminate vice…than Beavers ever did."; "White Slave Charge Is Ruled From Testimony," *Atlanta Journal*, 8 November 1917, 4.

[40] "Police Board May Give Beavers Another Trial," *Atlanta Journal*, 12 March 1917, 1; "Vaughn Will Head Police Commission," *Atlanta Journal*, 13 March 1917, 5; "Ex-Chief Beavers Seeks Vindication, Not a Job," *Atlanta Journal*, 1 May 1917, 8.

[41] "Beavers is Reinstated Provided He'll Resign 'If Requested,'" *Atlanta Journal*, 9 November 1917, 1.

[42] "Denies Politics Charge in Case of Beavers," *Atlanta Journal*, 10 November 1917, 1

[43] In the *Atlanta Journal*: "Mayor Candler Will Go to Wilson's Inaugural," 19 February 1917, 3; "Loyal Legion and Drum Corps Leave For Inauguration," 3 March 1917, 1; "Leading Citizens of Atlanta to March in Inaugural Parade," 4 March 1917, 3; "Atlanta's Loyal Legion to Carry Big Flag in Parade at Washington," 20 February 1917, 3. The flag had been found in storage in City Hall. "Great Ovation Is Accorded Loyal Legion in Parade," 5 March 1917, 1. Wilson knew Judge Hillyer from his days as a lawyer in the city.

[44] In the *Atlanta Journal*: "Committee to Plan Welcome for Troops," 19 February 1917, 5; "Plans Are Formulated for Welcoming Troops," 20 February 1917, 2; "Atlanta Troops Advised of Plans for Reception," 4 march 1917, 3; "Secretary of War to Join Welcome To Artillery Boys," 9 March 1917, 1; "'Welcome Home' Fund Goes Past $1,000 Mark," 15 March 1917, 5 [and many similar items over the next few days]; "Atlanta Troops Are Given Great Ovation on Returning Home," 28 March 1917, 8; "Atlanta's Soldier Boys to Get Royal Welcome Tonight," 29 March 1917, 1; "Atlanta's Soldier Boys Are Royally Entertained by Proud Citizens at the Auditorium," 30 March 1917, 5; "Thousands Cheer as Atlanta's Soldiers Parade City Streets," 31 March 1917, 1.

[45] "Atlanta's Soldier Boys Are Royally Entertained by Proud Citizens at the Auditorium," *Atlanta Journal*, 30 March 1917, 5.

[46] "Exemption Boards Named By Candler To Select Troops," *Atlanta Journal*, 11 June 1917, 1. Those chosen to serve were known as "selectmen"—the term "draftee" evidently came into use in later times.

47 "People Gather at Five Points and Pray for Armies," 30 May 1918, 1.

48"Mayor Challenges Governor to Plowing Match Saturday After Great Gardening Parade," *Atlanta Journal*, 7 March 1918, 2; "Principals in the Plowing Contest Ready for Action on Saturday Afternoon," *Atlanta Journal*, 9 March 1918, 1; "Two Executives Battle to Draw in Plow Contest," *Atlanta Constitution*, 10 March 1918, 1.

49"Mayor Candler Allows Flags To Be Displayed on Candler Building," *Atlanta Journal*, 27 March 1917, 6;

50"Flag Floats From Top of Every City School" *Atlanta Journal*, 5 April 1917, 1.

51"Mayor Candler Speaks at the Raising of Flag at Peeple's St. School," *Atlanta Journal*, 12 April 1917, 21; "Colors on the Way, Rush Contributions to Mayor Candler Today," *Atlanta Journal*, 18 April 1918, 3; "Win-the-War Spirit Reigns At Annual Dinner of Chamber of Commerce at Taft Hotel," *Atlanta Journal*, 16 January 1918, 7. See also, "Current Events from a Woman's Point of View: The Symbol of the Flag," *Atlanta Constitution*, 17 March 1918, F-10.

52At least thirty articles related to the creation of Camp Gordon may be found in the *Atlanta Journal* for the first six months of 1917; although several specific stories are cited below, the over-all newspaper coverage forms the background upon which the following account is based.

53"Atlanta To Make Effort to Secure Government Camp," *Atlanta Constitution*, 15 January 1917, 1.

54"Mayor Actively Behind Move For Army Camp," *Atlanta Journal*, 6 April 1917, 16; see also, Candler, *Asa Griggs Candler*, 329-30.

55Cooper, *Fulton County*, 675; "Atlanta to Make Fight for Great Divisional Army Post; Would Bring 20,000 Here," *Atlanta Journal*, 15 January 1917, 4 (quotes General Leonard A. Wood's estimates).

56"Atlanta To Make Effort to Secure Government Camp," and "Football Stories Of Days Long Ago Recalled by Wood," *Atlanta Constitution*, 15 January 1917, 1. Wood had toured the south in 1916 promoting "preparedness" in the form of civilian training camps where business and professional men could experience "strenuous military life." See "Gen. Wood on Way South in Interest of Training Camp," *Atlanta Georgian*, 3 February 1916, Home edition, 3.

57Ivan Allen, "Locating the Quartermaster's Depot in the Candler Warehouse, World War 1 [SIC]" signed typescript, August 20, 1949, in box 4, Charles Howard Candler Papers, Emory. [Howard Candler used a portion of this manuscript in his biography of AGC.]

58Candler, *Asa Griggs Candler*, 314.

59 "Atlanta Feels Certain of Great Army Camp," *Atlanta Journal*, 13 April 1917, 9. The physical assets of the warehouse company, which had become the property of the Candler children, were sold in 1922, for $1.1 million; $885,512,36 had accumulated in the "reserves for depreciation account." The warehouse company then was liquidated.

60"Atlanta Gets Divisional Camp Site," *Atlanta Journal*, 18 May 1917, 1; "Atlanta To Get More Than 2 Army Divisions," *Atlanta Journal*, 30 May 1917, 19 (includes map); "Water Supply For New Encampment Won Atlanta Fight," *Atlanta Journal*, 11 June 1917, 1.

61"Will Ask Council For Money for Water Main," *Atlanta Journal*, 21 June 1917, 9; "City Will Reimburse Chamber of Commerce," *Atlanta Journal*, 26 June 1917, 3; "Camp Gordon, Rescued From Pastoral Acres, is Merging Into City of Great Activity," *Atlanta Journal*, 26 July 1917, 12; "Water Main to Camp Gordon to Be Ready For Use by Next Friday," *Atlanta Journal*, 27 August 1917, 10; WPA, *Atlanta*, 36.

62"Wake Up" [cartoon], *Atlanta Journal*, 1 July 1918, 1; "Additional Facts About Proposed Emergency Bonds" and "Reasons For Bonds Will Be Explained To Atlanta Voters," *Atlanta*

Journal, 3 July 1918, 1; "Welfare of Atlanta At Stake Wednesday in the Bond Election," *Atlanta Journal*, 7 July 1918, 1-L; "Mayor and City Officials and Bonds Will Be Voted On," and "Gordon's Expansion Is Being Retarded by Water Situation," *Atlanta Journal*, 7 July 1918, 1-H.

[63]"Atlanta's Welfare Demands Your Vote for Bonds," "4,023 Votes Cast in Primary At 2 P. M.; Bonds Endangered," and "Gen. M'Cain Says Future of Gordon Depends on Bonds," *Atlanta Journal*, 10 July 1918, 1.

[64]"Council Will Act Quickly To Improve City Waterworks," *Atlanta Journal*, 11 July 1918, 1.

[65]Ibid.

[66]Minutes of the Atlanta City Council, vol. 26, 12 July 1918, Records of the City of Atlanta on deposit at the Atlanta History Center Library/Archives; "Candler To Guarantee Water Improvement," *Atlanta Journal*, 12 July 1918, 1; "Waterworks Will Be Provided For Without Tax Levy," *Atlanta Journal*, 13 July 1918.

[67]The following account of the alleged blackmail attempt and its aftermath rests principally on the following newspaper stories from the *Atlanta Journal*, all on p. 1: "Attempt to Blackmail Mayor Candler Is Alleged" 14 February 1918; "Hirsch Sees Wife at Tower; She Weeps; Pastor There, Too," 18 February 1918; and a great many other minor stories from the period of February 14-18; further stories (again, some minor items are omitted) in the *Atlanta Journal* include "Former Husband May Testify in Hirsch Case," 26 February, 1; "Mayor Candler and Forrest Adair Tell Story of Alleged Blackmail," 27 February, 1; "Spectators at Cook Trial Bring Lunch; Courtroom Packed," 27 February, 18; "Candler and Adair Tell of Alleged Blackmail," 14 March, 1; "Mrs. Hirsch Weeps as She Tells Her Story," 15 March, 1; "Hirsch Case will Go to Jury Early in Afternoon," 16 March, 1; Mrs. Hirsch Expects To Make Bond, Her Attorneys Declare," 17 March, 1; "Hirsch Divorce Suit To Be Final Chapter in Case," 3 April, 4; the *Atlanta Constitution* coverage parallels that of the *Journal*; the issues of 28 February and 15-17 March 1918 contain large excerpts from testimony presented in the two trials.

[68]"Cook Acquaintance Instead of Friend, Says H. H. Hirsch," *Atlanta Journal*, 17 February 1918, 1.

[69]"Candler and Adair Tell of Alleged Blackmail," *Atlanta Journal* 14 March 1918, 1. A wide ledge embellishes the third-floor level of the Candler Building where this office was located; a person need not be a human fly to gain a position outside of the window.

[70]Ibid.

[71]Ibid.

[72]Ibid.

[73]"Mayor Candler and Forrest Adair Tell Story of Alleged Blackmail," 27 February 1918, 1.

[74]"Candler and Adair Tell of Alleged Blackmail," *Atlanta Journal*, 14 March 1918, 1.

[75]"Merely What Was Expected" [Editorial], *Atlanta Journal*, 28 February 1918, 8.

[76]Candler, *Asa Griggs Candler*, 334.

[77]Candler, *Asa Griggs Candler*, 325.

[78]AGC, "in an address made midway in his term" quoted in Candler, *Asa Griggs Candler*, 326-27.

[79]Page 18. Howard already was president of Coca-Cola and William, the youngest, was its secretary-treasurer; Asa, Jr. managed Asa G. Candler and Company, a real estate firm; Walter was cashier of Central Bank and Trust.

CHAPTER ELEVEN

First Citizen

When Asa Candler left his responsibilities as mayor behind and announced his retirement, only those closest to him knew that Lucy, his wife of over forty years, was dying of breast cancer. The reticence of the time has left most of the course of her ailment undocumented. Indeed, this fatal modesty may have contributed to her death. She concealed—or ignored—the symptoms of the cancer for two years, before discussing them with her daughter-in-law. When Asa became aware of the exact nature of his wife's condition remains unclear, but the fact that she was in some way seriously ill had become evident by the summer of 1916, when the Candlers made their visit to the spa in Michigan, before beginning the Mayor's race. During this time Mrs. Candler also was said to have severe arthritic or rheumatic pain, but her suffering probably had its origins in the spreading cancer.

In that same year, the Candlers moved into an elegant new house that they had built on Ponce de Leon Avenue in Druid Hills. Mrs. Candler decorated in a sumptuous style and the furnishings included an Aeolian organ that reflected her love of music. Although she had done little to pursue a prominent place in society, her appreciation of fine music regularly brought the Candlers to concerts and the opera.

In April 1917, when New York's Metropolitan Opera came to Atlanta for its annual week of performances, Lucy attended at least once, gowned in white lace, white satin and cloth of silver. This may have been her last opera. By June, Candler described his wife as "almost constantly suffering." The couple made another visit to a spa at Hot Springs, Virginia, "in the interests of Mrs. Candler's health," in the following July. At some point a radical mastectomy, the standard treatment at the time, was performed—possibly at Johns Hopkins Hospital—but it was too late to benefit her health. In late February 1919, she died in the new house in Druid Hills. Brief obituaries attributed her death to "rheumatism of the heart" and conventionally noted her devotion to husband, family and church. Lucy Candler's modest, quiet life left little material for the authors of obituaries. Only a few letters and reminiscences remain to reveal the good-humored and affectionate woman who planted nasturtiums and mended pockets and loved the opera.[1]

A lifetime of religious devotion could not prepare her husband to accept the implacable hand of death when it took his companion of four decades. He entered the vital statistic on the "Deaths" page of his family Bible: "Lucy Elizabeth dear wife of Asa G. Candler Sr. Died February 22nd 1919" and added the agonized question "Why so soon!!!" in large and shaking letters.[2] We cannot know the full depths of his grief, but even through the dark glass that history gives us, his pain is evident. Perhaps he turned the pages of his Bible to find consolation. Soon afterward he offered verses from II Corinthians 1:3-7 to a bereaved friend; they read, in part, "Blessed be God...Who comforteth us in all our tribulation...For as the sufferings of Christ abound in us, so our consolation also aboundeth by Christ."[3]

Asa Candler would greatly need consolation in the last decade of his life. The death of his wife began a series of unhappy, sometimes embarrassing events, some so dismaying that his son called this "a decade of tragic mistakes" but could not bring himself to write about them in detail in his memoir of Asa Candler's life. Instead, Howard

Candler characterized his father in his last years as "sick in mind, soul, and body" and found his actions during this time to be "completely out of character with the buoyant courage and the clear faith of the fruitful days that had gone before."[4] In fact, Asa Candler was a lonely widower who, in his old age, suffered two unhappy relationships with women. The troubles of the rich often provide amusement for the masses, so the public and the press took a lively interest in Candler's private life; however, even when his personal relationships became grist for the mills of scandal, he never abandoned his high standards of conduct. In spite of Howard Candler's opinion, his father faced the public scrutiny resulting from these two associations with a "buoyant courage" entirely in keeping with his earlier years.

For a time after his wife's death, Asa Candler carried out a typical widower's existence. He lived alone, socialized a bit, and traveled occasionally. As a man not given to brooding, he continued to participate in civic and philanthropic activities, even though he was nearly seventy years old. So it was, that in the autumn of 1919 he became involved in a Confederate reunion held in the city of Atlanta.[5]

Confederate Veterans, Sons of the Confederacy, Daughters of the Confederacy, and their friends and supporters jammed into every hotel room in Atlanta for a full week in October 1919. A tent encampment in Piedmont Park provided the hardier (and poorer) veterans with shelter. The quasi-military units that attended the events in Atlanta brought with them large numbers of women; some were young belles, called "sponsors," while married women served as their official "chaperons." Elaborate balls, receptions, teas, and luncheons diverted these women and their escorts.[6]

At some time during the reunion, probably in the lobby of the Piedmont Hotel, friends introduced Asa Candler to the chaperon attached to the staff of Louisiana's General Van Zandt. She was the striking, auburn-haired Onezima de Bouchel Roquet. Various sources described her as a leader of New Orleans society and a "suffragette," although, upon observation, both characterizations seem slightly overstated.[7] Later, de Bouchel reported that during the reunion Candler entertained her and several other ladies at the Druid

Hills Golf Club, at his home, and on drives around the city. In the course of these visits, he would have learned something of her unhappy marriage, which had led her to live apart from her husband Adolphe for long periods of time and to travel alone.[8]

Later in the month, Mrs. Roquet wrote a thank-you note to Candler that included a coquettish complaint: "I was quite, or to be truthful, considerably disappointed at your not ringing me up as I had requested...." She urged him to call on her if he came to New Orleans on business and informed him of her immediate travel plans (to Key West and Tampa) so that he might contact her.[9] He answered her letter, and over the next three years the friendly correspondence ripened into a romance. More than three hundred letters passed between Candler and the exotic (by Atlanta standards) New Orleans socialite before their relationship ended in the fall of 1922. The following year, on 22 February, Deputy Marshal Walter Ackerman handed Asa Candler documents informing him that de Bouchel had filed a breach of promise suit, demanding $500,000 damages. When the case came to trial a year later, the opposing lawyers read many of their letters in court. The newspapers quoted them in detail, creating a historical record of the Candler-de Bouchel affair.[10]

The effect of this lawsuit was to create a public record of the romance. Onezima de Bouchel's petition to the court and Candler's reply provide parallel summaries of their brief, failed courtship. Public statements made by de Bouchel immediately after the collapse of their engagement, and letters and other evidence presented in the trial contribute fragments to a mosaic reconstruction of their relationship.

Both de Bouchel's petition to the court and Candler's reply generally agreed on the circumstances of their first meeting at the Confederate reunion, but then the two stories diverge slightly. Mrs. de Bouchel, as plaintiff, declared that she "unreservedly welcomed the frank assurances of friendly interest extended by the defendant." Candler, as defendant, stated that after the reunion ended he did not attempt to contact her, nor did he know where she was, until she "voluntarily wrote the defendant two letters, one from New Orleans and one from Florida." In the words of the de Bouchel's plea, "Their acquaintance ripened into friendship and an intimate correspondence ensued…."

Whether or not her letters influenced him, Candler did go to Florida during that fall of 1919. Although he and de Bouchel did not meet in person, a flirtatious letter mailed from West Palm Beach found him on the yacht "Helena" at Daytona Beach. De Bouchel extolled West Palm Beach as "an ideal place for a winter Honeymoon." Evidently Candler had complained to her about the demands made on his time. She observed that "Atlanta business men do not seem to understand that you have retired," and asked, "Why remain in Atlanta and be annoyed?"[11]

In a New Year's greeting letter, written in 1920, de Bouchel expressed her disappointment at having missed Candler in Florida, but added, "I am, however, consoled by the thought that I shall have the pleasure of seeing you shortly." She planned to stop in Atlanta, "for the sole purpose of seeing you," while en route to a suffrage convention in Chicago. While in Atlanta, she said, "I expect your undivided attention, you—Gay Lothario." Evidently Candler had made some comment on her suffrage sentiments, because she also wrote, "Of course, you knew that I was 'one of them things.' All intelligent, progressive women are. I return thanks for the compliment, how kind of you? Ahem!" Whether they actually met on this occasion is unclear, but in any case, a letter written in April kept up the cozy mood. Apparently someone had speculated about buying a yacht. De Bouchel wrote, "Let's make a bargain. I'll furnish the ocean if you will furnish the yacht." The letter also included the interesting information that her husband, Adolphe Roquet, would soon leave for Mexico, while she planned a long trip on the Continent.[12]

Onezima de Bouchel, on her way to embark on the voyage to Europe, again passed through Atlanta in the late spring of 1920. She wrote to Candler, asking that he reserve a room at the Ansley hotel for her and said, "I cannot leave America without telling you goodbye." Candler accompanied her to the docks in New York City, but if they met in Atlanta or if he was already in New York when she arrived there remains unclear. He was one of five persons who had ordered roses placed in her stateroom, and she wrote that she loved his best of all, going on to compare him favorably to another gentleman of her acquaintance. She also wrote from Europe, and although she still employed a formal style in greeting him as "My dear Mr. Candler" she again compared him to her travel companions: "None of them measure up to you."[13]

She returned after several months: "[T]o my surprise...as I walked down the gang plank...he was the first person I saw, waving his handkerchief."[14] The two soon became much closer, a change that was apparent in the more intimate tone of their letters. Her letter of 26 November 1920 began with the salutation, "My Dearest Friend." "The beautiful little ring arrived today...I want to thank you for it and tell you how deeply I appreciate it and the fact that you wanted me to have it. It is on my finger now. I have put aside my other elaborate ring and replaced it with your precious gift, which shall always be one of my most prized possessions, because it came from you."[15]

Near the end of this letter, de Bouchel referred to their plan to meet again, apparently in the near future. She commented, "Twelve months is a long, long time, isn't it?" Her comment reflects the fact that she was seriously considering a Nevada divorce that would require her to establish a legal residence in that state. She was affectionately possessive: "Remember that I expect you to be true, so be polite to the ladies, but be very careful and do not flirt and allow them to believe that your intentions are serious. You must never forget that you belong to [signed] Sweet One."[16]

On 30 November, she told Candler that a friend already living in Reno called it "a miserable little typical western town." In this letter she reminisced about a four-hour drive the two had taken from Greenville to Atlanta, writing "how delightful it would be to take a nice motor ride out in the country together. It is most depressing to think how long it will be before we can go driving again."[17] Candler also found this motor excursion memorable, for more than one reason. He wrote that he had once taken a similar drive with "a sweet and beautiful girl," his deceased wife. He remembered that "the same passionate fondness characterized that journey," and asked, "is it possible that you are going to take an old man's arm and guide him the rest of the way through life…?" In this bittersweet mood, he worried that "perhaps I have set my goal too high."[18]

Gallantry and flirtation held sway only briefly before the first difficulties intervened in the love affair. December 4 had brought a letter from de Bouchel's husband, asking her for a reconciliation, although she had no further interest in him. She told Candler: "I just want to be part of the very fabric of your life." In a stormy confrontation with her husband Adolphe, she discovered that he opposed the divorce. Afterwards, de Bouchel wrote a long, emotional letter to "My Darling," reporting her husband's response to the new situation. When she rejected Roquet's protestations of love and his plea for reconciliation, "He stormed & raged and threatened until I really became frightened." Then he became calmer and demanded twelve thousand dollars for his share of their community property. It was more cash than she could easily muster, and she was convinced that Roquet made the demand to inconvenience and embarrass her. "Tell me what to do?…I love you & you only, my only hope of happiness is with you…." Should she pay or leave for Reno and "let the thunder break?"[19]

She had mailed the letter on the twelfth, saying that she would await his advice. Candler replied immediately in a letter dated 14 December, advising her to speak to her lawyer about a financial settlement: "[W]e will work it out with as little pain to you as possible." He also revealed the steel at the core of his character, describing to her the results of the 1917 blackmail attempt: "[T]hey got no money, only imprisonment…. I will not be held up."[20] By the time his letter reached New Orleans, de Bouchel was already on the train to Reno. En route, she sent him a wire and followed it with a letter, mailed in Denver on 17 December, expressing regret that she had written the earlier one. She told Candler, "I have decided to let the thunderbolt fall and defy the devil."[21]

De Bouchel soon learned that the divorce law in Nevada, although more liberal than most states, made some stringent demands on persons who wished to take advantage of it. Since the law applied only to Nevada citizens, she first had to establish a residence in that state six months before any papers could be filed. The residence requirement was no mere formality, but required her physical presence in the state. If she were to leave the state for a few days, the filing date of her divorce case would be postponed for that number of days. If her husband did not contest the divorce, the court would issue a final decree forty days after her hearing. Her lawyer advised that she continue at least a technically legal residence for six more months to avoid any charges that she had received the divorce fraudulently. De Bouchel wrote to Candler, explaining these conditions and closed the letter, "…so be a good boy and send a sweet love thought to your exiled Sweet One."[22]

Throughout the year they exchanged letters almost every day. Determined to make the best of her exile, de Bouchel signed up for college courses, played cards and went for automobile drives with other prospective divorceés who shared her exile. She decided not to take up horseback riding because she only used the sidesaddle and disliked the local custom of riding astride, but she expressed interest in learning golf. Candler sent chocolates and flowers regularly. The dozens of letters that became public in 1924 are flirtatious, affectionate, and informative. Their plan to marry can be inferred from de Bouchel's letter of 7 February: "I feel just as near and sacredly toward you as if I were already your wife."[23]

There is nothing particularly scandalous in the way they conducted their relationship, beyond the implications that can be read into the fact that Candler met her secretly in California in April 1921. Passing through Kansas City on his way to California, he visited Godfrey Plachek, who had been associated with Coca-Cola in its early days. Plachek admired Candler as both an exemplary American businessman and a modest and approachable human being, but thought the elderly gentleman, "seemed very lonely." Candler, who now lived alone with his servants, confided to Plachek "his life was quite empty. Above all he missed that close, human, sympathetic companionship he enjoyed with [his late wife] and seemed like a lost soul groping for a bit of happiness."[24]

Candler also conveyed some hint of his intentions to Plachek: "I gathered in a sort of sketchy way that he planned to marry again. Then the papers published some rumors and finally came word of his marriage—but I never saw him again."[25]

No such hints of his plans appear in the letters Candler wrote to Atlanta during this trip, although he told Howard that Mr. Plachek "carried me riding all over Kansas City and environs." A few days later in San Francisco he wrote of going to the opera and a midnight supper. He planned to travel to Los Angeles, but he gave no clue that Onezima Bouchel was to meet him there. His San Francisco letter also conveys something of a depressed mood for a man engaged in a romantic tryst: "I can't bring myself to a frame of mind that causes this life to be really joyous. I don't seem to be fit for any class of society…."[26]

He may have felt ill at ease in a situation so contrary to his usual behavior, but this last comment is in keeping with a prominent theme in many of his letters. He was weary after a lifetime of labor and service. "For many years since I was 21 years old, I have been constantly at work. Most of those years I was at the head of several large corporations—some public and some private—all required (as I thought) that my hands be never off the pilot wheel. I now regret that I was so occupied that my good wife had cause to complain that she had no companion."[27]

He answered even a granddaughter's letter in a valedictory spirit. "I realized that I must be ever in the end of the processions of the family of which once I was the progenitor, so when any one of you look down the line to salute me I rejoice in the recognition."[28]

Traveling west again in the summer, he wrote to Howard of the emptiness that had entered his life. He finally dropped a hint of his future plans; evidently he hoped to prepare his children for the decision that had already been made. "I once was counted with Atlanta's builders, Georgia's active sons, your advisor. Now I am companionless, not needed, not called to any Service and so I am wandering, with those who do not even know me. And this condition will abide till I have trod life's trail to the end....If I take a hand in mine to steady my tottering body as it wends its way down the path, know all of you that your mother's memory is as dear to me as to you for whom she lived & loved us all."[29]

He worked to disentangle himself from his responsibilities, but with difficulty. For example, in January 1921 he declined requests that he serve on a certain "educational campaign" of the Southern Methodist Church: "I am not situated so that I can avail myself of the high honor...."[30] Closing down his business interests proved to be more complicated. He continued his perennial duel with the Internal Revenue Service, a particular source of irritation: "If I do have to pay it, I will have to do some destructive financing."[31] De Bouchel responded sympathetically in a letter of 18 February. Answering his frequent expressions of fatigue she urged him to retire completely in order to be "free from all the worries that make you nervous, bring on insomnia and rob you of your peace of mind."[32] By the end of 1921, after almost a year of unwilling separation from de Bouchel, he declared, "There is only one business I intend entering soon, and that is the business of being your husband."[33] Again duty, or perhaps the Internal Revenue Service, thwarted his wish. Writing in February 1922, he commented on his frustrated plans to have retired "last November" and added: "But I must abandon my business this year. My aim in life is to be with you...."[34] Business matters did not play a large part in this correspondence, but occasional glimpses emerge. When de Bouchel wrote a passing comment on the price of cotton and congratulated him on the apparent success of Coca-Cola, Candler replied briskly: "The advance of cotton will not help us much. Some collections must be made. We have been forced to make some foreclosures to prevent total loss. As to Coca-Cola, I have given that to my children, else it would not have gotten into all the trouble it has been in the last twelve months."[35]

Not only had his connection to Coca-Cola ended, his children's involvement also had been greatly reduced. In 1916, a few months before he ran for mayor of Atlanta, Asa Candler had retired from the presidency of Coca-Cola and given most of its stock to his children, although he had continued as chairman of the board. In September 1919, without consulting their father, the Candler children sold control of the company to a syndicate of three banks led by the Atlanta-based Trust Company of Georgia. The elder Candler strongly disapproved of the move, although his public statements expressed acceptance if not enthusiasm.[36] If Coca-Cola "got into trouble" during the years immediately following the sale, the problems certainly had no long-lasting effects on its continuing success. In any case, the fact that Candler met Onezima de Bouchel a month after the sale provided other matters to occupy his thoughts. Evidently he did not brood over his family's surrender of control over the Coca-Cola Company.

In addition to his repeated expressions of being tired of the business life, Candler also let de Bouchel know that he was not so rich as many imagined: "It is said no woman your age and beauty would marry me except for my property. I have given practically everything I own away. I have kept only a small portion for myself."[37] In another letter, he wrote, "Nine-tenths of my possessions have been divided among my children, the church and charity. The remaining one-tenth will suffice for me."[38]

Candler's letters to de Bouchel also convey something of his social life and attitudes. Although he went out frequently, for example to attend the theater with friends, he remained somewhat puritanical: "I attended Atlanta's New year ball (so called) last night…. [A]s I sat with the "wall flowers" and watched the "witch flowers" of the hour…. I rejoiced and fairly patted myself on the brow because I had chosen for my future life a companion so unlike those giddy ones at whom I looked on as upon the zoological part of a circus—lovely animals, but careless in the make up."[39]

Although he visited Mrs. de Bouchel during her residence in Nevada, he worried that someone might recognize him or that if he registered in a hotel under his own name the newspapers would find out.[40] However, he also displayed his puckish sense of humor: "Don't say I am a flirt again. I just like nice, pretty ladies…."[41]

Above all, his letters speak with the voice of a man who was simply, helplessly in love: "Excuse an old man's folly," he wrote in August of 1921, "Love me because I love you." His happy marriage to Lucy led Candler to hope for another such relationship, for a "helpmate in all that I do" who would be "aware of the responsibility of becoming my wife."[42] In another letter, his first marriage again occupied his thoughts. "Forty-three years ago today I was married—forty one of which were as happy as ever man spent on this earth—I can't look back—I must look forward to the future. I see for us the possible haven of peace...."[43]

Sadly, no "haven of peace" awaited the lovers.

As early as January 1921, he heard gossip harmful to her reputation. He attempted to defend her while keeping their relationship secret and wrote to her, condemning the "vile falsehoods" which "mortified" him. Evidently the comments came from family members, because he also wrote, "so far I have acted affectionately towards all those who are near relatives; just how long I can maintain this state of mind I can't foretell." A few days later, he reassured her that he did not give credence to unfavorable reports about her.[44] In June 1921, he still believed that when his family knew of their plans, at least some of them would approve: "my three brothers and two old sisters will love you, but my children don't want me to marry anyone."[45]

Only in January 1922, did the engagement become official; Candler himself later set the date for the wedding as the following 20 September. Later that spring he wrote to de Bouchel that rumors about the two had led his family to question him. He answered affirmatively if anyone asked if he were engaged. In April, Candler reported the reaction of each of his sons; he had also informed his daughter of his plans but apparently had not solicited her opinion:

> I have talked with all of my boys about my marriage. Howard says "Sorry you are going to marry; I fear you are making a mistake, but the woman you marry will receive from us a cordial and affectionate welcome."...Asa G., Jr., said, "All I

have you gave me and when you need it is all yours. Your wife I will love and welcome. If she loves you and makes you happy I will love her."...Walter don't want me to marry anybody; his experience has not been happy. William, my youngest, considers that my marriage to anybody is not wise.[46]

In a succeeding letter, he added that he now knew "who it is that has raised the questions concerning our marriage, and I know what the questions are." There were three points: Could a woman of Spanish-French extraction be happy with an Anglo-Saxon husband? Could a Catholic be "happily joined" with a Protestant? Would the public, the courts, and the Candler family recognize her divorce? To all three questions Candler had answered yes, but he refrained from identifying their source. He added that the three questions "have not been raised by my children, although none of them want me to marry anybody."[47] The criticism moved de Bouchel to attempt to cancel the engagement. However, as her petition to the court later stated, Candler refused to release her and expressed "his sincere and unalterable desire to consummate the engagement by marriage." Candler assured his fiancée that he would persuade his family to accept the match. He reminded de Bouchel that he had made "great sacrifices...for members of his family throughout his life, ... recited evidence of the genuineness of his lifelong devotion to them, and mentioned the financial obligations under which he had placed them by voluntary gifts of a large portion of his great fortune."[48]

Although Candler refused to give de Bouchel the name of the principal source of objections to their match, he left a clue in a letter written to her in March 1922, when he called efforts to break up the match "an indignant fight against an indulgent brother."[49] In another letter Candler wrote of "unreliable people" who slandered her and added that he did not need a "spiritual adviser to advise me in the affairs of head or heart."[50] Either of Candler's Atlanta brothers, John or Warren, might have posed the "three questions," although their theological bent and the interest in Anglo-Saxonism point to Warren, as does the reference to a spiritual advisor. Furthermore, Warren, never intimidated by his brother's wealth and position, was one of the few persons to whom Candler had turned for advice in the past.

As word of the engagement spread, other friends and family took it upon themselves to proffer unsolicited advice. Candler wrote: "I anticipate a fight on me, [or] rather on you, to prevent our marriage." He anticipated rightly. After only a month passed, his frustration had grown: "My friends continue to annoy me. I love my city, my state and my country, but I am almost ready to leave them forever...I am almost ready to ask you to marry me at once."[51]

By this point, the gossip had traveled beyond Atlanta. He was surprised to learn from Mrs. de Bouchel that her New Orleans friends were aware of his family's "excitement" over the engagement. "This is evidently a cruel warfare on me," he wrote, adding that he planned to discuss the matter only with her and with his attorney.[52]

Whoever led the opposition to the marriage, some member—or members—of the Candler family determined to take action. An exhaustive investigation into de Bouchel's background began. Candler and de Bouchel in later court documents gave accounts of this development that differed on some details: Candler claimed that letters concerning de Bouchel came from New Orleans to him and to members of his family; these letters motivated "one family member" to travel there to "investigate the suggestions made in these letters." According to Candler these letters were passed on to de Bouchel's attorney, who did not return them. On the other hand, De Bouchel claimed that members of the Candler family initiated matters by personally visiting New Orleans to seek out the means to destroy the engagement. They hired detectives that "even went to the extent of cross-examining Negro servants who had been employed by [de Bouchel]." In a letter, Candler described the family member who visited New Orleans as his nephew; according to trial testimony, one E. V. Candler of Mississippi interviewed some de Bouchel acquaintances in New Orleans. The Candler family also hired a detective named Cochran to interview de Bouchel's Nevada acquaintances, seeking some evidence of her impropriety. The de Bouchel petition asserted, and Candler's answer admitted, that these investigators found nothing. Candler revealed the investigation to his fiancée, proclaiming "with expressions of pride" that his good opinion of her remained intact.[53]

During the summer of 1922, as the wedding date approached, de Bouchel shipped her furniture to Atlanta, ordered announcement cards, planned a reception, and ordered flowers; a clergyman was engaged to perform the service. The bride-to-be prepared a trousseau and privately announced the impending event to her friends. Candler wrote that he had ordered her wedding ring to fit his little finger, adding, "I hope it will be the right size."[54]

To safeguard the divorce process and to escape notoriety, Candler avoided public discussion of the matter. Nonetheless, rumors increased. Their plans finally became officially public when de Bouchel wired her confirmation of the story in response to questions from the *New Orleans States*. Candler then followed suit when questioned by the *Atlanta Journal*. A few days later, the *Journal's* society section added a report that the wedding would take place in San Francisco, the honeymoon would be in Honolulu, and the couple would "reside at the palatial home of Mr. Candler in Druid Hills."[55]

Candler had understood the power of publicity when he built the popular demand for Coca-Cola through sophisticated advertising. For decades, he had enjoyed a positive image in the press. Now he experienced the darker side of "public relations." In this period, Atlanta newspapers routinely carried flippant accounts of local divorce cases that made Candler uncomfortable: "I have never seen so much unrest and muckraking…this situation has induced a fiendish resentment in the public mind and no divorce is allowed to be just."[56] Because of his celebrity, members of the public presumed to share his private life, advising him on his plans to marry. Their comments, like those of family and associates, focused on de Bouchel, doubly vulnerable as a divorced woman and a Catholic. A complete stranger who had suffered a bad marriage to a Catholic woman sent a warning by way of Bishop Candler: "The Catholic Church is fully behind this match for its own special good, take this from one who knew them fully...."[57]

Neither public scrutiny nor intrusions such as these had ever affected Candler's decisions; having received a "nasty" anonymous letter, he shrugged it off when he wrote to de Bouchel: "During my lifetime I have received many anonymous letters."[58] On the other hand, the objections of those close to him cut deeply. James E. Dickey, an important Methodist clergyman, formerly president of Emory College and long time friend, wrote to "Dear Bro. Candler" in early September 1922 because he could not "remain silent when the lustre of your noble life is about to be dimmed by what the church cannot but think is a mesalliance." Dickey admonished Candler, "You are not your own, you belong to your country, to your friends, to your family, to your church, to the Blessed Christ who loved you, and gave himself for you. For the sake of all these, I pray you, refrain from your contemplated act."[59]

This letter outraged Candler. He wrote between the lines and in the margins, pouring out his sense of betrayal: "Et tu Brute," "Why the stab!" and "Amazed! Amazed at you!" To Dickey's expression of concern that "I have presumed too far, perhaps..." Candler interjected "you have" and after Dickey's closing, "Your long time fellow worker and friend" he scrawled a question mark. This sad document, redolent with anger and pain, Candler returned to its sender. Dickey then forwarded the letter to Bishop Candler with the comment, "Enclosed find the results of my effort to help. I seem some how to have been unfortunate in my expression."[60]

The public followed every detail of their plans. In mid-August, Candler hoped to be in Reno "by the 22d" (presumably of the same month) but a railroad strike interfered with his travel. Although he wrote that they must "submit patiently to circumstances," the *New Orleans Picayune* soon found other causes for a delay in their plans. The headlines of 25 August brayed, "Candler's Wedding Delayed by Bishop. Religious Differences said to Have Brought Strong Family Protest. Mrs. De Bouchelle Bares Opposition. Wait Until Storm Blows Over, Word Sent to Club Woman." She gave a statement, admitting that the family had some objection to the match on religious grounds. Although she stated that Bishop Candler disapproved of her Catholicism, her divorce, and her support of woman suffrage, she attributed the delay of the wedding to other factors. Evidently the headline writer had not read the story thoroughly.[61] Others shared this notion that the Bishop somehow governed his brother's affairs. A Methodist minister, writing on church business to Candler's brother, ended his letter of 29 August, "Give your brother Asa my love, and be assured I am praying for him that he may escape the net of the fouler [SIC]. I sympathize with him. We all need and shall ever need to watch."[62]

As the day of the wedding neared, Candler busied himself by having de Bouchel's furniture and household goods unpacked and placed in his house and by ridding himself of his last important business involvement: "I have sold my stock in the Central Bank and Trust corporation. Did not accomplish what I desired, but received in notes—not cash—about all it is worth. It's disposal disappoints the main purpose of my life. I wanted to hold it for my children's benefit, but could not."[63]

He sold his interest to Citizens' and Southern, a Savannah bank that had expanded into Atlanta in 1919; the sale brought its total capital to more than fifty million dollars, with thirty million in the Atlanta branch. For the last time, and perhaps without realizing he had done so, Asa Candler had played a major role in the region's economy. Citizens' and Southern grew to be one of Georgia's great financial institutions, strongly influencing Atlanta's development in the middle of the twentieth century.[64]

The day after he wrote to inform de Bouchel of the sale of Central Bank and Trust, Candler's somber mood continued: "I am far from being happy. If it were not for my dear old sister who approves everything I do, I could not stay here. She will cordially and affectionately welcome you as her sister."[65] After sending this letter, Candler dined with his son Walter and Walter's wife; the couple had recently reunited after a scandalous estrangement, much to the elder Candler's relief. He planned another dinner the following day with his daughter Lucy. Clearly he was continuing his efforts to reconcile his family to the coming marriage. But in any case, the plans were set; he intended to board the 6:15 A.M. train for Reno on Saturday, 16 September.[66]

It was not to be. By the time the westbound train pulled out of Atlanta, Asa Candler had broken his engagement to Onezima de Bouchel. In the lawsuit documents, de Bouchel asserted, but Candler denied, that in September his family had renewed their efforts to sabotage the wedding. In any case, on the day before his scheduled departure Candler wrote to de Bouchel a letter bearing no salutation:

> It almost killed me to have to wire you this morning. "Circumstances such impossible for me to leave Saturday... ." I am in a state of great perplexity.
>
> Information has just been brought to me from sources entitled to belief that there are two men living in Atlanta who claim to have in time gone by visited you by your invitation at night in your room at a hotel in this city. To marry you with these reports in force could not in any case be right or fair to either of us. Even though they be untrue.
>
> Your reception in Atlanta would be so painfully affected thereby as to make me unwilling to bring you here and have you subjected to slights by people you will have to meet.... I must and will be kind and fair to you. We must and will not do that which cannot be undone.... Nothing has ever so disheartened me as this.
>
> I wooed and won you because I loved you. My heart is yet pure and true. I will not subject you unjustly to indignant undeserved affront. Please think kindly of me as I now and ever more will of you.[67]

According to her petition, de Bouchel's reaction to the charge was anguished: "[S]he was inexpressibly shocked and humiliated by the unworthy grounds upon which defendant so abruptly announced his purpose to abandon the wedding which he had arranged." She turned to her lawyer, who contacted Candler. He learned only that her accuser was a traveling salesman. In her next communication with Candler, written on 28 September, she raged, "Do you expect me to let this hideous slander go unpunished? I'll publish it to the whole world and we will see if the world is as credulous as you seem to be, and as you expect me to be. If there are any such men…who make such statements, they have been paid to do it, and they shall go to the penitentiary along with those who hired them. This is a clumsy conspiracy that imposes on nobody but you."[68]

His next letter, written before he received her letter of the twenty-eighth, was several degrees cooler than the last; again there was no salutation:

> As promised, I am doing my best to get the actual truth of the statements made to me.... I have been told by a citizen of Atlanta that while you were a guest of the Piedmont Hotel during the reunion Convention of the U. C. V.…he saw you alone in the corridor or hall of the hotel, when he gave you his telephone number, later you telephoned him that you were alone in your room asking him to call. He declined saying that the hotel was very carefully policed, that he did not visit ladies at their rooms in hotels. You assured him it would be perfectly safe that he visit you. He did not go. You gave him your home telephone, invited him to visit you when in New Orleans.…I got the above statement by agreeing not to divulge his name until such time as he will consent.…[69]

The last letter between the two came from Candler on 5 October:

> [I]t is evident that nothing is being done towards relieving the difficulties that caused me to break my engagement with you for September 20. Whether there is truth in the statements made of you or not—we should not marry. I am sure you concede this. Whatever course you deem to be wise— your interest considered as primal—to pursue, the earlier

you begin action the sooner will you and I be relieved from a condition of suspense that is next to unbearable to us both. / Sincerely, / Asa G. Candler.[70]

As her precipitous flight to Reno had already proved, de Bouchel was a woman of action. According to her version of events, she first sent her lawyer, Harry Gamble, to discuss the matter with Candler, who refused to divulge the identities of his informants. He did convey the charge that her callers during the Confederate reunion had visited "for immoral purposes." At this news, she stormed into Atlanta to demand a final meeting with Candler, who came to her suite in the Winecoff Hotel accompanied by Asa, Junior. In the aftermath she held court in a hotel parlor where she issued a lengthy formal statement and repeated her story to every newsman who cared to hear it. De Bouchel reported that she had demanded to know the identity of her accuser so that she might defend her good name, but she had learned only that Howard Candler had first heard the story but that Asa, Junior, had been the person who passed it on to his father. The men had pledged not to reveal the identity of their source. The elder Candler, according to de Bouchel, broke into tears, telling her his heart was broken and that if he were related to her he would "take a pistol and go out and kill the man who started these tales." Asa, Junior, offered her a trip to Europe, but she rejected this and again demanded the name of her "slanderer." Again they refused. She ended the interview.[71]

Candler's attorney replied to her public complaints that "Mr. Candler sincerely regrets that Mrs. de Bouchelle should have given such publicity to an unfortunate private affair." From this point onward Candler and most of his family kept silent and virtually invisible.[72] De Bouchel made enough noise for all of them and showed herself to be a fair hand at slander in her own right. She suggested that Candler's family had fabricated the story against her because he intended to bequeath the remnant of his fortune to her. She compared her "ancient Bourbon family" to Candler's supposedly humble origins. For the better part of five days she played variations on the theme of the woman wronged, to the delight of her audience of reporters. She pointed out that she was alone in the world, having been orphaned at age eight and raised in convent schools. Furthermore, as a woman of property, she had no interest in obtaining financial gain from the Candler family, but only sought to preserve her good name. The New Orleans *Picayune* came to the defense of her honor on its editorial pages, while various peripheral figures also gave interviews and otherwise attempted to become part of the story.

Lost in the avalanche of accusation and denial was one fairly good point in her defense: hotel space had been at such a premium during the reunion that she had shared her suite with three other women, one of whom slept on a cot in her room. Certainly, the thought that anyone would attempt an immoral liaison in a hotel jammed with True Daughters of the Confederacy stretches credibility to its limits, but Candler remained unmoved, or at least unwilling to attempt to repair the irreparable.[73]

After spending the better part of a week in Atlanta, de Bouchel and her attorney returned to New Orleans and in a few months she filed the breach of promise suit. Throughout the entire matter she insisted that she had no desire to collect damages, but that her object was to discover the names of her accusers. She had learned that Howard and Asa, Junior, were involved in conveying the charges to their father, but it seems probable that there was more to this story. Some of Candler's last communications claim that he broke off the engagement to protect her from the unpleasant climate of gossip she would have to endure as his wife.

Why would he develop this sudden delicacy of feeling after he had fended off earlier assaults on Onezima de Bouchel's reputation and the objections of his family and friends for many months? The accusation must have been very persuasive, but without knowledge of its origins, its merits cannot be evaluated fully. When the case came to trial Candler continued to avoid revealing the identity of the "sources entitled to belief" and they remain a mystery. Clearly an efficient investigator had been at work, collecting enough evidence to persuade Candler of the truth of the charges against the woman he loved so deeply. One possible conjecture would point to Forrest Adair, Candler's long-time friend and business associate, who (along with Candler's two older sons and brother John) had played detective during the Heinz-Cook blackmail attempt. Also worthy of consideration, on the grounds of his professional contacts and his close ties to Candler, is Chief of Police Beavers. Both Adair and Beavers were to serve Candler in a similar capacity once more in the near future. The breech of promise case did not come to trial until early in 1924 and in the interval more romantic melodrama entered Asa Candler's life.

In the face of his personal disappointment and the public scandal, Candler's fellow citizens offered support; in December of 1922 a committee of leading citizens named him as the first recipient of an annual "Atlanta's First Citizen" award. A delegation from the Kiwanis Club visited him to offer a ceremonious invitation to join their organization. The Presidents' Club held a dinner in honor of his fiftieth year as an Atlanta resident. Loving cups, leather-bound testimonials, and editorials reiterated the city's gratitude and affection. Howard Candler remembered his father's "proud embarrassment" as he listened to Governor Slaton extol the elder Candler's "stewardship" at the President's Club dinner: "As I watched my father's face, by now grown old and lined with the suffering of three years, I saw the tears come often to his eyes behind the rimless glasses."[74]

His fellow citizens could recognize his achievements and honor his generosity, but silver loving cups stuffed with editorials and testimonials could not fill the lonely void at the intimate center of his life. He yearned for companionship and with characteristic courage reached out once again to find it. Mrs. May Little Ragin, a recently widowed mother of twin daughters, whose husband had died after a long illness, operated a stenography office in the Candler Building. There she met the elderly millionaire. If any love letters passed between the two, they have not been preserved. There is no window into this relationship, although it seems reasonable to assume that Candler was as lonely—if not more so—as he had been before. This time he kept his secret closely, concealing the relationship and his plans from his family as well as the public until a few hours before he and Ragin were married in June 1923.

If Candler's family had objected to de Bouchel, this new match must also have seemed less than desirable. However, Candler left no opportunity for opposition. He wrote to his son Howard who was in New York,

> Tomorrow I am taking to myself a life companion—one I believe who is interested in me and will be a comfort to me. I feel the need of such companionship. She will be only by marriage related to you. I have reason to believe her worthy of your respect—if she by right living prove this to be true. I bespeak for her your confidence and respect. She has been obliged to work hard to support herself and two daughters—10 years old. As a public stenographer she has been a tenant of Candler Bldg. She is well thought of: a member of Central Presbyterian Church. Dr. Lacy the pastor says she is a Christian lady. We will be in New York from about June 24th to July 2nd at Hotel Biltmore.[75]

The Reverend Ben R. Lacy united Candler and Ragin in a morning ceremony marked by "quiet simplicity" held in the chapel of the theology Building at Emory University. Only a few family members attended the wedding, which was so quiet that students in nearby rooms had no idea what had taken place. The newlyweds immediately left for a short stay at the New Willard hotel in Washington, DC. Howard sent flowers to the newlyweds, and Candler wired his thanks, adding, "YOUR RENEWED DEVOTION CONTINUED WILL ULTIMATELY JUSTIFY MY POLICY IN WITHHOLDING NAME DATE AND PLACE FROM YOU ALL PREVIOUS EXPERIENCE CAUSE FEAR OF HARSH CRITICISM UNDESERVED AND UNDESIRED."[76]

The wedding made front-page news in Atlanta in stories that reflected Candler's respected standing in the community. Less deferential newspapers elsewhere in the country smirked over the announcement of "Coca-Cola Magnate" Candler's marriage to Mrs. Ragin: "If they like Coca-Cola" the Chicago *Herald-Examiner* burbled, "Julia and Mary, 10-year old twins, would approve of the match made by their mother...." Pictures of mother and daughters accompanied the story. Even in Atlanta, sidebar stories carried renewed accounts of Onezima de Bouchel's pending breach of promise suit. Asked to comment, de Bouchel "merely smiled" as she informed an interviewer that she "knew nothing whatever" about Candler's marriage.[77]

Candler and his new wife settled into the elegant house on Ponce de Leon. The scandal-mongers found other amusements for the next few months, until the de Bouchel lawsuit came to trial during the last days of January 1924.[78]

At this time de Bouchel's legal residence still was Reno, Nevada. Because the parties resided in different states, the case was heard in federal court. Spectators learned to their disappointment that in Georgia the principals in breach of promise cases could not testify in their own behalf and that the federal court would observe the requirement of Georgia law. Candler and de Bouchel would remain silent onlookers during the proceedings. Candler's brother John accompanied him in court each day, and his sons Walter and Asa, Junior, usually were there. Likewise, Mrs. de Bouchel brought a few friends from New Orleans for support and cut a dashing figure in the courtroom. Each side presented testimony, depositions, and extensive extracts from the correspondence between the lovers.

De Bouchel's arguments aimed to defend her honor. Her attorneys argued that Candler had improperly broken the engagement on the basis of an unsubstantiated slander. Her petition pointed out that during the engagement, Candler several times offered "financial assistance," but de Bouchel "in every instance, promptly, firmly but courteously refused." She sought to establish the sincerity of the bond between the two and to establish that this relationship had been sabotaged, probably by Candler's family. Candler's lawyers filed an amendment to their earlier answer, claiming that because de

Bouchel's divorce had not been completed when she agreed to marry Candler, the engagement had no legal standing.

Albert Howell, chief counsel for Mrs. de Bouchel, read a considerable number of Candler's letters into the record with the salutation "Dear Sweetum" before a conference with the judge and a careful examination of Candler's awkward handwriting corrected the reading to "Dear Sweet One;" the correction came too late to forestall a headline in the New York Times of 31 January: "Love Letter Read at Candler Trial / Atlanta Millionaire Called Mrs. De Bouchel "Sweetum" in Ardent Letters." According to newspaper accounts of the trial, while attorneys read his love letters into the record, the elderly millionaire dozed peacefully as unseasonably warm breezes stirred through the open courtroom windows.

Although Candler's counsel characterized de Bouchel as the pursuer in the relationship, they very sensibly refrained from raising the charges of impropriety against de Bouchel. Instead, they rested their defense on the technical claim that the engagement itself had no validity because her divorce had not been completed at the time when she accepted Candler's proposal of marriage. Based on this issue, Candler's lawyers asked Judge Samuel H. Sibley for a directed verdict. He denied the motion, ruling that "the question of this plaintiff's intention in going to Nevada constitutes a question for the jury, and I therefore will have to overrule the motion for a directed verdict."[79] De Bouchel's legal residence—or lack of residence—in Nevada also called her divorce into question. The correspondence left no doubt that de Bouchel had never intended to become a permanent resident of Nevada.

De Bouchel and Candler, each looking on as the case went to the jury, did not have long to wait for the verdict. She went to lunch at the Piedmont hotel with a group of friends and before the meal ended learned that the jury had denied her claim. The news reached Candler, "as he stood surrounded by a group of friends in the lobby of the Candler Building."[80] Judge Sibley ordered de Bouchel to pay the court costs. She told reporters that she was surprised and disappointed by the verdict, but was "consoled" by the fact that the verdict rested on a legal technicality and that Candler's answer to her petition had admitted "under oath, substantially every assertion of my petition sustaining my character." Candler said, "I have no statement to make, except that I am very happy."[81]

Some of his happiness might have come from the fact that the case no longer dominated the headlines. The death of President Woodrow Wilson had taken precedence on the front page. Candler wrote to one of his sons, "I did not wire you yesterday as I knew the press was carrying the result of the law suit. I expected your wire—it reached me very early—Thank you!" He had nothing more to say on the subject; the rest of the letter contains trivial family news.[82] Another "verdict" of a sort came from the community at large: the Kiwanis Club of Atlanta, in a resolution headed "Lest We Forget," recounted a number of Candler's civic services and observed that Candler "has been the victim of a seeming relentless persecution of his life when he should bask serene in the consciousness of a work well done...."[83]

If life were as neat as fiction, this could have been the end of a bittersweet tale, with the old gentleman retired in comfortable obscurity, peacefully married to the affectionate widow. But life seldom is neat, and sour anticlimax may plague old age. Only three days after the conclusion of the breach of promise suit, Chief of Police James L. Beavers personally arrested and detained the new Mrs. Candler. Even the New York Times carried the story: "Take Mrs. Candler on Liquor Charge. Millionaire's Wife and Two Men Companions Accused by Atlanta Police. 'Having a Little Party.' That is the Explanation She is Reported to Have given the Police Chief." The following day the Times informed the world that Mrs. Candler had moved out of the house on Ponce de Leon Avenue. Mrs. Candler, W. J. Stoddard (president of the National Association of Cleaners and Dyers) and G. W. Keeling (head of a brick manufacturing concern) appeared before the Recorder's Court to answer charges that they had violated the city liquor law.[84]

Once again, Candler's private life became front page news. In early March, in the Recorder's court, reporters took notes while Mrs.

Candler sat on a stool in the corner of the crowded room, watching Chief Beavers testify: The Chief reported that less than a month before the arrest, Candler had contacted him to complain about his wife. His testimony revealed that Candler's friend and business associate Forrest Adair also took part in planning the arrest. Once again, as he had done in the Hirsch blackmail case, Adair was working to defend his friend's interests. He told the chief to be prepared for a telephone call. The password "Howell" would be his cue to go personally to a certain apartment and make arrests.

A person named Thomas H. Pitt, who had been following Mrs. Candler, made the critical call to Beavers. Identified as "a real estate man," Pitt evidently had been put on this job by Adair, who was one of the city's leading realtors. The chief brought Police Captain A. J. Holcombe with him and the two met Pitt at the corner of Juniper and Ponce de Leon. Pitt drove them around the block and pointed out Mrs. Candler's automobile and that of Stoddard. The real estate man waited outside of the apartment house at 48 Juniper Street while the officers entered and began their investigation, eventually knocking at the door of apartment seven at the end of the hall. Keeling answered the door and told the officers that he was "just visiting" and that the apartment belonged to a friend. Beavers entered the apartment and went down the hall to the living room. According to his testimony, "Mr. Stoddard was the first person I saw there. He was coming from the door that led into a little room about ten by twelve feet; it was the bedroom. The door to this room was being shut and so I stepped over, caught hold of the knob, pulled back the door and Mrs. Candler was holding to the knob on the other end."[85]

He attempted to confirm her identity and she said, "Tell me who sent you here and I'll tell you anything." The chief testified that he then told her that she was Mrs. Candler. He continued his account of their conversation, testifying that she asked: "Did the family or Mr. Candler send you?"

"Mr. Candler knows all about this and I am sorry. You ought to be ashamed of yourself to treat Mr. Candler this way."

"'I don't care. We are not the only folks doing this way.'"[86]

Beavers also testified to asking Stoddard "how long he had been going with Mrs. Candler," and he claimed that Stoddard had replied, "Chief, she was my stenographer for six years."

"Mr. Stoddard did your wife ever get after you about running around with her?"

"Well, yes chief, she has."

At this point, Stoddard interrupted the testimony to shout, "No, that's not right and you know that's not right." He was silenced by the court, but Beavers answered him: "You know that you did. You know I wouldn't lie for you or anybody else. That isn't all you told me either. You asked me how long I had known about this and when I told you I had known about it a month, you said: "I wish to God you'd tipped me off," and you know, Bill, that an honest officer couldn't do anything like that."[87]

In any case, Chief Beavers had continued his investigation, gingerly sniffing and tasting the nearly empty bottle on the table. It contained whiskey. At this point Stoddard admitted that they had all had a drink and asked the chief to let Mrs. Candler go, saying that he and Keeling would take responsibility for the bottle. Beavers was willing to accept this gallant solution, but in a revealing action, he returned to the street to consult with Pitt. This "real estate man," who acted on behalf of Candler's friend Adair, instructed the chief to arrest all three and take them to the station, in spite of the fact that they could have been given a written copy of the charges and released on the spot. Pitt said, "They want them all treated alike and want them all to give bond." "They" could only have been Adair and Candler.

Beavers charged all three with violation of section 1768 of the city code, a provision intended to prevent the operation of "dives," or illegal liquor clubs. The attorney for the defense argued that this law did not apply to the case: "There were no persons without visible support in the apartment. There were no immoral persons, no loiterers, no sellers of liquor. The apartment could not be construed as a dive, by any means." Recorder Johnson agreed, and released Mrs. Candler and Keeling; Stoddard's admission that the liquor belonged to him resulted in his being bound over to the grand jury and released under $300 bond.[88] Meanwhile the New York Times, which had passed along the news that "Mrs. Candler Leaves Home of Husband," added the delectable morsel, "Wife of Wealthy Georgian Is Said to Have Spent Night in Raided Apartment." The Times's gossip received support during the following year when the owner of the apartment house at 48 Juniper Street sued several principal parties involved in the incident for damages resulting from the scandal. She claimed that the notoriety caused her other tenants to leave and ultimately resulted in the forced sale of the building when she could no longer pay the mortgage. In a document related to the case, she charged that Mrs. Candler and Stoddard had occupied the apartment "clandestinely" for "immoral purposes" since the autumn preceding the arrest.[89]

The following June, Candler filed for divorce. The petition asserted that Candler had married Ragin because he loved her. He believed her statements that she loved him, but immediately after the marriage, "defendant showed clearly by her treatment of the plaintiff that she had no love for him ... her marriage had not been the result of love, but of other motives."[90] He claimed that she customarily left the house early and stayed away until night. These absences often were "spent in the company of a man," sometimes for automobile drives into the country or meetings in unidentified "other places." She "ignored, and indeed insulted" his friends. She "cursed and otherwise vilified and abused...without slightest cause" her elderly spouse. This situation undermined his health, Candler's petition claimed, but his wife "willfully persisted in the various acts of cruel treatment" until her "unbearable" conduct led to their separation.[91] May Little Ragin Candler did not oppose the divorce, perhaps for the reasons presented in an *Atlanta Journal* story that appeared in July: "Reports in courthouse circles Friday were to the effect that Mr. Candler had settled $100,000 on his wife, but it was understood that the actual figures were $60,000 and that she had waived all claim against him...."[92]

Once again, what appeared to be finis left another chapter to play out. Mrs. Candler continued to live in Atlanta, residing at her parents' home while she waited out the completion of the divorce process. About 5:30 on an early October evening, she drove her Cole Eight sedan around a curve in East Pace's Ferry Road; 250 feet beyond the curve, five-year-old Mary Elizabeth Lunsford left her playmates to cross the street and stepped into the path of the oncoming car. The child died of severe head injuries.

In a statement, Mrs. Candler said,

> I was not moving faster than twenty miles an hour.... I slammed on the brakes immediately in an effort to bring the car to a stop, but succeeded too late to avoid the crash. As well as I remember, Mary Elizabeth hit my fender and was thrown into the gutter.... My heart goes out to the little girl and her loved ones. I am not to blame for what happened. There were witnesses nearby and each of them agreed that I did everything in my power to avoid striking the child as she dashed into the street.[93]

Police and witnesses agreed with Mrs. Candler's claim that the accident had been unavoidable.[94] Mary Elizabeth's mother, Mrs. Elizabeth Lawrence Lunsford, in a damage suit against Mrs. Candler that was filed on 5 November, shortly after the accident, claimed that the car had been traveling through the residential district on the wrong side of the street at forty miles per hour. The following month Mrs. Lunsford initiated a second suit, this time including Asa Candler as a responsible party, because "the wrongful conduct of his said wife is chargeable as a matter of law to him." This dreadful incident and the resulting lawsuits may have had some connection with a reconciliation between the Candlers, which evidently took place about the same time that Mrs. Lunsford filed the second suit. What passed between the husband and wife remains private, but Candler dropped the divorce action. Shortly before 11 December Mae Little Ragin Candler, bringing her twin daughters with her, returned to the Ponce de Leon mansion. After several continuances, Candler settled the Lunsford suit privately in March 1926.[95]

Howard Candler's memoir of his father's life not only fails to treat any of these matters, it omits the second Mrs. Candler's name from the genealogical information in the back of the published work, offering mute testimony to the family's opinion of this marriage. The terms upon which Mrs. Candler returned to her marriage can only be conjectured, but nonetheless the two stayed together, although Candler's health began to fail. They made a trip to Europe, "largely in the interests of his health" in 1925, but a few weeks after their return in early September, he became seriously ill.[96]

When he had recovered sufficiently, his thoughts centered on Emory. In November 1925 he telephoned W. D. Thomson, secretary of the university and a partner in John Candler's law firm, asking him to come to his office in the Candler Building. He handed Thomson a list of securities that he said were worth about a million dollars. They were to be his last gift to Emory University. In this final act of stewardship, Candler insisted on complete secrecy. Only Thomson was to know the details of the arrangement. To accomplish this, Candler had placed the assortment of securities in safe deposit box 279 in the Trust Company bank. He instructed the bank to change the box from his name to that of Emory University and told his son Howard to take the key to Thompson. Thompson and Candler devised a plan to deliver the proceeds from the stocks and bonds to the university in comparatively small amounts since a large anonymous gift would lead to the inference that it had come from Candler. On 14 January of the new year, the two men concluded this million-dollar deal with the simplest of formalities. Thomson wrote a brief memorandum of their discussions and asked Candler to write a statement on the bottom of the list that he had handed over earlier: "I have this day given Emory University all the above listed Securities and have delivered them to W. D. Thomson secretary of said Emory University. /s/ Asa G. Candler Jan 13th 1926."[97]

Candler's secrecy may have come from simple modesty, but the numerous disappointments of his last years may also have taught him to avoid possible disputes. He had resolved to live on annuities amounting to $110,000 annually. He told Thomson that this amount was "all he would need, & more."[98] His last two surviving letters suggest both the quietness of his life and the fact that he still was not forgotten. He declined to serve on the board of the Stone Mountain Confederate Monumental Association and he expressed gratitude for a gift of flowers and a "kind letter."[99] Although he had ended his involvement in almost every other interest, he never resigned from service as the president of the board of directors of Emory University. In February 1926, when he had become too ill to attend its meetings, the board of Emory University voted to name its new library building in his honor, even though he had always resisted all efforts to attach his name to any aspect of the Emory campus. In moving to bestow this recognition on Asa Candler, a board member noted that Candler's total gifts to Emory amounted to seven million dollars.[100] He was unaware that another million dollars' worth of securities waited in a safe deposit box at the Trust Company Bank.

The lamp of Asa Griggs Candler's life flickered low in September 1926. A paralytic stroke plunged him into a coma from which he never recovered. Months turned into years as he lay in the Wesley Memorial Hospital, the institution that owed much of its existence to his efforts. There, on 12 March 1929, he died.[101] Front-page obituaries recounted his honors, services, and achievements. The *Georgian's* included an excerpt from an interview: "The one curse my wealth has brought me has been that through it people became interested in me who had no normal or natural interest in me or mine. My one regret is that I have not been able to live my life in the simplicity of my early years."[102]

Candler's faithful stewardship of this wealth meant that little of it remained at the time of his death. His will bequeathed to his children "my good name as it has come to me from an honorable and honest ancestor." Each of the children, he said, "has been dutiful and faithful to me. For this I am grateful. May they be as faithful and true to their and our God is my prayer." Candler's testament included a characteristic statement: "My chief aim in life has been to help and not hurt my fellow man. My soul I commit unto Him who gave it...."[103] About a year after her husband's death, the second Mrs. Candler signed a quit-claim on the Ponce de Leon house, having received "$10 and other valuable considerations." It became the property of Asa G. Candler, Incorporated, but no one in the family ever chose to live there again.[104]

[1] Charles Howard Candler, *Asa Griggs Candler* (Atlanta: Emory University, 1950) 200, 207-08, 215; "Box Parties for Grand Opera Week," *Atlanta Journal*, 15 April 1917, L-7; "Brilliant Audience Assembled at Premiere of Opera Season," *Atlanta Journal*, 24 April 1917, 13; AGC to Bishop John C. Kilgo, 28 June 1918, John C. Kilgo Papers, Duke University Archives, Durham, North Carolina ["suffering"]; "Mayor Candler and Wife Visit Virginia Resort," *Atlanta Journal*, 12 July 1918, 5; "Mrs. Asa G. Candler, Sr.. Dies Saturday Morning at Druid Hills Home," *Atlanta Journal*, 22 February 1919, 1; "Mrs. Asa Candler, Sr.., Dies Early Saturday After Long Illness," *Atlanta Constitution*, 23 February 1919, K-14; "Funeral Services for Mrs. Asa Candler, Sr.., Held Monday Morning," *Atlanta Journal*, 24 February 1919, 1; James O. Robinson, M. D., "Our Surgical Heritage: Treatment of Breast Cancer Through the Ages" in *American Journal of Surgery*, 151:3 (March 1986), 317-333. Pages 325-26 describe the type of treatment prevalent in Mrs. Candler's time. Information on the Druid Hills house, located at 1428 Ponce De Leon Avenue, which is now a Melkite Catholic Church, may be seen in the *Atlanta Journal* of 28 July 1946 and 13 February 1972.

[2] "Family Record—Deaths" electrostatic copy of page from Asa G. Candler's family Bible in "Candler" genealogy file, Georgia Department of Archives and History; "Mrs. Asa G. Candler, Sr.." *Coca-Cola Bottler* (March 1919), 22; Candler, *Asa G. Candler*, 207-208.

[3] See AGC to Mrs. Arthur Tufts, 20 February 1920, box 1, AGC papers, Emory. The pertinent verses from the King James translation are as follow:

3 Blessed be God, even the Father of our Lord Jesus Christ, the Father of mercies, and the God of all comfort;
4 Who comforteth us in all our tribulation, that we may be able to comfort them which are in any trouble by the comfort wherewith we ourselves are comforted of God.
5 For as the sufferings of Christ abound in us, so our consolation also aboundeth by Christ.
6 And whether we be afflicted, it is for your consolation and salvation, which is effectual in the enduring of the same sufferings which we also suffer: or whether we be comforted, it is for your consolation and salvation.
7 And our hope of you is steadfast, knowing that as ye are partakers of the sufferings, so shall ye be also of the consolation.

[4] Candler, *Asa Griggs Candler*, 422.

[5] "Veterans Will Be Asked to Hold Big Reunion in Atlanta," *Atlanta Journal*, 21 July 1919, 1, mentions Candler as participant in planning.

[6] For extensive coverage of the reunion, see the *Atlanta Constitution* and *Atlanta Journal*, 5-10 October 1919, passim. This topic drove almost every other topic out of the papers with the exception of the results of World Series games.

[7] "Gate City Is Packed with Gallant Old Vets and Beautiful Women," *Atlanta Constitution*, 7 October 1919, 16; "Luncheon in Compliment to Guests from New Orleans," *Atlanta Journal*, 8 October 1919, 18. Her photograph appeared with several others on the front page of the *Atlanta Journal*, Rotogravure Section, 5 October 1919.

8"Hoped for Ideal companionship But Not Love—Mrs. de Bouchelle," *Atlanta Constitution* 11 October 1922, 1; "Mrs. D'Bouchel Recounts Mr. Candler's Courtship and Facts of Divorce," *Atlanta Journal*, 11 October 1922, 1. Mrs. Roquet soon was to seek a divorce from her husband and resume her maiden name; de Bouchel is spelled in every possible way in newspaper coverage.

9O. deB. Roquet to AGC, October 1919, see Appendix. Extensive excerpts from their correspondence formed part of the testimony in de Bouchel's 1924 suit against Candler, which is treated below. The file of this case, preserved at the Federal Records Center in Atlanta, does not include a transcript of testimony, however. A calendar of these letters as reproduced in certain newspaper sources appears in an appendix at the end of this work.. The original letters, if they exist, are not available

10United States District Court, Northern District of Georgia, Northern Division, No. 619 Common Law, *Onezima de Bouchel v. Asa G. Candler*, filed 17 February 1923, Federal Archives and Records Center, Atlanta. The following account draws on the petition of the plaintiff and the defendant's answer and amendment, and on newspaper accounts of the letters and public statements made by various participants in the dispute.

11De Bouchel to AGC, 23 November 1919, see Appendix.

12De Bouchel to AGC, "Tuesday" [1 January 1920]; and 23 April 1920, see Appendix.

13De Bouchel to AGC, [June 1920], see Appendix; petition of plaintiff and defendant's answer, *de Bouchel v. Candler*; de Bouchel to AGC, "aboard HMS Royal George," [June] 1920, and [June-November] 1920, "postmarked foreign address," see Appendix.

14"Mrs. D'Bouchel Recounts...*Atlanta Journal*, 11 October 1922, 1.

15De Bouchel to AGC, 26 November 1920, see Appendix.

16Ibid.

17De Bouchel to AGC, 30 November 1920, see Appendix.

18AGC to de Bouchel, 10 December 1921, see Appendix.

19De Bouchel to AGC, 4 December and 12 December 1920, see Appendix.

20AGC to de Bouchel, 14 December 1920, see Appendix.

21De Bouchel to AGC, 17 December 1920, see Appendix.

22De Bouchel to AGC, 21 December 1920, see Appendix.

23Letters, January-April 1920, see appendix. In the letter of 27 April, de Bouchel notes that two weeks have passed since she last saw Candler.

24Godfrey Plachek to CHC, 8 January 1949, box 7, CHC papers, Emory.

25Ibid.

26AGC to CHC, Kansas City, MO, 6 April 1921, and AGC to "My dear Children," San Francisco, 12 April 1921, both in box 1, AGC papers, Emory. De Bouchel's letter of 21 March mentions their plan to meet in San Francisco; her letter of 27 April begins "Two weeks have elapsed since I had the pleasure of seeing you . . . ."

27AGC to de Bouchel, 1 February 1921, see Appendix.

28AGC to [Catherine Candler], 2 June 1921, box 1, AGC papers, Emory.

29AGC to CHC, Laramie WY, 22 July 1921, box 1, AGC papers, Emory.

30AGC to Bishop James Cannon, Jr., 20 January 1921, Cannon papers, Special Collections Department, William R. Perkins Library, Duke University.

31AGC to de Bouchel, 14 February 1921, see Appendix.

[32]de Bouchel to AGC, 7 February 1921, see Appendix.

[33]AGC to de Bouchel, 2 November 1921, see Appendix.

[34]AGC to de Bouchel, 6 February 1922, see Appendix. In July, 1922, the physical assets of the Atlanta Warehouse Company (principally the mammoth warehouse Candler had built to store cotton and then loaned to the government during the World War) were sold; the company, with an accumulation of over $800,000 in its depreciation account, was liquidated. According to Howard Candler, the stock in this company had been given to the Candler children in 1916 and 1917 so it is possible that the timing of the liquidation had nothing to do with Candler's other withdrawals from business activity. See Candler, *Asa Griggs Candler*, 312 and 314.

[35]AGC to de Bouchel, 16 September 1921, see Appendix.

[36]Trust Company of Georgia, manuscript of a report on the history of Trust Company prepared by Bethel Minter and Henry Harris, "Trust Company of Georgia" subject file, Atlanta Historical Society Library-Archives, Atlanta Georgia. Kahn, *The Big Drink*, 60, and Watters, *Coca-Cola*, 109, have superficial accounts of the sale.

[37]AGC to de Bouchel, 7 April 1922, see Appendix.

[38]AGC to de Bouchel, 1 June 1922, see Appendix.

[39]AGC to de Bouchel, 1 January [1921], see Appendix.

[40]AGC to de Bouchel, 1 March 1921, see Appendix.

[41]AGC to de Bouchel, 17 May 1921, see Appendix.

[42]AGC to de Bouchel, 3 August 1921 and 29 November 1921, see Appendix.

[43]AGC to de Bouchel, 15 December 1921, see Appendix. In fact, Asa and Lucy married in January. Without the original letter, it is impossible to verify the date on its face.

[44]AGC to de Bouchel, 10 January and 14 January 1921, see Appendix.

[45]AGC to de Bouchel, 21 June 1921, see Appendix.

[46]AGC to de Bouchel, 5 April 1922, see Appendix.

[47]AGC to de Bouchel, 20 April 1922, see Appendix.

[48]Petition of Onezima de Bouchel, paragraph no. 32. See also: "$500,000 Damages Asked by Mrs. De Bouchel in Breach of Promise Suit," *Atlanta Constitution*, 18 February 1922, 1.

[49]AGC to de Bouchel, 17 March 1922, see Appendix.

[50]AGC to de Bouchel, 18 May 1922, see Appendix.

[51]AGC to de Bouchel, 24 March 1922, and AGC to de Bouchel, 29 April 1922, see Appendix.

[52]AGC to de Bouchel, 21 May 1922, see Appendix.

[53]AGC to de Bouchel, 8 May 1922, see Appendix; "D'Bouchel Suit Will Go to Jury," *Atlanta Constitution* 5 February 1924, 1; "Intimates Shower Character Praises on Mrs. de Bouchel," *Atlanta Journal* 31 January 1924, 1; "Defense to Charge Fraud in De Bouchel Divorce," *Atlanta Constitution* 1 February 1924, 1; plaintiff's petition and defendant's answer, de Bouchel v. Candler.

[54]AGC to de Bouchel, 6 February 1922, see Appendix; Petition of plaintiff, de Bouchel v. Candler; AGC to de Bouchel, 31 July 1922, and AGC to de Bouchel, 8 September 1922, see Appendix.

[55]"Beautiful New Orleans Woman to Wed Mr. Asa G. Candler," *Atlanta Journal*, 4 August 1922, 1; "Candler-DeBouchelle Engagement of Interest," *Atlanta Journal*, 6 August 1922, Society section, 1.

[56]AGC to de Bouchel, 16 May 1922, see Appendix.

[57]A. B. Vaughn, LaGrange GA, to WAC, "Correspondence 1922, Aug. 15-31" folder, box 47, WAC papers, Emory.

[58]AGC to de Bouchel, 26 May 1922, see Appendix.

[59]James E. Dickey to Bro. Candler, ALS, 2 September 1922 "Correspondence 1922" folder, box 47, Warren A. Candler Papers, Emory.

[60]James E. Dickey to My Beloved Friend [WAC], "Correspondence 1922" folder, box 47, Warren A. Candler Papers, Emory.

[61]P. Z. Alexander to Bishop Candler, "Correspondence 1922, Aug. 15-31" folder, box 47, Warren A. Candler Papers, Emory; "Lawyer Is Retained By Mrs. de Bouchelle In 'Poison Letter' Case," *Atlanta Journal*, 24 August 1922, 1; AGC to de Bouchel, 15 August 1922, see Appendix; "Candler's Wedding Delayed by Bishop," *New Orleans Picayune*, 25 August 1922 clipping, in "Asa Griggs Candler Papers and Biography," The Archives, The Coca-Cola Company.

[62]A. B. Vaughn, LaGrange GA, to Warren A. Candler, "Correspondence 1922, Aug. 15-31" folder, box 47, WAC papers, Emory.

[63]AGC to de Bouchel, 11 September 1922, see Appendix.

[64]"Mr. Candler Retires," *Coca-Cola Bottler*, October 1922, 29; "C & S Chronological History," *The Southern Citizen* [a C & S house organ], 70th anniversary edition (1957), 8, in "C & S" subject file, Atlanta History Center Library/Archives, Atlanta.

[65]AGC to de Bouchel, 12 September 1922, see Appendix.

[66]AGC to de Bouchel, 13 September 1922, see Appendix. Walter Candler had loaned a couple named Byfield money to make a trip to Europe; he had separated from his wife, wanted to take his two daughters on a visit to the continent and thought that the company of the Byfields would make the trip more congenial. During the voyage, Byfield came into his and his wife's stateroom, found Candler there, and a scene ensued. The Byfields charged that Candler had made improper advances on Mrs. Byfield, while Candler charged that the incident was an extortion scheme. In either case, Candler wrote a large check to Byfield that was later replaced by a promissory note. Upon reconsideration, Candler sued for the return of the note. Coverage of these events were front page news in Atlanta's newspapers beginning on 15 August 1922.

[67]AGC to de Bouchel, 15 September 1922, see Appendix.

[68]De Bouchel to AGC, 28 September 1922, see Appendix.

[69]AGC to de Bouchel, 30 September 1922, see Appendix.

[70]AGC to de Bouchel, 5 October 1922, see Appendix.

[71]"Mrs. D'Bouchel Asks Explanation of Mr. Candler," *Atlanta Journal*, 10 October 1922, 1.

[72]"Hoped for Ideal Companionship . . . ," *Atlanta Constitution*, 11 October 1922, 1.

[73]The *Atlanta Journal*, 10-14 October 1922, and the *Atlanta Constitution*, 11-15 October 1922, carry daily front-page stories on the scandal, many illustrated with large photographs of de Bouchel.

[74]Candler, *Asa Griggs Candler*, 423-31; Quotation from CHC on 430. The appellation "First Citizen" had previously been applied informally to Samuel Inman, who had died a few years earlier.

[75]"Papa" [AGC] to My dear Son, 19 January 1923, box 1, AGC papers, Emory.

[76]AGC to CHC, 25 June 1923, box 1, AGC papers, Emory.

[77]"Asa G. Candler Sr.., Marries Mrs. May Little Ragin at Emory," *Atlanta Journal*, 20 June 1923, 1; "Asa G. Candler Sr.., Marries Mrs. May Little Ragin," *Atlanta Constitution*, 21 June 1923; "Coca Cola Magnate Weds Stenographer; Plans Kept Secret," Mason City Iowa *Globe*, 20 June 1923; "Asa Candler Weds Stenographer," Council Bluffs Iowa *Nonpareil*, 20 June 1922; "If They Like Coca Cola," Chicago *Herald-Examiner* 23 June 1922. Clippings of the last three are in box 7, CHC papers, Emory.

[78]The following account of the trial is drawn from the plaintiff's petition and the defendant's amended answer in de Bouchel v. Candler, and from the *Atlanta Constitution* and *Atlanta Journal* daily front-page coverage of the story between 30 January and 6 February 1924.

[79]"Directed Verdict Is Denied Candler; Jury to Get Case," *Atlanta Journal*, 4 February 1924, 1.

[80]"Mrs. De Bouchel Denied Damages In Candler Suit," *Atlanta Constitution*, 6 February 1924, 1.

[81]"Clear Moral Victory Won, Mrs. De Bouchel's Lawyer Declared Upon Departure," *Atlanta Journal*, 6 February 1924, 10; "Mrs. De Bouchel Denied Damages In Candler Suit," *Atlanta Constitution*, 6 February 1924, 1.

[82]"Papa" [AGC] to "My dear Man, "ALS 6 February 1924, AGC Papers, Woodruff Library Special Collections, Emory.

[83]"Lest We Forget" typescript, box 7, Charles Howard Candler Papers, Woodruff Library Special Collections, Emory.

[84]"Take Mrs. Candler on Liquor Charges" *New York Times*, 10 February 1924, 17; "Mrs. Candler Leaves Home of Husband," *New York Times*, 11 February 1924, 17; "Mrs. Candler Faces Court," *New York Times*, 13 February 1924, 9.

[85]"Mrs. Candler and Keeling Acquitted; Stoddard Is Held," *Atlanta Journal*, 3 March 1924, 1.

[86]Ibid.

[87]Ibid.; "Mrs. Asa Candler Freed By Court," *Atlanta Constitution*, 4 March 1924, 1. Parts of this exchange are found in each story; the blocked quotation from Beavers appears in the *Constitution* story.

[88]"Mrs. Candler and Keeling Acquitted; Stoddard Is Held," *Atlanta Journal*, 3 March 1924; "Mrs. Asa Candler Freed By Court," *Atlanta Constitution*, 4 March 1924, 1.

[89]*New York Times*, 11 February 1924, 17; Mrs. Harriet W. Pitchford v. Forrest Adair, Sr.., et al., docket number 63437, plaintiff's amended petition, 1 June 1925, Fulton County Superior Court, Atlanta. The original suit named Adair, Stoddard, Keeling, and Mr. and Mrs. Candler as defendants; the amended petition dropped the complaint against Adair and Asa Candler and added the accusation against Mrs. Candler and Stoddard.

[90]Petition of Asa G. Candler, Asa G. Candler v. Mrs. Mae L. Candler, docket no. 60607, filed 17 June 1924, Fulton Superior Court, Atlanta.

[91]Ibid.

[92]"Mrs. Asa G. Candler Not to Fight Divorce Suit of Her Husband," *Atlanta Journal*, 25 July 1924, 1.

[93]"Three Children Hurt in Auto Accidents, One victim Dies," *Atlanta Journal*, 9 October 1924, 9.

[94]Ibid.

[95]Elizabeth L. Lunsford v. Mrs. Mae Little Candler, docket number 62447, 5 November 1924, and Elizabeth Lawrence Lunsford v. Mrs. Mae Little Candler, et al., docket number 62800, 5 December 1924, both in Fulton County Superior Court, Atlanta; "Asa G. Candler, Sr.., and Wife Reconciled; Suit Is Withdrawn," *Atlanta Journal*, 11 December 1924, 3; "Candlers Make

Peace," *New York Times*, 11 December 1924, 3. The terms of the settlement of the Lunsford matter are not recorded; $25,000 damages had been demanded, a sum based on the companionship and services, valued at $25 per month, that Mrs. Lunsford received from her only child.

[96]"A. G. Candler Seriously Ill," *New York Times*, 23 September 1925, 50.

[97]"Securities put in box #276, Trust Co. of Ga. by WDT & CHC 1/14/26," memorandum with attached list, Series I, Board of Trustees, Emory University Archives, Emory University, Atlanta. Candler's estimate of $1 million in market value applied to a group of securities with a par value of about $250,000. They included some small school district and municipal bonds, $200,000 of Philippine government bonds, 639 shares of Coca-Cola preferred and 200 Georgia Railway and Power preferred shares.

[98]Ibid.

[99]Rogers Winter, Chairman to AGC, 23 April 1925, and AGC to Miss Jennison, 26 February 1926, box 1, AGC papers, Emory.

[100]Minute Book of Emory University, 1915-26, 25 February 1926, Emory University, Atlanta. Bishop Darlington made the motion.

[101]"A. G. Candler Seriously Ill," *New York Times*, 23 September 1925, 50; "Asa Candler In Coma," *New York Times*, 29 September 1926, 25; "A. G. Candler, Maker of Coca Cola, Dies," *New York Times*, 13 March 1929, 31.

[102]"Modesty Marked All Asa Candler's Career as First Citizen Here," *Atlanta Georgian*, special extra edition, 13 March 1929, 1.

[103]AGC Last Will and Testament, probated March 1929, DeKalb County, AGC papers, The Archives, The Coca-Cola Company.

[104]Indenture, 28 March 1930, fol. 5, box 12, AGC papers, Emory.

This Was Asa Candler

Imagine Asa Candler in a moment of quiet, turning the pages of his well-used Bible. In the tenth chapter of Mark he begins to read the account of Jesus' conversation with a rich man who asked how to inherit eternal life. Jesus' advice to the man to give up all his material wealth and "follow me," was more than that man could do: "...and he went away. sorrowful." Jesus then said that it is easier for a camel to pass through the eye of a needle than for a rich man to enter the kingdom of God. This moved his disciples to ask, "Then who can be saved?" Perhaps Jesus' answer, that "all things are possible with God," offered encouragement to the pious millionaire.

To begin with Asa Candler's beginnings, the "poor boy" myth must be laid to rest. Although he made his own large fortune, fulfilling the American paradigm of the self-made man, the simplicity of his origins has been greatly exaggerated. In fact, Candler's Villa Rica childhood, although rural and disrupted by war, was undeniably comfortable, providing him with the manners and education necessary for a smooth entry into the commercial world. Undoubtedly his father's activity as a successful merchant schooled young Asa in the business methods and work ethic that contributed to his own success. His widowed mother's assets provided a bit of capital for his first venture, and the Candler family's large and well-established place in the state of Georgia provided a network of information and associations that would not have been open to any anonymous country boy. Although his account of his arrival in Atlanta with less than $2 in his pocket may be accurate, Asa Candler's career demonstrates that the true distinction between poverty and wealth does not depend simply upon an individual's net worth at any one moment. Intangible assets, such as education, social connections, and access to credit constitute another kind of wealth that Asa Candler never lacked.

He also possessed a hard intelligence and an aggressive personality. Candler could set himself up as the chief competitor of the man who had given him his first job, slander the man's professional competence in advertisements, and elope with his daughter a few months later. As time went on, people "got to owing" him money and he got to *owning* their businesses. Whatever else he was, Asa Candler was a type much admired by Americans—a relentless competitor.

If Americans admire competitiveness in business or elsewhere, piety and generosity also stand high in the national estimation, and Asa Candler fit this pattern as well. Wealth, tradition, and religion united to mold his personality, and the greatest of these was religion. If he ever doubted his faith he left no record of the experience. The Southern Methodist belief acquired in his youth dominated his life's choices: what he did with his money, how he functioned as a citizen, how he related to the other people in his world.

When his economic success brought him a place among Atlanta's elite, Candler attempted to use his wealth and power responsibly, according to his religious beliefs. Few persons of means in the present time would publicly represent themselves as God's business agents in the world, but Asa Candler and a few other men of means who professed Christian belief at the turn of the century did exactly this. They saw themselves as custodians of assets that properly belonged to God. Candler's career demonstrates this concept of *Christian stewardship* as a way of life. The temptation to dismiss the whole business as so much hypocrisy is refuted by Candler's private papers, which testify to the sincerity of his religious belief. His surviving correspondence preserves numerous letters that launch into ecstatic declarations of religious passion. Hypocrites on vacation do not find sermons in the stone walls of the Grand Canyon. With no sense of contradiction, he asserted that "the Decalogue" and the "natural laws of trade" guided his life. He believed commerce to be innately ethical because "it disdains rewards without services rendered, and despises gains gotten without 'value relieved.'"[1]

If Asa Candler served God, he also served his community. His creative use of his own resources to shore up the local economy__ most notably with the cotton warehouse project—should not be confused with simple philanthropy, but undeniably served Atlanta. More than once he loaned his credit to advance some public improvement project such as the construction of the Auditorium-Armory or the creation of Camp Gordon during Word War I. Even his conventional business undertakings—founding The Coca-Cola Company and developing Druid Hills, Candler Park and other residential areas—benefited Atlanta. Its airport also began as a Candler holding. Even in business, Asa Candler often worked for something larger than his own immediate interests.

Private conduct, to the extent that it can be known, also bears witness for Candler's life of stewardship. His principles allowed a degree of comfort but not ostentation. Not a miser, he nevertheless took great care of his (and God's) money. He established a measure of security for his family but gave the bulk of his fortune to church-related causes. Financial issues seem to have played only a small part in Asa Candler's relationships with his family, probably because they understood his views on giving money away. After all, he had charged his sons interest on the money he loaned them for college. When Warren's son-in-law needed money, Candler charged six percent for a loan with a regular schedule of payments. He did give support to his brother Warren, whose name appears frequently among the smaller stockholders of his various business enterprises. But even to the Bishop, Candler was not a prodigal giver; on December, 1906, the bishop's wife Nettie complained to her mother that "Bro Asa did not give Sissie or Warren a thing on Xmas. He sent me a turkey."[2] Perhaps the greatest testimonial to his sincere belief in stewardship is that he did not die a rich man. At the end of his days, he arranged to transfer the last remnants of his fortune to Emory University.

This guardian of God's wealth also acted as a guardian of public morality. If he was a man of principle, his principles did not admit the proposition that other persons—his fellow citizens—might be permitted to make moral choices at variance with his own. His beliefs dictated that he defend Chief Beavers' anti-vice crusade, in spite of the fact that a large proportion of his social peers, as well as many other Atlantans, held an opposing position. Candler never doubted his own convictions.

Like many others of his time, Asa Candler lived in the midst of widespread injustice and suffering, but simply did not perceive them as significant. His attitudes toward African-Americans, forged in a slave-owning household of the mid-nineteenth century, never grew beyond the amiable, paternalistic racism typical of his class of southerner. He did not hate blacks, but saw them as patently inferior. Furthermore his own Anglo-Saxon heritage, in his mind, elevated him above the mass of humanity, including most whites. He deplored the race riots of 1906, but the idea of changing the status of blacks in his world never occurred to him. Disorder offended him, if race prejudice did not. He seems hardly to have noticed the large class of affluent, educated blacks whose presence has enhanced the city Asa Candler loved. The best that may be said for him is that he was no worse than most and better than some of his contemporaries in his failure to perceive the essential humanity of his non-Anglo-Saxon neighbors.

Paternalism also limited his understanding of the women in his life and of the working people under his supervision. Only after her death did he recognize (by his own admission) his neglect of his first wife. Although he took great care to see his sons established in business, he never thought to involve his daughter in their management. He consulted his sons about his plan to marry Mrs. de Bouchel; he informed his daughter. His condescension towards de Bouchel's mild feminism further demonstrates that he saw women entirely in traditional roles.

He took a similar authoritarian and ultimately disrespectful attitude toward employees, imposing his religion (and occasional doses of medicine) on them. Christmas gifts do not replace respect for an individual's autonomy in private life. Although a fair examination of the record shows that he publicly opposed child labor, he may not have understood the difference between a farm boy's regular chores and intensive industrial labor performed by a child of similar age. The union organizer Pollard accused Candler of personally directing police actions against the streetcar strikers—not an unreasonable allegation.[3] His Anglo-Saxonism also came into play at this time, when he characterized labor organizers as "foreigners."[4]

Candler remained a well-intentioned paternalist to the end, not because he arbitrarily resisted change, but because nothing in his experience suggested to him that change might be needed. No cloud of ambiguity troubled his presumptions. His economic success protected his convictions from most challenges. Evidently, no one pointed out to him the weaknesses of his view that commerce was innately ethical. Mr. Candler told others the "wholesome truths" he thought they ought to heed. For the most part, those who did challenge him spoke from the margins of his society. He easily disregarded their voices. With the exception of campaigns for moral uplift, any need for fundamental social change entirely escaped his comprehension.

Candler's long career of public and private success left him poorly prepared for the blows that fell in this last decade of his life. His children bartered away the company that had been the foundation of his fortune and did not trouble to consult him. (His letters to Mrs. de Bouchel suggest that not being asked his opinions, rather than the actual sale of Coca-Cola, pained him greatly.) After his dutiful and affectionate wife died, he twice reached out for companionship and love and twice failed. In addition to the public scandals arising from his relationships with Mrs. de Bouchel and May Ragin—which he faced with public stoicism—one of his children became embroiled in a sexual scandal that provided additional entertainment to newspaper readers around the country.

Had Candler experienced more failure and frustration earlier in life he might have tempered his convictions in the crucible of experience to render them flexible and able to cope with new challenges. Instead, he held fast to the old way of things. His relationship with Onezima de Bouchel could not withstand the demands of propriety in spite of his obvious love for her. Deeply wounded by this experience he briefly committed a kind of petty rebellion by concealing his next courtship, but the resulting marriage disappointed him deeply. The best he could do was to call on the old team of friends and relatives that had defended him from the blackmailers of the past, to expose his new wife's misbehavior.

Until his final decade he lived as a confident and contented man. He wielded his authority in ways he believed to be just and managed his wealth according to his religious principles. He set an example of modesty, dignity, and service. Sincerity, however, should not be confused with pure goodness. A dark side of this life of single-minded dedication arises from his complacent, uncritical acceptance of the traditional beliefs acquired in his youth. He thus became a steward not only of God's wealth but also of the status quo. Some who examine Asa Candler's life and works may fault this decent man for not being a better one, but the final verdict must be that Asa Candler was neither a protestant saint nor a heartless capitalist, but rather, a man who did his duty as he understood it, without counting the cost.

---

[1] "Notable Address Delivered by Mr. Candler," *Atlanta Journal*, 31 December 1907, 5.

[2] Nettie to "My Dear Mother," written on the back of another letter headed "Gainesville, Fla, Dec. 20, 1906," box 13, WAC papers, Emory; [Andrew Sledd] to "My Dear Bishop [Candler]," 25 February 1908, fol.8, box 14, WAC papers, Emory. "Uncle Asa" accepted sixteen notes "endorsed by my friends" for $150 each, payable every thirty days at 6 percent, hardly an act of charity. The immediate cause of Sledd's trouble is discussed in chapter 7.

[3] See ch. 9, note 39.

[4] See ch. 9, note 45.

Calendar of de Bouchel-Candler Correspondence

This table chronologically lists each letter, excerpt or paraphrased excerpt quoted in newspaper coverage of the *de Bouchel v. Candler* suit. After the date, the letter [d] indicates a letter written by de Bouchel and the letter [C] marks a Candler letter. The next entry cites the sources of the letters, using the following abbreviations: *Atlanta Journal* [AJ], *Atlanta Constitution* [AC] *New York Times* [NY]; almost all of these stories begin on page 1. A descriptive comment is included to assist in identifying most of these items; parts of one letter may be found in more than one source, so the phrase "*Same letter…" must not be construed to mean "identical quotation."

Date of letter	author	source	comment
?? October 1919	d	AJ 01 Feb	thank you, but disappointed
5 November 1919	d	AJ 31 Jan	*Same letter as cited in previous line.
23 November 1919	d	AJ 31 Jan	"honeymoon" "why be annoyed"
23 November 1919	d	AJ 01 Feb	*Same letter as cited in previous line.
1 January 1920	d	AJ 31 Jan	to suffrage convention via Atlanta
1 January 1920	d	AJ 01 Feb	*Same letter as cited in previous line.
23 April 1920	d	AJ 31 Jan	will go to Europe
[June 1920]	d	AJ 31 Jan	"Saturday"; will pass thru Atlanta
[June 1920]	d	AJ 01 Feb	*Same letter as cited in previous line.
June 1920	d	AJ 31 Jan	aboard HMS *Royal George*
[June-Nov.] 1920	d	AJ 01 Feb	"post marked, foreign address"
26 November 1920	d	AJ 31 Jan	NY C. sapphire ring. "sweet one"
26 November 1920	d	AC 01 Feb	*Same letter as cited in previous line.
30 November 1920	d	AJ 01 Feb	
4 December 1920	d	AJ 01 Feb	rec'd. letter from Mr. Roquet
10 December 1920	C	AJ 01 Feb	automobile ride
12 December 1920	d	AJ 01 Feb	Mr. R. wants money; wants advice
14 December 1920	C	AJ 01 Feb	advises settlement
17 December 1920	d	AJ 01 Feb	regrets letter, en route to Reno
21 December 1920	d	AJ 01 Feb	divorce law
1 January 1921	C	AJ 01 Feb	misdated 1920; discuss gossip
3 January 1921	d	AJ 01 Feb	in Reno for 2 weeks
12 January 1921	C	AJ 01 Feb	

*The two papers gave different dates, but portions of each quotation are identical to one another.

Date of letter	author	source	comment
14 January 1921	C	AJ 01 Feb	he is saving her letters
14 January 1921	d	AJ 01 Feb	who sorts your mail?
16 January 1921	C	AJ 01 Feb	"vile falsehoods"
22 January 1921	d	AJ 01 Feb	friends approve
24 January 1921	d	AJ 01 Feb	life in Reno
25 January 1921	d	AJ 01 Feb	possible AGC visit
1 February 1921	C	AJ 01 Feb	desires retirement; wife was lonely
2 February 1921	d	AJ 01 Feb	discretion. AGC to California?
7 February 1921	d	AJ 01 Feb	"as if I were already your wife"
8 February 1921	C	AJ 01 Feb	Werlein, Holmes
14 February 1921	C	AJ 01 Feb	Valentine; suffrage
18 February 1921	d	AJ 01 Feb	'liberty bond,' Mrs. Holmes
1 March 1921	C	AJ 01 Feb	use pseudonym in hotel
6 March 1921	d	AJ 01 Feb	gifts; plan meeting
11 March 1921	C	AJ 01 Feb	"nerves shake"
21 March 1921	d	AJ 01 Feb	condolences; discuss meeting
27 April 1921	d	AJ 01 Feb	"two weeks since I saw you"
2 May 1921	d	AJ 01 Feb	
17 May 1921	C	AJ 01 Feb	NY C; "don't say I am a flirt"
21 June 1921	d	AJ 01 Feb	Roquet still a problem
24 June 1921	C	AJ 01 Feb	re: his bros. & sister
25 June 1921	d	AJ 01 Feb	possible meeting?
1 July 1921	C	AJ 01 Feb	advice on her property in N.O.
26 July 1921	d	AJ 01 Feb	
2 August 1921	C	AJ 01 Feb	Isaac & Rebecca
20 August 1921	C	AJ 01 Feb	sapphire ring
26 August 1921	d	AJ 01 Feb	plan to meet
30 August 1921	C	AJ 01 Feb	"old man's folly"

Date of letter	author	source	comment
10 September 1921	C	AJ 01 Feb	
11 September 1921	d	AJ 01 Feb	
12 September 1921	C	AJ 01 Feb	
16 September 1921	C	AJ 01 Feb	
1 October 1921	C	AJ 01 Feb	special delivery
7 October 1921	d	AJ 01 Feb	wedding trip plans
9 October 1921	d	AJ 01 Feb	plan to meet
10 October 1921	C	AJ 01 Feb	plan to meet
1 November 1921	d	AJ 01 Feb	must live in Reno until March
2 November 1921	C	AJ 01 Feb	wants to concentrate on her
21 November 1921	d	AJ 01 Feb	"when we meet next month"
15 December 1921	C	AJ 01 Feb	recalls wedding anniversary
6 February 1922	C	AJ 30 Jan	desires retirement an marriage
17 March 1922	C	AJ 30 Jan	opposition; "indulgent brother"
24 March 1922	C	AJ 01 Feb	rumors; family questions
5 April 1922	C	AJ 01 Feb	childrens' attitudes
20 April 1922	C	AJ 01 Feb	"three questions"
21 May 1922	C	AC 05 Feb	Roquet dangerous, cruel warfare in family
29 April 1922	C	AC 05 Feb	wants to leave Atlanta
[April/May] 1922	C	AC 05 Feb	more family problems
8 May 1922	C	AJ 30 Jan	nephew investigates
7 May 1922	d	AC 05 Feb	GA divorce laws
18 May 1922	C	AJ 30 Jan	
26 May 1922	C	AC 05 Feb	re investigation of deB.
1 June 1922	C	AJ 30 Jan	catholic influence; prevent marriage
1 June 1922	C	NY 31 Jan	*Same letter as cited in previous line.

Date of letter	author	source	comment
?? June 1922	C	AJ 30 Jan	next letter; "born rejuvenator"
31 July 1922	C	AJ 30 Jan	21 days; wedding ring
13 August 1922	C	AJ 31 Jan	strike; wed in early September
8 September 1922	C	AJ 31 Jan	discussed wedding plans
8 September 1922	C	AC 01 Feb	Sell CB&T stock
11 September 1922	C	AJ 31 Jan	*Same letter as cited in previous line.
12 September 1922	C	AJ 31 Jan	Re: Atlanta paper; sister approves
13 September 1922	C	AJ 31 Jan	sees Walter; will leave on 16th
15 September 1922	C	AJ 31 Jan	AGC breaks engagement
15 September 1922	C	AC 01 Feb	*Same letter as cited in previous line.
28 September 1922	d	AJ 31 Jan	"hideous slander"
30 September 1922	C	AJ 31 Jan	elaborates charges against d
30 September 1922	C	AC 01 Feb	*Same letter as cited in previous line.
3 October 1922	C	AJ 31 Jan	"painful to deny your demand"
5 October 1922	C	AJ 31 Jan	"we should not marry"
nd/1922	C	NY 31 Jan	
nd/1922	d	AC 05 Feb	

BIBLIOGRAPHY

Primary sources—archival materials; rare publications; public records:
Allen, Ivan. "Locating the Quartermaster's Depot in the Candler Warehouse, World War 1[SIC]." Signed type-
script, 20 August 1949, in box 4, Charles Howard Candler Papers, Special Collections, Robert W.
Woodruff Library, Emory University.
"Atlanta Architecture: A survey of the architecture of Atlanta for the last hundred years prepared by students
of the School of Architecture, Georgia Institute of Technology, Winter Quarter, School Year 1948-49."
Bound typescript cataloged in book collection, Atlanta History Center Library/Archives.
Atlanta Chamber of Commerce. Minutes of the Board of Directors. Chamber of Commerce Research
Department, Atlanta.
Atlanta City Directories. Atlanta History Center Library/Archives.
Atlanta, City of. Registry of Merchants, 1873-1886. City of Atlanta records on deposit at Atlanta History
Center Library/Archives.
_____. "Annual report of the Chief and Board of Fire Masters of the Atlanta Fire Department for the Year
1917." City of Atlanta records on deposit at Atlanta History Center Library/Archives.
Atlanta Civics (November and December 1917). Asa Griggs Candler Papers. Robert W. Woodruff Library,
Emory University.
Baylor, H. B. and E. B. Latham. *Baylor Atlas, 1873.* Atlanta History Center Library/Archives.
Candler, Asa Griggs, Papers. Robert W. Woodruff Library, Emory University, 1851–1929.
Candler, Asa Griggs, Papers and Biography. The Archives, The Coca-Cola Company, 1873–1950,1873–1950.
Candler, Charles Howard. *Asa Griggs Candler.* Atlanta: Emory University, 1950.
Charles, Howard. Papers. Robert W. Woodruff Library, Emory University, 1878–1957.
———. Papers and Biography. The Archives, The Coca-Cola Company, 1895–1950.
_____. "Thirty-three Years with Coca-Cola." Typed manuscript, The Archives, The Coca-Cola Company,
1932.
_____. "The True Origin of Coca-Cola: Additional Facts Relating to Its Early History." Typed manuscript
[1952], Charles Howard Candler Papers and Biography, The Archives, The Coca-Cola Company.
Candler, D[aniel] B. "A Brief History of Coca-Cola." Daniel B. Candler file, The Archives, The Coca-Cola
Company, nd.
Candler Family Papers. The Archives, The Coca-Cola Company, 1897–1967.
Candler, John. Untitled biographical sketch of Asa Candler. Typed manuscript, [1929], Charles Howard
Candler Papers, Special Collections, Robert W. Woodruff Library, Emory University.
Candler, Lucy Beall, Papers. Robert W. Woodruff Library, Emory University.
Candler, Warren Akin, Papers. Robert W. Woodruff Library, Emory University, 1897–1941.
Cannon, Bishop James Papers. Special Collections Department, William R. Perkins Library, Duke University.
Coca-Cola Company, The. *Coca-Cola: Opinions, Orders Injunctions, and Decrees Relating to Unfair
Competition and Infringement of Trade Mark.* Bound volume, 1923, The Archives, The Coca-Cola
Company, Atlanta.
Coca-Cola Company, The. Opposer vs. The Koke Company Company [SIC] *of America, Appellant, Before the
Examiner of Interferences.* Printed transcript, vol. 1, The Archives, The Coca-Cola Company, Atlanta,
1929.

Connally, Joseph Brown, Scrapbook [MSS 45]. Atlanta History Center Library/Archives, Atlanta. Carroll County, Georgia. Court of Ordinary, Book G, Appraisements and Vouchers, 1874-1876 [microfilm]. Georgia Department of Archives and History, Atlanta.

DeKalb County, Georgia. Tax Digests, 1880-1929 [microfilm]. Georgia Department of Archives and History, Atlanta.

Edgewood, Georgia. "Minutes of the Town of Edgewood from Feb. 2, 1889 to August 13, 1906." City of Atlanta records on deposit at Atlanta History Center Library/Archives.

Emory College. Microfilm of Minutes of the Board of Trustees of Emory College, vol. 5, Emory University Archives.

Fulton County, Georgia, Superior Court, Office of the Clerk of the Court. Index to Land Suits, 1854-1914, vol. N-R; Minute Books 57, 61, 133; and Writs Book 100.

Fulton County, Georgia. Tax Digests, 1880-1929, [microfilm]. Georgia Department of Archives and History, Atlanta.

Garrett, Franklin. Personal communication: eyewitness description of Asa Candler c. 1917-1918. Historian, Atlanta History Center.

Georgia Department of Defense. Records of the Office of the Adjutant General. Georgia Department of Archives and History, Atlanta.

Hart County, Georgia. Tax Digests, 1900, 1901, [microfilm]. Georgia Department of Archives and History, Atlanta.

"History of the Atlanta Police Department." Published by the Policemen's Relief Association, Atlanta, Georgia, 1898. Repr., with introduction by Herbert T. Jenkins, 1976. Cataloged as a book in Atlanta History Center Library.

Institute for Southern Studies. "Georgia Methodism and Coca-Cola" [pamphlet]. 88 Walton Street, Atlanta: Institute for Southern Studies, 1972.

J. C. Hart, Attorney General v. Neal Bank, et al., docket number 16535, Fulton County Superior Court.

Maddox, Robert F. Papers [MSS 143]. Atlanta History Center Library/Archives.

Maxwell, Mrs. Alva G. "Story of the Methodist Children's Home, Decatur, Georgia" [pamphlet, c. 1938]. Georgia Collection, Atlanta-Fulton Public Library, Atlanta.

Megahee, Grover, compiler. Dividend No. 3 (1911). Cataloged as a book in Atlanta History Center Library.

Minter, Beth and Henry Harris. [untitled report on the history of the Trust Company Bank]. "Trust Company" subject file, Atlanta History Center Library/Archives.

Minutes of the Board of Directors of the Coca-Cola Company. The Archives, The Coca-Cola Company.

R. G. Dun & Company Collection. Baker Library, Harvard University Graduate School of Business Administration.

Travelers' Protective Association of America, Georgia Division. A Commercial History of the State of Georgia. Edgar Harvey, ed. (1897). Special Collections Department, Atlanta-Fulton Public Library.

United States Bureau of the Census. Manuscript returns for Carroll, DeKalb, Fulton, and Hart Counties, Georgia, including the years 1840, 1850, 1860, 1870, 1880, 1900, 1910 [microfilm]. Federal Archives and Records Center, Atlanta.

United States v. Forty Barrels and Twenty Kegs of Coca Cola, 241 US 995 (22 May 1916); original transcripts of testimony in the US District Court for the Eastern District of Tennessee, Southern Division, Chattanooga, (1911). Federal Archives and Records Center, Atlanta.

Willard, Samuel. [Untitled history of Coca-Cola, 1891-1903]. Samuel Willard file, The Archives, The Coca-Cola Company. [Possibly the manuscript for a series published in the Coca-Cola Bottler.]

Secondary sources—Published materials, maps, theses and dissertations:

American Institute of Architects Guide to Atlanta, Kermit B. Marsh, ed. Atlanta Chapter of the AIA, 1975.

Anderson, William G. "Progressivism: An Historiographical Essay." The History Teacher. (May 1973): 427-52.

(Atlanta) Journal of Labor.

Atlanta Constitution.

Atlanta Independent.

Atlanta Journal.

Atlanta Georgian.

Bartley, Numan V. The Creation of Modern Georgia. Athens: University of Georgia Press, 1983.

Bauman, Mark K. "A Famous Atlantan Speaks Out Against Lynching." Atlanta Historical Bulletin (Spring 1976): 24-32.

_____. "The Inherent Disposition of Racial Consciousness: Bishop Candler's Changing Attitude Toward Lynching," Atlanta Historical Bulletin (Fall 1977): 24-31.

_____. *Warren Akin Candler: The Conservative as Idealist.* Metuchen NJ: The Scarecrow Press, Incorporated, 1981.

Beard, Rick. "Hurt's Deserted Village: Atlanta's Inman Park, 1885-1911." *Olmsted South: Old South Critic, New South Planner,* Dana F. White and Victor A. Kramer, eds., Contributions in American Studies, Number 43. Westport CN: Greenwood Press, 1979, 195-221.

"Big Ten's Map of Georgia Gold." Cocoa Beach FL: Big Ten, Incorporated, n. d.

Bolden, Willie Miller. "The Political Structure of Charter Revision Movements in Atlanta during the Progressive Era." Ph. D. dissertation, Emory University, 1978.

Bonislawski, David F. "Business Leadership in Atlanta during World War I." M. A. thesis, Georgia State University, 1984.

Bonner, James C. *Georgia's Last Frontier: The Development of Carroll County.* Athens: University of Georgia Press, 1971.

Brandeis, Louis D. *Other People's Money and How the Bankers Use It,* new edition with foreword by Norman Hapgood. New York: 1914; Reprint, Frederick A. Stokes Company, 1932.

Brubacher, John H. and Willis Rudy. *Higher Education in Transition, An American History: 1636-1956.* New York: Harper & Brothers Publishers, 1958.

Burton, T. Eldin. "The Music Festival of 1909." *The Atlanta Historical Bulletin* 9 (July 1939): 199-202.

Campbell, Steve B. "The Great Fire of Atlanta, May 21, 1917." *Atlanta Historical Journal* 13/2 (1968): 9-14

Candler, Allen D. *Colonel William Candler: His Ancestry and Progeny.* Atlanta: Foote and Davies, 1896.

"Carroll County Slave Owners of 1860 as taken by George W. Awtry beginning 5th June 1860, Second District: Post Office—Villa Rica." Reprinted in *Carroll County Genealogical Quarterly* (Spring 1981):12-13.

Cashman, Sean Dennis. *Prohibition, the Law of the Land.* New York: The Free Press, 1981.

Chandler, Alfred D., Jr. *The Visible Hand: The Managerial Revolution in American Business.* Cambridge MA: The Belknap Press of Harvard University Press, 1977.

Cherrington, Ernest S. *The Evolution of Prohibition in the United States of America: A Chronological History of the Liquor Problem and the Temperance Reform in the United States and from the Earliest Settlements to the Consummation of National Prohibition* Publication No. 40: Patterson Smith Reprint Series in Criminology, Law Enforcement, and Social Problems. 1920; Reprint, Montclair NJ: Patterson Smith, 1969.

"Child Labor and Social Progress: Proceedings of the Fourth Annual Meeting of the National Child Labor Committee." *Supplement to Annals of the American Academy of Political and Social Science,* n. 22 (July 1908). Philadelphia: The American Academy of Political and Social Science, 1908; Reprint, New York: Kraus Reprint Co., 1970. [Supplement may be bound separately from the corresponding volume of the *Annals.*]

City Builder magazine. Atlanta Chamber of Commerce.

Clarke, E. Y. *Illustrated History of Atlanta.* (1877; Reprint, Atlanta: Cherokee Publishing Company, 1970.

Coca-Cola Bottler magazine.

Cooper, Walter G. "Fifth Chapter in the History of the Atlanta Chamber of Commerce—Sam D. Jones' Administration." *City Builder* (April 1929): 16.

_____. "Sixth Chapter in the History of the Atlanta Chamber of Commerce—J. Wylie Pope's Administration." *City Builder* (May 1929): 17.

_____. "Seventh Chapter in the History of Atlanta Chamber of Commerce—Asa G. Candler's Administration." *City Builder* (June 1929): 32.

_____. *Official History of Fulton County.* Atlanta: Walter Brown Publishing Company, 1934.

Crowe, Charles. "Racial Violence and Social Reform—Origins of the Atlanta Riot of 1906." *Journal of Negro History* 53 (July 1968): 234-56.

Cushman, Robert E. "The Wesleyan Tradition." *Encyclopedia of Religion in the South,* Samuel S. Hill, ed. Macon GA: Mercer University Press, 1984.

Davidson, Elizabeth H. *Child Labor Legislation in the Southern Textile States.* Chapel Hill: University of North Carolina Press, 1939.

Deaton, Thomas Mashburn. "Atlanta During the Progressive Era." Ph. D. dissertation, University of Chicago, 1969.

_____. "The Chamber of Commerce in the Economic and Political Development of Atlanta from 1900 to 1916." *Atlanta Historical Bulletin* 19/3 (1975): 19-33.

_____. "James G. Woodward: The Working Man's Mayor." *Atlanta History* (Fall 1987): 11-23.

Dictionary of Georgia Biography. Coleman, Kenneth and Charles Stephen Gurr, eds. Athens GA: University of Georgia Press, 1983.

Dinnerstein, Leonard. *The Leo Frank Case*. Athens GA: University of Georgia Press, 1987.

Dittmer, John. *Black Georgia in the Progressive Era, 1900-1920*. Urbana: University of Illinois Press, 1977.

Doyle, Don H. *New Men, New Cities, New South: Atlanta, Nashville, Charleston, Mobile, 1860-1910*. The Fred W. Morrison Series in Southern Studies. Chapel Hill: The University of North Carolina Press, 1990.

Du Bois, W. E. Burghardt. "The Tragedy at Atlanta, from the Point of View of the Negroes." *The World To-Day* (November 1906): 1169-1172.

Edge, Sarah Simms. *Joel Hurt and the Development of Atlanta*. Atlanta: Atlanta Historical Society, 1955.

Engelbourg, Saul. *Power and Morality: American Business Ethics, 1840-1914*. Contributions in Economics and Economic History, n. 28, Robert Sobel, ed. Westport CN: Greenwood Press, 1980.

Encyclopedia of Southern Culture. Charles Reagan Wilson and William Ferris, eds. Chapel Hill: University of North Carolina Press, 1969.

Encyclopedia of Religion in the South.

English, Thomas W. *Emory University, 1915-1965*. Atlanta: Emory University, 1966.

Field, G. Lowell and John Higley. *Elitism*. Boston: Routledge & Kegan Paul, 1980.

Fink, Gary W. *The Fulton Bag and Cotton Mills Strike of 1914-1915: Espionage, Labor Conflict, and New South Industrial Relations*. Ithaca NY: ILR Press, 1993.

_____. "We Are City Builders, Too: Atlanta Typographers and New South Boosterism, Atlanta Style." *Atlanta History* (Winter 1993): 40-53.

Galishoff, Stuart. "Atlanta's Water Supply, 1865-1918." *The Maryland Historian* (Spring 1977): 5-22.

_____. "Germs Know No Color Line: Black Health and Public Policy in Atlanta, 1900-1918." *Journal of the History of Medicine and Allied Sciences* (January 1985): 22-41.

Garofalo, Charles Paul. "Business Ideas in Atlanta, 1916-1935." Ph. D. dissertation, Emory University, 1972.

Garrett, Franklin M. *Atlanta and Environs: A Chronicle of Its People and Events*. Volume 2 of 2 Volumes. Athens: University of Georgia Press, 1954.

Georgia Writers' Project [WPA]. *Atlanta, A City of the Modern South*. American Guide Series. Sponsored by the Board of Education of the City of Atlanta; 1943; Reprint,. n. p.: Smith & Durrell St. Clair Shores MI: Somerset Publishers, 1973.

Gibson, Thomas. "The Anti-Negro Riots in Atlanta." *Harper's Weekly*, 13 October 1906, 1457-59.

Gournay, Isabelle. "Area 15, Emory University (EU)." *AIA Guide to the Architecture of Atlanta*. Athens GA: University of Georgia Press, 1993.

Grantham, Dewey W. *Southern Progressivism: The Reconciliation of Progress and Tradition*. Knoxville: University of Tennessee Press, 1983.

Graves, John Temple. "The Tragedy at Atlanta, from the Point of View of the Whites." *The World To-Day* (November 1906): 1173-74.

Hall, Bob. "Case Study: Coca-Cola and Southern Methodism." *Southern Exposure* 4/3 (1977): 98-101.

Harris, Julian. "Asa G. Candler: Georgia Cracker." *Uncle Remus's Home Magazine. Emory University Quarterly* 7/4 ((November 1909; Reprint December 1951): 196-207.

Hartshorn, Truman, et al. *Metropolis in Georgia: Atlanta's Rise as a Major Transaction Center*. Cambridge MA: Ballinger Publishing Company, A Subsidiary of J. B. Lippencott Company, 1976.

Holli, Melvin G. "Urban Reform in the Progressive Era." *The Progressive Era*. Lewis L. Gould, ed. Syracuse University Press, 1974, 133-152.

Hudson, Winthrop S. *Religion in America: An Historical Account of the Development of American Religious Life*, Second edition. New York: Charles Scribner's Sons, 1965, 1973.

Hunter, Floyd. *Community Power Structure: A Study of Decision Makers*. Chapel Hill: University of North Carolina Press, 1953.

Isaac, Paul E. *Prohibition and Politics: Turbulent Decades in Tennessee, 1885-1920*. n.p. University of Tennessee Press, 1965.

Jarrell, Dr. Charles C. *Oxford Echoes*. n. p.: Historical Society of the North Georgia Conference and the Wesleyan Christian Advocate, 1967.

Jones, Alton DuMar. "The Child Labor Reform Movement in Georgia." *Georgia Historical Quarterly* 48 (1965): 396-417.

Judson, Edward. "The Church in Its Social Aspect." *The Annals of the American Academy of Political and Social Science* 30 (November 1908).

Kahn, E. J., Jr. *The Big Drink*. New York: Random House, 1950.

Klima, Lloyd. "Land Barons Ride the Rails: Real Estate Speculators and Street Railways in Late Nineteenth Century Atlanta." M. A. thesis, Georgia State University, 1977.

Knight, Lucian Lamar. *Reminiscences of Famous Georgians*. 2 Volumes. Atlanta: Franklin-Turner Company, 1908.

Krout, John Allen. *The Origins of Prohibition*. New York: Alfred A. Knopf, 1925.

Kuhn, Clifford M., Harlon E. Joye, and E. Bernard West. *Living Atlanta: An Oral History of the City, 1914-1948*. Atlanta: The Atlanta Historical Society and Athens: The University of Georgia Press, 1990.

Lefever, Harry G. "The Involvement of the Men and Religion Forward Movement in the Cause of Labor Justice." *Labor History* (Fall 1973): 521-35.

Levine, David O. *The American College and the Culture of Aspiration, 1915-1940*. Ithaca NY: Cornell University Press, 1986.

Lyon, Elizabeth A. "Frederick Law Olmsted and Joel Hurt: Planning for Atlanta." *Olmsted South: Old South Critic, New South Planner*, Dana F. White and Victor A. Kramer, eds., Contributions in American Studies, Number 43. Westport CN: Greenwood Press, 1979, 165-193.

Lyon, Elizabeth Anne Mack. "Business Buildings in Atlanta: A Study In Urban Growth and Form." Ph. D. dissertation, Emory University, 1971.

Marlin, Rev. Lloyd G. *The History of Cherokee County*. Atlanta: Walter W. Brown Publishing Company, 1932.

Martin, Jean. "Mule to MARTA, Volume I." *Atlanta Historical Bulletin* 19/2(1975): 1-112.

Mathias, William J. and Stuart Anderson. *Horse to Helicopter: First Century of the Atlanta Police Department*. Community Life Publications: Criminal Justice Series, School of Urban Life, Georgia State University, 1973.

Mims, Edwin. *History of Vanderbilt University*. Nashville: 1946; Reprint, Vanderbilt University Press, Arno Press Collection, The Academic Profession, Walter P. Metzger, ed. New York: Arno Press, A New York Times Company, 1977.

Mixon, Gregory Lamont. "The Atlanta Riot of 1906." Ph. D. dissertation, University of Cincinnati, 1989.

Mixon, Wayne. "Georgia." *Encyclopedia of Religion in the South*, Samuel S. Hill, ed. Macon GA: Mercer University Press, 1984, 289-304.

New York Stock Exchange. "Cotton and Cotton Futures" [pamphlet]. 1952.

Nesbitt, Martha Tovell. "The Social Gospel in Atlanta: 1900-1920." Ph.D. dissertation, Georgia State University, 1975.

Nielsen, A. E. *Production Credit for Southern Cotton Growers*. Morningside Heights NY: King's Crown Press, 1946.

Norwood, Frederick A. *The Story of American Methodism: A History of the United Methodists and their Relations*. Nashville: Abingdon Press, 1974.

Otwell, W. Larry. *Panning Georgia's Gold: The Gold Panner's Guidebook*. Cleveland GA: Rainbow Sequoia, Publishers, 1985.

Porter, Earl W. *Trinity and Duke, 1892-1924: Founders of Duke University*. Durham NC: Duke University Press, 1964.

Rainey, Glen Weddington. "The Race Riot of 1906 in Atlanta." M. A. thesis, Emory University, Atlanta, 1929.

Rensi, Ray C. and H. David Williams. *Gold Fever: America's First Gold Rush*. Georgia History and Culture Series. Atlanta: Georgia Humanities Council, 1988.

Robinson, James O., M. D. "Our Surgical Heritage: Treatment of Breast Cancer Through the Ages." *American Journal of Surgery* 151/3 (March 1986): 317-33.

Rogers, Alan. "Rise of Asa G. Candler from Poverty to Wealth." *Atlanta Constitution* 12 June 1907, 6.

Russell, James Michael. *Atlanta, 1847-1890: City Building in the Old South and the New*. Baton Rouge: Louisiana State University Press, 1988.

Rudolph, Frederick. *The American College and University: A History*. New York: Alfred A. Knopf, 1962.

Rumbarger, John J. *Profits, Power, and Prohibition: Alcohol Reform and the Industrializing of America, 1800-1930*. SUNY Series in New Social Studies on alcohol and Drugs, Harry G. Levine and Craig Reinarman, eds. Albany: State University of New York Press, 1989.

Sanborn Insurance Maps of Atlanta (1911)

Schiesl, Martin J. *The Politics of Efficiency: Municipal Administration and Reform in America 1880-1920*. Berkeley: University of California Press, 1977.

Street, James H. *The New Revolution in the Cotton Economy: Mechanization and its Consequences*. Chapel Hill: The University of North Carolina Press, 1957.

Studenski, Paul and Herman E. Krooss. *Financial History of the United States: Fiscal, Monetary, Banking, and Tariff, Including Financial Administration and State and Local Finance*, second edition. New York: McGraw Hill Book Company, Inc., 1952, 1963.

Talmadge, John E. *Rebecca Latimer Felton: Nine Stormy Decades*. Athens: University of Georgia Press, 1960.

Tedlow, Richard S. *New and Improved: The Story of Mass Marketing in America*. New York: Basic Books, Inc., 1990.

Timberlake, James H. *Prohibition and the Progressive Movement, 1900-1920.* Cambridge MA: Harvard University Press, 1963.

Tindall, George Brown. *The Emergence of the New South, 1913-1945.* A History of the South. 11 Volumes. Wendell Holmes Stephenson and E. Merton Coulter, eds. Baton Rouge: Louisiana State University Press and The Littlefield Fund for Southern History of the University of Texas, 1967.

Veterans of McDaniel (Curtis Camp) and the Annie Wheeler Chapter, United Daughters of the Confederacy, sponsors, *Carroll County, Georgia: Souvenir—Historical Edition.* Carrollton GA: R. Lee Sharpe-Modern Printing Company, 1908. Repr. Carroll County Genealogical Society, 1988.

Warnock, Henry Y. "Andrew Sledd, Southern Methodists, and the Negro: A Case History." *Journal of Southern History* 31/3 (August 1965): 251-271.

Watters, Pat. *Coca-Cola, An Illustrated History.* Garden City, NJ: Doubleday, Inc., 1978.

Watts, Eugene J. *The Social Bases of City Politics: Atlanta 1865-1903.* Contributions in American History, Number 73, Jon L. Wakelyn, ed. Westport CN: Greenwood Press, 1978.

White, Dana F. "Landscaped Atlanta: The Romantic Tradition in Cemetery, Park, and Suburban Development." *The Atlanta Historical Journal* 26(Summer-Fall 1982): 95-112.

White, Raymond Everett. [title unknown, Leslie's Weekly. September 1916]. Repr. "Writer in Leslie's Weekly Tells of Election of Asa G. Candler." *Atlanta Constitution,* 21 September 1916, 8.

Whitlaw, Lt. Col. Lowell E. "Buick No. 10." *The Horseless Carriage* (January-February 1957): 21.

Wiebe, Robert H. *Businessmen and Reform: A Study of the Progressive Movement.* Chicago: Quadrangle Paperbacks, Quadrangle Books, 1962.

Wingo, Horace Calvin. "Race Relations in Georgia, 1872-1908." Ph. D. dissertation, University of Georgia, 1969.

Wilkinson, Charles F. "Asa G. Candler, Pioneer-Capitalist," *Buildings and Management* (September 1915): 56-57

Willard, S. J. "The Early History of Coca-Cola as I Know It," part 5. *The Coca-Cola Bottler,* (May 1930): 45.

Williams, David L. "The Development and Consolidation of Atlanta's Street Railways, 1866-1891." M. A. thesis, Georgia State University, 1975.

Woodward, C. Vann. *Origins of the New South, 1877-1913,* vol. 9 in *A History of the South,* Wendell Holmes Stephenson and E. Merton Coulter, eds. First paperback edition. Baton Rouge: Louisiana State University Press and The Littlefield Fund for Southern History of the University of Texas, 1951.

_____. *The Strange Career of Jim Crow,* Revised Edition.. New York: Oxford University Press, 1974.

Woolston, Howard B. *Prostitution in the United States, Prior to the Entrance of The United States into the World War,* (1921). Repr., Publication No. 29: Patterson Smith Reprint Series in Criminology, Law Enforcement, and Social Problems. Montclair NJ: Patterson Smith, 1969.

Wright, Gavin. *Old South, New South: Revolutions in the Southern Economy Since the Civil War.* New York: Basic Books, Inc., Publishers, 1986.

Wrigley, Steven Wayne. "The Triumph of Provincialism: Public Life in Georgia, 1898-1917." Ph. D. dissertation, Northwestern University, 1986.

Wyllie, Irvin G. *The Self Made Man in America: the Myth of Rags to Riches.* New Brunswick NJ: Rutgers University Press, 1954.

Research facilities and types of materials consulted in each:

The Archives, The Coca-Cola Company, Atlanta: various Candler family papers, records of the Coca-Cola Company.

Atlanta Chamber of Commerce, research department. The earliest of the Chamber records were hand-written in a ledger book; after the turn of the century, typewritten minutes, reports, subscription lists, correspondence, and occasional ephemera were pasted in chronological order in large ledger or invoice books, scrapbook style. In a few cases the records of a particular committee were placed in a separate volume.

Atlanta History Center Library/Archives: manuscript collections; subject files on Candler family members, Atlanta businesses; rare publications on local history; maps.

Baker Library, Harvard University Graduate School of Business Administration: R. G. Dun and Company Collection.

DeKalb County Historical Society: subject files on Candler family, residences.

DeKalb County Public Library, Decatur Branch: rare publications in local history; microfilm of *Atlanta Constitution* and *Atlanta Journal.*

Federal Archives and Records Center, Atlanta: manuscript census returns, federal court records.

Fulton County Clerk of the Court: Atlanta City Court and Superior Court records.

Georgia Department of Archives and History, Atlanta: Candler family subject files, tax digests or probate records of Georgia counties; records of the Georgia Adjutant General.

Pullen Library, Georgia State University: microfilm of *Atlanta Journal, Atlanta Constitution, Journal of Labor,* and *New York Times.*

Special Collections Department, Woodruff Library, Atlanta University Center: subject files on the riots of 1906.

Special Collections Department, Woodruff Library, Emory University: collected papers of Asa G. Candler, Charles Howard Candler, Warren Candler; other Candler family papers; records of Emory College and Emory University.

Special Collections Department, William R. Perkins Library, Duke University: Miscellaneous correspondence associated with Warren Candler.

Special Collections Department, Atlanta-Fulton Public Library: rare publications relating to local history; microfilm of the *Atlanta Georgian* and *Atlanta Independent* newspapers.

INDEX